Why Conservatives Tell Stories and Liberals Don't

Parts of political stories may be told in images (for example, via television) rather than in words (for example, via books and magazines). Thus on May 1, 2003, President Bush, wearing a fighter pilot's flight suit, flew to the USS *Abraham Lincoln,* a nuclear aircraft carrier sailing in Pacific waters near San Diego. While dressed as a modern warrior—complete with helmet and goggles—the president was photographed on board with some of the ship's crew members, who also wore combat clothing. Later, and dressed as a civilian, the president appeared in television reports while (1) announcing from the *Lincoln*'s flight deck, (2) against the backdrop of a sign reading "Mission Accomplished," that (3) "major military operations in Iraq have ended." In these circumstances, George W. Bush must have looked, to some viewers, like a seasoned and energetic commander, presiding over courageous and popular armed forces, confidently and reliably leading the nation to "victory" over "terrorism." That Mr. Bush had learned to fly while enrolled in a National Guard unit designed to keep him, and other privileged young men, out of combat during the Vietnam War, was not part of the projected image and perhaps not known to, or recalled by, the same viewers.

Why Conservatives Tell Stories and Liberals Don't

Rhetoric, Faith, and Vision on the American Right

David M. Ricci

Paradigm Publishers
Boulder • London

Published in the United States by Paradigm Publishers, 2845 Wilderness Place, Suite 200, Boulder, CO 80301 USA.

Paradigm Publishers is the trade name of Birkenkamp & Company, LLC, Dean Birkenkamp, President and Publisher.

Library of Congress Cataloging-in-Publication Data

Ricci, David M.
Why conservatives tell stories and liberals don't : rhetoric, faith, and stories on the American right / David M. Ricci.
p. cm.
Includes bibliographical references and index.
ISBN 978-1-59451-873-7 (hardcover : alk. paper) — ISBN 978-1-59451-874-4 (pbk. : alk. paper)
1. Conservatism—United States. 2. Conservatives—United States—Language. 3. Storytelling—Political aspects—United States. 4. Rhetoric—Political aspects—United States. I. Title.
JC573.2.U6R53 2010
320.520973—dc22
2010015819

Printed and bound in the United States of America on acid-free paper that meets the standards of the American National Standard for Permanence of Paper for Printed Library Materials.

Designed and Typeset by Straight Creek Bookmakers.

14 13 12 11 10 1 2 3 4 5

FOR IRY

אשת חייל

Contents

Introduction 1

Part I Rhetorical Ploys

One *Rejections* 11
Two *Irrefutables* 29
Three *Promotions* 55

Part II Articles of Faith

Four *Enemies* 81
Five *Enchantments* 105
Six *Stories* 131

Part IIII Reality Checks

Seven *A Tale Against Tales* 159

Notes 183
Index 251
About the Author 271

Introduction

News reports since the 2008 election have centered, for the most part, so spectacularly on President Barack Obama that some readers may have difficulty remembering that between 1980 and 2004, conservatives captured the presidency five times, controlled one or both houses of Congress repeatedly, scaled back or canceled signature programs of the New Deal and the Great Society, appointed a series of right-leaning judges to the Supreme Court, and, in February 2003, propelled the nation into a war in Iraq that has taken tens of thousands of lives and may cost $3 trillion before it is over.[1]

In 2006 and 2008, right-wing candidates slipped electorally. All things considered, though, it is clear that in recent decades, and despite receiving less media attention today than they did until virtually yesterday, people animated by conservative ideas have notably influenced public life in America. Historically, then, conservatives have been strikingly successful, in a project fashioned by men and women (1) who are thoroughly committed to their principles, (2) who are regrouping across the land—most obviously now at Tea Parties—and (3) who will surely, as they have done after setbacks in the past, reassert themselves culturally, economically, and politically.[2]

The Vision Thing

Now, what interests me most about this performance is not the maneuvering that accompanied it—say, the Republican Party's southern strategy[3]—but the ideas that conservatives have advocated and will continue advocating to enlist voter support.[4] For example, in 2004, after starting a controversial war, and after generating enormous federal deficits, and while promoting an economy that severely widened income gaps,[5] the conservative George W. Bush, barely elected in 2000, was elected again. With so many potential strikes against him, was not the president's victory a triumph for whatever inspirational message—"the vision thing," his father had called it—the candidate managed to project?

Under the circumstances, the 2004 election can be interpreted by saying that Bush II won by staying on script.[6] But in that case, the conservative script must be very powerful. Indeed, it was so powerful in 2008 that when John McCain and Sarah Palin followed it, more or less, their poll ratings, even while the war dragged on, were similar to those of Barack Obama and Joseph Biden until Lehman Brothers Holdings Inc. collapsed on September 15 of that year and a looming economic disaster seized the nation's attention less than two months before election day.

Conservative Talk

So let us consider in this book the conservative script. Here is the special discourse within which many conservative politicians, journalists, and activists go about their work and sometimes win elections. Here are the terms that project right-wing principles and priorities, together adding up to a vision about how the country got to where it is, what it is doing now, and where it should go from here.[7]

Other people will write about conservative chronologies, personalities, fund raising, election campaigns, organizational networks, lobbying, legislative agendas, judicial strategies, and more—that is, about various aspects of political ups and downs on the right stretching from Barry M. Goldwater to George W. Bush and beyond. Some have already done so.[8] I will write, instead, about a verbal dimension of those events, to show how right-wing propositions link up and hold together to constitute a powerful force in America's political conversation today.

Accordingly, I will not explain in detail what conservatives think about, say, poverty, with examples from writings by Charles Murray, George Gilder, Marvin Olasky, Newt Gingrich, Irving Kristol, Jerry Falwell, William Buckley Jr., Glenn Beck, and so forth. The same is true for other interesting matters such as feminism, the origin of life, supply-side economics, immigration, and constitutional intent. Rather, I will show, with reference to such matters—but also to welfare, race relations, abortion, family values, the optimal level of taxation, and other important topics—that when conservatives talk about social and economic situations, they tend to deploy particular arguments, sometimes effective, that show up repeatedly in what they say about a wide range of public issues.

In other words, although conservatives grapple with affairs of great consequence, I will not describe fully *the* right-wing view of anything in particular. I will say something, and not just in passing, about what conservatives believe. But I will not analyze conservatism as if its ideas unfold along a straight line, with people on the right starting somewhere in principle, marching along together after that, discussing first one thing and then arriving at another, and finally wrapping up their deliberations with a comprehensive and consistent philosophy of life. On the contrary, in Chapter Four we will see that conservatives in public life do *not* project such a philosophy. They have, nevertheless, created a matrix of talk that works very well compared to liberal arguments that often do not mesh effectively. After showing this to be so, I will remark later on why, when political polemics are conducted, liberalism has in many recent years performed poorly.

The Conservative Mind

All this can be placed in historical perspective. In 1953, Russell Kirk wrote about "the conservative mind" and meant by that phrase roughly the sum of what leading conservatives believed to be true.[9] Trying to write similarly today is not feasible. First, because there are now more American conservatives than there were in Kirk's time, not agreeing entirely with one another, from Pat Buchanan to Mike Huckabee, from William Kristol to Sarah Palin, from Lindsey Graham to Kay Bailey Hutchison. And second, because the political issues they confront, including health care and the economic crisis, are so dynamic that there is no way to decide exactly what, in current terms, "conservatives" believe and what they do not.

It is possible, however, to consider writings by a wide range of people known as conservatives and to find in those writings shared ways of thinking, of analyzing situations, and of talking in public, often about why liberal ideas are wrong.[10] In this sense, it is possible to describe a right-wing mind that has evolved considerably since Kirk analyzed the subject. This mind offers precepts for thinking about social problems and formulas for dealing with them, and it employs rhetorical techniques that help conservatives promote policy proposals that may differ somewhat from one advocate to another but usually clash with those proposed by people on the left.

Here, then, is an intellectual entity that can be described not so much in terms of exactly what conservatives together regard as true but more as a matter of how, as a class of thinkers, they confront their critics and policy opportunities. This is the conservative mind that liberals encounter when they engage right-wingers in debate or campaign against them for office. Beyond catchy slogans aimed at immediate targets of opportunity—where slogans are wielded by conservatives *and* by liberals—people on the right tend to express a distinctive range of ideas (1) selected from particular thinkers in history, including men such as Aristotle, Jesus, John Locke, David Hume, Adam Smith, Patrick Henry, Alexander Hamilton, James Madison, Alexis de Tocqueville, Abraham Lincoln, and Pope John Paul II, and (2) interpreted by modern intellectuals such as Allan Bloom, C. S. Lewis, James Wilson, Robert Bork, Thomas Sowell, Paul Johnson, Harry Jaffa, Michael Novak, and Milton Friedman.[11] In modern politics, the mind behind those ideas is a singular presence, and as such we will analyze various aspects of it in chapters to come.[12]

The Major Analysis

But how to proceed? First, I will explain how various conservative propositions buttress one another in ways that many Americans regard as timely and relevant to their concerns. Thus this book's subtitle—"Rhetoric, Faith, and Vision on the American Right"—indicates that we will see, via elements of *rhetoric* and *faith,* how right-wing talk relates to models, economic reasoning, individualism, anecdotes, correlations, rational discrimination, mediating structures, Tax Day, family values, creative destruction, and so forth. The analysis will culminate in a consideration of how right-wing stories translate into an overall narrative—a forceful *vision* of freedom in national life—in an era when inspiring stories can produce political success. Yet finally, in Chapter Seven we will see how, at least in the Iraq War case, such stories can be painfully misleading.

The Story Gap

As my analysis unfolds, it will suggest an important generalization to be treated especially in Chapters Five and Six. This generalization suggests that, on the whole, conservatives are more likely than liberals to think traditionally. Accordingly, right-wingers tend to describe the world and our concerns in it via stories. Some of these they may see as absolutely true—the Creation, for example, or the Invisible Hand—and others, as in Ronald Reagan's folksy use of anecdotes, they may regard as not literally accurate but credible for illustrating large verities. What is most important for our purposes is that conservative activists and candidates tell many stories that come together, in ways we cannot sketch precisely, to project a large-scale tale, a cultural narrative, a vision of what America is and what it should do to prosper socially, economically, and politically.

Liberals, by contrast, prefer to create concepts and practices that challenge long-standing beliefs based on what Max Weber called "enchantment." In their lives and work, liberals therefore tend to look for theories rather than stories, for mathematical explanations rather than theological axioms, for data rather than anecdotes, and for statistics rather than homilies. The bottom line here, which impacts powerfully on everyday politics, is that (1) even if liberal activists and candidates for public office would know they should counter every conservative story with one of their own, (2) personal inclinations would make it difficult for them to believe in, and consistently promote, such stories—and beyond them a large-scale story, narrative, or vision—even if they might try to fashion those tales themselves.

In short, to the extent that stories are important in public life, there is a sense in which liberals, while committed to disenchantment, are disadvantaged in contemporary American politics. Drew Westen, a psychology professor and political consultant, sees here a major stumbling block for Democrats. The Left, he says, "has no brand, no counterbrand, no master narrative, no counternarrative. It has no shared terms or 'talking points' for its leaders to repeat until they are part of our political lexicon. Instead, every Democrat who runs for office, every Democrat who offers commentaries on television or radio, every Democrat who even talks with friends at the water cooler, has to reinvent what it means to be a Democrat, using his or her own words and concepts."[13] Columnists have noted the same deficit. Thus Frank Rich argues that Barack Obama used a narrative of change and hope to campaign successfully in 2008. But after a year in office, says Rich, the liberal president promotes "no consistent, clear message to unite all that he is trying to do," and therefore he governs "without a powerful vision" to enlist support for the programs he seeks to enact.[14]

There may be, however, a corresponding downside for conservatives in this situation. On the one hand, stories can help candidates win elections. There is the Right's advantage. On the other hand, stories may persuade voters to endorse inspired but unrealistic public policies. Yet what that last capacity indicates, as we shall see in Chapter Seven when considering the war in Iraq, is that conservatives, as adroit storytellers, may be vulnerable to critics who insist that right-wing stories, sometimes capable of dominating elections, may eventually cost the country more than it wants to pay.

What Is Missing?

I will not explore right-wing soul-searching over current issues such as Afghanistan and bank regulation. CNN is reporting on these important matters as I write. But this book seeks to describe a right-wing vision promoted in a distinctive sort of talk. To that end I assume that, even though some conservatives will differ among themselves in the short run, say on what to do about illegal immigration, those same people will continue to call themselves conservatives and probably not move into the Democratic Party. What I will explore, in short, is the structure of a macro-reality—the persistence of what we call right-wing political ideas—rather than a sometimes fleeting series of micro-elements in the larger world. In that approach, to review controversies that are now unfolding, and whose outcomes is uncertain, would be to risk getting sidetracked unnecessarily by trying to predict the course of events that may evolve into something else even as this book goes to press.[15]

Recent Events

In sum, the following chapters will explain how and why political conservatives tell stories that help them to win elections and help us to understand what they do in office. That being my aim, a disclaimer should appear before I begin. The election of 2008 provoked great popular interest and constituted an important milestone in American public life. Yet beyond supporting widespread speculation about what caused the outcome, the same election can add little, so far, to our understanding of whether right-wing talk, and the vision it conveys, "works." On November 4, 2008, Barack Obama and Joseph Biden defeated John McCain and Sarah Palin for the offices of, respectively, president and vice president of the United States. Serious practical consequences followed. But no one, until now, can say for sure why the Democrats won.

Why is that so? Especially via e-mail, mobile phones, blogs, chat rooms, and other Internet relationships, Obama and Biden raised more money and reached out to voters more effectively than any previous candidates for national office. Such were matters of technique. Yet with regard to substance—that is, to largely liberal propositions of Democrats versus mainly conservative claims of Republicans—it is not clear that Democratic messages triumphed. Rather, shocking events in the fall of 2008, including the subprime mortgage crisis, the slump in stock prices and real estate values, and rising rates of unemployment, probably angered enough swing voters to turn them against Republicans regardless of exactly what Democratic candidates said to evoke electoral support.

One inference here is this: Against a backdrop of economic turmoil greater than any since the Great Depression, the victory of Obama and Biden—who received 365 electoral votes against 173 for McCain and Palin, and who took 7 more percentage points in the popular vote than their Republican adversaries did—was not unusually impressive.[16] Democrat Franklin Delano Roosevelt, for example, running against a Republican president accused of causing, or at least not repairing, the Crash of 1929, defeated incumbent Herbert Hoover by 18 percentage points in the popular vote and 472 to 59 electoral college votes. By comparison, it is possible that McCain and Palin—who advocated mostly conservative principles and projects—might have defeated Obama and Biden if Wall Street had not tanked late in the Bush II presidency.

All this being so, it is reasonable to regard national events during 2008 as having overwhelmed political talk. Yet if they did, and if we want to locate durable examples of how right-wingers present their case, it makes sense to focus less on what anyone said in 2008 and more on what conservatives claimed and wrote previously. So that is what I will do in the chapters to come, citing works by founders such as Barry Goldwater, William Buckley Jr., and Phyllis Schlafly, and adding to them premises, aspirations, and expectations promoted by politicians, publicists, and activists during the Republican ascendancy stretching from Ronald Reagan to Newt Gingrich and on to George W. Bush.

A Final Note

In the Digital World where everyone now lives, hard copy books face massive electronic competition from virtual articles, books, encyclopedias, documents, videos, blogs, chat rooms, and more, all delivered online free. One result so far is that, for technical and financial reasons, hard copy footnotes are increasingly being transformed into hard copy endnotes. In that publishing solution, supplementary information no longer appears at the bottom of text pages. Accordingly, *Why Conservatives Tell Stories and Liberals Don't* is extensively annotated and augmented not with footnotes but with endnotes. Those especially explore social, economic, and political ideas which challenge those promoted by conservatives. I therefore invite readers to regard my endnotes on pages 183–250 below as (1) a running commentary, (2) punctuated with striking examples, (3) about what they read in the text. Such notes are, I think, worth consulting frequently.

Part I
Rhetorical Ploys

Chapter One
Rejections

We begin with a practical difficulty. Right-wing thinking is neither inscribed in a catechism nor expounded by certified practitioners. Moreover, it does not inform the platform of a national party with card-carrying members who can be asked how firmly they believe in what that platform proposes. Consequently, scholars have no technique that can reveal exactly what American conservatism is. In fact, we cannot always say for sure who is a conservative and who is something else, because some political thinkers, elected officials, voters, and activists, no matter how conservative they may seem to neutral observers, insist they are not.[1]

The Conservative Story

Accordingly, one can offer only a plausible interpretation of the subject.[2] To that end, we may start by noting that in books, articles, research reports, talk shows, speeches, sermons, and judicial decisions, American rightists promote a fairly consistent story of how their country got to where it is and how it should move beyond that point prosperously. On the one hand, the conservative story praises capitalism for stimulating economic growth and facilitating scientific progress, and for enabling Americans to acquire private property that helps them resist governmental encroachments on freedom. On the other hand, it recommends tradition and long-standing values, which are important to personal well-being but can also inspire Americans at work and in business—that is, within the framework of capitalism—to treat other members of their community decently.[3]

Basic Propositions

George Bush I may have believed that a "vision thing" could emerge from this conservative story, but scholars would call the same story simply a "narrative."[4] Of course, it is not a straight-line affair like *Little Red Riding Hood*. It is, instead, a matter of returning repeatedly to propositions that appear in what conservatives say, in many forums, about American history and current events. It is the propositions that create a story line, that make one right-wing item after another seem to support many of the rest, that help the public to understand that conservatives have a vision of what America has been and can be in the future.

A typical example of such propositions appeared in 1955, when William Buckley Jr. founded *National Review*. Buckley promised in the inaugural issue that the *Review* (1) would strongly oppose "the growth of government," (2) would refuse coexistence with the "satanic utopianism" of communism, (3) would resist the "cultural menace" of "intellectual cliques" (liberals) in education and the arts, (4) would ferret out "Fabian operators" (liberals) intent on controlling America's major parties, (5) would combat "politically oriented [liberal] unionism," and (6) would oppose "fashionable concepts of world government" embodied in "Liberal elite" support for the United Nations.[5] After the Soviet Union collapsed between 1989 and 1991, the *Review* targeted radical Islam as America's chief enemy abroad. Other than that, Buckley and his colleagues after 1955 stuck to their story line, showing the *Review*'s readers again and again, via Buckley's original precepts, what was right and wrong in America and how conservatives should relate to both.

A later example of right-wing propositions, also projecting important parts of the standard conservative vision, appeared in Newt Gingrich and Dick Armey, *Contract with America* (1994).[6] Gingrich and Armey claimed that five principles form what they called the "basic philosophy of American civilization." These are: "individual liberty," "economic opportunity," "limited government," "personal responsibility," and "security at home and abroad." Assuming that the Republican delegation in Congress endorsed the same principles, Gingrich and Armey proposed advancing them in a right-wing legislative agenda. Thus Congress should enact a "Personal Responsibility Act" that would prohibit welfare payments to unwed mothers under the age of eighteen, a "Taking Our Streets Back Act" that would authorize police to gather evidence in ways not now permitted by the Supreme Court, a "Job Creation and Wage Enhancement Act" that would cut the federal capital gains tax for those who own corporate stocks, and a "Common Sense Legal Reforms Act" that would limit the amount of damages citizens might claim in court from manufacturers of dangerous or defective products. Similar propositions abound in other conservative writings.[7]

Democracy

Two common denominators underlie this tale. First, it is inherently democratic. Early American conservatives, such as Russell Kirk, James Burnham, and Richard Weaver in the 1940s and 1950s, did not believe that mass voting is likely to express political wisdom.[8] They thus resembled classic Europeans on the right, like Edmund Burke, Louis De Bonald, Joseph de Maistre, Matthew Arnold, and James Fitzjames Stephen.[9] But since Barry Goldwater's presidential campaign in 1964 encouraged grassroots organizing on his behalf, most American conservatives have praised democracy[10] and exhorted ordinary people to support candidates committed to capitalism and traditional values. Therefore, this point of principle now inspires writings by conservative politicians, preachers, scholars, activists, talk show hosts, journalists, and others.

Truth

Second, the conservative story projects what its advocates regard as permanent truths. Religious rightists, of course, assume that such truths are available via theology and should spur citizens to shape public policy accordingly. Thus Ben Kinchlow says that "[w]e need to restore truth to the people. Do you know that most of our children have no idea about the true history of America?" Such children cannot fulfill their civic responsibilities, Kinchlow believes, because "[t]hey have no idea [that for the Founders] . . . Christianity was the order of the day."[11] Or consider Charles Colson, who insists that in public life "Christians ought to boldly maintain the reality of absolutes." There are, he says, "laws for human behavior just as there are laws for the physical world," as compelling as the "effects of gravity."[12] To embody such laws in public policy is Colson's goal, and H. Edward Rowe agrees with him. "In a certain sense there are only two classes of people" says Rowe, "those who live by the truth and those who do not." It follows that "[t]he movement to apply Christianity in our nation will succeed because it is rooted in basic reality—the truth of God."[13]

In less theological terms, secular rightists also promote what they regard as always true. Thus Barry Goldwater declares that his classic book, *The Conscience of a Conservative* (1960), "is not written with the idea of adding to or improving on the Conservative philosophy. Or of 'bringing it up to date.' The ancient and tested truths that guided our Republic through its early days will do equally well for us."[14] That being the case, "[w]hat is required of us," says Frank Meyer, "is a conscious conservatism, a clearly principled restatement in new circumstances of philosophical and political truth."[15] Or, as Jeffrey Hart advises his compatriots, "We don't need new ideas nearly as much as we need new techniques to spread tried and true ideas."[16]

Rejections

In general terms, conservatives offer to Americans a large story, or vision, about freedom, efficiency, private property, individual responsibility, and so forth. We will return to that story especially in Chapters Five and Six, where we will discuss why conservatives are effective at storytelling while liberals usually have little inclination or talent for that practice—in which case the liberals are seriously disadvantaged in politics today. For now, however, and especially in Chapters Two, Three, and Four, we should linger on our way to the later discussion in order to get a sense of what sorts of propositions conservatives talk about and thereby project as eventual building blocks for their larger story.

Let us note, then, as a point of departure, that the conservative conviction that people in their camp expound what is True has a corollary, which is the belief that a liberal view of the world must be False—that is, it must misrepresent or misinterpret some elements of reality that, in the right-wing view, are known and immutable. Accordingly, Albert Hirschman claims that conservatives since the Enlightenment have opposed many liberal projects—intended to improve social and economic life—in order to achieve three aims.[17] These are (1) to forestall perverse results, (2) to avoid jeopardy, and (3) to abstain from futility. Here is a starting point for the conservative vision in that to seek such ends, as Hirschman points out, is to warn, firmly and repeatedly, that, no matter what liberals may hope to accomplish, their proposals are either dangerous or useless and therefore worthless.

Perversity

Hirschman cites arguments advanced mainly by Europeans such as Edmund Burke, Joseph de Maistre, Herbert Spencer, and Gaetano Mosca. As he points out, though, the same arguments appear in some American conservative writings today. Thus Hirschman explains that, in both the Old World and the New, the assumption of *perversity* suggests that attempting "to push society in a certain direction will result in its moving all right, but in the opposite direction."[18]

Accordingly, Milton and Rose Friedman observe that late nineteenth–century legislators designed the Interstate Commerce Commission and the Sherman Anti-Trust Law to promote competition. Unfortunately, they continue, these efforts at reform "had perverse effects," such as when existing industrial firms persuade government regulators to prevent new firms from entering the market.[19] Similarly, Edward Banfield claims that most proposals for reforming urban public schools "may be expected to produce results exactly the opposite of those intended; that is, hasten the movement of the well-off from the city, increase unemployment and poverty, [and] widen the chasms of class and race."[20] And James Wilson notes that "[t]hings never work out quite as you hope; in particular, government programs often do not achieve their objectives or do achieve them but with high or unexpected costs."[21]

That things get out of hand is inevitable according to what Wilson and Gertrude Himmelfarb call "the law of unintended consequences."[22] For example, New Dealers may have wanted to help people stricken by the Great Depression. But because to do so FDR's colleagues fostered what conservatives regard as undesirable growth of government, Larry Burkett concludes that "the short-range benefits given to the thirties' generation were provided at the expense of future generations."[23] Similarly, liberals who enacted Medicare and Medicaid aimed at extending health insurance to millions of Americans who had none. But by authorizing government agencies to pay doctors' bills, says David Frum, they unintentionally inflated medical expenses and thereby produced "the most gargantuan example of unintended consequences in the whole sorry history of modern welfarism."[24]

Good Intentions

Concerning such cases, conservatives often hold that good intentions are inadequate.[25] As Friedrich Hayek says, "Is there a greater tragedy imaginable than that, in our endeavor consciously to shape our future in accordance with high ideals [social compassion], we should in fact unwittingly produce the very opposite [government oppression] of what we have been striving for?"[26] Rush Limbaugh agrees. It is counterproductive, he says, to enact "policies that have the superficial appearance of compassion, but do nothing to solve the problem, and often make it worse."[27] Bill O'Reilly reinforces this point by naming victims. "The road to hell is paved with good [liberal] intentions," he says, "and you know what? Those intentions are being paid for big-time [via taxes and affirmative action] by all working Americans."[28]

Welfare

Welfare programs are particularly likely, say conservatives, to produce perverse policy results. Thus people on the right claim that when government provides financial support for the "undeserving poor"—that is, for those whom conservatives describe as able but unwilling to work—it encourages them to shirk personal responsibility, live on the dole, and behave so haplessly as to perpetuate a culture of poverty. Marvin Olasky, for example, who prefers private to public philanthropy, argues that giving aid to poor people is not enough. Only private agencies, he says, often based on religious faith, can provide the steady and personal contact between giver and receiver that will inspire the receiver to mend his or her ways, leave sloth behind, and become a productive and successful member of the community. Aid lacking such contact only perpetuates dependency.[29]

Charles Murray describes the culture of poverty as, in his opinion, based on perverse incentives, that is, on paying people not to work, on rewarding them for bearing children out of wedlock, on encouraging the unemployed to regard themselves as victims of discrimination, and so forth. That being the case, weaker members of society remain sufficiently poor to be miserable but insufficiently ambitious to make their way in modern life.[30] During many years of government aid to the poor, says Murray, "things got worse rather than better."[31] Consequently, he concludes that "the entire federal welfare and income-support structure for working-aged persons" should be scrapped, leaving such people "with no recourse whatsoever except the job market, family members, friends, and public or private locally funded services."[32]

Restating the point, Michael Bauman suggests that Americans who promote government welfare programs are like "dangerous Samaritans," who "unintentionally injure the poor."[33] The problem here, says Gertrude Himmelfarb, is that welfare entitlements send the wrong "message." For example, some people stop feeling responsible for elderly parents who will receive government aid, and some feel free to conceive children whom the state must support. In light of such moral failures, Himmelfarb contends that when relief, now called welfare, "became a legal right," the "unwitting effect of this policy was to undermine the traditional family."[34]

Conservatives are especially concerned, they say, that poor people may refuse to marry so that their single-parent children will qualify for child support. George Gilder, for example, argues that there is no escaping this destructive result for so long as parents can easily calculate that it pays to remain single. As he says, "AFDC [Aid to Families with Dependent Children] already offers a guaranteed income to any child-raising couple in America that is willing to break up, or to any teenaged girl over sixteen who is willing to bear an illegitimate child."[35] Under the circumstances, a poor man realizes that "when all is said and done his wife and children can do better without him."[36] So why marry?

The Minimum Wage

Beyond condemning welfare payments, conservatives argue that when liberals promote a minimum wage to raise lower-class income, they inadvertently penalize poor people. As Ronald Nash says, "Minimum wage laws are a good example of how interventionist policies are counter-productive."[37] The sequence here, according to Milton and Rose Friedman, is that a minimum wage will cause employers to "discriminate against persons with low skills."[38] That is, the law may set $2.50 (in the 1970s) as the minimum legal wage that can be paid, even when some potential workers offer competence worth only $2.00 per hour. In such circumstances, say the Friedmans, those people will remain jobless for so long as employers are legally barred from paying them the lower rate for doing work they can do.[39]

It stands to reason then, as Edward Banfield claims, that "the way to solve the employment [unemployment] problem in the city is to allow the price of all labor, including the least valuable, to fall to a level at which it will be purchased. If a ditch digger's work is worth no more than $1.00 an hour [in the 1970s] to anyone and if a fifteen-year-old dropout's work is worth no more than 50 cents an hour, these should be their wages."[40] In the real world, instead, minimum wage laws prevail and from time to time are amended to increase the pay levels prescribed. The outcome, according to conservatives, is particularly painful for African Americans whom liberal reformers seek to help, because every time the minimum wage is raised, say rightists, among the first to be discharged, or never hired to begin with, are black teenagers who are not yet skilled enough to compete for higher wages.[41]

On this point, James Watt claims that while "laws mandating higher minimum wages have been passed, black youth unemployment has risen from 25.3 percent in 1966 to 47.3 percent in the 1980s."[42] Yet if the minimum wage in 1980 would have been lowered from $3.10 to $2.25, says Richard Viguerie, "hundreds of thousands of black youths who have no job experience or skills could get a job, get off welfare and the streets and learn a trade and become productive, tax paying and proud members of their community."[43] Justice Oliver Wendell Holmes condemned this sort of laissez-faire argument—which justifies allowing employers to offer deplorable working conditions to unemployed individuals—when he dissented in the Supreme Court case of *Lochner v. New York* (1905).[44] Nevertheless, Mark Anthony concludes that overzealous government agencies should not prosecute Burger King for "allowing teens under the age of 16 to work beyond 7:00 p.m."[45]

Feminism

Many Americans worry that family life is less intimate than it used to be, that divorce rates are uncomfortably high, that teenagers are less respectful of their elders than they were years ago, that many children are failing in school, and that drugs and crime sometimes wreck young people's lives. Liberals have various ideas about why such things happen, while many conservatives believe that "feminism" is a major culprit. Thus Gertrude Himmelfarb observes that, from the 1960s to the 1990s, while women sought economic independence and social empowerment, the percentage of mothers working outside their homes rose from about 30 percent to about 60 percent. There were good intentions here, she thinks, but also "ambiguous effects," such as children becoming problematic due to "government-subsidized day care" that is "inferior to ordinary parental care."[46]

Other conservatives reinforce the image of feminism plagued by perverse results. Carol Ianonne recounts her change of heart as a young feminist who eventually recognized "the extent of damage feminism has done to women and to our cultural life."[47] George Gilder charges unconventional women across the board with failure and claims that "[e]ven feminist sociologists now concede that the *independence effect* [women becoming financially autonomous] conferred by high female incomes is an important cause of family breakdown among men and women of all races and educational levels."[48] Robert Bork goes even further. As he puts it, "Radical feminism is the most destructive and fanatical movement to come down to us from the Sixties.... Totalitarian in spirit, it is deeply antagonistic to traditional Western culture and proposes the complete restructuring of society, morality, and human nature."[49]

Feminists strongly promoted the Equal Rights Amendment.[50] But in the 1970s conservatives predicted for it perverse outcomes. Phyllis Schlafly, for instance, argued that if the proposed amendment were adopted, it would invalidate state laws that require a husband to support his spouse, it would compel states to permit homosexuals to marry and act as parents, it would force governments to abolish veterans' benefits that go mainly to men, it would require the Pentagon to assign combat tasks to female soldiers, and it would compel single-sex colleges to accept students of the other sex.[51]

Religious rightists agreed with such forecasts but also warned that the ERA would destroy first families and then churches. Jerry Falwell, for example, held that feminists undermine stable family life because they have "never accepted their God-given roles," i.e., because, as he and John Whitehead observed, the Bible clearly describes families not as egalitarian associations but as partnerships in which wives should "submit themselves" to husbands because "the husband is the head of the wife, even as Christ is the head of the church."[52] Rosemary Thomson adds that the sort of equality promoted by the ERA will not only shatter Christian families, it may also undermine churches that inspire Christian commitment in those families, because a federal requirement of equality between the sexes might lead to depriving some churches of their tax-exempt status for upholding tradition rather than equality, say, by refusing to ordain women.[53]

Jeopardy

Jeopardy complements perversity in conservative writings. According to Hirschman, the *jeopardy thesis* asserts that in public affairs "the proposed change, though perhaps desirable in itself, involves unacceptable costs or consequences of one sort or another."[54] For example, William Buckley Jr., who opposed the Supreme Court's decision in *Brown v. Board of Education* (1954), argued that to integrate classrooms, thus forcing white Americans to attend schools with black Americans, was to risk "jeopardizing the good nature [good will] of the white majority."[55]

Slippery Slopes

The jeopardy thesis appears when conservatives argue against government programs that, they say, place America on slippery slopes to ruin. For example, George Roche notes that "Progressives," by whom he means liberals, support "the centralization of authority ... and increases in public services provided by governmental agencies." Consequently, "we may find ourselves progressing toward a spiritual collectivization and proletarianization."[56] Or, as M. Stanton Evans notes, "twentieth-century liberalism has failed," but "the resulting concentrate of power ... has led us steadily toward authoritarian practice."[57] Donald Lambro amplifies the charge. "Freedom," he says, "is not lost all at once, except, perhaps, through violent revolution. Liberties are lost bit by bit through a process of attrition often imperceptible to the general population—until it is too late."[58]

Other slippery slopes are more specific. Rus Walton sees welfare payments as implicitly establishing a right of the poor "to share in somebody else's income." Yet if that is the case, "there is no logical stopping place in distributing money and favors to them, short of the point where this brings equality of income for all."[59] In another version of this allegation, Harold Brown argues that we must not accept "adultery and homosexual behavior" as "alternative lifestyles." There, too, a slippery slope beckons, for if long-standing sexual prohibitions are permitted to lapse, we will "find it hard to think of plausible reasons for condemning bribery."[60]

In fact, sex issues abound with predictable deterioration. Irresponsible intimacy can lead to abortions, from which it follows, says Jesse Helms, that, once government has approved of doing away with expendable young people—that is, by abortion—"euthanasia is the logical sequence."[61] Similarly, Ronald Reagan held that "[w]e cannot diminish the value of one category of human life—the unborn—without diminishing the value of all human life."[62] His remarks to this effect, and his opposition to *Roe v. Wade* (1973), were published together with C. Everett Koop's anti-abortion essay entitled "The Slide to Auschwitz."[63]

Same-sex liaisons are also dangerous, for various reasons. Not least among these is their capacity for starting things rolling downhill. William Dannemeyer insists that state laws against sodomy must be reinstated because a failure to condemn homosexual behavior leads inevitably to less support for "the American family and its central place in our society."[64] Or, as William Donohue says,

"Tolerance for sexual behavior of every kind [homosexuality] knows no finish line. It is a slope so slippery that, once stepped upon there are no brakes: it's a sheet of ice. Everything goes, including pedophilia."[65]

The Excluded Middle

Some slippery-slope arguments appear together with right-wing claims that the possibilities under consideration include only two genuine alternatives, in which case nothing viable exists in the space between those two. When Barry Goldwater accepted the Republican Party nomination for president in 1964, he declared that "[e]xtremism in the defense of liberty is no vice. Moderation in the pursuit of justice is no virtue."[66]

Rhetoric aside, what Goldwater really suggested was that one could be entirely in favor of liberty and justice, whatever those might be, or entirely opposed to them. The implication was that anything between being totally for or against these ideals—something like temperance, compromise, prudence, and taking all things into account—would be an unconscionable concession to expediency.

Many compatriots follow Goldwater on this score. For example, Milton Friedman explains that "[f]undamentally, there are only two ways of coordinating the economic activities of millions. One is central direction involving the use of coercion—the technique of the army and the modern totalitarian state [fascism, communism]. The other is voluntary co-operation of individuals—the technique of the marketplace [democratic capitalism]."[67] Or, as George Roche says: "Only two methods exist to organize productive human activity. One is coercive, governmental, and dictated by State authorities: this is the bureaucratic method [fascism, communism]. The other is free, private, and voluntary, and is directed by all consumers.... [T]his is the profit method [democratic capitalism]."[68]

Then there is Michael Novak, who recommends democratic capitalism and claims that "the empirical effect of socialism [communism] has been to give ... unparalleled power and privilege to a small elite, while keeping the living standards of the poor well below those obtaining in free societies of comparable culture.[69] He offers no discussion of social democracies. Robert Bork extends the analysis: "There is really no alternative to a capitalistic, bourgeois society other than some form of socialism [Marxism]. But socialism is widely, almost universally, recognized to be a practical and intellectual failure."[70] Bork does not discuss apparently popular collectivist projects, such as the Canadian national health system. Or consider Joshua Muravchik, who learnedly describes what is at stake: "The contest between them [democratic capitalism and communism] constitutes the overriding political question of our epoch.... When I said just that in a debate with Frances Fitzgerald once, she accused me of holding a Manichean point of view. My answer can only be that this is a Manichean reality."[71]

Under the circumstances, right-wingers often regard middle-ground actions as unsustainable. And so they note that democratic states like Sweden, France, and Singapore have decided to be *somewhat* socialistic. However, conservatives say, such states cannot maintain that compromise in the long run. Instead, says Friedrich Hayek, once they move away from capitalism per se, they will inevitably gravitate toward what conservatives sometimes call socialism, although they mean by that communism.[72]

Ronald Nash agrees and cites another Austrian economist. "The fundamental weakness of the mixed economy," says Nash, "was uncovered by Ludwig Von Mises. According to Mises, no logical third alternative to a free market and socialism [communism] is possible.... 'Step by step it [expansion of government intervention] must continue until it [government] finally seizes control over production from entrepreneurs and capitalists.... The ultimate effect refutes the notion that there is a middle form of organization, the "regulated" economy, between the private property order and the public property order.'"[73] William Simon argues along similar lines by asking what will happen if one will try to mix "the polar systems of political-economic organization," that is, capitalism and communism. In that case, says Simon, in regimes sometimes known as the welfare state, or social democracy, or democratic socialism, and so forth, political liberty will decline, creativity will fade, and wealth will contract.[74]

Truth and Error

In economic affairs, in short, conservatives argue that being a little socialistic is as impossible as being a little pregnant. Danger on the spiritual front, however, is just as great. There, too, dichotomies beckon, usually as some contemporary version of Good versus Evil. Thus Brannon Howse submits that "[w]e as a people will either embrace the Christian worldview or the secular humanist worldview. There is no middle ground."[75] Edward Rowe repeats the contention when he says that "[t]here are only two movements in history—God's and man's. God's movement has been revealed in the Holy Scriptures.... It is theocentric: God is at the center. Man's movement is humanism.... It is anthropocentric: Man is at the center."[76]

Logically speaking, commitment to the word of God as it appears in Scripture makes middle-ground areas exceedingly difficult to occupy.[77] If one possibility is Truth—that is, Christianity—and the other possibility is Error—that is, humanism—then the middle ground is compromise—that is, a little of both, now and then. But to admit that compromise is feasible, is to imply that the Truth is not always True. Thus when Clarence Darrow asked William Jennings Bryan—who testified to biblical veracity during the Scopes trial in 1925—whether he believed that a whale swallowed Jonah, Bryan said that he did so believe. After all, to express doubts about the truth of even so unlikely a story would have been to permit the logical inference that if one part of the Bible was not entirely true, other parts might be somewhat false as well, including the Genesis story of a miraculous Creation.

This sort of reasoning inspires some conservative opponents of abortion. For example, Ronald Reagan quoted Malcolm Muggeridge, a British conservative, who argued that "[e]ither life is always and in all circumstances sacred [Truth], or intrinsically of no account [Error]; it is inconceivable that it should be in some cases the one, and in some the other."[78] Pro-choice advocates say that in some situations abortions should be permitted. But pro-life people, like Reagan and Muggeridge, cannot easily endorse a middle ground implicit in the concept of "some." For them to agree that in *some* cases abortions make sense is to start down the slippery slope that leads to believing human life lacks absolute value. In their view, such a belief is immoral (Error), and would leave no ethical barrier (Truth) against sanctioning abortions, to say nothing of accepting euthanasia and the Holocaust.

Futility

Conservatism's third rejection theme is *futility*, and Hirschman sums up that thesis as a notion "that the attempt at change is abortive, that in one way or another any alleged change is, was, or will be largely surface, façade, cosmetic, hence illusory, as the 'deep' structures of society remain wholly untouched."[79] The beginning of wisdom on this score, as Barry Goldwater says, is that "the first obligation of a political thinker is to understand the nature of man."[80] Here, surely, one searches for a "deep structure." To posit some sort of human nature, however, is to introduce a presumption of invariance into human affairs, where many proposals for social and economic amelioration will seem unpersuasive because they anticipate an improvement in people's behavior—say, a learning curve—that is, a priori, impossible. This is the pessimistic message conveyed by David Horowitz's categorical assertion that "[m]any things change, but people do not."[81]

Sometimes the very titles of conservative books and articles suggest how unlikely learning curves are. For example, Edward Banfield's book *The Unheavenly City: The Nature and Future of Our Urban Crisis,*[82] evokes the imperfection of St. Augustine's two cities, implying that America's urban problems cannot be solved because they flow from character flaws that permanently hobble human projects. Similarly, Roger Kimball's book *Experiments Against Reality: The Fate of Culture in the Postmodern Age,*[83] evokes an image of irrevocable facts standing opposite organized efforts to improve modern life, suggesting that liberal policy proposals are based on misunderstanding human nature and therefore must fail. The same premise, that it is futile to believe that people can intentionally and substantially improve social conditions, resonates in the title of James Wilson's article, "A New Approach to Welfare Reform: Humility."[84]

Human Nature

In other cases, we must look into conservative writings to see how deeply futility arguments are embedded there. On the one hand, religious conservatives regard most people as morally imperfect and not much given to improvement. Therefore, the Christian Right is convinced that biblical standards should motivate both voters and politicians so that, with electoral mandates and moral exhortation, America may in public life deliberately check powerful undercurrents of ambition, greed, arrogance, and a propensity to sin by any other name.[85]

Harold Brown speaks to this concern when he says that "American society, like every other society, needs some kind of generally accepted consensus on values to function," and this means that "the present trend of government in America to participate in the active eradication of traditional Christian values ... will ... make government as we ... know it in America impossible."[86] To this way of thinking, we should fear not just backsliding government but also a general climate of irresponsibility. Thus newfangled notions of situational ethics and moral relativism, and perhaps even feminism, are dangerous because they erode social bonds that unite communities. It is true, says Thomas Lane, that even some church authorities "have embraced foolish notions about changing the nature of man by humoring his passions." Yet to do so can only encourage a "reversion to barbarism"[87]

On the other hand, some secular conservatives believe that people are economically rational. Thus one first stipulates that a man's wants are insatiable and then assumes he may best pursue them in a competition for scarce resources that assigns prices to things that can be exchanged for money.[88] In such a view, economic events flow from irrepressible impulses. In the words of George Roche, "[E]conomics cannot be changed. Market activity is ruled by iron laws. When we interfere with supply and demand, say, we may not know exactly what will follow, but we know it will be unpleasant."[89] Ronald Nash says much the same thing: "There is a basic core of economic concepts and theories in positive economics that applies to all nations and to all economic systems. A nation that adopts institutions and legal frameworks to support communism does not negate a basic economic principle such as supply and demand."[90]

To this way of thinking, markets take into account innumerable bits of information and desire, combining them via Adam Smith's "invisible hand," as individuals, no matter how rational, are incapable of doing. It follows that government, composed of the same individuals, can regulate production and consumption only to the point where citizens will obtain less utility, less satisfaction, and less happiness than if legislators and bureaucrats will refrain from attempting the impossible task of knowing better than supply and demand vectors how to combine efforts and resources most effectively. Milton Friedman was a leading exponent of this point of view.[91] William Simon was another.[92]

Conservatives who posit human nature as economically rational tend to regard the costs of material progress—costs that Joseph Schumpeter attributed to "creative destruction"[93]—as a sort of slippage that cannot usefully be avoided. Over time, they say, compensating individuals such as blacksmiths, elevator operators, typesetters, cotton pickers, vaudeville acrobats, and cobblers, who lose their jobs to such destruction, can only diminish the overall gains made from creativity by society at large. Years ago, Friedrich Hayek noted that while technological progress can unfairly displace workers in every sort of enterprise, helping them by using public money to subsidize obsolete forms of labor would amount to squandering national resources best used for expanding economic production.[94] Or, as George Gilder said later, while praising the pursuit of wealth, "creative destruction is always the essence of [economic] growth."[95]

Genes and Gender

We will explore additional futility arguments later. For now, one such approach to race relations is worth noting. This is the case made by writers such as Richard Herrnstein and Charles Murray,[96] and apparently endorsed by Dinesh D'Souza,[97] that African Americans suffer a genetic flaw that leaves their average IQ roughly fifteen points below many other Americans. Assuming this genetic factor exists and affects IQ as much as conservatives believe, the implication is that little can be done to help African Americans as a group—say, via affirmative action—to study and work more effectively and thereby qualify for better jobs and careers in modern society.[98]

Similarly, conservatives bracket feminism by intimations of futility because they tend to regard men and women as naturally different.[99] If we assume that such differences are inevitable, we may conclude that biological imperatives determine human capacities and that people should express those in traditional gender roles. Thus Phyllis Schlafly describes women as inherently eager for marriage and motherhood, in which case feminism is a futile endeavor to change what nature has wrought.[100] And Midge Dector assures us that every woman "wants to marry." That is, she "requires both in her nature and by virtue of . . . her immediate practical need . . . the assurance that a single man has undertaken to love, cherish, and support her." Women's Liberation, on the other hand, according to Decter is driven by women who refuse to grow up to the role of child rearing and who recommend "nothing less than the radical alteration of nature itself."[101]

Utopianism

The logical sequel to right-wingers claiming they understand why left-wing ends cannot be achieved is to denounce liberals for assessing human nature unrealistically. Hirschman does not stress this point, but American conservatives often describe liberals as people of utopian inclination, as if they believe that "the evils of society . . . are the results of ignorance and faulty social institutions or arrangements," in which case "obstacles to the good society" are "remediable" and one should believe in "progress" and "historical optimism."[102] William Buckley Jr. takes up this cudgel when he maintains that liberals "are men and women who tend to believe that the human being is perfectible and social progress predictable, and that the instrument for effecting the two is reason."[103]

Rael and Erich Isaac extend the indictment when they refer to liberals as "coercive utopians" who would use state power to force citizens to act out a social vision that assumes "that man is perfectible and the evils that exist are the product of a corrupt social system."[104] Roger Kimball attacks the archetypical liberal, John Stuart Mill, and complains that "the great defect" of "Mill's doctrine of liberty" is that it implies "too favorable an estimate of human nature."[105] Irving Kristol sweepingly condemns people of baseless optimism (liberals) in an essay entitled "Utopianism and American Politics."[106] And David Horowitz portrays Democrats as people who "favored an arms control agreement [with Moscow] because, as liberals, they believe in the fundamental good intentions of most human beings."[107]

The Bottom Line

Perversity. Jeopardy. Futility. Conservatives expound these concepts in a steady drumbeat of talk that justifies resisting almost every liberal sentiment or policy proposal. Yet the rightist project does not stop there, because Hirschman's typology, reaching back over two hundred years, overlooked one very practical but recent idea. Thus, perhaps unexpectedly, the ultimate rejectionist ploy is to cut taxes. After all, if government will lack money to fully fund regulation, entitlements, and public works, liberal proposals to do so can be dismissed as unrealistic out of hand, without discussion.

Cutting Taxes

Now, to some extent, tax cuts need no justification, because many people are happy to pay less, none regret getting a rebate, and some will enthusiastically support politicians who advocate easing their burden. Nevertheless, tax cuts for individuals and corporations, enacted by Congress when urged by Ronald

Reagan and George W. Bush, are also justified, for purposes of policy debate, by a theory of supply-side economics expounded by conservative writers such as Jude Wanniski and Paul Craig Roberts.[108]

The theory observes that if affluent people will pay lower taxes, government will suffer a temporary shortfall in revenue and therefore incur a budget deficit. On the other hand, those same people will save more money than before the tax cuts took effect, and they will invest that money in profitable enterprises that will expand employment, raise the National Product, bring in more tax revenues, and eventually balance the budget. This theory is not a central truth in mainstream economics, for reasons too complicated to explore here.[109] But it is acclaimed by conservative politicians and publicists even though its theoretical "proof" in the Laffer Curve—to which we will return in Chapter Two—is so unempirical that no one knows how that diagram relates to real economic behavior.

The Deficit Ploy

Inspired by supply-side enthusiasts like Jack Kemp,[110] Ronald Reagan urged Congress in 1981 to lower tax rates to stimulate the economy. Simultaneously he insisted on higher defense spending, and he left popular social programs, such as Medicare and Social Security, mostly intact. The result was a budget deficit that lasted throughout the 1980s and became an enormously powerful conservative weapon in the political conversation.

What happened, though probably unintentionally, was that government accounts went so far into red ink that no public money was available for improving old social programs or implementing new ones.[111] Yet if that were the case, there was no need to conduct a serious national debate about the merits of doing either, since with no wherewithal, any proposal along those lines, presumably from liberals, would seem unrealistic if not naive. Accordingly, an advantage in debate would go to those on the Right, since they wanted anyway to cancel government programs and, under budgetary pressure, would be relieved of having to try to persuade their opponents that cutting back would be prudent and equitable.[112]

Some conservatives learned this lesson quickly, even though they had for years advocated budgetary caution and fiscal restraint.[113] Without reminding voters of his support for Reagan's tax cut in 1981, Congressman Newt Gingrich explained in 1984 that "balancing the budget is vital."[114] Nothing new there. Then in 1994, in the widely publicized *Contract with America,* he called for a constitutional amendment that, if enacted, would have compelled Washington to balance the national budget.[115] Again, nothing new. But in 1998, sharply reversing himself, Gingrich remarked that "one of the key values of most conservatives is opposition to tax increases. This is not only right in itself, but helpful as well, because it protects us from all sorts of temptations that the liberals love to place before us."[116] In even plainer terms, Paul Krugman describes Republican support for tax cuts as designed to forestall government activism by "starving the [governmental] beast."[117]

The Conservative Mind

Written sources do not indicate that rhetorical rejections in right-wing America flow from a conscious effort to fashion interlocking arguments designed for public debate. Nevertheless, they serve that function and do so powerfully. Whoever tries to do liberal X will get undesirable Y. That's perversity. If we believe that Y will be dangerous, we should desist. That's jeopardy. And if we know in advance that liberal Z cannot endure if established, why try to achieve it in the first place? That's futility.[118]

And what if none of this silences the opposition? Then cut taxes so deeply as to incur a deficit and prevent spending on public projects. Here is the ultimate rejection because, at that point, liberal proposals for using government constructively will seem obviously impractical and, to many Americans, not worth discussing. George W. Bush inherited from Bill Clinton in 2001 a federal budget surplus and serious public debate over how to use the extra money. The new president and his Republican allies in Congress quickly enacted tax cuts and generated massive budget deficits.[119] The debate subsided and played no significant role in the election of 2004 or 2008. Part of it may return, though, via accusations of fiscal irresponsibility, if Barack Obama and his Democratic colleagues will try to fund job creation and health care reform while Washington's financial resources are strained by war costs and massive deficits flowing from commercial bailouts authorized in Congress after the Crash of 2008.

Chapter Two
Irrefutables

So far, we have considered a negative mood that spurs conservatives to regard all liberal proposals as flawed by qualities of perversity, jeopardy, and futility. Propositions to this effect underlie the right-wing political vision we will explore in Chapters Five and Six. Meanwhile, to examine here some positive propositions—about models, rational individuals, personal responsibility, racial color-blindness, unencumbered people, and so forth—is to begin to see how, with considerable optimism, conservatives explain that an amalgam of capitalism, Judeo-Christian ethics, and democracy is desirable for promoting maximal freedom and human happiness.

A word of caution: Some of the items we are about to consider look like they are designed to be debated. That occurs, for example, when fundamentalists ask schools to permit children to compare the notion of "intelligent design" to the theory of evolution, as if pupils might judge one explanation for human origins to be more persuasive than another. In such cases, conservatives rarely intend to put themselves at risk of being proved wrong by critics. Instead, they proceed as if much of what they believe is so true as to be immune to ordinary testing.[1] And therefore many of the claims, assumptions, and demonstrations we will explore in this chapter serve less to promote debate and more to deflect criticism from right-wing precepts. In this sense, some of these new items are more "irrefutable" than they are open to challenge, and that explains the title of this chapter.

Religious Invulnerability

A good point of departure is what religious rightists believe about America. For the most part, theological claims are philosophically irrefutable. Consequently, we need not spend much time considering them here because, although a Christian take-off point is assumed by many modern conservatives, its non-negotiability is clear to both its advocates and their critics.

On the one hand, Christian rightists may depend on faith in a Truth—that God and His will are present in America—that cannot be disproved because its Author is unimpeachable. Many examples bear on this point, and among them we find Jerry Falwell, who says, "I strongly oppose homosexuality. I believe it is wrong because the Bible says it is wrong, because it undermines the family [created by God], and because it violates what God has designed: one man for one woman for a lifetime."[2] Accordingly, Falwell wants laws that withhold legitimacy from homosexuals. Similarly, Randall Terry, a leading foe of abortion, observes that "[a]cross our country thousands of believers are peacefully blockading so-called 'women's health clinics' to bring an end to the slaughter of innocent babies."[3] They are animated, he says, by the biblical admonition that, even where abortions are legal, "[w]e must obey God rather than men."[4] Robert Dugan extends this refrain. "As believers," he says, "we must ... recognize that government receives its authority from God and is accountable to Him. Even though others might not acknowledge God's rule over the whole of life or that ours is a nation 'under God,' we must as Christians assert this truth and not apologize for it."[5]

On the other hand, Christian rightists sometimes go beyond God's immanence and make predictions about American life that cannot be falsified. For example, they may claim that if and when laws will enjoin Christian behavior, good times will certainly come. Ralph Reed, while with the Christian Coalition, delivered this sort of message frequently. As he put it, "If religious conservatives took their proper, proportionate place as leaders in the political and cultural life of the country ... [f]amilies would function again; marriages would work; children would be considered a blessing rather than a burden; neighbors would be neighbors again; government would be the servant instead of the master of a free and educated citizenry; [and] revitalized communities would radiate from compassionate churches and synagogues."[6]

D. James Kennedy expresses similar sentiments and assures us that "[i]f all of the Christians in America simply led one person to Christ this year, this nation would once again be overwhelmingly Christian, and most all [*sic*] of the problems of society would vanish like snow before the rising sun. The solution to those problems is for us to become involved in our culture and to proclaim the Gospel of Jesus Christ. If Christians would do those two things, this nation and this world would be transformed almost overnight."[7] Pat Robertson says much the same. "How revolutionary it would be," he proclaims, "if the nations of the world truly walked in the ways of the God of Jacob. The voluntary application of just one of His principles, called the Golden Rule, would cause air and water pollution to cease, crime to cease, divorce and child abuse to cease, economic exploitation to cease, the narcotics traffic to cease, human rights abuse to cease, and war to cease."[8]

The Role of Models

More subtle cases projecting irrefutability flow from economic reasoning, which promarket conservatives use to advance claims that cannot be challenged empirically. The strategy here is to deploy an analytic model and then argue that because the model seems persuasive, reality must resemble it. Such models can be irrefutable in the sense that Neil Postman describes some advertisements—such as pictures of people cheerfully eating McDonald's hamburgers—as irrefutable, that is, as seeming to imply some conclusion but actually making no statement of fact and therefore permitting no disproof.[9]

Thus Milton and Rose Friedman tell us that under conditions of what they call free trade, "the terms at which any transaction takes place are agreed on by all the parties to that transaction. The transaction will not take place unless all parties believe they will benefit from it. As a result, the interests of the various parties are harmonized."[10] Here is a model that sounds logical. And it is attractive for seeming to describe traders as profiting fairly in proportion to the worth of what they bring to an exchange. But what if *real* trade is not *free,* and what if some *real* traders, who look like they are acting voluntarily, are compelled by force of circumstances to make what are, for them, bad bargains? What happens in fact, by practice and not by theory, in this complicated world of making and selling, getting and spending, where we live?

The Friedmans deflect this sort of criticism when they say, of another model case, that "[t]he actual situation is, of course, more complicated than this hypothetical example.... However, the principle is the same."[11] Thomas Sowell agrees. As he puts it, "The elimination of ... complicating possibilities ... allows the basic analysis to be presented in its skeletal simplicity. Once this underlying skeleton is understood as determining the basic form, then the flesh-and-blood complications of reality can be added—enriching, but not fundamentally changing, that form."[12]

Slighting Evidence

Specific reliance on models rather than evidence appears in other conservative works praising the market and its effects. Thus the Laffer Curve, which presumably justifies Republican tax cuts in the name of supply-side economics, is used by Jude Wanniski to demonstrate that "[t]here are always two tax rates that yield the same [government] revenues."[13] There is a higher rate that will yield, say, $100 million in tax revenues, and there is a lower rate that will also yield $100 million in tax revenues, because at the lower rate, (1) people will work harder than at the higher rate in the knowledge that (2) they will keep most of their income,[14] in which case (3) more work than before will increase output and (4) the lower tax rate on that output will yield as much government revenue as a higher tax rate on less output. The policy implication of all this, according to Wanniski, is that we can (a) choose the lower tax rate, (b) work harder, (c) make and sell more goods, (d) earn more profits, and (e) still have enough public money to pay for government programs that many citizens regard as desirable.

But the Laffer Curve is a model that does not measure the facts of life. And therefore no one knows where, if at all, the lower yet maximally efficient point of taxation may be in any particular country—say, in Japan, Sweden, India, Mexico, or the United States—depending on whatever domestic and foreign policy agendas that country's people see as legitimate and worth funding.[15] Critics might charge that responsible people should not use such indirect reasoning to justify tinkering with government revenues and therefore public services. But Wanniski defends himself against such criticism when he says that he "does not pretend" that what he writes "is a 'correct' model but [he] offers it merely as one that he has found more reliable than competing models as a way of looking at the world."[16]

From Models to Reality

Conservatives who recommend them claim that models can help Americans understand how people behave. But the matter does not end there because, in right-wing talk, some models are promoted as if they are not just possible explanations but mirrors of reality.[17] And when that happens, citizens may unwittingly accept as true and desirable what are, after all, only hypotheses generated by someone trying to score debating points.

Henry Hazlitt, for example, writes about "How the Price System Works."[18] In the process, he fashions a hypothetical scenario starting from examples such as *Robinson Crusoe* and the *Swiss Family Robinson*, in which simple economic exchanges begin, expand between individuals, and eventually grow to millions of buyers and sellers—ergo, "the price system." This system Hazlitt praises and recommends. He does not say, though, that what he calls the price system is only a model rather than the American economy today. Yet such is the case, because what Hazlitt writes about is not the situation we live in. That is, he does not write about a world where the totality of prices in any real place, including countries that call themselves capitalist, is subject to social, economic, and political pressures that can shape trading opportunities in favor of some people and deny them to others.

Or take Michael Novak, who describes "democratic capitalism" as "a predominantly market economy; a polity respectful of the rights of the individual to life, liberty, and the pursuit of happiness; and a system of cultural institutions moved by ideals of liberty and justice for all."[19] Defined that way, democratic capitalism sounds magnificent and therefore Novak advises us to support it. But is he talking about an existing entity, or is he talking about a model, a sort of Platonic Idea of what well-intentioned men and women should strive to achieve according to conservative lights? No matter. Novak insists that "[s]ocial systems like those of the United States, West Germany, and Japan (with perhaps a score of others among the world's nations) illustrate the type."[20] One cannot know which twenty additional countries Novak has in mind, but the clear implication of this passage is that readers should endorse what obtains in America because, according to Novak, it is, more or less, what the model says it is.

Or, as Ronald Nash writes: "The word *market* . . . [describes] the set of procedures or arrangements that prevail throughout a society that allows voluntary exchanges. . . . No one invented the market process. It is an impersonal social institution in which individual people make economic choices in accord with their personal value scales within a framework of rules." What Nash describes here is a model, that is, a benchmark referring to no particular place or era. But then comes the blurring of categories. "Without help from any group of central planners," Nash continues, "the impersonal market system does a remarkable job of supplying the countless wants of countless numbers of people."[21] *Does*? Does as in "does" today and "will do" tomorrow? At this point, the market that was hypothetical becomes, rhetorically, something real that presumably can be found only in countries that reject the doctrines of what Nash calls "socialism."

The same blurring can take place in reverse, moving from actual events to an irrefutable model. Thus Paul Weaver says that the capitalist arrangements that most Americans see around them, which he calls "the corporate state," are unfair and dishonest compared with what he calls "the moral bedrock of capitalism—the free and independent individual, the rule of law, and the market economy."[22] In this case Weaver in effect suggests we should ignore the world we know in favor of a model. Yet this model is a stipulated simplification that recognizes only individuals and ignores many of the institutions, including ethnic groups, sects, corporations, and governments, that individuals create.

Something similar happens when Richard Viguerie turns his back on everyday America in favor of a model. As he puts it, "The so-called capitalism [what America really has] supported by the corporate and political elite entails government subsidies, minimum and maximum prices, tax loopholes for politically-favored activities, and preservation of the status quo (which, as Ronald Reagan used to say, is Latin for 'the mess we're in')." But all that, according to Viguerie, is not real capitalism. "True capitalism," he says, "is an economic system free of governmental interference, to which all businesses, big and small, are free to succeed—or to fail."[23] In this view, critics of modern enterprise are irrelevant. Such critics say that what they call "capitalism" requires fixing when, in fact, "true" capitalism is the model and needs no repair.

Economic Reasoning

When conservative models and reality do not seem tightly linked, part of the problem is that a major strand in conservative thinking relies so heavily on economic concepts as to slight or ignore some things we know from, say, political science, sociology, psychology, and history. The imbalance leaves critics uneasy, but conservatives who emphasize an economic view of the world score rhetorical gains from making reality look more simple and comprehensible than it is.

Rational People

Thus one economic concept shows up when many right-wingers assume, according to models such as those we have noted, that people behave rationally in the special way economists have in mind when they talk about "rational men" who somehow compute the size of advantages and disadvantages in any course of action. Where this notion holds sway, the tendency is to argue that social problems, such as the rate of crime, or the failure of children in school, or the extent of poverty, flow from personal calculations made by, say, poor people and various delinquents.

This is the case, for example, in writings on crime by James Wilson, who stipulates that "[t]he average citizen hardly needs to be persuaded of the view that crime will be more frequently committed if, other things being equal, crime becomes more profitable compared to other ways of spending one's time. Accordingly, the average citizen thinks it obvious that one major reason why crime has gone up is that people have discovered it is easier to get away with it.... Such opinions spring naturally to mind among persons who notice ...

that people take their hands off hot stoves, shop around to find the best buy ... and change jobs when the opportunity arises to earn more money for the same amount of effort."[24]

Newt Gingrich applies similar thinking to the problem of children who perform poorly in school. Leaving aside factors such as broken families, neighborhood segregation, the pressures of social class, the distractions of television, the outsourcing of parents' jobs to foreign factories, and the gap between educational spending in center cities and suburbs, Gingrich argues that children's performances can be improved if we will fashion a proper "reward system." As he says, "One experiment worth trying would be to offer a $500 bonus for any child who enters the first grade reading at a fourth-grade level. If we combine that with an October 'Achievement Sunday' in some local churches at which the bonus winners are recognized, we will have created a social and economic reward system that can have real impact in poor neighborhoods and change the reading patterns of entire communities." After all, "when children learn that basketball players may earn $1,000,000, while studying reading gets you a grade on paper, it's no wonder the summer is spent playing basketball instead of reading."[25]

Like Gingrich, William Simon analyzes human behavior narrowly and therefore sees bureaucrats as deplorable across the board. "The bureaucrat's first objective," says Simon, "... is preservation of his job." This follows from assuming that such men have no work ethic and act only after calculating their personal gain. "Whether real-world problems get solved or not is of secondary importance," Simon continues. In fact, "bureaucrats have a vested interest in not having problems solved. If the problems did not exist (or had not been invented), there would be no reason for the bureaucrat to have a job."[26]

Charles Murray uses comparable calculations to argue that child support programs for single mothers should be abolished. To demonstrate why this is so, he says, "Our guides are a young couple—call them Harold and Phyllis.... She is pregnant. They will have a child together. They will face the kinds of painful decisions that many young people have had to face. What will they decide? What will seem to them to be 'rational' behavior?"[27]

Actually, Harold and Phyllis are analytical constructs rather than our friends and neighbors—parts of a model, really. Murray does not ask real people, as sociologists might, why they get married, and he cannot ask Harold and Phyllis what they intend to do because they do not exist. Instead, he proceeds to calculate "rationally" and concludes that, so long as government provides even low levels of support to unmarried mothers, "[i]t is difficult to think of a good economic reason from Phyllis's viewpoint why marriage might be attractive."[28] So Phyllis won't marry, according to Murray, and her child will have no father at home. But if that is the case, payments to single mothers in the real world should be abolished because, as he says, "transfers are inherently treacherous [by which he means perverse or counterproductive]."[29]

Racism and Employment

Economic reasoning may also show up when right-wingers talk about racism in America. Here, the general argument matches a "rational man" theory advanced by economist Gary Becker.[30] Conservatives who accept Becker's line of reasoning assume that racism in employment does not pay. After all, if efficient and unemployed workers belonging to a minority group are available for work, alert businesspeople will hire them and profit from their productivity. Where such a structure of incentives exists, the fact that potential workers are black, red, yellow, or white is irrelevant, economically speaking. And that means that, in a capitalist society where economic considerations are supposed to rule employer calculations, workplace discrimination must be absent, weak, or on its way to being phased out as more employers get on the bandwagon.

Parts of Becker's approach appear in works by conservatives ranging from Thomas Sowell[31] to Robert Bork,[32] Paul Roberts, and Lawrence Stratton.[33] But wholesale adoption of the thesis is best illustrated in Dinesh D'Souza's discussion of racism. Thus D'Souza cites Becker as demonstrating that to refuse to hire the best-qualified people "makes no economic sense" because employers who do so will "suffer relative to their competition."[34] Building on this hypothesis, D'Souza says it is reasonable to "expect that it [such a refusal] would be relatively infrequent in a competitive market."[35]

Here is an assumption, apparently justified by social science, that is crucial to D'Souza's overall view of race relations in America. If he can demonstrate that it makes sense for employers to hire African Americans, he can go on to infer that a painfully high rate of unemployment for African Americans today must be caused by idle workers rather than potential employers. That is, if businessmen hire few African Americans, they must have good reasons for ignoring the rest.

This step in D'Souza's syllogism leads him to the concept of "rational discrimination." To discriminate rationally is to refuse to hire people because you know something negative about them or the group to which they belong.[36] In other words, taking into account knowledge of a particular unemployed person and/or knowledge of where his or her group ranks in indices of work history, family life, educational achievements, personal comportment, and ambition or lack thereof, you may, according to D'Souza, reasonably believe that hiring such a person is a risk your business can't afford.[37]

We will return to D'Souza's view of discrimination in America. What we have seen so far, though, is that he uses economic reasoning to conclude that African Americans are largely responsible for their own circumstances. Not surprisingly, then, when D'Souza turns to American slavery, he uses the same reasoning to find that people who once owned African American workers were less despicable than historians might say they were. Thus D'Souza stipulates that "it was not in the interest of the owners to carry the abuse of slaves too far. Remember that the defining characteristic of the slave was that he was legally classified as property. Most people, and Southern planters were no different, try to take care of their property.... In summary, the American slave was treated like property, which is to say, pretty well."[38]

Environmental Fixes

Economic reasoning leads some conservatives to argue that liberals worry too much about the environment. Arguments along these lines usually discount what ecologists claim to know—for example, what they have discovered about climate change—because conservatives are especially interested in finding the right balance between the state of nature and the benefits of modern production. As Milton and Rose Friedman put it, "The real problem is not 'eliminating pollution,' but trying to establish arrangements that will yield the 'right' amount of pollution: an amount such that the gain from reducing pollution a bit more just balances the sacrifice of the other good things—houses, shoes, coats, and so on—that would have to be given up in order to reduce the pollution. If we go farther than that, we sacrifice more than we gain."[39] Similarly, Rus Walton holds that "the desire for economic revival should not be an excuse to debauch our lands or foul our nests; yet it is reason to balance environmental considerations with concern for economic impact. What one person rejects as pollution hundreds of others may view as a sign that the factory is still running and their paychecks are still coming."[40]

On the other hand, some conservatives concede that ecologists may occasionally be right and that perhaps drastic steps should be taken, now and then, to rein in pollution and other forms of environmental degradation. Here, though, a problem arises because, if something must be done, that act must limit all members of the community, in which case government must impose restraint. And because most conservatives fear that any government tends to grow tyrannical, some of them promote economic arguments designed to postpone the inevitable.

The first conservative argument to this effect is the dollar fix. It insists that environmental protection is contrived mainly by people of ample means, who are not threatened by poverty, and who therefore can afford to take conservation seriously and sacrifice on its behalf. This being the case, we should encourage economic growth so that such people will be able to afford to repair its environmental results. Aaron Wildavsky captures this syllogism in an essay entitled

"Richer Is Safer."[41] He shows, while ignoring ecological deterioration, how health and wealth have risen along with economic growth in recent times. It follows, he argues, that additional growth will lead to even longer and better lives by permitting, through generous funding, whatever environmental precautions will have to be taken somewhere down the road. There is the dollar fix. For now, growth should continue so that wellbeing will accrue to more people even if they will use more natural resources and create more pollution.[42]

The second conservative argument in this realm holds that science and technique can overcome apparent ecological limitations. In other words, one assumes that a technological fix will appear. For example, scientists and engineers will discover new stocks of natural resources, and they will substitute, for scarce and expensive materials, others that are plentiful and cheap. Conclusions to this effect, say, in the work of Julian Simon, are based on the history of prices, which have for some resources dropped over time,[43] and on the common-sense notion that, just as industrialists have solved many problems in the past, they will continue to do so if new problems, including ecological deterioration, will arise in the future.[44] This notion of a technological fix complements assurances of a dollar fix because the assumption is that people will discover solutions to ecological problems for so long as, from economic growth, we will have enough money to pay for scientific research and development.[45]

The third environmental argument rests on a market fix. Like the previous two, it recommends no immediate action. What it claims is that if and when ecological dangers arise, they will call forth innovative solutions via free enterprise if only government will minimize regulation and permit commercial flexibility. Market fix solutions may not yet exist, but right-wingers claim they will be discovered when needed, by private profit seekers whose pursuit of gain caused ecological degradation to begin with. Thus George Gilder insists that if entrepreneurs are given freedom to do so, they will, via "dynamic . . . innovation," overcome the "tragedy of the commons" and fix whatever "externalities" (in this case, ecological damages) are created by "free markets."[46] And thus R. Emmett Tyrrell complains that environmental "catastrophists" are remiss for not relying on supply and demand. As he puts it, "[W]hen prices rise consumers begin to seek alternatives even as suppliers seek to serve their customers either with more of the resources in question [say, oil] or with alternatives [say, unconventional energy]."[47]

Ceteris Paribus

Economic reasoning of this sort is hard to refute because of an important assumption underlying many conservative writings. Economists recognize this assumption with their qualification of ceteris paribus. By claiming that what you say about society is true "if all other things are equal," it is possible to posit many things that may look true—such as what causes crime, or what perpetuates poverty, or what will reverse global warming—but have no necessary bearing on actual events. Along these lines, we saw that James Wilson believes that, "other things being equal," people will commit crimes if crime seems profitable. That sounds reasonable, but what "other things" in America must be held constant for it to be so? Also as we saw, Charles Murray relies on the same qualifier when he says that, "other things being equal," there will be more crime when risks associated with committing it go down. Yes, but once again, what "other things" in the real world might change this equation?

The Normal Setting

The ceteris paribus argument is rhetorically important. To say that you understand some social event, such as the crime rate, on the condition that all other things are equal, is to assume that human life takes place in a normal setting that is occasionally but insignificantly punctuated by exceptions to the rule. Julian Simon, for example, insists that the growth of world population will not provoke a social crisis because—and here is the normal setting—science and technology will continue as usual and are capable of improving agriculture to the point where it will produce food for whoever needs to eat.

Of course, Simon knows that some people don't receive much of this abundance due to slip-ups and bottlenecks or other social obstacles. Thus he notes that "[t]he sharp food-price rise in the early 1970s was caused by *a chance combination* of increased Russian grain purchases to feed livestock, U.S. policies to reduce 'surpluses' and get the government out of agriculture, a couple of bad world harvests, and some big-business finagling in the U.S."[48] Here are important departures from the norm, which in this case is the reign of technological progress. Or, as Simon says earlier in the same book, "some countries' experiences [in food production and consumption] have been tragically different from the general trend, usually because of politics and war. More about these *special cases* later."[49] Ergo, the rule is again plagued by exceptions.

Now the interesting thing about such exceptions is that, to the economic way of thinking, they are regarded by right-wingers as occasional aberrations whereas for sociologists, historians, political scientists, and anthropologists, the world is full of exceptions that include wars, corruption, untimely deaths, divorces, bureaucratic incompetence, faulty data, deliberate deceptions, assassinations, group think, ethnic tensions, religious fanaticism, floods, plagues, drought, and, not least of all, creative destruction—that is, the social disruption caused by economic evolution. Consequently, to people who take seriously the findings of empirical research, economic reasoning based on *ceteris paribus* assumptions may suggest an occasional insight into human affairs but should not be taken as conclusive until the dots are connected and the blanks get filled in. Anything less would cause us to forget that, in a way, what *ceteris paribus* regards as abnormalities, deviations, digressions, diversions, anomalies, irregularities, eccentricities, and aberrations are, to many scholars—to say nothing of novelists—the sometimes mysterious, and often unpredictable, yet ordinary and inescapable stuff of life itself.[50]

We will see more of ceteris paribus, but a few additional examples are worth noting now. Thus conservatives can say, in favor of piety, that "[w]ith all other factors being equal, inner-city residents who go to church are far less likely to commit a crime or use drugs or drop out of school and are more likely to hold a job."[51] Maybe this is true. Certainly it sounds attractive to religious conservatives. But what "other factors" actually operate in this city or that? And how do they influence local indices of crime, drugs, school attendance, and employment? And what should we do about them?

Or you can claim that "Adam Smith's key insight was that both parties to an exchange can benefit and that, *so long as cooperation is strictly voluntary,* no exchange will take place unless both parties do benefit."[52] The implication is that markets are praiseworthy, but in how many real markets are exchanges truly voluntary? And what should society do, if anything, about exchanges that are not? Or you can assert that "[l]ike consumers, citizens prefer more to less, other things remaining constant or equal."[53] The assumption is that citizens care little about collective ends but vote and lobby to seek personal advantage—say, tax reductions—via public policies. But is that entirely true? Are there no "other things" beyond private gain that citizens occasionally take into account, such as national pride, neighborhood solidarity, ecological sanity, cultural continuity, and mutual responsibility? And if these things are desirable, how may support for them be evoked?

Individualism

We will come back to economic reasoning. But let us turn now to the concept of individualism. European conservatives, such as Edmund Burke, tend to assume that society is an organic structure composed of interlocking groups. But American conservatives prefer to regard society as a collection of discrete individuals.[54] For example, Russ Walton stipulates that his book on America is "not . . . about groups, or sections or segments or however some would slice and slot our society today. *It is a book about individuals—and individuality.*"[55] Dick DeVos lives in a similar world. As he describes it, "Upholding freedom takes honesty, reliability, fairness, compassion, courage, humility, reason, and a great deal of self-discipline ... [as well as] optimism, commitment, initiative, work, perseverance, accountability, cooperation, and stewardship."[56] Here is a list that commends individual efforts, i.e., the trees, but virtually ignores collective projects, i.e., the forest.

William Simon barely sees America. As he says, "There is no such thing as the People; it is a collectivist myth. There are only individual citizens with individual wills and individual purposes."[57] Irving Kristol is close behind. "It is the basic premise of a liberal-capitalist society," he says, "that a 'fair' distribution of income is determined by the productive input ... of individuals into the economy.... [Therefore] a liberal-capitalist order does not—except in extraordinary circumstances—concede to any authority the right to overrule the aggregate of individual preferences on this matter."[58] Or, as Frank Meyer describes the outlook of authors in his conservative anthology: "For all of the contributors, the human person is the necessary center of political and social thought."[59]

Putting the individual first is what Barry Goldwater does when he accepts the Republican nomination for president in 1964 and proclaims that "[i]n our vision of a good and decent future ... there must be room for the liberation of the energy and the talent of the individual.... We must know the whole good as the product of many single contributions."[60] The same preference for individual pursuits over the "whole good" animates George Roche. "We are bombarded," he says, "by such notions as society, race, class, gender, public and countless others groupings like them. To one school of thought [liberals], these aggregates are as real as the gods were to the Greeks.... However, the concepts are all fictions.... I am here to tell you that the individual is the primary human reality. Everything that is conceived and accomplished is done by individuals."[61]

Personal Responsibility

Emphasizing the importance of individuals goes hand in hand with insisting they must tend to their own fate. Here, the key concept is what conservatives call "personal responsibility." Thus right-wingers tend to argue that people of few accomplishments in life, such as the poor, the unemployed, the unskilled, and the uneducated, must do more to improve their situation rather than claim they are victims of forces—say, racism, urban renewal, suburbanization, downsizing, outsourcing, and globalization—beyond their control.

Lawrence Kudlow makes this point by describing "personal responsibility" as a vital moral code. "It is up to each of us," he says, "to behave in socially responsible ways. And that includes *accepting the consequences* of our actions. Blaming others when events go against us, often called victimization, is one of the worst of the liberal-left dogmas of the past thirty years."[62] Harvey Mansfield promotes the same proposition. For him, affirmative action programs too often "come to regard American citizens as victims rather than free agents [responsible individuals] and to substitute the imposition of punitive justice [court decisions] for the democratic choice of policy." The unfortunate consequence, Mansfield continues, is that so-called victims "are not expected to do or understand anything on their own."[63]

From one policy issue to another, conservatives emphasize that personal effort is required. Alan Keyes, for example, worries about abortions and deplores the pro-choice conviction "that encourages young women to believe it's better to take a human life than to take personal responsibility for the consequences of their actions."[64] Stuart Butler and Anna Kondratas oppose welfare and argue that "[g]overnment programs should not prop up the pathology of poverty. We should insist that the poor, like anyone else, must take responsibility for their actions and frame policies accordingly."[65] Ralph Reed notes the crisis in American health care and attributes much of it to immoral behavior that necessitates enormous expenditures for taking care of crack babies, cases of lung cancer (from smoking), drug disorders, AIDS patients (from irresponsible sex), and hospital emergency rooms that deal with "victims of gang wars, drive-by-shootings, and domestic quarrels."[66]

Racial Color-Blindness

Support for personal responsibility leads many conservatives to oppose affirmative action, whose advocates believe that some groups of Americans suffer from discrimination that entitles them to special treatment. For example, David Horowitz links support for individualism to a rejection of affirmative action when he says that "[i]ndividual responsibility means that individuals should win jobs and educational places on merit, not on race or gender. It is the basic American principle of nondiscrimination and fairness to all."[67] Rush Limbaugh endorses the same principle when he says, "There is no question that this country has severe blemishes in its past (slavery) with respect to equality of treatment and access to opportunity. But the way for us to overcome that, in my opinion, is to strive toward racial color-blindness," that is, to treat people as individuals rather than as members of groups.[68]

The historical argument on this score proceeds by stages. First the U.S. Supreme Court decided, in *Brown v. Board of Education* (1954), that school segregation should cease because children suffer when they are assigned to schools by race. Thus the Court accepted, say conservatives, the reasoning of Justice John Harlan, who criticized the Supreme Court decision in *Plessy v. Ferguson* (1896) for ruling that separate but equal facilities are permissible in public services. Harlan insisted, instead, that the Constitution is color-blind and, correctly interpreted, regards all citizens as equal before the law.[69]

Second, Martin Luther King Jr. and his colleagues marched and protested, according to conservatives, to overcome race-conscious laws on behalf of Harlan's principle that all nonwhite Americans should be treated in accordance with their individual merits.[70] This political activism helped the Court to strike down segregation in shopping, public transportation, employment, beaches, hospitals, and libraries, and it evoked support for anti-discrimination legislation, such as the Civil Rights Acts of 1964 and 1965. Third, President Lyndon Johnson noted, in his Howard University speech on June 4, 1965, that it is not enough to open the gates of opportunity to people weakened by generations of discrimination. More must be done to ensure that everyone will be able to walk through those gates.[71]

And fourth, some activists, bureaucrats, and politicians, building on earlier sentiments such as those expressed by the president, proposed affirmative action programs. These were intended to operate in, for example, higher education, employment, housing, and federal contracting, there to assist some groups who presumably could not make their way successfully without special support from government agencies. But these new programs, say conservatives, endanger a trend reaching back to the Middle Ages, whereby American democracy came to be characterized by the principle that civil rights should derive not from one's status as a member of some group but from each person's possession of a natural right to the pursuit of happiness.[72] As Terry Eastland describes this postfeudal achievement of American democracy, "colorblind law provides equal protection for individuals in every racial or ethnic group by denying to any group a position of favoritism or subordination."[73]

Encumbered People

Individualism is a powerful rallying cry in America. Many people feel comfortable with the idea that individuals are important partly because it helps them to feel special and partly because, on occasion, it justifies their shedding some of the inhibitions that attach to traditional obligations. Individualism also promotes, when the world seems too much to us, a heartening image of men and women in control of their destinies, like when Nancy Reagan famously encouraged children to take charge of their lives and "just say no" to drugs.

Nevertheless, the conservative stress on individualism is not entirely persuasive, and Michael Sandel's discussion of encumbered and unencumbered people highlights one reason why this is so.[74] From political science, Sandel challenges philosopher John Rawls's strategy of fashioning a theory of justice by first hypothesizing an "original position." Rawls claims we can reach that position by stepping back mentally from our surroundings, after which we can discover in our minds an abstract principle of justice and then decide to apply that principle to public policy decisions that will shape everyday events.[75]

Sandel argues, instead, that people live in a world of specific circumstances from which they often cannot detach themselves. That is, people live in a world of history, a world of languages, a world of cultures, a world of families, a world of neighborhoods, a world of friends, a world of work, a world of art and spiritual inspiration. To some extent each of us enjoys, or suffers, his or her own combination of such "encumbrances." But to some extent, and with important political consequences, groups of people are encumbered in similar ways, say by tribalism, ethnicity, religion, or nationalism. From this point of view, to offer a model of social interaction—that is, individualism—which ignores encumbrances but recommends drastic policy changes as if men and women are all the same, is to promote a caricature of reality, a world of stick figures that is mostly irrelevant to sober policy debate.[76]

So here is one outcome: When conservatives assume that society is composed of individuals and then call upon those people to exercise personal responsibility, little attention gets paid to encumbrances. Thus Richard Herrnstein and Charles Murray write more than six hundred pages in *The Bell Curve* to argue that little can be done—say, via better housing, better jobs, and better schooling—to change the fact that African Americans on average receive lower IQ test scores than whites, Asians, Italian Americans, Jews, and so forth.[77] What their book downplays or ignores are encumbrances of history, of family, of neighborhood, of employment, and of social discrimination.

In this regard, the argument from IQ amplifies conservative presumptions noted in Chapter One about human nature, as if some average IQ scores denote inherent and limited capacities of certain individuals regardless of their encumbrances. Herrnstein and Murray insist on this point: "As far as anyone has been able to determine, I.Q. scores on a properly administered text mean about the same thing for all ethnic groups."[78] No encumbrances there. Yet this means that elected officials should base public policy on an index that captures a moment in time without reference to what surrounds that moment, and without reference to how, beyond personal and perhaps extraordinary exertion, a momentary performance might be improved.

On this score, the conservative insistence on a "colorblind" interpretation of existing laws shows little regard for social differences. Everyone can agree that all students, including African Americans, should strive to succeed even without special help. But white children, on average, do not necessarily do better than black children because they try harder and thereby display superior character. After all, many minority children in America come to life's journey—unlike, say, William F. Buckley Jr. or George W. Bush—hampered by racial discrimination, bad schools, ill health, broken homes, tough neighborhoods, poor parents, and more.[79] Yet this is the sort of larger picture that William Bennett discounts when he places "moral considerations" at the center of the drug problem. Why, Bennett asks, do "root causes" (encumbrances) fascinate liberals? The main thing is to get more police, more jails, and more courts so as to combat crime more energetically and more decisively.[80]

Voluntary Exchanges

Encumbrances are absent, of course, when conservatives extol the spontaneous trades said by them to characterize capitalism, free enterprise, or the same thing by any other name. Postulates on this score, without reference to extenuating circumstances, are advanced frequently. Thus Milton Friedman says that "both parties to an economic transaction benefit from it, provided the transaction is bi-laterally voluntary and informed." Accordingly, "A working model of a society organized through voluntary exchange is a free private enterprise exchange economy—what we have been calling competitive capitalism."[81]

Ronald Nash amplifies this paean: "The reason people enter market exchanges is because they believe the exchange is good for them. They take advantage of an opportunity to obtain something they want more in exchange for something they value less. Capitalism then should be understood as a voluntary system of relationships that utilizes the peaceful means of exchange."[82] George Roche elaborates further. "In legitimate business," he says, "all exchanges are two-sided, value given for value received. All parties to an exchange enter it voluntarily, and all do so expecting to better their condition by doing so.... In short, everybody comes out ahead, each according to his own scale of values and priorities."[83]

Sometimes conservatives seek to nail down the case for voluntary exchanges by arguing, like Rush Limbaugh, that "we do not believe that the American economy is a zero-sum game—in other words, if I have more, that means someone else will have less."[84] Robert Bork echoes Limbaugh when he affirms that capitalism is not a zero-sum game and therefore "[t]he millionaire's wealth does not cause the pauper's poverty."[85] For both men, the zero-sum analogy is false because, if exchanges are voluntary, each trader gets something of value to her, in which case both sides wind up with more value than they had before. Dinesh D'Souza agrees. Of course the rich are getting richer, he notes. But they are not doing so at the expense of the poor, because "the rich are creating new wealth that didn't exist before." So what if "we live in a society where the rich are getting richer and the poor are also getting richer, but not at the same pace?" At that point, says D'Souza in 2000, "is it a big deal if you drive a Mercedes and I drive a Hyundai?"[86]

The Edgeworth Box

Talk of voluntary exchanges is particularly persuasive if one relates little to real world transactions, where *ceteris* is not *paribus,* and where social encumbrances accompany every trade. Economists have a theoretical construct called the Edgeworth Box which provides one starting point for discussing such matters. But that box does not appear in the conservative writings we have cited here, and its absence says something about the right-wing mind.

Without getting too technical, let us say that the Edgeworth Box uses a graph drawing to show two individuals facing each other in a situation permitting them to trade. Each is represented in the box by her own indifference curve, which measures her preferences for a particular commodity in terms of how much she is willing to pay and what quantity she expects to receive at that price. Where the curve of one individual touches that of the other, the two are likely to trade. Most significantly, the Edgeworth Box shows how, between touching points on two such curves, there is usually room for negotiation to set a price at which an actual trade will take place. That means that if one party is stronger in negotiation than the other, the two will settle on a price that gives the stronger most of what she wants, while the weaker gets something of what he wants but less than what the stronger could afford to yield.

In this situation, one can see the relevance of encumbrances, which are not all equal. Conservatives assume that trades within capitalism are "voluntary." Perhaps most of them are if one defines voluntary as action taking place in the absence of violence or even a threat to wield it. Beyond that, however, what we regard as "voluntary" exchanges depend on relative bargaining strengths, and sometimes those vary substantially.

In the classic case of employment contracts, for example, accepting or not accepting a wage offer is not like buying a tie or doing without it. After all, workers of little means, who must eat and support their families, are not entirely free to reject a meager wage offer from, say, the well-heeled CEO of a major cigarette manufacturer.[87] This is especially so in an era of downsizing. Even workers who increase their strength by joining a union may be constrained by an employer's implicit or explicit threat to send their work elsewhere if his or her wage offer, no matter how skimpy, is rejected. This is one meaning of outsourcing. In both cases, the gains from making a deal are not necessarily summed up by Irving Kristol's declaration that, "in a free market, self-interested transactions between consenting adults are mutually advantageous."[88]

Moreover, "voluntary" exchanges can seem particularly attractive if one looks at each of them separately and ignores their cumulative results. Thus Dinesh D'Souza assumes that no one gets hurt if some people gain a great deal from trades while other people gain less. Yet in the long run, this means that some people will accumulate wealth while others will be able to save little or nothing. We should note, then, that wealth has serious consequences in any society.[89] One is political power, because where wealth is not needed for immediate consumption, it can be invested in politics—for example, via lobbying, campaign contributions, and soft-money advocacy—to induce legislators to revise marketplace rules so that future exchanges, even more than those today, will favor the affluent.[90]

Of course, to speak of political power is to notice how rooted it is in encumbrances, and conservatives would rather not open that Pandora's box. Their preference helps us to understand how Julian Simon can maintain that under conditions of "free trade," Western states cannot "exploit," in the proper sense of that word, third world countries. The assumption, never stated, is that commercial transactions between strong and weak people are voluntary, in which case both sides get what they deserve, ethically speaking. As Simon says, an analogy on this score is when Chicago, a manufacturing center, buys soybeans from farming counties in downstate Illinois.[91] Here is an example that, via *economic* reasoning, ignores the *political* fact that all other things are *not* equal, that Chicago and downstate Illinois trade under conditions set democratically by the state and federal legislatures they share. The same is not true for trade between, say, Parisians and Jakartans. But to point this out is to raise issues of political power that conservatives, wielding a simple model of individual exchanges, prefer to ignore.

Spheres of Justice

Right-wing arguments based on God's will, economic models, rational men, ceteris paribus, individualism, unencumbered people, and so forth have a capacity for deflecting charges raised by liberals against conservative claims. This we have seen in particular cases. Let us now see how and why in such cases something very important may get lost. On this score, it is useful to consider what political philosopher Michael Walzer calls "spheres of justice."[92]

Walzer claims there is no single definition of justice, of values, of performance, of proper agents, and of worthy ends, that can be applied usefully to all realms of human life. What he means is that we should not assume that social affairs can be explained or warranted by any single proposition, such as when some conservatives claim it is the nature of men to sin, or when other conservatives insist that everyone acts rationally in an economic sense.[93] Walzer suggests, instead, that there is an appropriate way of looking at religious affairs; that there is another standard by which we should build armies and assess their work; that a funeral cortege is not a Thanksgiving parade; that celebrating a birthday is not the same as commemorating the Fourth of July; and that, in the business world, managers work according to the bottom line.

Most important, in this scheme of things, standards in one realm may differ from those in another. Thus we would not hire a bishop for his athletic prowess; we would not appoint a battalion commander for his theological acuity; we would not choose a cardiologist because she plays the piano beautifully; and we expect CEOs to behave like Sam Walton rather than Albert Schweitzer. Indeed, as Walzer points out, people in every society agree, as a matter of justice, that some spheres must be kept separate from others.

In democratic societies this recognition of differences shows up in shared understandings that some things should not be for sale, that is, that some possible purchases, regardless of economic "rationality," must be forbidden or "blocked."[94] These include the purchase of people, the purchase of political power, the purchase of criminal justice, the purchase of marriage and procreation rights, the purchase of police protection, the purchase of prizes and honors, the purchase of friendship, and the purchase of ecclesiastical or military rank. Just to consider such a list is to sense that good lives are composed of various spheres, each with its own goals and imperatives.[95]

At the highest level of generality, Walzer in effect claims there is no absolute Truth because each sphere has its own truth. Conservatives are uncomfortable with that sort of reasoning, and we will explore their distress in Chapter Four. For now, it is enough to note that the concept of multiple spheres of justice bears not just on issues of Truth but also on mundane aspects of right-wing talk. Thus Walzer's insight applies to cases where conservatives say that one sort of human relations dominates the whole, or is the cardinal rule in social affairs. Walzer might argue, in his terms of reference, that to make a claim based on one factor is philosophically unjustified. Justified or not, however, in such cases conservatives, wittingly or unwittingly, make it difficult for critics with knowledge of other interactions—that is, other spheres of justice—to press their arguments.

For example, commitment to a monolithic rather than a pluralistic universe of social ingredients is demonstrated when conservatives choose to regard society as composed only of individuals. The difficulty there is that regarding individuals as the principal actors in social theory is like recognizing only trees rather than the forests and thickets they live in, or like seeing only a pile of identical building blocks rather than an enormously complicated matrix of individuals, families, nations, sects, ethnic groups, corporations, political parties, interest groups, labor unions, neighborhoods, and more.[96] In Walzer's terms, at least some of these collectivities can only be understood as shaped by circumstances not easily described in the language of individualism, and maybe not much related to one another either.

The Marketplace

Because individualism underlies much of conservative talk, we will return to it. For the moment, let us note examples of right-wing analysis that raise a sphere issue because they are couched very narrowly. These examples illustrate the tendency of conservatives, while talking about various public policy issues, to use economic terms that do not fully assess all that happens socially. Consequently, in case after case, right-wing talk takes little account of real world events, institutions, and motivations that, beyond the commercial and financial, are regarded as vital in scholarly fields such as international relations, sociology, anthropology, psychology, history, and literature.

The stake here appears when, for example, conservatives discuss marketplaces, where they use economic terms as if those describe citizens adequately and therefore concepts familiar to, say, political science need not be considered. Thus Milton and Rose Friedman argue that when Washington in 1980 guaranteed $1.5 billion in loans for the Chrysler Corporation, the money could have been used more "productively" elsewhere. As they put it, "the market has a far better record than government in judging what are the most productive uses of capital."[97] Productive of what? Microchips, maybe. But sports utility vehicles? Cancer research? Hoop skirts? Old age pensions? Libraries? Pet rocks? Cigarettes? In this case, the Friedmans ignore the ethical nature of a national community, the political mechanisms by which citizens who live together sometimes choose to "produce" some elements of civilization itself, i.e., choose to help or protect one another in ways that they, rather than a marketplace, decide are desirable.

Or, see Irving Kristol when he criticizes liberal activists for wanting to "shape our civilization—a power which, in a capitalist system, is supposed to reside in the free market."[98] Is Kristol so indifferent to what constitutes a civilization—where civilization is a matter of political concern—that he would, say, permit entrepreneurs to peddle machine guns, hard drugs, snake oil, and shares in the Brooklyn Bridge because selling such items to voluntary buyers passes the market test of profitability? In truth, the man known as the godfather of neoconservatism is made of sterner stuff. Thus Kristol elsewhere proposes that the principle of free speech should yield to censorship in the case of pornography, which he considers so patently reprehensible that even consenting adults should not, in his opinion, be entirely free to buy and sell it in America.[99]

And what about Newt Gingrich, who insists that "We must rethink our competition in the world market.... We must rethink all the things that inhibit our ability to compete: regulation, litigation, taxation, education, welfare, the structure of our government bureaucracies."[100] Why should Gingrich, then Speaker of the House of Representatives, think economically rather than politically? In a modern democracy, are his constituents not entitled to ask Congress how, in line with America's social and not commercial contract, it might protect them from the corrosive effects of creative destruction? Congress might insist, for instance, that Third World countries will safeguard human rights, including the right to unionize, so that American workers will not have to compete against what is sometimes, in places like modern China, tantamount to peonage.

Or take Melvyn Krauss, who says that "[i]f Microsoft ... has its products stolen by Chinese counterfeiters, as it apparently does, the problem is essentially Microsoft's."[101] Among other things, he probably means that Washington should not retaliate with sanctions against Beijing because doing so might hurt American consumers by slowing the influx of cheap Chinese goods to American stores such as Target and Walmart. But in the language of international politics, counterfeiting is a crime, in which case the culpable party should be punished as a matter of principle and long term prudence regardless of short term material inconvenience. On this score, does Krauss know nothing of the state and its responsibilities, or of how Admiral Stephen Decatur in 1815 forced the Barbary Coast pirates to sign treaties assuring the safety of American ships in the Mediterranean?[102]

Then there is Jude Wanniski, with his claim that "[b]ecause 'quality' of life is a matter of subjective judgment, the only conceptually satisfying way to measure it is to have individuals do it [the measuring] themselves."[103] Wanniski must be aware that by ratifying the Constitution, Americans created a government to "establish justice, insure domestic tranquility, provide for the common defense, promote the general welfare, and secure the blessings of liberty to ourselves and our posterity." Does he believe such ends can be achieved by individuals' making "quality of life" choices in private markets? Will those markets, rather than taxes and legislation, preserve for them the commons and provide public goods like highways, parks, schools, libraries, safe air, clean beaches, and drinkable water?

Admiration for markets also inspires Patrick Buchanan when, fearing a loss of national power, he worries about declining birthrates in America. The "elite," he says—meaning liberals—who promote conservation and ecological balance claim the world would be better off with fewer residents. But there are 6 billion people in the world today, he observes, and they live better and longer than 2 billion did in 1930. From the fact that people live now so well, comparatively speaking, it follows that we may safely encourage more births in America because it is only "political incompetence and criminality, foolish ideas and insane ideologies" that cause "starvation and misery, not people."[104]

Buchanan can preach endless population growth because he relies on economic reasoning that assumes that commercial progress is normal while politics are an aberration, because he assumes that economic growth can continue indefinitely without piling up consequences that scientists fear may cause irreparable harm to civilization.[105] In effect, Buchanan rejects Walzer's idea that distinct spheres of knowledge and experience can generate various imperatives, among which we must choose and mix depending on real world circumstances. Can there be any doubt, for example, that recent purchases of petroleum by India and China, representing more than 2.5 billion people who increasingly seek to enjoy a modern lifestyle, have driven up the price of that resource and heightened international competition for influence and control of Middle East oil fields? How can such competition be controlled, if at all, by political means? Does the war in Iraq have nothing to do with this by-product of population growth?

Micro and Macro Conditions

In short, where controversies arise between right-wingers and their critics, it helps to concentrate the mind if one can discuss people without reference to, say, what many political scientists, historians, anthropologists, sociologists, and psychologists believe they know about various collectivities those people form.[106] What happens, analytically speaking, is that conservatives tend to assume there is a micro-level substance to society (composed of individuals) that, by growing slowly but steadily, evolves into a macro-level reality (composed of collective entities) that embraces all the bits and pieces that were there to begin with.

In this view, the absence of a link between micro and macro phenomena is especially clear in the thinking of those who praise capitalism as if a description of personal transactions can satisfactorily account for the most important elements of collective life. For example, Tom Rose wrote *Economics: Principles and Policy From a Christian Perspective* (1977),[107] which discusses microeconomics, and then he wrote *Economics: The American Economy from a Christian Perspective* (1985),[108] which discusses macroeconomics. Both praise free markets and private enterprise. But Rose provides no analytical link between the two books and their subjects, between, say, what happens first to people making a living and what happens next in the larger economy of national interest rates and trade balances. In real life, there must be some connection between the one and the other, but Rose does not feel obliged to explicate it.[109]

Milton Friedman accepts the same disjuncture when he says that "[i]n its simplest form … [a working model of capitalism] consists of a number of independent households—a collection of Robinson Crusoes, as it were.… Despite the important role of enterprises and of money in our actual economy, and despite the numerous and complex problems they raise, the central characteristic of the market technique of achieving co-ordination is fully displayed in the simple exchange economy that contains neither enterprises nor money."[110] Ronald Nash is more forthcoming when he says that the activities of groups such as "unions, societies, organizations, and nations" may be of interest to a scholar who thinks economically. He concludes, though, like Friedman, that "the actions of these groups are explained best by concentrating on the actions of the individual human beings that make up the groups."[111]

Libertarians are not the only conservatives who make such assumptions about the economy. George Roche, for example, talks about economic life as if it consists of individuals exchanging money and commodities according to what seems to them, separately, worthwhile. "Such is the nature of all exchanges in the market, no matter how complicated they may seem in their details. It is invariably a matter of two (or more) people trading something they value less for something they value more."[112] Irving Kristol makes similar assumptions. The problem with liberals, he claims, is that "they are at bottom rejecting a liberal [by which he means capitalist] civilization which is given shape through the interaction of a countless sum of individual preferences."[113]

The Fallacy of Composition

The idea entertained by Rose, Friedman, Nash, Roche, and Kristol, that a modern society of roughly 300 million Americans—with money, corporations, scientific research, superstores, networked computers, fast food chains, televised preachers, credit cards, environmental regulation, advertising, and stock market gyrations—goes about making a living and buying commodities like a collection of Robinson Crusoe households, is very powerful as a rhetorical device. We may assume that because simple examples and small-scale ideas are comprehensible to most people, some who hear such an argument may believe that whoever promotes it understands what he or she is talking about.

Nevertheless, the same idea is also a classic example of what philosophers call "the logical fallacy of composition," where if the parts of a whole have a certain quality, the whole is deemed to have the same property. Reality does not work that way, as if, when individual men and women get together, there are no nations, no tribes, no sects, no crowds, no stereotypes, no committees, no mass hysterias, no fashions, no brand loyalties, and no economic bubbles. Furthermore, to suggest that America can be understood without concepts drawn from noneconomic disciplines—like the power plays and social contracts that political scientists analyze, the role playing and functional rationality that sociologists study, the risk assessments and group thinking that psychologists explore, and the myths and taboos that anthropologists investigate—is to ignore Walzer's central point about how spheres of justice, via different values, agents, and ends, make different contributions to our understanding of life. Of course it is difficult to argue against an economic view that seems neat and tidy. But the same view does not explain how societies cohere and thrive. It simply assumes that if individuals will look out for themselves, civilization will appear and endure.[114]

The Conservative Mind

Conservatives frequently advance arguments ranging from what sorts of models can accurately describe a free society, to how people act rationally in various realms of life, to what is the nature of economic transactions, to how such transactions between citizens are the key to understanding what happens throughout the country. These arguments, and others we will note, speak of an America founded in individualism and personal responsibility rather than feudalism and collective solidarities, of an America maintaining an economy of private property and free enterprise rather than some measure of capitalism tempered by an occasional socialist project, of an America committed to democracy and political consent rather than big and sometimes meddling government, and of an America infused with principles derived from Christianity rather than from secular and scientific relativism.

That being the story so far, what does it tell us about the conservative mind? Mainly, we know now that arguments in support of the larger vision may be so bounded that critics are hard-pressed to challenge them. In some cases, like when right-wingers use models to represent reality, facts are not advanced and therefore cannot be disproved. In other cases, where some facts are introduced to draw conservative conclusions, other facts are ignored, as when the ceteris paribus assumption of "all other things being equal" is stipulated.

Furthermore, we now know that conservative arguments are rhetorically powerful because they tend to simplify, because they speak mostly in terms that are uncluttered and comprehensible, to say nothing of, perhaps, confirming common expectations. And we also know that, underlying and strengthening this capacity for simplification, there is a preference for leaving aside encumbrances and overlooking many insights that flow from various fields of knowledge and experience.

Now, to a considerable extent, those fields in modern society are powerfully informed by the findings of social science research, often conducted at leading colleges and universities and not much admired by conservatives. Eventually, however, I will suggest that small conservative interest in encumbrances, and the rejection of relative truths that clash with conservative axioms, are not just academic matters. After all—and this we will see in Chapter Seven—they can affect public policy as, for example, when a right-wing vision drove America to war in Iraq without taking into account that that country is inhabited by people encumbered by ethnicity and sectarianism to the point where no one knows how to establish among them a democracy based on tolerance and equal rights for all citizens.

Chapter Three
Promotions

Conservative arguments do not appear in a sequence that makes their overall meaning plain. Nevertheless, I have suggested that right-wing talk starts, so to speak, in notions about perversity, jeopardy, futility, and human nature. We then explored lesser rhetorical items—such as models, the ceteris paribus assumption, economic terms of reference, and individualism—which are noteworthy separately but also powerful in public debate because they are to some extent irrefutable—that is, difficult to engage directly and to test conclusively.

These small pieces of right-wing talk contribute to a larger political vision—of freedom unfolding in America and around the world—which we will review in Chapters Five and Six. On the way to that end, however, and to an understanding of how conservatives and liberals differ in the realm of talk, let us now consider how additional propositions, claims, and demonstrations help to establish earlier rhetorical items on the right as credible. There are no hard and fast distinctions to be drawn here, but we may regard these additional items as promotional devices—as bits and pieces of information deployed to buttress broader arguments.

Anecdotes

For example, on behalf of promotion many conservatives embellish their talk with anecdotes. Ronald Reagan was a master of this tactic, and Russell Kirk, introducing a typical right-wing book, explains why anecdotes are a preferred rhetorical device. "The authors' method of rousing the great sleepy public," says

Kirk, "is the true narration ... [or] illustrative anecdotes extracted from our newspapers and magazines.... From these vignettes of what has been done to our neighbors, we learn what may be done to us, and soon."[1]

Accordingly, conservatives often enliven their writings with anecdotes like the following: "Someone once estimated that there are 502 taxes of one sort or another on a pair of shoes; each one levied at a different stage of production and distribution and sale by a different governmental agency."[2] Or, "It is indicative that Janet Reno, [President] Clinton's Attorney General, devoted more public comment to the rights of criminals than to defending the legitimate rights of crime victims and the community at large."[3] Or, "In the climactic hours of the Communist fall [1989–1991], someone—Boris Yeltsin perhaps—remarked that it was a pity Marxists had not triumphed in a smaller country because 'we would not have had to kill so many people to demonstrate that utopia does not work.'"[4]

Such anecdotes cover many subjects. Thus: "The federal government once held up a license for a residential project because the bureaucrats in charge wanted to protect a wetland. The wetland they were guarding was .0006 acres—about the size of a ping pong table."[5] And, "In the last years of the Clinton administration, 26,000 very special Americans received $8.5 million in food stamps. The reason that these Americans were special is that they were dead at the time the food stamps arrived."[6] And, "Dr. Bruce N. Ames ... recently commented on the proposed ban on commercial pesticides by the EPA. I didn't record his exact words, but the gist was: There are more carcinogens in a cup of coffee than in all the foods you eat in an entire year."[7]

Or, to condemn what he regards as unfair cases of product liability, one rightist reports that "a gymnast missed his one-and-a-half rollout in a trampoline, hurt himself on landing, and sued the manufacturer of the mat. He was awarded $14.7 million in the initial case."[8] Against "humanism" regarded as an inclination to ignore traditional standards of decency, another rightist tell us that "[a] father, dying of kidney failure, artificially inseminated his 16-year-old daughter with the help of her physician. Seven months into her pregnancy, the child was taken from her uterus by Cesarean section. The newborn baby's kidneys were removed surgically and transplanted into the father. Then the innocent new infant was cruelly left to die of uremic poisoning."[9]

In all of this, conservatives know that, as pictures can be worth thousands of words, so a story may affect readers more powerfully than many pages of logical or philosophical analysis. This is what William Bennett has in mind when he notes that he relies often on anecdotes in his work because "behind almost every political ... story there is a moral sentiment, a mind-set that influences and often dictates the judgments made about particular issues."[10] Or, as Steve Forbes says, "The statistics [on family life] are grim enough. But the anecdotal evidence hits home."[11]

The Matter of Truth

Many right-wingers are committed, then, to telling anecdotes.[12] Yet what if some of those are framed with a little exaggeration here and a little poetic license there? Ronald Reagan, for example, illustrated his worldview with many stories that treated facts carelessly. Thus he told visitors to the Oval Office that he personally sensed what had happened in the Holocaust because he was present when American soldiers liberated German concentration camps.[13] This Reagan recounted even though he did his entire Army service during World War II in the United States.

No one could be sure that Reagan's stories were true.[14] His popularity did not suffer as a result, though, because Reagan understood, better than those who complained about his "facts," that stories are effective when listeners judge them to express a truth that is more important than whether one ostensible fact or another advanced in any particular story is entirely demonstrable.[15] Furthermore, Reagan knew that conservatives tend to believe they already know the Truth, in which case if a story confirms it, one need not be too fussy about whether or not the story is as accurate as the equation that says two plus two makes four.[16]

In other words, only a pedant insists on precision. Perhaps with that thought in mind, Midge Decter tells what she calls "exemplary stories" about parents and children, mainly to scold the children. These stories "are not 'true' stories," she says, "in the sense of being about individuals known to me or interviewed by me or whose case studies have been presented to me." They are "true stories nevertheless," as Decter says, in the sense of conveying something that she, and perhaps her readers, know to be true about what relationship parents and children should maintain.[17]

The Lack of Citations

But what if liberals, hoping for rhetorical gain, insist that right-wing stories should be tested for accuracy? In that case, the chances are that such critics will encounter a conservative tendency to protect the plausibility of their anecdotes by not providing citations. In this way, after all, a protagonist in debate can make claims with instant emotional appeal even while he or she prevents detractors, say, in the scholarly world, from checking to see if those claims—like the one about "Boris Yeltsin perhaps"—are true.

Liberals are frustrated, then, when confronted by conservative statements such as "Schools are no exception to the generalization that anything government does tends to cost twice as much as it costs if done in the private market."[18] Anything? Twice as much? Without footnotes—that is, without reference to recorded facts—

why believe such a claim? Or, "Given that the average inmate has committed an estimated 187 crimes in the year before going to prison, at an average cost of $2,300 per crime, society gets a pretty good return on a $70,000 [per jail cell] investment."[19] Who is this average inmate? Are such numbers reliable? Where do they come from? Or, in opposition to environmental pessimists, "There are more acres of forest land in America today than when Columbus discovered the continent in 1492."[20] Really? Does the U.S. Forest Service confirm that figure? Are the trees hardwood or soft, old growth or new? Are they in biodiverse forests or are they growing in rows for Christmas?

Then there is the story, told by Phyllis Schlafly and Chester Ward to mock federal employees, that something called the Board of Economic Warfare during World War II tried "to buy up all the rabbits in Europe, and thereby cause the German troops to freeze to death in Russia [for lack of warm clothing made from rabbit fur]." The strategy failed, according to Schlafly and Ward, because the rabbits bred faster than they could be removed from the market.[21] Was there a Board of Economic Warfare? Yes, between December 1941 and July 1943. Did it pursue such a strategy? That is hard to believe, if only because at that time the board had no access to most of Europe.

And what about teenage abstinence? "How do we know kids can say no?" ask John Ankerberg and John Weldon. "Because for most of human history the vast majority of teenagers have waited for sex until marriage.... Teenagers adopt this behavior all over the world. In China the vast majority of teenagers—95 percent—remain chaste until marriage."[22] Leave aside the vagueness of "most of human history" and "the vast majority of teenagers." Is the number for China credible—95 percent?

And what should be done with problematic children? "We have had for over a century now, in this country and elsewhere," says Irving Kristol, "an infinite variety of juvenile delinquency programs. They have all been studied exhaustively by sociologists, criminologists, and social workers, and the findings are dismal. Not a single such program works better than no program at all."[23] There were *no* programs that worked? Not a single one? Not even one that worked a little? And this is confirmed "exhaustively" by "sociologists, criminologists, and social workers"? Do most members of these disciplines agree with Kristol? If not, why not?

Self-Validating Stories

Apart from whether they are true, or whether citations support them, conservative anecdotes often display powerful elements of style. Many conservative writers—especially in comparison with liberals—display significant talent for infusing their anecdotes with verve and panache, for placing a construction on little stories that makes them leap forcefully off the page and directly into a reader's mind. Such stories, like artful advertisements, are likely to evoke a strong emotional response, a feeling that the teller has identified a point of principle that cannot be denied. We may think of these anecdotes as stories that seem so obviously true, at least to people on the right, that they are, in a sense, self-validating.

To see what is at stake here, let us consider, without checking for veracity, examples from a range of conservative writings. Some of these challenge the separation of church and state. Thus Pat Buchanan says that "[i]f you wish to reshape American society through law, says the [Supreme] court, you may use as guides the books written by Karl Marx, Rachel Carson, Betty Friedan, or Al Gore, but not the books written by Matthew, Mark, Luke, or John."[24] William Donohue is equally caustic when he notes that "Angela Kaye," a high school senior, was "banned from giving a valedictory address because her speech included a quotation from Jesus. Had she decided to quote Larry Flynt, editor of *Hustler*, that would no doubt have been acceptable."[25] Or, "What the American people don't understand," says William Bennett, "is that a group of students can ... get together and say, 'We must all advance the Marxist revolution.' ... But they can't get together and say, 'Our Father, who art in heaven, hallowed be Thy name.'"[26]

Abortions are another target. Thus George Roche describes a liberal as "one who deplores the killing of baby harp seals and defends the killing of baby humans with equal vigor."[27] Along similar lines, Jerry Falwell says that "[s]urely there is something very wrong with a society that protects owls and eagles' eggs, but offers no protection for precious unborn human life."[28] Ronald Reagan agrees, when he tells us about "a young pregnant woman named Victoria," who says that "[i]n this society we save whales, we save timber wolves and bald eagles and Coke bottles. Yet, everyone wanted me to throw away my baby."[29]

Harold Brown is shocked that "[a]lthough a minor girl could not have her ears pierced without their written consent, her parents have nothing to say about whether the state provides [her with] an abortion."[30] Randall Terry finds it strange that "[w]hile schools cannot dispense an aspirin to a student without written permission, they can make an appointment for a young girl to have her child killed—a major medical procedure that could leave permanent physical and emotional scars—and her parents would never know."[31] John Whitehead offers the following: "Today's gatekeepers of information [the liberal media] show no reluctance about depicting in frank fashion, with overt condemnation, the slaughter of baby seals or the threatened existence of the snail darter. However, when it comes to coverage of the slaughter of unborn children, a double standard of morality sets in."[32]

There are also miscellaneous cases. Michael Medved, who wants less sex and violence in movies, says that of course Hollywood studios have a right, by free speech, to make any sort of movie they might choose to make. But could we really defend their choice if they filmed "a revisionist view of Holocaust victim Anne Frank that portrayed her as an out-of-control teenage nymphomaniac who risked capture by the Nazis night after night to satisfy her raging hormones?"[33] Irving Kristol complains that "in the United States today, the law insists that an 18-year-old girl has the right to public fornication in a pornographic movie—but only if she is paid the minimum wage."[34] And Gertrude Himmelfarb condemns the "liberals who advocate the largest freedom for artists . . . [yet] also tend to support, in the name of the same freedom, the strictest separation of church and state—with the curious result that the photograph of a crucifix immersed in urine can be exhibited in a public school, but a crucifix not immersed in urine cannot be exhibited."[35]

Correlations

In Chapters Five and Six, we will return to the promotion of anecdotes as a sort of storytelling in which conservatives display an aptitude unmatched by liberals, with crucial implications for modern American politics. For the moment, let us continue here to note that right-wing rhetoric is especially powerful when its anecdotes entail what may be called persuasive correlations. Technically, two things are correlated when they occur in tandem, as when umbrella sales rise during rainy seasons. In that case, we may conclude that rain causes those sales to thrive. However, correlation is not the same as causation. For example, children's math scores and children's shoe sizes go up together. There is the correlation. But what does that signify for causation? Does the correlation show that big feet are a predictor of intelligence? Or does it show only that older children with big feet will score higher on a standard test in mathematics than younger children with small feet? In fact, what such examples demonstrate is that, while a correlation of two factors may point toward conclusions having to do with causation, we will know if those conclusions are reasonable only if we will know something of the circumstances that surround those two factors.

General Examples

In light of these fundamentals, it is clear that many conservative correlations pay little attention to the logic of causation. They seem to suggest important conclusions. But they do so mainly by focusing on a limited range of trends and ignoring many possibly relevant conditions. For example, look at what Pat Buchanan says about the decline of the British Empire. "It is no coincidence," he observes, "that the passing of Britain as a great power, and the decline of the British nation proceeded . . . with the rise of British Socialism."[36] The culprit here is "socialism." Does that mean that World War I and World War II had nothing to do with Britain's decline?

Beyond socialism, Jude Wanniski attacks a favorite right-wing target when he argues that raising income taxes for, among other people, opera singers makes it unprofitable for Mary S. to continue to sing and more likely that she will enter the sex business. The result, as he puts it, is that "an increase in the government wedge [taxes] decreases the quality of opera and increases the supply of prostitutes."[37] Does this mean we should blame modern government if the number of women selling sex rises? Are there no other causes?

Or, Irving Kristol notes that "the tremendous expansion of government during these past three decades has not obviously made us a happier and more contented people. On the contrary, there is far more sourness and bitterness in our lives, public and private, than used to be the case."[38] In other words, government growth is the cause of modern discontent rather than, say, television commercials, recorded announcements, outsourcing, downsizing, climate change, understaffed superstores, traffic jams, call waiting, fast food fat, Windows Help, delayed flights, cell-phone addiction, and fear of nuclear war.[39]

George Will is like Kristol for being critical of "government" in general. And so Will declares that "[a]s government has become more determinedly ameliorative, it has fallen in the esteem of the public whose condition it toils to improve."[40] Will does not say what time frame he has in mind. What is clear, though, is that he will not promote what is surely true as a simple correlation, that the federal government has fallen in esteem, according to survey research findings, while Republicans (and conservatives) have gained more and more commanding positions in it since the election of Richard Nixon in 1968.[41]

Crime

Additional examples of partisan correlations abound. On crime, there is Myron Magnet noting that "[a]s it became possible to suppress key evidence and literally get away with murder, crime took off. In the sixties, the overall crime rate doubled."[42] In other words, more crimes were committed because thuggish people learned about new rules of evidence. These would include the Miranda warning that informs suspects they have a constitutional right to remain silent and consult a lawyer. This is something that Enron executives and Bernard Madoff knew all along but that, Magnet may suppose, many other incipient felons did not. Then there is Dick Armey, with his contention that "crime pays." Statistics, he says, bear him out on that point: "A murderer can expect a mere 1.8 years in jail. A rapist, just sixty days in the hoosegow." Thus "[a]s punishment goes up, crime goes down—and vice versa."[43] Armey offers no footnote to permit anyone to check the source of these numbers, see what they represent, and observe whether they are rising or falling over time, in relation to what.

On matters criminal, both men prescribe an active government, and both are challenged by Milton and Rose Friedman. The Friedmans say that criminal events and expenditures on law enforcement have increased together. There is the correlation. What it proves, according to the Friedmans, is that "throwing money at the problem has been no more effective in curbing crime than in improving education."[44] In other words, Magnet and Armey are wrong: More police officers (funded by rising law enforcement budgets) to catch more criminals, and more prison facilities (similarly funded) to keep them locked up longer, have no effect on the criminal mind.

Schools

In this charge, the Friedmans prepare us for a conservative correlation that says spending for education is unrelated to children's performance. William Bennett, who served as secretary of education (1985–1988) under Ronald Reagan, visits this contention repeatedly. In one book he observes that between 1950 and 1989, spending per pupil rose almost 300 percent in real terms, while from 1963 to 1980, average Scholastic Aptitude Test (SAT) scores declined from 980 to 890.[45] In other words, when spending goes up, performance goes down. In another book, Bennett notes that between 1960 and 1980, spending on education doubled, with average class size shrinking and teachers' credentials improving. But SAT scores fell 85 points in the same years, even while the homicide rate for young people more than doubled.[46] Therefore, again, as spending goes up, performance goes down.

To correct this state of affairs, conservatives often propose dispensing school vouchers. With such vouchers in hand, each worth thousands of dollars, parents will not have to send their children to neighborhood schools but will be able to shop around for a school elsewhere. Presumably this technical device will force schools to compete for vouchers, in which case, according to conservatives, the schools will perfect their product and children's performance will improve.[47]

Here is the conservative preference for market arrangements. However, to say that vouchers will work is to assume that money conveyed by vouchers can make a difference in education, which contradicts what conservatives say to begin with. Furthermore, other factors that might cause poor performance in school—such as television watching, computer addiction, parental indifference, juvenile violence, students' working part time, poor command of English, high rates of divorce, neighborhood fragmentation, and more—do not appear in right-wing correlations that focus on average educational spending and average scholastic performance.[48] Thus the rightists we have cited do not suggest how better to spend specific sums of money, in school or out, to deal with such impediments, and others, successfully.

Sex Education

The rhetorical road from schools to sex, paved with persuasive correlations, is short. Jerry Falwell states the basic proposition plainly: "Since Planned Parenthood–type programs began in 1970, unwed pregnancies have increased 87 percent among eighteen- and nineteen-year olds."[49] That is, more sex education causes more pregnancies. William Dannemeyer makes the same claim. As he puts it, "[E]ven as the amount of sex instruction has risen over the years, so has the pregnancy rate—not just the number of pregnancies, mind you, but the *rate* at which unmarried girls are becoming pregnant."[50] John Ankerberg joins the chorus. We must ask, he says, "what happened in our society as a result of these sex education classes in the last 20 years." The answer is that "over 50 percent of all 15 year olds have had sex. This is compared to 10 percent 30 years ago."[51]

William Donohue offers a qualification. "It is striking," he says, "to note the correlation between the expansion of sex education and unwanted teenage pregnancies: the more we have of the former, the more we have of the latter. No one doubts that the correlation is true, the only question is whether there is a cause-and-effect relationship. It is impossible to know for sure, but what is not uncertain [i.e., what is certain] is the fallaciousness of the proposition that more sex education yields fewer unwanted teenage pregnancies. Yet this is precisely what Planned Parenthood recommends."[52]

The significance of this anecdote hinges on what meaning should attach to the phrase "fewer unwanted teenage pregnancies." If it means fewer pregnancies than occurred years ago, Donohue may be right. But if it means fewer pregnancies than would have occurred without sex education, in an era where teenagers are titillated relentlessly by sexual images in popular and commercial culture, Donohue may be wrong. Ironically, the finger is, in effect, pointed at him by Michael Medved, who deplores how Hollywood exploits sex more openly now than in the past.[53] From Medved we get a sense of how teenage pregnancies might be inspired by surrounding factors—in this case, movies—which are missing in the correlation that Donohue describes.

Religion

From sex to piety, conservative anecdotes are again buttressed with persuasive correlations. Larry Burkett, for example, says that the Supreme Court in 1962 struck down school prayer and thereby forbid mentioning God in the classroom.

Since then, he notes, children use more drugs, are more likely to contract venereal diseases, are more violent, and are more likely to commit suicide. That is, when God leaves school, immorality enters. "And we call this progress," Burkett observes dryly.[54] Harold Brown brings the same reasoning to bear on crime. A "marked increase in crime," he says, "... happens (does it 'just happen'?) to coincide with a systematic turning away from the principles of our Judeo-Christian spiritual heritage in law, the courts, the schools, and the media."[55] That is, when Americans reject God, they embrace sin.

John Ankerberg and John Weldon paint the same picture. "In the last thirty years," they say, "we have increasingly removed God and absolute moral values from our national culture. Since then we have experienced a dramatic rise in [the] divorce rate, illegal drug use, crime, child abuse reports, suicide levels, educational decline, political corruption, teenage pregnancies, economic dislocations, sexually transmitted diseases, pornography, abortion, and many other social ills."[56] As before, less faith encourages more turpitude.

Reverse Sequences

Some particularly persuasive right-wing correlations are driven by reverse sequences. These show up when conservatives reject liberal propositions by turning them around. For example, liberals tend to argue that poverty is a major cause of immorality, in the sense that want drives some people to crime. Here the assumption is that efforts to ease poverty will, by forestalling crime, enhance public safety. Conservatives argue exactly the opposite, that immorality causes poverty. That is, steady aid will not lift poor people out of poverty. If they would commit to God, however, they would work harder, earn more, sin less—that is, commit fewer crimes—and emerge from deprivation.[57]

As for schooling, liberals are likely to argue that America is a pluralistic society, where different groups live side by side. Here is the rationale for multicultural education, for the proposition that life in America will improve if schools will accept the fact of cultural diversity and discuss with students the views and aspirations of people different from themselves. Once again conservatives argue the opposite, that America is collapsing into a cacophony of clashing voices and values. In their opinion, this descent takes place not because pluralism already exists but because schools are enamored of multiculturalism, in which case they foster pluralism by failing to unify students via teaching them precepts that are essential to America's way of life.[58]

Environmental degradation inspires its own reverse sequence. Liberals sometimes accuse capitalists of polluting the world we live in. The charge may seem to them reasonable because great corporations shop around, inside and outside

America, in search of "good business climates" maintained by governments, local or national, that enforce antipollution laws weakly or not at all. The inference is clear: Capitalism is an ecological danger that must be regulated so that some profits, by government order, will either be foregone in the interest of environmental protection or put aside to pay for ecological repair.

Conservatives tend to say just the opposite. For example, Aaron Wildavsky argues that throughout history, only affluent people have had the time, money, and emotional energy to draw up pro-environmental policies and enforce them.[59] The inference is again clear: Profit-making should be subject to little or no restraint because commercial success is not an ecological villain but the source of private wealth that will overcome environmental problems should they arise.

As for health care, liberals are inclined to believe that medical expenses rise in modern societies largely because science and technology provide pills and operations, pacemakers and prosthetics, vaccines and MRI scans and disposable hospital equipment. These improve the quality of life but impose enormous bills for health care. Under the circumstances, many people cannot afford medical insurance; therefore, government should create entitlement programs that, by earmarking tax support and spreading the risk, ensure to every citizen health care when necessary.

Again, conservatives believe that things are the other way around. Like liberals, conservatives note a correlation between rising health bills and the growth of Medicare and Medicaid. Unlike liberals, they then conclude that state and federal insurance programs cause expenses to go up, which is the reverse of what liberals claim. The chain of effect seems clear to right-wingers: When governments rather than patients pay doctors and hospitals, citizens lose track of how much health care costs, use too much of it, and demand even more. Fueled by this irresponsible consumer behavior, medical prices rise.[60]

The Great Reversal

Among reverse sequences, one stands out not only for the effort conservatives make to promote it but also for the plausibility it has achieved in American social thought. The sequence, explicated at length in right-wing writings, holds that high rates of poverty and unemployment in African American communities are due in large part not to racism practiced by other Americans, as liberals might claim, but to offensive behavior displayed by African Americans. Where this line of reasoning is regarded as true, it may help the Republican Party to acquire electoral strength at least in America's southern states. There, since the Goldwater campaign, many white voters have left the Democratic Party and support Republican candidates for local and national offices.[61]

The clue to what happens on this score is a lively right-wing interest in the Kerner Commission Report, which most Americans have probably forgotten. President Lyndon Johnson appointed Illinois Governor Otto Kerner in 1967 to chair the National Advisory Commission on Civil Disorders that studied riots in Detroit and Newark. In 1968 the commission reported that racism caused the riots. Ergo, the national civil rights problem was rooted not in destruction wreaked by rampaging blacks but in discrimination practiced by bigoted whites.[62] From the commission's report, indeed, liberals could infer that if black Americans had *not* rioted, had *not* broken the law, and had *not* acted out their conviction that peaceful complaints were powerless to overcome injustice, then no progress in the field of civil rights would have occurred.

Conservative writers tend to condemn the Kerner Report.[63] Charles Murray, for example, holds that it charged "white racism" with responsibility for the 1965–1968 riots but "presented no proof of this statement."[64] Stephan and Abigail Thernstrom named their massive work on race relations *America in Black and White: One Nation, Indivisible*,[65] thereby implying that the Report of the Advisory Commission wrongly forecast growing de facto segregation in America. Then, in the book, they specifically criticize the report on various grounds.[66]

Thomas Lane argues that "[t]he charge of white racism levied in the Kerner Report was a typical Marxist attack on the free society."[67] His point is that democratic capitalism permits all citizens, white or black, to work hard and get ahead. Where, then, is the Marxian ruling class that exploits African Americans? David Horowitz complains that the Kerner Commission invented the liberal concept of "institutional racism," which locates discrimination in patterns of housing, schooling, and employment. Thus, he says, the commission's report justified violent rebellion against democratic institutions, after which it promoted programs of affirmative action that subvert the principle of equal legal treatment for individuals. All this the report did, according to Horowitz, when the vast majority of Americans are not racists but "accept African-Americans as fellow citizens and full partners in America's civic contract."[68] Similarly, Dinesh D'Souza condemned the report for reinforcing liberal preconceptions. "For liberals," he says, "the document which expressed the belief in a systematic and entrenched racism was the Kerner Commission Report."[69]

Defining Racism

So liberals charge that racism exists and has deplorable consequences, while conservatives claim that racism does not exist or is so weak as to have no serious results. The reverse sequence on this score starts with conservatives defining racism as a conscious commitment to discriminate against people one disdains. Thus D'Souza claims that "[r]acism is a doctrine of innate or biological superiority.

In its classic form, it leads to discrimination."[70] Here, doctrine is the culprit. In another place, D'Souza says that "racism is an ideology of intellectual or moral superiority, based upon the biological characteristics of race."[71] There, ideology is at fault. But whether the covering term is *doctrine* or *ideology*, the effect of such definitions is to portray racism as present not because it inheres in discriminatory acts but only when it reflects open devotion to hostile beliefs.

From this launching point, the reverse sequence continues with right-wingers claiming that racism has little or no purchase in America today. That is, having defined racism as a matter of attitudes rather than deeds, conservatives go on to observe that white Americans usually believe in no racist doctrine or ideology. In fact, in public opinion interviews and questionnaires, white respondents claim they are tolerant. Thus Stephan and Abigail Thernstrom note that by 1972, "97 percent of whites said they believed blacks should have equal opportunities to get a job.... Likewise, by the early 1970s, 80 percent of whites believed that African Americans were of equal intelligence; 84 percent favored racially integrated schools; and 85 percent had no objection to having a black neighbor of the same social class."[72] If such figures are valid, even Rush Limbaugh comes across as broad-minded when he says that "[c]onservatives believe that the great majority of people are capable.... There's room for everyone to make it here.... The American Dream still works. I know, because I've lived it."[73]

But does not racism exist because, whatever their doctrine may be, right-wing voters oppose African American needs and public policy preferences?[74] Here, a further piece of the reverse sequence falls into place when Robert Whitaker argues that white southerners and blue-collar northerners who left the Democratic Party to vote for Ronald Reagan were not racists but people animated by a philosophy of "social conservatism." Such people are not driven by racial prejudices, says Whitaker. Instead, social conservatives oppose government help to African Americans not because the recipients are black but because social conservatives condemn *any* government activism that constitutes "social engineering" of America's "structures and values."[75]

Government Help

Should citizens authorize government to promote social change? Whatever the correct answer to this question might be, conservatives say that liberal intervention, when tried, has failed. Therefore, as we have seen, conservatives oppose government programs of welfare and affirmative action intended to help African Americans. Welfare generates perverse incentives, according to writers like Charles Murray. In effect, it tells poor people they need not work hard because, after all, social relations infected by racism guarantee that their efforts will fail and they will remain poor. Proper motivations, say conservatives, can be evoked only by personalized aid to needy people, say, via religious organizations, to be extended on the condition that recipients will make every effort to help themselves.[76]

Affirmative action also generates perverse incentives, say conservatives. For example, it lowers academic standards and therefore demands less of minority students than they are capable of doing. Moreover, by treating individuals as members of targeted groups, affirmative action thrusts some of them into places—for example, top universities—where they are unqualified, unable to compete, and therefore likely to fail.[77] The proper alternative is to call for colorblind law enforcement. Americans should insist, say right-wingers, that private and public agencies treat individuals—house them, feed them, school them, and employ them—exactly in proportion to what their personal efforts entitle them to receive.

Social Class

When conservatives decry government aid, they do not mean it cannot work for anyone. There are always destitute people, as during the Great Depression, who receive help, regard it as temporary, and eventually get back on their feet. That is true for, say, many Asian refugees who arrived in America penniless after the Vietnam War. So the real problem, as conservatives see it, is that there are some people who respond badly to government aid, who seem unable or unwilling to use it to tide themselves over until they can seize an opportunity, work hard, and succeed in life. This is especially the case according to Edward Banfield, who wrote *The Unheavenly City* (1970) to explain why inner-city residents as a group are unlikely to do what they must to emerge from poverty into the mainstream of American life.

Banfield's key concept is "social class," which he defines as a collection of people "who share a 'distinct patterning of attitudes, values, and modes of behavior.'"[78] He assumes that in America there are four such classes, which he calls the upper, middle, working, and lower classes. Upper-class people, says Banfield, exert themselves and plan ahead, whereas middle-class, working-class, and lower-class people have, respectively, less and less regard for the future, to the point where lower-class individuals think ahead hardly at all. Accordingly, people from the upper class are most likely to work hard, to save, to invest, and to cultivate their children's long-term interests, while middle-class people are less likely to do these things, working-class people do them minimally, and lower-class people prefer not to do them at all.

As Banfield describes the most irresponsible, "the lower-class individual lives from moment to moment.... Impulse governs his behavior, either because he cannot discipline himself to sacrifice a present for a future satisfaction or because he has no sense of the future. He is therefore radically improvident.... His bodily needs ... and his taste for 'action' take precedence over everything else.... He works only as he must to stay alive, and drifts from one unskilled job to another.... The lower class individual has a feeble, attenuated sense of self.... He feels no attachment to community, neighbors, or friends.... He is a nonparticipant: he belongs to no voluntary organizations, has no political interests, and does not vote unless paid to do so."[79] In short, his behavior is "pathological."[80]

The Banfield Thesis

The bottom line in this analysis is clear, powerful, and enormously important to the conservative case. It is not racism, caused by whites and highlighted by the Kerner Report, that holds many poor African Americans in their places. Rather, it is dysfunctional behavior, perpetuated by lower-class people, that keeps many poor African Americans down. Here is a thesis—which assumes the main thing is class, not race—that reverses the liberal view of how whites relate to blacks in America. The liberals, after all, say that race is a cardinal feature of American life, or that racial discrimination can itself cause objectionable class characteristics.[81]

After Banfield places class at the center of urban relations, other conservative writers follow suit and repeatedly expand on shortcomings in black behavior. Dinesh D'Souza, for example, says that African Americans are proportionately more likely than whites to commit crimes, after which they will more often serve jail time.[82] He adds that many African American children perform poorly in school, presumably because lower-class parents fail to discipline them properly, or because the children decide to pursue gratification immediately rather than invest in hard work that will pay off in the future. The Thernstroms offer similar data on crime rates, on illegitimate births, and on school performance, showing African Americans leading whites on the first two indices and trailing them on the last.[83]

Updating Banfield's terminology, D'Souza and the Thernstroms speak less about "class" and more about a hapless "culture" of poverty, rooted in perverse incentives promoted by welfare, affirmative action, and the liberal canard that racism is so powerful a force in American life as to impose tyrannical conditions on minority ghettoes and justify there rage, violence, alienation, illegitimacy, and sloth. The locus of guilt may move, then, from "class" to "culture" in conservative writings. But the thing condemned is the same and, most important, belongs to the poor, not to those who criticize them. Besides which, some conservatives continue to stress the importance of class. Thus George Gilder says that the way people live in America is a reflection of their "economic class," whereby lower-class people who are perennially poor maintain the wrong values, refuse to work hard, and refuse to "make sacrifices for their children."[84]

Rational Discrimination

The final plank of the great reversal is what Dinesh D'Souza calls "rational discrimination."[85] The move to this concept unfolds logically. First comes a definition of racism that emphasizes doctrines and thereby sets aside acts that might be regarded as loading the dice against minorities. Then comes the postulate of a lower class that has apparently chosen to ignore what others regard as rules of the game. Next comes a good deal of information, summed up in impressive tables, charts, and graphs, showing how extensively the lower class violates those rules. And finally, conservatives describe the process of rational discrimination as a sort of prudent calculation by which many successful Americans, often white and alarmed by how some blacks behave, relate to African Americans in ways that might previously have been called racist.

Now, what are some of the character traits, from class or from culture, that can justify alarm? The list is a familiar litany of conservative complaints about how the poor tend to live and why.[86] These people are not getting married enough; they have too many illegitimate children; they commit more than their share of violent crimes; they disdain work for low wages; they do not save; they do not invest; they lack audacity in business; they do not press their children to behave well in school; they permit property, theirs and the landlord's, to deteriorate; they demand government handouts; they respond ungratefully to what they are given; they speak crude or even offensive English; they dress outlandishly; they degrade, if that is possible, MTV; they are clannish; they riot for no good reason; they demand entitlements that working people must fund; they won't take responsibility for their lives. It is no wonder that prosperous people prefer not to live among such misfits, in what the Thernstroms call "impoverished, dangerous, deteriorating neighborhoods."[87] It is understandable, too, that people of quality tend to congregate apart from their social inferiors, prefer not to hire them when more diligent workers are available, and are offended by having to pay taxes for government programs that only perpetuate the problem.

In short, white people who treat African Americans with some discrimination are simply behaving as one might expect a "rational man" to behave. In colleges and universities, for example, white students may resent the fact that some black students are present thanks to an admissions policy that favors minorities; it may also irritate whites that blacks tend to sit with other blacks in libraries and lunchrooms.[88] In these circumstances, some white students will reject their black peers.

This rejection D'Souza does not praise. But he says that "[t]he old racism was based on prejudice, whereas the new racism is based on [rational] conclusions. Prejudice ... means prejudgment, judgment in the absence of information.... The new bigotry is not derived from ignorance, but from experience. It is harbored not by ignoramuses, but by students who have direct and first-hand experience with minorities in the close proximity of university settings." Then he continues: "The 'new racists' do not believe they have anything to learn about minorities; quite the contrary, they believe they are the only ones who are willing to face the truth about them."[89]

In this view, in short, if white students exclude blacks, they probably have good reasons for doing so. The principle carries over into other realms. Thus on the issue of whether to hire workers from a community that, by his tables, charts, and graphs, scorns America's work ethic, D'Souza says that employers face "a choice in which the claims of morality are on one side, and the claims of productivity are on the other."[90] And how should such a dilemma be resolved? Well, "[r]ational discrimination against young black men [that is, refusing to hire them] can be fully eradicated only by getting rid of destructive conduct by the group that forms the basis for statistically valid group distinctions."[91] In other words, blacks should shape up.

Distractions

Anecdotes with or without footnotes,[92] self-validating stories, persuasive correlations, reverse sequences,[93] the great reversal: One promotional device follows another in right-wing talk. Most of them avoid direct engagement with liberal critics because they appear in such a way as to make disproof difficult if not impossible. That we saw. But in addition, conservatives offer arguments designed to divert attention from criticism and thereby focus debate on matters that are either peripheral or irrelevant to the critical point at hand.

Killing the Messenger

Some efforts at distraction, adjusted to fit diverse targets of convenience, employ the rhetorical tactic of "killing the messenger." Here the goal is to so disparage the bearer of liberal news as to persuade voters that there is no need to consider the message itself, no need to place it on the public agenda maintained by every nation to discuss matters that seem to it important.

Killing the messenger shows up, for example, when Robert Bork argues that law professors who disagree with his concept of "original intent" in the Constitution are expressing an opinion that is "political."[94] The implication is clear. To be "political" vis-à-vis legal principles is, according to Bork, to express a personal opinion that ignores what he posits as historical fact—that is, what he thinks the Founders intended—and is therefore worthless. Killing the messenger appears again when Edward Banfield, speaking of ghetto poverty, argues that "Negro leaders cannot be expected to explain that [racial] prejudice is no longer *the* obstacle."[95] Such leaders, according to Banfield, thrive from galvanizing other black Americans to confront even imagined adversity and therefore have a vested interest in preserving their role by citing racism as the major cause of inner-city misery.

Liberal proposals in many public policy realms can be brushed aside with similar arguments. "What is our greatest obstacle to solving the homeless problem?" asks Rush Limbaugh. "Simply put, the liberals don't want the problem solved. They are interested in power, and the way they maintain their power is to build up a giant network of government programs that employ their friends."[96] Or, "What [Ralph] Nader and his allies seek is not reform, but power," says Pat Buchanan. "They want a new economic system where final decision-making authority over the nation's business and industry no longer resides with the corporate officers or boards of directors, but in Washington, where Mr. Nader and his allies can influence or make those decisions themselves."[97] The same applies to those who opposed the theory of supply-side economics. "The fight over the economics models," says Paul Craig Roberts, "went on so long and so hard because ... [t]he real issue was political power. A supply-side tax cut would reduce the size of government relative to the private sector [but] ... [t]he political careers of many liberals depend on government action replacing private action."[98]

The Red Herring

To make liberals look bad, some conservatives accuse them of sympathy for communist principles or practices. This "red herring" is actually a variant of the "killing the messenger" ploy. Thus the purpose of applying such terms as communist or pro-communist, says Joshua Muravchik, "is to be able to stigmatize them [liberals]. Not to stigmatize them as subversives, but as people whose political perceptions or moral values are so deeply flawed that their counsels deserve no weight."[99]

That liberals are like communists is frequently postulated. Rael and Erich Isaac, for example, insist that "[i]n so far as the utopians [liberals] have real life models, they are places like Cuba, Vietnam, Nicaragua and China (at least until it moved toward the West)."[100] See also Phil Kent, who notes that "[m]any latter-day politicians [liberals] bristle at the charge of being socialistic, but under its basic definition—the sharing of all earned income by those who did not help earn it—they are squarely in the camp of socialism, if not Marxism."[101] Similarly, Rush Limbaugh attacks civil rights activists: "It is neither farfetched nor unfair to draw an analogy between the civil rights leadership and the Soviet Communist leadership, insofar as exploitation of their people is concerned. The leaders of both enjoy the privileges of class at the expense of the masses."[102]

Universities and professors are especially remiss. "There's but one place left on the face of the earth," says Bob Grant, "where widespread belief in the goodness and rightness of the principles of communism still endures.... It's in American universities."[103] William Simon agrees. As he puts it, "[T]he academic community probably remains the last, great bastion and fertile ground for Marxist thought and teaching in America today."[104] R. Emmett Tyrrell concurs. The theory of "Dr. Marx," he says, "is totally convincing at least for those whose ultimate goal is to knock off millions of fellow citizens or to join the faculty of the Harvard Law School."[105]

Liberals Hate America

If red herrings fail to distract, conservatives may charge liberals with hating America, in which case, presumably, they are dastardly people and their opinions are irrelevant to public debate. This motif appears frequently in right-wing talk. For example, Norman Podhoretz says that "what finally alienated me from the radical movement of the '60s was its hatred of America."[106] Here is his way of apologizing for left-wing sentiments earlier in life. Robert Bork shares Podhoretz's disdain. "Many people attribute the student frenzy, civil disobedience, and violence of the Sixties to the war in Vietnam," says Bork. But "the evidence seems clear that Vietnam was more an occasion for the outbreaks than their cause. The war at most intensified into hatred a contempt for American civilization that was already in place."[107] Not just counterculturalists are at fault, though. For example, the same pathology animates liberal educators who, by conservative definition, have destroyed decent schooling in America. Accordingly, William Donohue concludes that "it is impossible to understand the mentality of those [liberals] who wrecked the schools without referencing [*sic*] the profound contempt they had for American society."[108]

To lump together liberals—who include John Dewey, Franklin Roosevelt, Adlai Stevenson, Martin Luther King Jr., Arthur Schlesinger Jr., Hubert Humphrey, Lyndon Johnson, Barbara Ehrenreich, Ted Kennedy, Robert Reich, Michael Walzer, Ralph Nader, Robert Kuttner, Henry Waxman, and Jonathan Kozol, plus George McGovern, the United Auto Workers, and the Americans for Democratic Action[109]—as people who hate their country cannot be factually accurate.[110] But it can spur a distaste for liberals that invites Americans to ignore them as people who, immoral themselves, can produce only worthless ideas. Ann Coulter epitomizes this approach to political debate. As she says, "Liberals hate America, they hate 'flag-wavers,' they hate abortion opponents, they hate all religions except Israel (post 9/11). Even Islamic terrorists don't hate America like liberals do. They don't have the energy. If they had that much energy, they'd have indoor plumbing by now."[111]

Where so much hatred exists, it will emerge in deeds, and so Coulter points out that when it comes to action, "[l]iberals have a preternatural gift for striking a position on the side of treason. . . . Whenever the nation is under attack, from within or without, liberals side with the enemy."[112] Here are no ifs, ands, or buts. As Coulter says, "Whether they are defending the Soviet Union or bleating for Saddam Hussein, liberals are *always* against America. They are either traitors or idiots, and on the matter of America's self-preservation, the difference is irrelevant."[113]

The Conservative Mind

Conservative concepts inspire negative talk in opposition to liberal schemes and sentiments. Then right-wingers go beyond rejecting the Left to promote powerfully their own schemes and sentiments. Colorful anecdotes invigorate the message, keeping audiences focused on federal boondoggles, welfare deadbeats, sexual oddballs, bureaucratic tyrants, feminist harpies, and other stock situations and characters that anyone can love to scorn.

These anecdotes express truths that, to conservatives, are known or suspected, and thus they serve as morality tales that, lacking identifiable sources, may be difficult or impossible to refute. But what if such tales fail to convince? Then one may turn the attention of citizens elsewhere. People who suggest liberal projects are personally flawed, say conservatives, so we need not take seriously what they recommend to the country. Such people are known, to the conservative mind, for aiding and abetting America's enemies, sometimes from malice and sometimes from naïveté. For hating America, they and their ideas deserve mainly contempt.

If none of this works, then the fallback, as we have seen, is to praise supply-side economics and enact tax cuts. The economy may bounce back to healthy equilibrium sometime down the road. Meanwhile, the cuts will generate budget deficits and limit spending on government programs. Here is the ultimate deflection because, when public coffers fail to fill, debate over social and economic policies will subside.

Agenda Setting

All of this contributes to what political scientist John Kingdon called agenda setting.[114] That is, it amounts to trying to maintain a public dialogue whose terms will keep participants focused on conservative proposals rather than liberal projects. It remains, then, for us to note only how what conservatives do *not* say makes it difficult for liberals to challenge conservative control over the rhetorical playing field, makes it difficult for critics to move the terms of debate leftward, and makes it difficult for them to persuade voters to stop thinking about right-wing postulates and consider liberal concepts instead. In short, some things are significantly missing from conservative rhetoric.

Surrounding Factors

And what might these be? Conservatives rely heavily on stories and anecdotes, all designed to suggest a conservative view of the world, and many based on correlated factors. These factors usually come two at a time like, say, sex education and teenage pregnancy, or minimum wages and minority employment, or teachers' unions and low SAT scores—in which case one is regarded as a cause and the other as an effect.

As we saw, such stories can be very persuasive. Because that is so, liberals try to draw attention away from stories that conservatives tell. They do this especially by saying that right-wing tales are incomplete, that things unmentioned in those stories influence their central characters, that moving beyond the events and processes that conservatives describe will bring Americans to understand which actors, motivations, trends, and institutions really, and crucially, affect public life. Such matters, usually absent in conservative stories, may be called "surrounding factors."[115]

Without always noting this challenge explicitly, conservatives may respond to it indirectly by injecting into their writings an occasional qualifying phrase, such as "all other things being equal," or "other things remaining equal." To do so is to seem intellectually responsible, is to appear less than doctrinaire, is to sound like someone willing to consider unforeseen possibilities, in which case critics may look unnecessarily severe for harping on a point, or factor, that conservatives are already taking into account. In fact, though, ceteris paribus disclaimers are not common in conservative writings. Moreover, they are mostly unaccompanied by consideration of the surrounding factors they denote and how those might undermine the moral of the story.[116] Instead, conservatives tend to ignore such factors, and they usually avoid mentioning or discussing them. Meanwhile, people on the right press on with an outpouring of conservative anecdotes, all driving home, again and again, simple but powerful elements of right-wing sentiment.

Yet here is a major rhetorical deflection. It is customary to think of rhetorical efficacy as a quality flowing from *what is said*. In this case, however, the opposite is true, for efficacy lies in *what is not said*. In debate, after all, leaving surrounding factors aside serves conservative purposes well. Why admit before the public that conservative correlations project a limited view of reality? To do so would be rhetorically generous. But it would also make rightists seem less decisive, less committed to what counts, and less forceful than how they want to be seen by their audiences.

In fact, too many warnings of the ceteris paribus sort would be rhetorically counterproductive, because they might make conservatives sound like the liberals and academic scholars they decry. Those, according to right-wing anecdotes, are people who are *not* decisive. They are, for example, Democrats who can't get their act together, scholars who regard tentativity as an academic art form, professors who don't seem committed to one thing more than another, teachers who have no clear message about what is true or false, pluralists who dither over which culture is best, and relativists who cannot decide where to draw the line, morally speaking.

Discounting Encumbrances

The second thing missing from right-wing talk is serious consideration of what Michael Sandel called encumbrances. Encumbrances are a special sort of surrounding factor, a matter of social ingredients that are *not* equal for all people but *do* count importantly where they, the encumbrances, are present. To talk of encumbrances is particularly unhelpful to conservative ends because, if Americans were to dwell on the likelihood of encumbrances shaping people's behavior, they might come to believe that what conservatives call human nature, individual motivation, and personal responsibility can be trumped, in real life, by social environments. Voters might come down, in short, on the wrong side of the nature/nurture equation.

On this score, slighting encumbrances occurs in conservative writings associated with "the great reversal." We saw that Edward Banfield strongly implies that lower-class behavior rather than white racism accounts for most of the plight of poor African Americans in inner-city neighborhoods. But here is how he makes this point: "That physically distinguishing characteristics [one class of encumbrances] do not necessarily stand in the way of acceptance and upward mobility is evident from the example of Orientals. The median family income of urban Japanese-Americans in 1969 ($12,794) was considerably higher than that of urban whites ($11,203) and their unemployment rate (2.1 percent) was considerably lower (4.7 percent). The same was true, although not in the same degree, of Chinese-Americans."[117] That Asian Americans are not black, that they are not regarded as such by white Americans, and that they have a history of family life very different from African Americans—on these aspects of ghetto life, Banfield does not comment.

Similarly, Stephan and Abigail Thernstrom avoid what is, for conservatives, an encumbrance trap. Seeking to drive home the point that neither racism nor poverty is accountable for what they regard as dysfunctional behavior in poor black neighborhoods, here is what they say: "More than 16 million immigrants have entered the United States in the past quarter of a century, many of them coming with very little education, no capital, and no command of English.... Few of these newcomers have been unable to find jobs, even though they often live on the same block as African Americans who do not seem employable."[118] Like Banfield, the Thernstroms do not stress how such people might differ, by language, family, religion, tradition, and historical experience, from American descendants of people who endured human bondage, lynchings carried out by the Ku Klux Klan, and peonage imposed on southern tenant farmers.

Dinesh D'Souza extends the indictment. Looking at different sectors of the African American community, he remarks on how many black immigrants from Caribbean islands do better in their adopted country than blacks descended from American slaves.[119] To D'Souza, the fact that some blacks succeed more than others in America shows that racism is not a major problem there. But he does not ask what encumbrances, of language, family, and shared history, might underlie the disparity in performance. Instead, like Banfield, D'Souza is impressed by how much better non-Caucasian immigrants are doing than African Americans. Therefore, he summarizes the situation as follows: "Many liberals are having trouble providing a full answer to the awkward question: 'Why can't an African American be more like an Asian?'"[120]

We may ask why D'Souza, born and raised in India, would so easily discount the centuries of social encumbrances that make many African Americans different from many Asian Americans and vice versa. Whatever the reason might be, like other conservatives D'Souza prefers to leave encumbrances out of his analysis. To treat them seriously might permit various liberal claims, about history, institutions, and social environments, to divert attention from the sort of individualism that conservatives praise—that is, from the idea that every person, and no one else, is responsible for his or her situation and standing in society.

Back to Iraq

To assume that all individuals are basically the same—in which case collective circumstances do not really encumber anyone because they can be thrown off by force of character—is one reason why conservatives do well in debate. The view of human nature thus projected is simple, the markets it praises are uncluttered, and the stories it tells are inspiring. To some members of the audience, this sort of talk must seem both insightful and persuasive.

In practice rather than in talk, however, we shall see in Chapter Seven that right-wingers who counted encumbrances for nothing decided to destroy Saddam Hussein's government while believing that Iraqis were exemplars of those self-sufficient people, unburdened by local circumstances, who conservatives assume live everywhere. And this translated, in the conservative mind, into thinking that (1) Iraqis were unencumbered by Middle Eastern history, sectarianism, and family ties, from which it followed that (2) they were autonomous lovers of freedom who, once Saddam Hussein was deposed, would do everything necessary to replace the old regime with frequent elections, competitive parties, minority rights, free speech, religious tolerance, independent courts, and all the other great and hard-won institutions of democracy.

Part II
Articles of Faith

Chapter Four
Enemies

Rhetorical elements appear repeatedly in a wide range of right-wing books. Further items of talk, however, are not so much matters of rhetorical presentation as of fundamental conviction. Therefore what we will begin to explore now are references to what Americans on the right assume that modern life is and should be about. These additional aspects of conservative thinking signal faith in suppositions that cannot be proved but that, when accepted in principle and promoted with passion, constitute a sort of spiritual mortar that unites conservatives and gives meaning to their lives.

Without, then, drawing too sharp an analytical line between the ideas we have explored already and the ones we are about to consider, let us say that in Chapters Four, Five, and Six, we will see how articles of faith, promoted here and there with rhetorical flourishes, eventually become parts of a powerful story about how Americans may live together successfully. That story offers a political vision that projects well in an age dominated by electronic media that thrive on stories. Compared to such a right-wing capability it is a matter of no small importance, to which we shall return, that liberals, for reasons we will note, have neither fashioned nor promoted a strong alternative to the story their opponents tell.

Sources of Tension

We have seen that right-wing talking points help ward off critics. But some of those points also threaten one another because, between social and economic ideas on the right, tensions arise constantly.[1] These flow chiefly from the fact that capitalism continually updates itself, destroying the old to make way for the new, inventing unforeseen products, discarding familiar skills, discharging previously essential workers, and undermining support for long-standing habits and traditions. Under the circumstances, progress constantly challenges order.[2] Thus the car, the credit card, television, contraceptives, fast food, jumbo jets, personal computers, suburban subdivisions, mobile phones, 24/7 news, and superstores are promoted by capitalists, revolutionize social relations, and weaken attachment to long-standing precepts and practices.[3]

Critics of capitalism often claim that conditions of stability and incidents of change are incompatible.[4] But some conservatives also make this point. "In showering necessities, optional goods, and luxuries upon virtually everyone living under it," Harold Brown remarks, "capitalism stimulates self-interest, selfishness, and self-indulgence to a degree that ... Americans have come first to disregard, and finally to repudiate, the values upon which their wealth was based."[5] Irving Kristol sees the same paradox. The bourgeois citizen, he says, "has been killed off by bourgeois prosperity, which has corrupted his character from that of a citizen to that of a consumer. One hears much about the 'work ethic' these days.... But the next time you hear a banker extolling the 'work ethic,' just ask him if he favors making installment buying illegal."[6] And Thomas Fleming reminds compatriots that "[t]he hardest task for [social] conservatives will be to convince our capitalist allies [economic conservatives] that ... the land, the home, and the church—not the marketplace—are the only proper foundations for a healthy society."[7]

Such examples usually show capitalist innovations weakening attachment to traditional values. Thus automobiles became common in America and, when driven by young people, made chaperoning of teenagers by adults more difficult to achieve than previously. However, it is also true that promoting tradition, say, by social conservatives who recommend using government to prevent abortions, can undermine devotion to laissez-faire ideals favored by economic conservatives, who want to limit government regulation and foster free choices in life. On this score, traditionalists can compromise capitalists rather than vice versa.[8]

In fact, then, tension between their social and economic ideas runs both ways and is deeply troublesome to rightists. Electorally, it threatens to unhinge their voting coalition—strong among evangelicals, white men, gun enthusiasts, managers, professionals, and antifeminists—that dominated the House of Representatives from 1995 to 2006, that sometimes rules the Senate, and that won the White House in 1980, 1984, 1988, 2000, and 2004. Ideologically, it threatens to confuse the widespread agglomeration of think tanks, magazines, Web sites, blogs, talk shows, and other forums where right-wing spokespeople work tirelessly to shape public opinion so their candidates will win elections.

Bridging Solutions

In short, while social and economic conservatives believe that they understand the nature of American life, their beliefs do not sit well together. Indeed, with the mismatch in mind, Norman Mailer unkindly suggests that to be conservative in America is "to live as an oxymoron."[9] Consequently, people in the two camps need somehow to bridge the gap, if possible, to gain peace of mind or, failing that, to maintain at least an appearance of partisan solidarity.

Christian Economics

Jesus warned that a camel can pass through the eye of a needle more easily than a rich man can enter heaven.[10] Nevertheless, one effort at reducing tension among conservatives finds them promoting Christianity not as in conflict with, but as complementary to, capitalist enterprise. Thinkers on the right who are enthusiastically Christian often pursue this objective energetically. Moreover, because both capitalism and Christianity are complicated entities capable of evoking various interpretations, conservative talk offers many ways of connecting the two.

Thus some right-wingers say there are now, and have been for centuries, only two economic systems in the world. In this view, one is pagan and the other is Christian. The first assumes that a "man's value depends upon his worth to the State," while the second regards man as "a free agent, accountable to God." According to this typology, socialism perpetuates the pagan idea, while capitalism lets men realize their divine potential for free will and responsibility by striving for individual achievement and excellence. In the latter system, markets can be defined in biblical terms, with citizens owning private property according to the Eighth Commandment, which forbids theft, and with the same citizens exchanging goods voluntarily according to the Golden Rule of doing for others what we hope they will do for us.[11]

From here, two possibilities unfold. On the one hand, Christian rightists may say that conscience, character, and good deeds can take shape only when people make decisions voluntarily. In this sense, God intends us to be free so we may exercise responsible choices. And since that is the case, where markets provide freedom they deserve praise.[12] On the other hand, freedom may tempt people to make bad choices and act immorally. Thus the biblical fall of Adam and a subsequent tendency to depravity go hand in hand. Accordingly, against dangers such as envy, greed, and sloth, some conservatives argue that capitalism and competitive markets, by rewarding prudence and efficiency, restrain a human propensity to sin.[13]

On a related plane, those who link Christianity and capitalism emphasize that markets may be economically effective but morally flawed. Against this downside, conservatives may insist that biblical values can inspire people to behave well when making and selling, getting and spending. To this end, Lawrence Kudlow interprets Adam Smith to have argued "that the commercial spirit must be fused with the moral spirit. Freedom does not mean rebellion, defiance, disobedience and disrespect. It must be rooted in moral virtues."[14] Michael Novak agrees when he observes that where free enterprise may so accelerate the rate of social change as to disrupt personal and communal ties, the commercial system "needs taming and correction by a moral-cultural system independent of commerce."[15] Similarly, George Roche holds that markets should reflect "our spiritual values as well as our free economic choices.... Recent scholarship by George Gilder and others has established the moral and altruistic basis of entrepreneurial capitalism."[16]

Missing Corporations

Where religion is less of an issue, conservatives may minimize the tension between social and economic ideas by saying little about certain parts of economic life. The effort to this end does not aim directly to resolve right-wing differences of approach but is more a matter of out of sight, out of mind. Thus many conservatives steer clear especially of corporations. For example, Milton and Rose Friedman claim that *individuals* in *free* markets earn more or less what their efforts and resources are worth. A critic might argue that *corporations* dominate many *real* markets, in which case the terms they offer there will determine the wages that real workers receive. But the Friedmans say that "the existence of the modern corporation does not alter matters," because the corporation is an aggregation of individual stockholders, in which case its income is their income, alongside the income of workers.[17] So much for the dynamics of globalization, as well as for the life and times of specific corporate entities, such as, say, British Petroleum, Enron, Exxon Mobil, Disney, Toyota, Walmart, Halliburton, Microsoft, Lehman Brothers, and Goldman Sachs.

George Gilder insists that "[t]he only dependable route [away] from poverty is always work, family, and faith."[18] He does not mention corporations in this context. Robert Bork condemns the Supreme Court for banning prayers in public schools and adds that "[t]he application [actually misapplication, according to Bork] of the Bill of Rights to the states in this and other matters has done much to alter the moral tone of communities across the country."[19] He does not blame business entities that glamorize outrageous behavior, like on the Jerry Springer show or in movies like *Pulp Fiction* or *Hostel*. William Bennett says that "a reform-minded and thoughtful social agenda" should include proposals for more prisons, for national educational standards, for forcing fathers to "take responsibility for their children," and so forth.[20] He does not suggest considering how citizens might together confront a world economy led by soulless corporations[21] and characterized by downsizing, outsourcing, deindustrialization, contingent labor, ubiquitous advertising,[22] leveraged buyouts, mass media mergers, ecological destruction, and environmental pollution.

Mediating Structures

Just as useful as overlooking corporations is to misplace them. This happens when conservatives praise what they call "mediating structures." Here the general idea is that people live for the most part privately, with little institutional support, even while public life is dominated by what Richard Neuhaus and Peter Berger call "megastructures." These megastructures include the state, "conglomerates of capitalist enterprise," labor unions, and bureaucracies such as those in education and the professions.[23]

In this view, "[m]eaning, fulfillment, and personal identity are to be realized in the private sphere."[24] It follows that because citizens are somewhat alone in private life and sometimes alienated from megastructures, they will best be able to pursue happiness if they will participate in strong and vibrant "mediating structures." Among these, Neuhaus and Berger list "neighborhood, family, church, and voluntary associations."[25] Other conservatives, such as William Bennett,[26] Ronald Nash,[27] Robert Bork,[28] Stuart Butler, and Anna Kondratas,[29] endorse the same list or parts of it. Such mediating institutions are, they think, what Edmund Burke had in mind when he praised "little platoons" for helping men to unite their affections.[30]

Yet here is where corporations get misplaced. Instead of regarding them as one sort of megastructure among others, we could easily categorize corporations as mediating institutions because they dominate workplaces that stand between individuals and government. However, if we were to see them as mediating institutions, the implications of that term would suggest that we should focus on them, much like conservatives such as Jerry Falwell, Rick Santorum, and Rebecca Hagelin focus on families.[31] We would then want to know, as their neighbors, customers, stockholders, and employees, how corporations influence the world of work, where many citizens spend as much waking time as at home, and where "meaning, fulfillment, and personal identity" are created as powerfully as in what Neuhaus and Berger call "private" life.[32]

Indeed, while moving corporations into the analytic column of mediating structures, why not move labor unions into the same column, perhaps worth fostering via public policy for their capacity sometimes to generate social solidarity and promote interests shared by otherwise isolated workers?[33] And what of political parties? Neuhaus and Berger do not list parties as mediating institutions. One hopes this is merely an oversight, because surely parties can help citizens to combine their aspirations and, on occasion, tell megastructures such as government what to do, even unto regulating corporate activity to advance public interests.

Dealing with Disagreement

Social and economic conservatives believe strongly in their respective understandings of what happens in America, and they will not forsake commitments—in favor of tradition, in favor of change; in favor of communities, in favor of markets; in favor of patriotism, in favor of globalization—they have made, personally and in public policy, based on their beliefs. Yet inconsistency persists at the heart of American conservatism, and attempts to overcome it are unlikely to succeed in a philosophical sense because the relevant commitments clash severely.

Conservatives know this, even while they look for bridging solutions.[34] Thus Garry Wills, a former *National Review* staffer, notes the tension between what he calls "authoritarians" and "libertarians" among conservatives he worked with in the Goldwater era. William Buckley Jr., he remarks, professed loyalty to both Catholicism and capitalism—that is, to tradition and to markets. "But the fact," says Wills, "that men can live with contradiction does not remove the contradiction—it just makes the contradiction go philosophically 'underground' and play funny games there."[35]

Yet where two inconsistent principles inspire the faithful, how can right-wing alliances flourish? On the one hand, in public life it is not always necessary to resolve contradictions with philosophical rigor. Ronald Reagan, for example, got elected because he was so effective a salesman that he could charm audiences with heartwarming anecdotes about small towns and material progress even though he never explained exactly how Main Street and shopping malls can sponsor the same excellent values. In politics, then, there is always room for at least some constructive fuzziness.

On the other hand, unity cannot rest only on salesmanship, because not every Republican candidate can promote his or her creed as attractively as Reagan did. Accordingly, there is a sense in which social and economic conservatives are united less by what they believe in than by what they oppose. That is, though they affirm clashing aspirations, they target common enemies, and this shared hostility helps keep their coalition together.[36] To make common cause by attacking outsiders may not resolve philosophical difficulties. But it can ease cognitive dissonance and also energize partisans by focusing on areas where agreement reigns.

Shared Enemies

Ergo, a campaign against rascals is the program for unity. Thus for many years conservatives despised and denounced communists.[37] Such enemies easily united Christian rightists who abhorred atheism and free marketers who cherished private property. But communism collapsed in Eastern Europe and the Soviet

Union during the late 1980s, whereupon antipathy fell more upon government, which conservatives had never liked, and especially on government in Washington. As Republican strategist Don Fierce said then, "Washington is financially and morally bankrupt and because of that it is the glue that binds economic and social conservatives. These are people that love their country but hate their federal government. Where is the evil empire? The evil empire is in Washington."[38]

Variations on this theme abound. James Watt says that "[t]he focus of the battle has become the dignity of the individual versus the domination of the government."[39] Jack Kemp says that "[o]pportunity, the chance to make it and to improve your life, that's what the American Dream was and is all about. What poisons that dream is when government stands in the way, throwing up roadblocks that are really unnecessary."[40] Those are blanket charges, but conservatives also rebuke specific agencies. Thus Thomas Lane says that "American citizens who cherish our long-established tradition of honesty and responsibility in personal behavior and of honesty and the rule of law in public affairs must come to realize that the Supreme Court is today the most deadly enemy of these cherished ideals."[41]

Pithy maxims are available. Dick Armey says that "[t]he market is rational and the government is dumb."[42] William Bennett says that "[t]he American people are fine. Washington is not."[43] Ronald Reagan says that "[i]n the present crisis, government is not the solution to our problem; government *is* the problem."[44] Or, to sum up these sentiments with an anecdote, Marvin Olasky recounts a farmer's daughter story: "'Momma,' the young lady called out [from the yard, where she was milking the family cow], 'there's a man here to see you.' The mother looked out the kitchen window and replied, 'Haven't I always told you not to talk to strangers? You come in this house right now.' The girl protested: 'But Momma, this man says he is a United States senator.' The wise mother replied, 'In that case, bring the cow in with you.'"[45]

Government Produces Nothing

In conservative theory, Washington is contemptible for, among other things, taxing citizens while government usually produces little or nothing in return. Here the idea is that government, by levying taxes and offering services, in effect merely transfers money from one person to another. There is no plus in this sequence since, as Donald Lambro observes, "government can put into the economy only what it first takes out."[46] Restating the same point more formally, George Gilder argues that "[g]overnment cannot significantly affect real aggregate demand through policies of taxing and spending.... All this shifting of wealth is a zero sum game."[47]

Gilder might concede that public spending for hospitals, schools, and scientific research can enhance people's lives to the point of stimulating "real aggregate demand." Yet he writes as if private investors will generate this demand even if government spends little. In such circumstances, nothing vital emerges from most public activity, and that is what George Roche has in mind when he says that "[p]olitics cannot build or create; it can only rearrange existing wealth (certainly not least into the hands of politicians and their friends)."[48] Rush Limbaugh packages the same thought for popular consumption: "The government can't create wealth; it can only destroy it or confiscate and redistribute it."[49] In which case, as Dinesh D'Souza says, "[i]f the new president changed into his pajamas every afternoon and took a long nap, like Calvin Coolidge, this would probably be good for the market and good for the country."[50]

Such formulations reject the Keynesian thesis that government can will into existence goods and services when it decides to run programs or occasional deficits so that investor confidence will thrive and, consequently, economic output will grow beyond where it might stop without government intervention.[51] Accordingly, many conservatives assume that, as Larry Burkett says, "When money is diverted from private hands and given to the government, it simply means there is less spending in the private sector. This eventually results in a slower economy, less industry, and lower employment."[52] The same scorn for government projects inspires Bob Grant, who noted in 1996 that the federal government collects $1.3 trillion in taxes annually. "Just think," says Grant, "of what $1.3 trillion could do if it were left in the hands of the people who earn it. Think of all the goods and services you'd purchase with the money now going to taxes."[53]

Arguments to this effect overlook Washington's role in subsidizing railroad development, agriculture, universities, highways, airlines, the merchant marine, suburban housing, miracle drugs, satellite communications, the Internet, and many other vital elements of American life. Furthermore, they ignore many things—from schools to bathing beaches, from libraries to parks, from small business loans to genetic mapping—that Americans request from their representatives via frequent elections. Yet the goods and services provided by government surely include some that would not otherwise exist unless, after voters make known their will, taxes will be levied to force "free riders" to help pay for things they hope to enjoy but cannot or will not buy individually and voluntarily.

Tax Day

To forestall consideration of such matters, right-wing talk encourages taxpayers to regard themselves as victims. Barry Goldwater starts this ball rolling in his *Conscience of a Conservative*. "The average American," says Goldwater, "is ... working one-third of the time for government: a third of what he produces is not available for his own use but is confiscated and used by others who have not earned it."[54] Conservatives as various as William Simon,[55] Dick Armey,[56] Mark Anthony,[57] Phil Kent,[58] Jerry Falwell,[59] Rush Limbaugh,[60] and Grover Norquist[61] cite similar figures, and Jesse Helms adds that the "typical taxpayer works from January 1 to April 30 solely for the benefit of the government.... Taxes are the largest item in the family budget, and more than food and housing combined."[62] And that means that "none of us are free in the original sense of the word," says Charlotte Twight. "With 'tax freedom day' moving ever later into May," she notes, "Americans now work on average over four months out of every year just to satisfy the tax claims of governmental authorities."[63]

As William Hoar describes it, the period of forced labor may be even longer. When the costs of tax collection and government regulation—amounting annually to hundreds of billions of dollars by conservative calculation—are added to whatever money Americans are directly assessed, the same people, according to Americans for Tax Reform, "work from 1 January to 9 July to pay for the cost of government."[64] As usual for the Right, when Hoar relates to public finance in this way he says nothing about what taxpayers receive in return, such as schools, police, roads, parks, scientific research, courts, libraries, sewer systems, air traffic control, weather forecasting, postal service, garbage collection, Medicare, work safety, Social Security, environmental protection, and national defense.

Government Injures Women

Conservatives often condemn feminism.[65] But some sympathize with women who, they say, are injured by excessive taxation in America. Newt Gingrich and Dick Armey made this point after Republicans captured the House and the Senate in 1994. "Today," they say, "the average family spends more on taxes than it spends on food, clothing, and shelter combined. Many families now need a second earner [probably female] not to support the household, but to support the government."[66] This charge against government has the advantage, by conservative estimate, of blaming Washington rather than private enterprise for inducing women to abandon homemaking and thereby undermine family life. Thus mothers work and, on occasion, may neglect their children not to make do in the modern economy but to keep afloat in a sea of cruel and unnecessary taxes.

Ralph Reed concurs when he says that "[h]igher taxes have torn at the fabric of the American family. In many families, both parents must work just to make ends meet" because "roughly two-thirds of the wife's earnings are taken by the federal government."[67] Pat Robertson also finds government at fault when he notes that "the number of working mothers has skyrocketed from 32.8 percent in 1948 to 66.6 percent in 1990, much of that caused by government-induced inflation and the resultant drop in the real incomes of male head-of-family wage earners."[68] One gets no sense here of families struggling to keep up with private sector costs in, say, housing, transportation, day care, and health insurance.[69]

The New Class

In short, Washington is normally wicked. Nevertheless, conservatives do not usually claim that government is inherently evil, since some people who staff it they admire, such as Barry Goldwater, Ronald Reagan, Newt Gingrich, Jesse Helms, Dick Armey, Trent Lott, William Bennett, Henry Hyde, Tom DeLay, John Ashcroft, Antonin Scalia, Clarence Thomas, George W. Bush, Donald Rumsfeld, Lindsay Graham, Sam Brownback, and more. To explain, then, why government often behaves badly, or so they say, right-wing writers sometimes hold that a "new class" has arisen in America, encouraging government to evil works, and sometimes seeking public employment to do the job personally and get paid to boot.[70]

Composition

The concept of a new class arose in the 1960s and 1970s and refines what conservatives generally suspect. Many modern intellectuals, they believe, are incorrigibly opposed to right-wing ideas and political projects. Therefore, some conservatives posit a new class even while others, without using that term, envision a conglomeration of well-educated thinkers, opinion leaders, and activists who obstruct conservative aspirations. Irving Kristol, for example, says that "the new class" includes "scientists, teachers and educational administrators, journalists and others in the communication industries, psychologists, social workers, those lawyers and doctors who make their careers in the expanding public sector, city planners, the staffs of large foundations, the upper levels of the government bureaucracy, and so on."[71]

Elsewhere, Kristol describes the same people as "scientists, lawyers, city planners, social workers, educators, criminologists, sociologists, public health doctors, etc.—a substantial number of whom find their careers in the expanding public sector rather than the private."[72] And Charles Murray, who speaks of "the intelligentsia" but has a new class in mind, includes in that category "the upper levels of ... academia, journalism, publishing, and the vast network of foundations, institutes, and research centers that has been woven into partnership with government during the last thirty years."[73] He adds that "[p]oliticians and members of the judiciary ... and bankers and businessmen and lawyers and doctors may be members of the intelligentsia as well, though not all are."[74]

In passages such as these, Kristol and Murray condemn intellectuals who, they say, disparage capitalism and promote the welfare state in America. The danger on this score especially worries economic conservatives. But right-wingers intent on tradition and inherited values also find intellectuals to condemn. Thus Robert Bork assigns various jurists to what he calls the "new class" or the "knowledge class" because they reject what he calls the jurisprudence of "original intent" and thereby ignore, in his eyes, principles of wisdom that America's Founders wove into the Constitution.[75]

Marvin Olasky adds to the category of dangerous intellectuals those social workers who have abandoned the insights of faith-based philanthropy for secular professionalism.[76] Rael and Erich Isaac, via an attack on "utopians," show how unsound intellectuals are found in organizations like the National Council of Churches, the American Friends Service Committee, the Department of Education, the Legal Services Corporation, the Corporation for Public Broadcasting, the Friends of the Earth, and Environmental Action.[77] John Ankerberg and John Weldon extend the indictment to Planned Parenthood, People for the American Way, and "the national Democratic Party."[78] And William Donohue concludes that "the history of the ACLU represents the emergence of the 'new class' in the twentieth century."[79]

Outlook

Such claims reveal that right-wingers do not define the new class according to empirical reference points—like sociologists might recognize classes by income or education[80]—but by its outlook on life. For example, not all lawyers, journalists, teachers, and social workers belong to the new class. Rather, you become a member of that entity not because you and your neighbor study law but because you conclude, perhaps from your studies, that certain kinds of social problems should be handled by government. Or you become a member of the new class not because you and your neighbor study journalism in college but because you decide, perhaps while there, that women are entitled to more rights than they legally enjoy, in which case existing laws should be changed accordingly.

Outlook is the defining quality, and it permits conservatives to identify as members of the new class people who, by right-wing interpretation, tend to reject private and/or traditional ways of handling social circumstances and prefer to advocate public and/or unconventional paths to progress instead. Such people may exercise great power in modern societies by helping to shape the symbolic universe in which we live and make sense of our lives. Thus, as Jeane Kirkpatrick says, it is not so much the "highest officeholders" who join the new class but those who surround, sustain, and condition those at the top. "The importance of this second-level stratum of the political elite," she continues, "should never be underestimated. Under conditions of political freedom, it can shape debate, determine agendas, define standards, and propose and evaluate policies."[81]

A Tactical Coup

Here, then, is the sequence. Conservatives do not talk much about how, as a collective political persona, they simultaneously recommend—as if all the following were compatible—tradition *and* change, Main Street *and* Walmart, stable communities *and* capital mobility, family values *and* television, patriotism *and* globalization. Instead, they invest their energies in offensive operations. In this project, positing the new class is a tactical coup for right-wingers because, while citing that term and others related to it, social and economic conservatives can join forces to attack a common enemy.[82]

Convenient Rhetoric

When right-wingers talk about a new class, it sounds like they are speaking about something that exists beyond their preferences and inclinations. But since they do not define this entity dispassionately, it actually includes only people they regard as members of it. This is convenient because if they were to propose for that class clear taxonomical criteria—such as advanced education, professional training, job occupations, and concern for policy debate—the public might see what conservatives hope it will overlook, namely, that many of the accusers are themselves new class people. Robert Bork, for example, describes intellectuals he does not like as "part of the chattering class."[83] But right-wingers chatter no less, and on this score there is no difference between Bork and Noam Chomsky, Milton Friedman and Michael Walzer, George Will and Robert Kuttner, David Brooks and Paul Krugman, Bill O'Reilly and Keith Olbermann, Mike Huckabee and Hillary Clinton.

As defined by conservatives, then, the vessel they call a "new class" looks like a neutral receptacle but in fact contains only those whom right-wingers want to quarantine there as people dangerous to society. Accordingly, new class members are the same adamant fools whom conservatives condemn as liberals in other contexts. Thus James Wilson complains that "the intelligentsia, the upper-middle class, the educated persons, [and] the literati" are people who promote an unrestrained sense of "self-expression" that, in his opinion, encourages criminal activity in America.[84] In the conservative universe, such people are presumably liberals. And thus Robert Bork perceives moral standards deteriorating in courts, in labor unions, in universities, in journalism, and in academia, all of which he attributes to Americans whom "[Irving] Kristol calls the New Class." This occurs, he continues, when those institutions are staffed by people who are animated by "modern liberalism."[85]

Condemning Liberalism

Since the term *new class* sounds objective, it makes liberals look worse than if someone would censure them in patently partisan language. The term's power does not stop there, though, because it also helps right-wingers to work together against those they detest, that is, to avoid talking about what might divide them and especially about various painful consequences of capitalism.

In this project, many charges are filed. Gertrude Himmelfarb, for example, argues that poor people can make a good living if they will try harder to succeed in life. She thinks they are persuaded not to do so, however, by new class members who scorn personal traits, such as prudence, perseverance, moderation, and steadfastness, that can lift poor people out of poverty.[86] Similarly, Charles Colson complains that many television journalists, as well as most writers and producers in Hollywood, belong to the new class, which exalts "individual gratification" and "rebellion against authority." Such people entertain an outlook he describes as secular and liberal in contrast to the Christian worldview of America's traditional and responsible leaders.[87] Liberalism also subverts public education, says Richard Viguerie, who blames poor performance in high schools on "the National Education Association and similar liberal groups" that "have insisted that it's more important ... to do away with grades, not worry about discipline, and protect teachers from fitness tests than to teach pupils how to read, write and do arithmetic."[88]

Beyond details, one can charge generally that new class people are responsible for almost everything undesirable in America. This accusation gives little weight to much that is happening in essential realms of modern life, including those linked to science, technology, consumerism, mass communications, globalization, and the environment. Thus James Burnham skips over many historical details but encourages solidarity on the right when he proposes that the West, including America, is spiraling into decline because of liberal sentiments, because it has lost a sense of purpose, because it is led by men and women who, regardless of institutional imperatives and configurations, feel guilty about their society's material and military power in the world.[89]

Modern trends are likewise absent when David Lebedoff argues that nothing works anymore, that things are out of control, and that such deterioration is caused by the rise of a "new elite" whose members correspond roughly to those whom Irving Kristol assigns to the "new class."[90] Similarly, David Frum argues that "abortion, the slippage of educational standards, foreign policy weakness, federal aid to handicapped schoolchildren"—all these are "expressions of a single creed," which he identifies as liberalism.[91] Gertrude Himmelfarb ices this cake when she argues that for half a century, the main problem of American "liberalism" (by which she means her sort of conservatism) was how to defend itself against "totalitarianism." But now, she continues, the urgent problem is "how it can defend itself against itself," that is, against "liberalism" (by which she means a radical "new class").[92]

The Counterculture

Comfortable with condemning the new class, conservatives went on to argue that it encouraged a "counterculture" to rise during the 1960s and early 1970s. In this view, people of that outlook, mostly young but with a sprinkling of adult enthusiasts who were sometimes professors and always dangerously new class in character,[93] spurred urban riots, opposed the Vietnam War, supported affirmative action, promoted environmental protection, denounced what they regarded as political irresponsibility by universities, danced to incomprehensible music, set up house without bothering to wed, and, throughout all this, defied the law by using drugs. This was, in short, the Woodstock Generation that conservatives later saw as epitomized by Bill Clinton.[94] To social conservatives it was as if unpatriotic barbarians had breached the gates of civilization, and to economic conservatives it was as if capitalism were under fire from people who hated both corporations and impulse buying.

Right-wing complaints against counterculturalists are various, numerous, and sweeping. Patrick Buchanan, for instance, argues that America, as part of the West, is sliding down hill because its population is falling. "In 1960," he notes, "people of European ancestry were one-fourth of the world's population; in 2000 they were one-sixth; in 2050, they will be one-tenth." From this perspective, deterioration gathered strength during the counterculture era. Among its causes, Buchanan is especially critical of birth control pills and legal abortions, the first marketed and the second adjudicated in the 1960s and 1970s. Both were originally endorsed and promoted by feminists and campus radicals who rejected what Buchanan calls "the Judeo-Christian moral order." Marriage, family, and children have gone out of fashion, says Buchanan, and he condemns *Sex and the City* as a sign of all that started going wrong in those crucial years.[95]

Charles Colson and Jack Eckerd describe how, as they put it, "[t]hings aren't working well here in America." What they mean is that many American products are shoddy and defective, and that, due to their low quality, American exports have suffered and the country's standard of living has fallen. The fault, they say, does not lie with those who lead American industry and commerce, such as managers and board members at General Motors. Rather, the culprit is disdain for the Protestant Ethic—which entails "thrift, investment, savings, respect of property, and charity toward others"—by people increasingly in thrall to a "cultural elite" that participated in a "revolution" of values starting in the 1960s. This elite denies, and it has inspired other Americans to reject, transcendent principles in favor of the idea that men and women can build a "just order" without God. It is such nihilism, born in the 1960s, that accounts for the country's parlous condition today.[96] To the religiously literate, it is as if "every man did that which was right in his own eyes."[97]

Additional scorn for the counterculture comes from William Donohue, who is especially critical of artists and writers who challenged long-standing moral precepts in the 1960s. Artists led a fervent assault on "bourgeois culture," according to Donohue, expressing "a raging desire to trample, mutilate, and destroy the norms, values, beliefs, and sentiments of established culture." But writers were equally destructive. Counterculture icons like Paul Goodman, Herbert Marcuse, and Charles Reich assaulted "the very meaning of society. Marriage, the family, sex roles, tradition, custom, religions—all the institutions, norms, and values that are the stuff of society—were attacked as instruments of repression." And about feminists, like Betty Friedan and the National Organization of Women, Donohue says that "revolution" was the prescription for "childrearing, education, marriage, the family, medicine, work, politics, the economy, religion, psychological theory, human sexuality, morality, and the very evolution of the race. Nothing was worth saving."[98]

Other denunciations were available. For example, Harvey Mansfield celebrated Ronald Reagan's election in 1980. It was, he said, "a general repudiation of the [counterculture] values of the 1960s." What particularly offended him, he describes as "lack of patriotism, abandoning one's friends, lack of self-restraint, easy abortion, interchangeability of the sexes, atheism in schools, increased rights for criminals, respectability for homosexuals, contempt for producers, forced busing, reverse discrimination, license to pornographers, and living off others."[99] Similarly, Gertrude Himmelfarb charges that counterculturalists "liberated" many Americans from virtues that used to stabilize society. "It is no accident," she notes in a typical right-wing correlation, "... that the rapid acceleration of crime, out-of-wedlock births, and welfare dependency started at just the time that the counterculture got under way."[100]

Killing Messengers

When they considered everything that had gone wrong, conservatives were seriously annoyed by young people who joined the counterculture, and they were especially distressed to see such people in the 1960s and early 1970s demonstrating, sometimes violently, on university campuses and in Washington streets, mainly for civil rights and against the Vietnam War. Ire increased as university administrators conducted what the Right saw as unseemly negotiations with student leaders, and as some of those leaders promoted not just particular demands but also wider visions of America as tyrannical and immoral. In both cases, of consorting with hooligans who broke the law and of kowtowing to unpatriotic rowdies, conservatives felt that hallowed standards and practices were being abandoned.

Now, to some extent, conservatives dealt with this cultural insurrection by criticizing its messengers. Thus Newt Gingrich says that "[i]t is normal for the young to rebel" against elders temporarily. But in the 1960s and 1970s, he thinks, when youthful suspicions were fueled by segregation, Vietnam, and Watergate, what started as, in these terms, a normal outbreak of specific rebellions hardened into a wide-ranging attack on the system itself. And although Gingrich insists that he holds no brief for segregation or the Vietnam War and regards Watergate as "disgraceful," there was no justification, in his eyes, for rejecting the system as a whole.[101]

Burton Pines denounces campus rebels along similar lines. What triggered their radicalism and demonstrations, he leaves for "another study." But "a major contributing factor," he says, "surely was the record-breaking number of restless, rebellious middle-class youngsters in the bulging baby-boom cohort as they reached adolescence." These were the people who scorned democratic resolutions of policy disagreements because, he observes, "[a]s do nearly all adolescents, counterculturalists mainly revolted against authority and rules, notably those enforcing traditional rites of passage into adulthood."[102]

Midge Decter says much the same thing.[103] What sort of children are these? she asks rhetorically. Some of them grew up in good and comfortable homes of diligent and successful parents who might even have been neoconservatives. Yet they seem to have no tolerance for difficulty in life, she says; they think mostly of themselves; and they expect other people to support them financially while they tear down what those people have built up. Why do they not understand that they have been trained and equipped to someday enter "positions of power and prestige in this society"?[104] Why are they willing to live in communes or drive taxicabs or clean houses, as if to throw away all their advantages?[105] Perhaps, she muses, the real fault lies with timid parents, who demanded of their irresponsible offspring too little and gave them too much.[106]

Exaggerations

Such criticisms give students little credit for working hard to make their case, as if the country would have promoted civil rights and withdrawn from Vietnam even if young people had not called attention dramatically to those issues. Moreover, some conservatives even argue that, in the era of mass demonstrations and urban riots, there were no issues that justified a radical response. Thus Irving Kristol says it is difficult to understand the counterculture because we keep looking for causes and find none. In fact, says Kristol, "[i]t is fair to say that *nothing happened* to provoke this rebellion—there was no visible crisis, or even any sense of crisis, in the economies, the societies, the politics of the West."[107] In which case, by elimination, the counterculture must have emerged from some quirk of the rebels rather than from any defect in the situation.

Samuel Huntington expands this thesis into an entire book.[108] He divides American history into successive eras and contends that each of them shows how the nation experiences recurring challenges to public authority fueled more by exaggerated censure than by government acts that deserve special condemnation. This "arrogance of morality,"[109] as he calls it, can cause government officials who feel threatened by such challenges—for example, Richard Nixon—to abuse their authority, thereby provoking more challenges. But that is a side point. The main problem is that recent protesters rebelled against a wide range of social and political leaders even though abuses of authority, such as existed, were no more serious than those tolerated prior to the counterculture era. In which case, what happened "lies not so much in the behavior of officials as in the temper of their times and the extent to which the American psyche [occasionally] becomes possessed by moralistic demons outraged at the gap between ideal and practice."[110]

Multiculturalism

The next useful enemy was multiculturalism. By conservative reckoning, counterculturalism grew during the Vietnam era and gave birth to multiculturalism especially on college campuses in the 1980s and 1990s.[111] Multiculturalism may be defined as "a philosophy of education that stresses the unique contributions of different cultures to the history of the world."[112] Those who promote this philosophy are encouraged to do so, they say, by social circumstances. Research shows, in this view, that many immigrants to America have not turned into Anglo-Saxons via the "melting pot" mechanism in American life. Instead, the United States is becoming more pluralistic than in the past, composed of different sorts of people who have much to learn about one another, hence the talk today about being more tolerant and respectful of cultural differences than previously.

The Canon

Conservatives see multiculturalists not as recognizing diversity but as extending the counterculture, as mistakenly rejecting long-standing values and therefore dangerous to both tradition and free enterprise. Support for this argument entails, among other things, the premise that universities should teach students the great ideas promoted by Western civilization via a series of books known together as "the canon."

Right-wingers frequently praise this canon, which Roger Kimball defines as "the unofficial, shifting, yet generally recognized body of great works that have stood the test of time and are acknowledged to be central to a complete liberal arts education."[113] According to people on the right, the canon suffers from many problems today. One is that not enough of it is being taught, because items of lesser stature are increasingly replacing great works while universities like Stanford cancel core curriculum courses. This is the meaning of instructing students to get acquainted with Franz Fanon instead of John Locke,[114] or *The Color Purple* instead of *Othello*,[115] or *Kramer vs. Kramer* instead of *Anna Karenina*.[116] Along with Kimball, conservatives like Allan Bloom,[117] William Bennett,[118] and Dinesh D'Souza[119] make this argument.

A second canon problem is that what professors today teach about even good books is troublesome because it embodies the multicultural notion that human beings are so fallible as to be unable to recognize the truth even if they believe that "the truth" may be said philosophically to exist. Here is where conservatives come down especially hard on postmodern professors like Geoffrey Hartman, Richard Rorty, and Stanley Fish, who seem to believe that texts have no fixed significance beyond whatever meaning readers attribute to them. Kimball, for example, claims that the canon offers "the best that has been thought and said," and he insists that insights embedded in various texts, visible for all to see, are in some sense absolutely true.[120] When modern professors reject this philosophy of education, says Allan Bloom, their students will be unable "to distinguish between the sublime and trash, insight and propaganda."[121]

A third canon problem is that professors behave irresponsibly by refusing to teach from presumably "great books" what patrons of higher education want their children to learn. This is the argument, made famously by William Buckley Jr., that legislators, trustees, and parents are entitled to decide what they will buy, in which case those who supply educational commodities should be more responsive to public demand.[122] It is a pro-marketplace argument that implicitly rejects Michael Walzer's "spheres of justice" principle—which was enunciated later—because Buckley insists that people outside of universities, who may know little of how knowledge is generated inside them, are nevertheless entitled to tell professors how to conduct research and what to teach students.[123]

Telling the Right Story

What they regard as contempt for the canon especially angers conservatives because it seems to encourage universities to spend more time talking about "identity," "difference," and "gender" than about the principles and convictions that, according to the Right, first made the West, and then America, great. On this score, Alvin Schmidt concedes that to teach young Americans about other cultures is legitimate. But he argues that such "multicultural education" is often inspired by a "leftist political ideology" that "sees all cultures, mores, and institutions, as essentially equal." In this sense, multiculturalism "encourages immigrants and other minorities to retain their foreign cultures by not assimilating into the Euro-American culture."[124]

The Americanism that conservatives hope to instill in young people starts with admiration for Western precepts and projects and then goes on to praise America's version of those cultural achievements. It is the West, in this view, that created and promotes science, technology, free speech, religious tolerance, civil rights, social mobility, economic opportunity, and more. In contrast, non-Western societies are still plagued, although not entirely so, by ethnic vendettas, social stratification, corrupt officials, religious animosities, and various depredations against women, such as clitorectomy and polygamy.

Here is a partial description of the Third World from Bob Grant: "Tyranny. Tribal uprisings. Anarchy. Repression of the many by the few. Revolving dictatorships. Revolution. Murderous religious warfare. Class warfare. Race warfare. Civil strife. Officially sanctioned slaughter. Guerrilla death squads. Juntas right and left."[125] Against a backdrop of such horrors, say conservatives, it is no wonder that immigrants flock to America rather than the other way around. Indeed, that they vote with their feet shows that the real choice, as Roger Kimball puts it, "is not between a 'repressive' Western culture and a multicultural paradise, but between culture and barbarism."[126]

As conservatives describe the country, immigrants from Europe infused their American lives with solid Western values. That being so, Daniel Flynn complains that multiculturalism in universities is actually "a code word for anti-Americanism." In other words, "multiculturalism is rarely about promoting other cultures. It is more often about debasing our own."[127] What bothers Flynn, then, is what he sees as universities encouraging women and minorities to believe they are victims of some oppressive impulse built into American society. Everywhere people live there is room for improvement, say conservatives like Flynn. But, they add, America is, comparatively speaking, more ethically attractive than other societies.

On this score, right-wing writers compare lists of national pluses and minuses to make the case for a more America-centered liberal arts agenda, and they write books with chapter titles like "Some Cultures Are More Equal than Others,"[128] and "All Cultures Are Not Equal."[129] The implication is that although no country is perfect, some Americans talk too much about being shortchanged by their society. From this point of view, even the descendants of former slaves should be thankful for having benefited from America's great moral principles. After all, is not the United States one of the Western countries that led the world in banning slavery, a practice not invented in the New World but eventually stamped out there?[130]

The Uncertain Center

Conservatives charge the new class, counterculturalists, and multiculturalists with sins committed in personal behavior, in education, in professional consulting, in journalism and movies, in literature and the arts, in fashion and design, in lobbying and demonstrations, and so forth. These are all linked, however, by related assumptions that right-wingers see at the center of liberal activity and that they regard as dangerous to core values that have sustained America and enriched the country's life for hundreds of years. These assumptions, which conservatives attribute to liberals, are labeled variously in right-wing talk.

Cultural and Moral Relativism

Thus conservatives criticize liberal support for what they call "relativism," by which they mean the idea that every culture has special virtues and achievements, whereupon "all ways of life" have "equal value."[131] Bill O'Reilly sees this sort of diffidence in what he calls "the gradual contagion of nonjudgmental acceptance," whereby Americans are increasingly willing to accept "behavior that would have been roundly condemned forty years ago." As a case in point, he tells of "hundreds" of people who sympathized with two college students who killed their newborn baby and left the corpse in a trash can.[132] Charles Colson focuses on a sexual abstinence curriculum that recommends to young people that they say no but notes they are also entitled to say yes. The endorsement of a right to say yes in such circumstances he describes as "relativism" in American education.[133]

James Wilson traces what he calls "cultural relativism" to the discipline of anthropology. Ruth Benedict's *Patterns of Culture* (1934), he says, discussed cannibalism "without explicitly condemning it" and thereby left the impression that local customs "can make anything right and anything wrong."[134] Allan Bloom argues that students at his university are committed to moral "relativism," which he defines as a "replacement for the inalienable [immutable] natural rights that used to be the traditional American grounds for a free society."[135] Along the same lines, John Lofton observes that universities are so set against upholding moral standards that "pluralism," by which he means relativism, has become their "absolutism."[136]

Dinesh D'Souza finds "cultural relativism" deeply entrenched in America because many people deny that "race is a meaningful category" and hold that "all cultures are equal."[137] As a result, "cultural relativism" spills over into "moral relativism" in the sense that, when all cultures are considered equal, a culture that fails to maintain moral standards is excused from making the effort.[138] And that, says D'Souza, is why relations between many whites and blacks in America are strained, because the black community, especially in its underclass, is not culturally equal to the white and suffers from what D'Souza calls "a civilizational breakdown." When that "civilization gap" will be closed, he says, "the race problem in this country is likely to become insignificant."[139]

Secular Humanism and Situation Ethics

Under the labels of "humanism" and "secular humanism," conservatives may condemn expressions of relativism that focus on theology rather than culture. Some on the right trace this view to philosophers such as John Dewey who taught, they say, that "[m]orals are relative to changes in society. The Bible is merely a collection of literary expressions from various stages of developing Hebrew and Christian societies."[140] Specifically, this sort of philosophy was proposed, with Dewey's endorsement, in the *Humanist Manifesto* (1933) and updated in the *Humanist Manifesto II* (1973). There, says H. Edward Rowe, humanists deny God as creator of the universe and reject the notion that values must find sanction in divine will.[141]

The problem with humanism, says Samuel Blumenfeld, is that it "considers the complete realization of human personality to be the end of man's life," whereas "we believe the purpose of life is to glorify God."[142] Phyllis Schlafly agrees and protests against secular humanism in America's schools, where it "denies the Bible and divine revelation and teaches that man's reason is all we need to accomplish everything."[143] In the Christian Right's vocabulary, secular humanism rejects the "Judeo-Christian worldview." It thereby denies that human beings are made in God's image, and it further denies that certain kinds of behavior—marriage, monogamous sex, the work ethic, and so forth—are absolutely good because God commands them.[144]

As a corollary to humanism, what they call "situation ethics," or something close to it, repels some conservatives. To that way of thinking, they say, God does not lay down ethical imperatives, and therefore one must assess the particular shape of every situation to decide what behavior seems appropriate to it. Accordingly, Rus Walton describes "situational ethics" as rampant in schools, to the point where "whatever fits is right, baby. Whatever turns you on. Morality is a rubber yardstick. Stretch it as you will. Any ends justify any means."[145] James Hefley recalls Judges 17:6, where every man does what is right in his own eyes. Then he insists that America's legal system was not founded on such "situation ethics" but on injunctions derived from English common laws, which were themselves inspired by Christian faith in the Ten Commandments.[146]

As we might expect, anecdotes illustrate conservative propositions along these lines. Ben Kinchlow, for example, tells of "a recent survey" in which 65 percent of the boys and 40 percent of the girls said that after a young couple has been dating for "at least six months" it is permissible for the boy to rape the girl. Moreover, according to Kinchlow, 25 percent of the boys said "it's okay to rape her if you spend at least $15 on her. Sixteen percent of the girls agreed." Furthermore, close to 75 percent of the boys said "it's okay to rape her if you're going to be married, anyway. Sixty-seven percent of the girls said, well, you might as well." Horrified, Kinchlow asks: "Where does that come from?" It comes, he answers, from "situation ethics." From having "[n] o absolutes."[147]

The Conservative Mind

In short, right-wingers claim that modern society no longer recognizes indispensable moral precepts.[148] This ethical flexibility is deplorable, they say, because it challenges fixed elements of faith that make life meaningful for conservatives. These are numerous and inspiring. On the one hand, right-wingers insist on preserving families, stopping abortions, censuring gay relations, praying in public schools, canceling affirmative action, cleaning up movies and television shows, and, say, promoting creationism. On the other hand, conservatives also insist on encouraging competition, rewarding entrepreneurship, reducing environmental protection, privatizing public services, sanctioning outsourcing, and, say, expanding world trade.

The problem is that arguments to these ends, each persuasive to some people by itself, do not always mesh well. Under the circumstances, conservatives attack people they regard as shared enemies. These include the new class and its offspring, i.e., counterculturalists and multiculturalists. Conservatives condemn both the behavior and the ideals of these people, to whom they attribute cultural and moral relativism, secular humanism, and situation ethics. And therefore they eventually conclude that the real sin of such enemies is that they refuse to accept ethical absolutes.

Creative Destruction

Now, what is actually happening here? As we have noted, the greatest threat to conservative intelligibility comes from the capacity of capitalism for what Joseph

Schumpeter called "creative destruction."[149] Everyone wants the creativity that generates antibiotics, networked computers, digital television, extraordinary agriculture, marvelous transportation, satellite communications, miracle fabrics, genetic mapping, and, say, low prices at superstores. But few want the destruction of modern families, falling water tables, dwindling rain forests, shrinking polar ice, dangerous neighborhoods, vacant stores on Main Street, the export of factory jobs, cancellation of company pensions, and, say, shredding of the social safety net. And so, to thwart suspicions that they might be responsible for some of these painful conditions, conservatives either declare or intimate that the destructive side of creative destruction—all that is wrong lately with America, why nothing works anymore in America—is caused not by capitalism, which most right-wingers praise, but by a particular kind of people whose behavior and ideas set into motion many kinds of deterioration in American life.[150]

The Theological Version

The culprits in this case are people who are difficult to identify and impossible to count, people such as the "new class" or "multiculturalists." Moreover, although one can attribute to them cultural relativism and secular humanism, it is not clear, even to their own ranks, what such people believe in. Precision aside, though, what emerges plainly from right-wing talk about such things is a sense that some modern citizens have lost their grip on something vital, in which case, for conservatives who feel most comfortable speaking from religious conviction, what those citizens lack is a commitment to transcendental values.[151]

Thus putative members of the new class, variously defined, are those who deny moral absolutes that come, in the conservative lexicon, only from God. After all, "[w]ithout God everything becomes morally possible and permissible as first Communists, and then Nazis, demonstrated."[152] After all, "ethics must be defined by a power which he [the moral person] knows transcends the individual person. That power, of course, is God."[153] And after all, "[a] [Hollywood] war against standards leads logically and inevitably to hostility to religion because it is religious faith that provides the ultimate basis for all standards."[154]

In this lexicon, the enemy are people who, while not believing in absolutes, mistakenly assume that America can today behave decently, as presumably it did in the past, even though it has "no anchor to give stability to its decisions."[155] Thus "the secular state will inevitably lead to authoritarian government in one form or another. Such a state has no absolute reference point."[156] And thus "if chance is our creator, then no universalistic code of moral absolutes exists.... It is no mere coincidence that the modern deterioration of morality has occurred contemporaneously with the advance of evolutionary philosophy."[157]

The Bourgeois Version

In a secular version of this notion, conservatives may claim that social problems arise because liberals disparage bourgeois values. This argument comes in two parts. First, what conservatives call bourgeois values—such as thrift, prudence, and fidelity—are described as those that made America great and can extricate the country from its present sea of troubles.[158] Various lists of such values are noted,[159] and one is encouraged to suspect that liberals are guilty (1) of rejecting these, say, in the counterculture era,[160] and (2) of inciting other people, say, the poor who receive welfare, to turn their backs on those same values. This is a convenient rubric because, although one can speak about bourgeois values as a neutral force, many religious Americans who are listening can easily understand that most people who admire those values are actually committed to Christian principles as in, say, the Protestant Ethic. Thus extolling bourgeois rectitude is less provocative than when some Christians promote public righteousness in a country that honors separation of church and state. But the message is similar.

Second, conservatives who praise bourgeois values tend to describe them as admired by most ordinary men and women. On this score, right-wingers project an image of the new class, or liberals by any other name, as people holding themselves aloof from the crowd, keeping apart from rank-and-file citizens, and mocking wisdom shared by a majority of plainspoken and right-thinking Americans.[161] This image has enormous rhetorical power. To dismiss liberals as a sort of self-appointed smart set is to project, by contrast, an appealing image of right-wing democrats, but not usually Democrats, that fits well with the populist overtones of modern American conservatism. Thus, unlike Edmund Burke, right-wingers such as Ronald Reagan, Pat Buchanan, Newt Gingrich, William Bennett, Sean Hannity, Rush Limbaugh, and Sarah Palin tend to describe themselves as ordinary folks who speak for a great hinterland of sensible public opinion.[162]

Chapter Five
Enchantments

Conservatives claim to speak for most Americans.[1] But no one knows exactly what citizens believe because sometimes they equivocate. And one cannot calculate precisely why citizens vote as they do because sometimes even they do not know why that is. Moreover, as political scientists Jacob Hacker and Paul Pierson explain, a majority of Americans say in opinion polls that they believe in liberal or moderate principles and projects. But then, say Hacker and Pierson, from media reports and Republican candidates such citizens receive a good deal of persuasive but sometimes inaccurate information—right-wing talk, actually—about campaigns, parties, government agencies, and public policies. The result is that many people, liberal at heart, wind up voting, on the basis of this information, against what they think they are supporting with the ballots they cast.[2]

So rather than trying to decide, as between attitude surveys and voting results, how many Americans are really and truly conservative,[3] let us continue to explore messages that appear in right-wing talk. These have been promoted by many candidates to public office since Barry Goldwater's presidential campaign. Therefore, regardless of how many citizens might endorse what those candidates say, their messages project an important political vision that is offered to everyone.

Inclinations

Right-wing thinkers close ranks by criticizing liberals, including members of the new class, counterculturalists, multiculturalists, humanists, and so forth, whom both economic and social conservatives regard as enemies of a good society.[4] If we take this aversion to liberals as given, we know *whom* conservatives regard as working against social well-being. But if we want to understand *why* those people are guilty, we must take into account more than what we have seen so far about what conservatives believe their enemies are guilty of. And as we expand on that subject, we will see that right-wing charges against liberals reflect a conservative resistance to some elements of modernity,[5] a vision that rests on elements of faith—or enchantment—rather than on matters that anyone can speak of with objective certainty.

Accordingly, let us consider now inclinations that spur conservatives to speak up against their enemies. Here are perceptions that define America's situation and urge conservatives to repair it. Here are beliefs that help conservatives maintain solidarity with other conservatives even if they disagree on the exact culpability of this or that liberal person or policy. Here are factors, in short, that cause advocates on the right first to sense serious difficulties in national life and second to feel they should express their views on such matters together.

Resentment

One powerful inclination is resentment.[6] Conservatives say that many Americans are angry about how they and their values are disparaged by new ideas and the proponents of those ideas.[7] For example, Burton Pines is concerned for parents worried about ineffective public schools, for evangelicals horrified by abortions, for professionals who favor stronger national defense, and for "humbler folk" worried about family decline and homosexuality. "What all these groups share," he says, "and what transforms their individual actions into a semblance of a movement is the similar way that they have responded to being pushed to the brink. They have reacted by reacting, by trying to recapture a previous value or quality which they believe has been lost."[8] Ralph Reed speaks directly for the besieged. "The [Christian] movement," he says, "is best understood as an essentially defensive struggle by people seeking to sustain their faith and their values."[9] Similarly James Wilson, who sympathizes with "ordinary men and women," says that such citizens wish to make moral judgments but are told by "people who have had the benefit of higher education"—that is, the new class—that "morality has no basis in science or logic."[10]

The refrain is picked up by other conservatives. Terry Eastland observes that white applicants to higher education may be rejected in favor of black and Hispanic applicants with lower academic qualifications. "Affirmative action . . . is bound to breed resentment," he concludes.[11] Donald Lambro writes about polls indicating that "67 percent of all Americans believe that 'what you think doesn't count much anymore.' An almost identical percentage," he says, "agreed with the statement that 'the people running the country don't care what happens to you.'"[12] And according to Patrick Buchanan, even though liberal intellectuals portray themselves as "benefactors of the working class, it is the working class, dirt farmers and factory hands, who come to their feet cheering and stomping, when George Wallace takes off after the 'pointy-headed pseudo-intellectuals who can't park a bicycle straight.'"[13]

Most important, the people who offend rank and file conservatives seem, by right-wing lights, firmly in charge of America. Thus Charles Murray is convinced that "in the 1960s and 1970s there was an elite wisdom [in the intelligentsia] that shaped the direction of social policy, [and] there was also a popular wisdom [against welfare, affirmative action, "lenient judges," and "socially conscious schools"] about why things were falling apart." According to the latter, deterioration set in because "government is meddling far too much in things that are none of its business."[14] Clyde Wilson sharpens this point. The American "republic," he says, is deteriorating into an "empire" because "our institutions are now managed in the spirit of and for the interests of ... [an] imperial class" ruling from Washington. "This class is decadent and must be replaced ... if we are to survive. It may be that abrogating the narrowness of small town morality was at some point a good thing. But liberation has not brought the Acropolis to Main Street, it has brought the Massage Parlor."[15]

Being Left Behind

Critics who described the "radical Right" during the 1950s sometimes talked about such people as being "dispossessed."[16] Alternatively, we can say that conservative resentment flows, in some cases, from "creative destruction."[17] Resentment may be caused by social and technological transformations that downgrade old values and old skills, and that undermine the status of people committed to them.[18] Consequently, we usually think of creative destruction as emerging from industrialization. This explains the anguish of nineteenth-century Luddites who protested against mechanization in English textile factories. But in a society undergoing rapid change, people in every walk of life—from farming to the armed forces, from teaching to the ministry, from commerce to the family—can be downsized, outsourced, bypassed, and otherwise relegated to positions of less importance, influence, and legitimacy than they previously possessed.

Under the circumstances, conservative publicists encourage some Americans to resent being left behind during times of "progress."[19] For Irving Kristol, modern life is promoted by liberals who scorn bourgeois precepts and practices. Yet "how can a bourgeois society survive," he asks his readers, "in a cultural ambiance [liberalism] that derides every traditional bourgeois virtue and celebrates promiscuity, homosexuality, drugs, [and] political terrorism?"[20] Samuel Francis makes the same point broadly. The current elite, by which he means liberals, are united by "what may be called the 'cosmopolitan ethic.' This ethic expresses an open contempt," he says, "for what Edmund Burke called the 'little platoons' of human society—the small town, the family, the neighborhood, the traditional class identities and their relationships—as well as for authoritative and disciplinary institutions—the army, police forces, parental authority, and the disciplines of school and church."[21] Rush Limbaugh presses the same charge. "Remember this about liberals," he says. "They survive and thrive on a fundamental belief that the average American is an idiot—stupid, ignorant, uninformed, unintelligent, incapable of knowing what's good for him, what's good for society, what's right and what's wrong."[22]

Disenchantment

To recognize that anger over being left behind can crop up as society evolves is not yet to understand which acts and values are at stake. To that end, much of conservative resentment today may be illuminated by Max Weber's concept of "disenchantment." Weber argued that disenchantment (*Entzauberung*)—or the reign of reason—is the hallmark of a modern society.[23] This was his way of suggesting that how Westerners lived in the nineteenth and twentieth centuries is an extension of how, in the seventeenth and eighteenth centuries, people of the Enlightenment turned away from mystification.[24]

More specifically, Weber meant that he expected modern developments in science, technology, and administration to rest on rational calculations rather than on arcane forces known best from theology and medieval philosophy. Success in making such calculations—leading to antibiotics, automobiles, television, plastics, miracle grains, heart surgery, computers, and more—would confer great prestige on scientists, inventors, and managers. It followed that, where much of our surroundings are understood rationally, some people will stop explaining the facts of life as if they are created and controlled by supernatural forces. It followed also that religious beliefs and traditional morality will seem less persuasive to modern people than in the past because those old guidelines often recommend behavior that is justified by revelation rather than experimentation.

The Faithful

What Weber described is around us to the point where scholars talk about McDonaldization as a symptom of how rational calculations and dispassionate configurations are replacing enchantment and tradition in modern life.[25] But that does not mean that everyone who lives in modern times will want to be entirely modern. Instead, some people still prefer old and familiar verities. When they are on the right, such people condemn "secular humanism" for seeing man, rather than God, as the measure of all things.[26] They challenge a woman's right to abortion, for example, holding, like Antigone, that they cannot obey a law of the land if it conflicts with higher laws.[27] They were shocked by the 1960s and fear that children will go astray in a permissive society praised by counterculturalists.[28] And they oppose multiculturalism because they believe that Western civilization deserves special credit for promoting principles capable of sustaining freedom and justice for all nations.[29]

Such people believe the stakes are high. As Harold Brown says, the contest today is not between left and right but between the "conservative" who seeks "to preserve the authentic deposit of our cultural heritage in all of its transcendental and historical aspects" and the liberal, or, more precisely, the "rationalist," whose rationalism "derives from an 18th century movement [the Enlightenment] that denies our spiritual origins and sets up man and human reason as the sole rule of a purely material universe."[30] In this scheme of things, Brown and many other conservatives see the world via theology and not science. Thus when he wants to advance a moral claim, Brown refers to scripture rather than sociology,[31] and when he seeks wisdom he looks more to Church Fathers than to discoveries made by Darwin, Freud, or Einstein.

Realms of Enchantment

Resentment and enchantment are often related. After all, rightists hope to preserve a considerable measure of enchanted knowledge. Consequently, they resent the status of, and the influence wielded by, people—in the new class, among professors, and more—who claim that modern society is best off for not relying on traditional explanations and understandings, and for not especially empowering the people who espouse them.[32]

This being the case, conservatives tend to support enchantment both in religion and in economic thought. On the one hand, such support appears when a large cohort of right-wing Americans evoke God's will and argue that it should animate laws concerning, say, abortion, homosexuality, sex education, prayer in schools, and the teaching of evolution. We will address this commitment first. On the other hand, some conservatives praise certain economic propositions with mystical fervor and recommend that citizens will instruct government to incorporate those propositions into domestic and foreign policies. Here is where conservatives promote faith in a "free" market that does not exist in the real world. To that project, we will return shortly.

Religious Enchantment

One can sympathize with pious Americans when they feel that Weber's modern people show less respect than in the past for what the devout call "revealed truth." However, the totality of conservative writings that touch on religion suggest formidable intellectual dilemmas to those who do not believe. Partly, this is because the validity and usefulness of sacred injunctions become difficult to determine when various religions compete for allegiance.

How to Choose?

For example, if one calls on liberals, as Stephen Carter does, to take Christian principles more seriously than secular-minded people do today, it is not clear which principles the skeptical should espouse. Should they show sympathy for the notion of "witches as supernatural beings," which is a belief that Carter himself rejects?[33] Or should they lobby for reinstatement of "blue laws," whereby state legislatures will forbid shopping on Sundays in deference to principles espoused by some of their Christian neighbors? Furthermore, if skeptics are asked to admire the "Judeo-Christian ethic" for expressing transcendent truth in America, is there any reason, beyond faith, why that "truth" should be judged more valid than other religious precepts, such as, say, the Buddhist doctrine of reincarnation?

Moreover, what lessons should be learned from the street demonstrations that broke out during 2006 in Muslim countries following the publication in Western newspapers of political cartoons depicting Mohammed? Should (1) American Catholics, who draw inspiration from paintings and statues of Jesus, accept the Muslim injunction against making images of God and the Prophet? And if they do accept it, should they redecorate their churches? Yet if they do not, is their rejection of Islamic truth any less disrespectful of another people's faith than the indifference expressed by secularists toward religion in general? Or, (2) should lawyerly conservatives, some of whom revere the Constitution as divinely inspired, decide that its hallowed right of free speech for individuals created in God's image should be limited by what other people prefer we will not say?

And how should rationalists assess the idea that religious commitments are important as a bulwark against tyrants who refuse to recognize moral absolutes that might be used to condemn their actions?[34] Surely there is some truth in this contention. One thinks, for example, of how many lives could have been saved if more Germans had stood up for unswerving decency as did Pastor Dietrich Bonhoeffer, who participated in the 1944 plot to assassinate Hitler and was hanged in retaliation. The same perception gives little weight, though, to the fact that religious beliefs have justified many persecutions in human history, including repeated violence against people regarded as "heretics" and centuries of brutality against Native Americans and African Americans in the New World.

The Origin of Things

In such matters, skeptics may challenge right-wing piety but cannot prove it is wrong because, to some extent, theological propositions are matters of opinion rather than fact. And who, in a democracy, is not entitled to his or her opinion? Under the circumstances, conservatives are almost rhetorically unassailable in the realm of values. Occasionally, however, people who accept enchantment use it to postulate facts. And when conservatives do that, they draw criticism from men and women who favor reasoning based on, say, census data, language analysis, astrophysics, genetic mapping, and laboratory experiments.

An example of disagreement arising from disputed facts concerns the issue of where Earth and its inhabitants come from. Some religious conservatives endorse the biblical story, which they regard as a theory of creation, that is, "creationism." Having stipulated that that story is a theory, they then argue that evolution is also a theory.[35] Consequently, they propose that public schoolteachers should allocate equal class time to both "theories."[36] As James Watt says, "We believers in the Old Testament want the theories of both evolution and Creation taught. We modern conservatives are not afraid of discussing all the possibilities of unproven theories."[37] If the two are compared, they say, it will be seen that the theory of evolution assumes various "link" creatures whose fossils have never been found, in which case evolution is no more "scientific" than creationism.[38]

When espousing creationism seems too sectarian, those who believe in a Creator may advocate the technical idea of what they call "original design." The contention here is that many things, such as DNA or the human eye or the Apollo moon rocket, are too complicated to exist by any reasonable degree of chance. Furthermore, they say, there are some things, such as a bird's wing, that cannot have slowly evolved from a previous thing serving another purpose because the in-between stages would have had neither function nor viability. Scott Huse sums up what he regards as the necessary inference on this point: "The existence of a creation necessitates the reality of a Creator. Intricate design requires a careful and intelligent master designer; organization requires an Organizer. This is pure and simple logic."[39]

Omissions

The vision to this point may be inspiring but is not really logical because, in the chain of causation, the Creator makes the world but nothing makes the Creator. Under the circumstances, belief in Creation and a Creator entails commitment to some sort of mystery, and that commitment can be sustained by faith without much public justification or elaboration. In a sense, then, further analysis here might be superfluous in that, like taste, there is no accounting for faith. On the other hand, like Sherlock Holmes, we should note when this dog does not bark. In other words, right-wing talk may gain part of its persuasiveness by not much noticing some important things that happen in the world.

The Separation Issue

For example, in the case made for religion in public life, people on the right slight some of the historical reasons for separating church and state in America. Thus, according to conservatives, America's Founders enacted the First Amendment to ensure that Congress would establish no state church in America. Here, their intent was to protect the free practice of religion from government. The same amendment, conservatives observe, does not say that Americans should exclude faith from the public square. That is, the Founders did not believe that government had to be protected from religion. From this historical perspective, what counts is that the Founders were mainly devout men who carried religious precepts into their public lives and therefore could not have intended to restrict application of those precepts to private affairs.[40]

In fact, this hindsight is seriously incomplete. Early American understandings of how religion and the state should coexist were strongly influenced by events in Europe, from where most white Americans came. In brief, the relevant European experience concerning religion was shaped in large part by the Reformation, when sixteenth- and seventeenth-century wars between Protestants and Catholics, or between Protestants and other Protestants, via governments that they dominated, raged for more than one hundred years until some Europeans decided that government should withdraw substantially from godly affairs. Their aim was to stop provoking violent resistance to religious ordinances that would be seen, inevitably, by some of their neighbors as sectarian oppression.

And so European statesmen and political philosophers, such as Jean Bodin in *Six Books of the Commonwealth* (1576) and Thomas Hobbes in *Leviathan* (1651), argued that (1) sovereign governments may rightfully establish a state church but that, in the interests of prudence, (2) they should not oblige all citizens to worship there. This policy of not imposing orthodoxy on all citizens acquired the name of toleration, as in John Locke's "Letter on Toleration" (1690). Americans later extended the policy by deciding that not only would Washington exercise toleration, it would also forgo maintaining a state church.

All this conservatives may acknowledge. But in their eagerness to infuse public life with moral imperatives, they tend to slight part two of the Reformation equation. The lesson that inspired the Treaty of Westphalia (1648) to endorse a policy of toleration, hesitant and incomplete as that policy was at first, teaches that government should not demand religious conformity. Accordingly, since most European governments at the time were princely regimes, contemporary language framing the lesson focused on what rulers can or should do. But once democracy took increasing hold in Western countries, mainly in the nineteenth century, the same ban on imposing religious conformity became, logically speaking, applicable also to citizens expressing their religious opinions in public life. This was because where elections take place, voters tell rulers which laws to enact. And in that event, if government after Westphalia should refrain from imposing religious conformity, then modern citizens should not ask government to enact rules that would violate such a ban.

To see American history this way, with an eye to what informs political philosophy, is to shed light on the right-wing hope for religious inspiration in elections, legislation, and administration. On the one hand, conservatives argue that religious guidelines are needed to improve the quality of civic life, in which case we should choose government officials for their dedication to transcendental values even though such screening might offend, in spirit, the constitutional ban on religious tests for federal office.[41] On the other hand, conservatives claim that people of faith have a moral right to express that faith in public affairs,[42] even though dissenters who promoted toleration, like Roger Williams in seventeenth-century Rhode Island, opposed mandating godly acts and behavior not because the dissenters belittled transcendental values but because they feared the results of trying to impose particular beliefs on people who marched to a different drummer. On both counts, conservatives criticize liberals, the new class, counterculture radicals, humanists, and so on for inventing a principle of separation that, they say, the Founders did not intend and that Thomas Jefferson proclaimed only years after America ratified the Constitution.[43]

The bottom line is that such conservatives discount the dark side of piety[44] and attribute to religion, or to what they call the Judeo-Christian ethic, various good effects as if only such will ensue if Americans will bring religion to bear on public life.[45] Thus they credit Christianity with "the first hospitals ... [and] the first universities"[46] but skip over the Inquisition, the forced conversion of South American Indians, and the Salem witch trials. Thus they praise the Southern Christian Leadership Conference as theologically inspired but, at the same time, say little about the Anti-Saloon League that lobbied to impose its vision of Christianity on a nation that would not stop drinking. And thus they extol religion for infusing American life with the idea that "slavery is evil, and [that] human life is sacred,"[47] but they slight the fact that white Christians, including clergymen, promoted first slavery and then segregation in the South.[48]

Families

So conservatives overlook the Reformation's full import—which the Founders did not[49]—in which case their approach to injecting elements of faith into democratic politics may sound more convincing than it might otherwise. But conservative oversights, or omissions, do not stop there, because right-wingers go on to argue that, apart from how it can improve the tenor of public life, faith should strongly animate private lives. This is especially true when they recommend that American families stick to traditional values. Jerry Falwell, for example, says that modern families are under assault from forces that include "the cult of the playboy," which disdains matrimony, and the "feminist revolution," which disparages traditional relations between men and women.[50] Elsewhere, he attributes family strains to "gay liberation, radical feminism, uncontrolled materialism, and political liberalism," and then he adds Planned Parenthood, the National Abortion Rights Action League, and the American Civil Liberties Union, which he describes as "dominated by a Marxist/Leninist influence."[51]

Speaking more secularly, Phyllis Schlafly deplores broken homes and blames the decline of stable families on people with bad ideas and weak character rather than on powerful economic trends. As she says, "The worst thing ... a woman can possibly do is take a 'women's studies' or some other sociology or psychology course in college. Some of these courses should be called 'How To Break Up a Marriage.'" They constitute "a psychological red-light district where fundamental values are exchanged for fleeting stimulants at an exorbitant price."[52]

While promoting such messages, people on the right pay little attention to real-life families as entities that may benefit from exhortation but would surely welcome tangible relief from some of the severe pressures brought on by what is commonly called economic progress. Instead, right-wing writers idealize what they call "the bourgeois family." That social unit contains a mother, a father, several children, and perhaps some grandparents, all devoted to one another and to values such as "hard work, delayed gratification, and self-imposed restraints on personal behavior."[53]

According to conservatives, the bourgeois family dominated social life in Western countries during earlier generations of the modern era, and it long provided strong support for democracy and capitalism.[54] Its existence in America is now threatened, says the Right, by liberals who promote permissiveness, and its decline is apparently accepted with equanimity by Democrats like President Jimmy Carter. Carter, says William Donohue, hosted a White House Conference on Families and during it signaled his endorsement of pseudo families—headed by, say, single parents, ad hoc lovers, or gay couples—by defining a family as "any group of people living together in a climate of caring."[55]

With these ideals in mind, conservatives champion public policies they think will strengthen traditional—that is, bourgeois—families. Proposals to this end appear, for example, in the Contract with America that Republicans promoted when they won control of the House of Representatives in 1994. These include tax reductions for parents raising children, abstinence education in schools, prosecution of fathers who refuse to pay child support, tax credits for people who discourage abortion by adopting otherwise unwanted children, severe sanctions against child pornography, incentives to spur welfare mothers to work, lower income taxes for married couples, and improved Individual Retirement Accounts.[56]

Stuart Butler and Anna Kondratas,[57] Bryce Christensen,[58] William Donohue,[59] William Bennett,[60] and Rick Santorum[61] advance similar proposals. None of these writers suggests using government to temper various manifestations of creative destruction so as to reduce its sometimes devastating power over families. Santorum, for example, argues that enacting laws like those the Contract proposed will help families generate the "social capital" that political scientist Robert Putnam regards as necessary for maintaining democracy.[62] Santorum's vocabulary is impressively up to date. But he ignores Putnam's major research finding, which is that the greatest threat to social capital today is not government activism but the fact that citizens watch so much television as to isolate themselves from families and friends.[63] Is television a manifestation of "progress" that we should fear? Does something about this mostly private project require public regulation? Santorum does not say.

Scientific Findings

By slighting what Putnam discovered about television's social impact, Santorum reveals that when conservatives address matters involving faith—such as the origins of life or the family's need for "values"—they tend to neglect what many scholars who practice science believe they have discovered about such matters. Conservatives talk often about science. They may say that it is a matter of discussing things with an open mind,[64] that scientists are as fallible as other people,[65] that what is regarded as scientific truth can reflect cultural biases,[66] and that what scientists believe is based on a majority vote among practitioners.[67] None of this goes to the heart of the matter, however, which is that testing defines scientific work.

On this score, Karl Popper describes an ideal scientific community where empirical tests are performed and where theories are accepted as tentatively true by one's colleagues for as long as they are not falsified in those tests.[68] Alternatively, Thomas Kuhn describes a history of science where paradigmatic hypotheses are accepted among colleagues who then spend considerable time and effort trying to confirm or disprove them experimentally.[69] Most important, for both Popper and Kuhn science is an enterprise centering not on *what* scientists believe—say, the theory of relativity or that of evolution—but on *how* they decide what to believe. In this sense, science is a matter of method, of men and women working together, of some people making informed guesses, of other people certifying some of those guesses by reference to materials available to all, of each generation hoping to know more than its predecessors about the world and how to live prosperously in it.

In short, science is the flagship of Weberian disenchantment, a mechanism by which men and women apply reason to dispel mystery, the modern world's hallmark institution for discovering new knowledge and undermining old understandings. As such, it cannot be congenial to people who believe they know already what needs to be known, who are looking for examples that will confirm what they regard as truths discovered long ago, and who want to maintain traditions formed in bygone societies.[70] On this score, science is the opposite of advocacy based on insight, and that explains why William Buckley Jr. says we should rely less on "technicians" and more on "men of poetic intuition."[71]

Furthermore, science, with its emphasis on laboratory results and statistics, is a polar alternative to social thinking based not on experiments but anecdotes. Here the conservative approach to public life is especially significant. George Will says that "a sufficiency of anecdotes makes a pattern that confirms a theory."[72] No scientist worth the title would agree. John Ashcroft says he knows the death penalty "saves lives" because, among other things, Ronald Reagan used to tell about a shopkeeper preventing his own murder by reminding the knife-wielding man robbing his store that, just the week before, a murderer had been executed in California.[73] Again, no scientist would accept this reasoning as a chain of evidence.

Instead, science emerged in Western society as an antidote to trying to understand the world via anecdotes, or time-honored tales, or revelations, or articles of faith, or intimations, or trances, or epiphanies, or myths, or premonitions, or theological stipulations.[74] Thus David Myers speaks on behalf of many academic colleagues when he says that "[a]s an experimental social psychologist ... I'm not much persuaded by anecdotes, testimonials, or inspirational pronouncements. When forming opinions about the social world, I tell people, beware those who tell heart-rending but atypical stories.... One can marshal dramatic stories to support any contention, or its opposite. The truth of human experience, I believe, is better discerned by surveys that faithfully represent the population and control for complicating factors, and by careful experiments."[75]

Free Market Enchantment

We have seen so far that conservatives may feel that people who are modern in the Weberian sense do not sufficiently respect people of faith or their works. The faith they themselves espouse appears in what conservatives say and do not say about, for example, the origins of life, the situation of families, and the efficacy of scientific communities. It also appears, let us note now, though not always for every conservative, in the right-wing approach to capitalism.

Some scholars insist on this point: Wholesale praise for free markets, they say, which is epitomized by enthusiasm for an "invisible hand," often entails powerful elements of enchantment.[76] The flavor of this enchantment is described by Harvard theologian Harvey Cox who concluded, in an article entitled "The Market as God," that "[t]he lexicon of *The Wall Street Journal* and the business sections of *Time* and *Newsweek*" bears a "striking resemblance to Genesis, the Epistle to the Romans, and Saint Augustine's City of God. Behind descriptions of market reforms, monetary policy, and the convolutions of the Dow, I gradually made out the pieces of a grand narrative about the inner meaning of human history, why things had gone wrong, and how to put them right. Theologians call these myths of origin, legends of the fall, and doctrines of sin and redemption."[77]

The Model

To understand right-wing talk in this regard, let us start from the fact that because societies shape *real* markets, no one has ever seen a *free* market. Indeed, no such market has ever existed, and what we sometimes call "the free market" is no more than a model, invented by people who tend to forget it is only a mental construct. One must read conservative writings very carefully to keep these facts in mind. For example, George Roche says that "[f]irst, we must understand the [free] market and how it works. It is a remarkable regulatory device, when it is allowed to function."[78] Roche's first sentence refers to a thought experiment, because Roche never saw a free market. His second sentence, however, by using the word *is* twice, suggests to unwary readers that the free market is not just a concept but an entity that actually exists even though, unfortunately, government tends to suppress it.

In the language of economics, one can talk as if free markets are tangible by positing analytical models hedged in with frequent assumptions of ceteris paribus. This is because to assume that all other things are equal is, in many cases, to focus little or no attention on factors that prevent free markets from arising. In the language of political science, such factors are also discounted if we ignore social *encumbrances*. One thereby assumes that all humans are the same, in which case none of them will let varying degrees of ethnicity, nationality, sectarianism, family ties, and so forth stand in the way of striving chiefly to make money to obtain and consume every sort of commodity.

Based on such reasoning, which we explored in Chapter Two, economic conservatives believe that if government will leave people alone to buy and sell voluntarily, the market will generate an ever-rising National Product, which is desirable because it enables people to buy more of what they want. And who knows better than they what that is?[79] Accordingly, Dinesh D'Souza feels he should praise entrepreneurs, working imaginatively and competitively, for "producing things that make society better off."[80] One needs only to establish a market and good things will emerge from it.

It follows that many instances of collective behavior—such as institutional rigidities, ethnic and religious biases, jurisdictional disparities, paradoxes of social choice, and the existence of free riders—and how they might produce some "bads" rather than only "goods," are not worth much discussion. All these are, by right-wing lights, temporary annoyances rather than the permanent stuff of human life. In the real world they will be handled, some successfully and others less so, by local and national leaders making political decisions. But conservatives will have little to say about that because market models do not much describe such decisions.

In this view, instead, the main thing is to keep one's eye on a very attractive ball, which George Gilder describes as follows. Capitalism, he says, is "a drama most essentially not of measurable money and machines, aggregates and distributions, but of mind and morale. Above the vast architecture of production, and surrounding it, is a statistically invisible atmosphere of moods and ideas, a phantasmagoria of images and visions of the future, which either admit, or eclipse, the sustaining light and power of the sun: the life-giving faith in the possibility that free enterprise can prevail among the unpredictable forms of wealth in the unknown world to come."[81] Is Gilder describing a model of capitalism or the thing itself? No matter; in the annals of conservative thought, he is here updating rather than innovating. Calvin Coolidge, for example, had already assured Americans that business "rests on a higher law.... It has as its main reliance truth and faith and justice. In its larger sense it is one of the greatest contributing forces to the moral and spiritual advancement of the race."[82]

More Omissions

Right-wing talk about free markets offers a stirring vision of efficiency and virtue. But that vision entrances few liberals, who are more likely to admire progressive taxation, Medicare, Social Security, and environmental regulation. And they are mostly immune to its charms because when conservatives talk about *free* markets, they say little about *real* markets. That is, within the totality of conservative propositions and demonstrations, a good deal of what happens in real markets is left out when right-wingers criticize members of the new class, radicals, humanists, and liberals by any other name. Some of these things, which conservatives might mention but do not describe adequately, are matters we touched on in earlier chapters. So let us now consider them a little further, along with additional parts of the right-wing vision.

Capitalism

For example, as we have seen, conservatives write frequently about capitalism, or free enterprise, or private property. But by leaving out many details, they actually neglect this important subject. Milton Friedman offers a *model* of capitalism;[83] Jude Wanniski offers another *model*;[84] Michael Novak describes the *spirit* of capitalism;[85] and George Gilder praises *faith* and *altruism* as hallmarks of capitalist behavior.[86] But these are examples of inspirational literature rather than accounts of what actually happens when people make a living. On this score, the usual sequence is that conservatives first contend that various agents cause America's social problems and then fail to highlight capitalists among those agents.

Thus Tammy Bruce fears that "[t]he mass media are among the most important foot soldiers for the Left Elite.... Television news and entertainment, the film industry, and even theater all present, day after day, night after night, material that reinforces moral relativism, the death of tradition, and the destruction of values."[87] She does not point out that most American media outlets are owned by entrepreneurs, driven by financial imperatives, and therefore impelled to produce material that, however outrageous, will maximize profits. Instead, she assumes that media liberals are responsible for deplorable performances and broadcasts.

The same perception animates John Ankerberg and John Weldon, who decry themes of extramarital relations in soap operas and in talk shows hosted by people like Jerry Springer, Oprah Winfrey, and Phil Donahue. It adds up, they say, to children being "indoctrinated with a liberal view of sex."[88] Moreover, that indoctrination is reinforced from beyond the small screen, they note, by "dozens of powerful media personalities—rock stars, TV stars, and movie stars—openly proclaiming their liberal sexual attitudes."[89] Again, liberalism is guilty rather than some impulse arising in lives seeking profits.[90]

Similar charges aim at other targets. Against government, for instance, George Hansen claims that "[a] substantial case can be made that the ills of American industry can be traced directly to the tax system and the burdens it imposes."[91] In this view, industrial problems are caused by politicians rather than businessmen, by senators trying to penalize polluters rather than Enron directors inflating their company's share prices or GM directors deciding to produce gas-guzzling SUVs. Burton Pines insists that "high tax rates . . . have slowed the rate of savings and investment, shrunk the pool of capital available for expanding and modernizing production, and gnawed at productivity."[92] He thus indicts government with no hint that the country's rate of savings might fall because of, say, installment buying and credit cards, both vigorously promoted by merchants and entrepreneurs rather than bureaucrats and legislators.

Then there is poverty. Stuart Butler and Anna Kondratas describe the able-bodied poor as miscreants who fail to support themselves because government welfare programs encourage moral irresponsibility.[93] Slighted here is the fact that some citizens are poor because even though they work—say, in superstores, motels, nursing homes, and fast food restaurants—they have become almost economically worthless in an extraordinarily productive civilization driven by science, technology, capital mobility, modern management, and cheap labor in the Third World. That is the message of recent books with titles like *Nickled and Dimed: On (Not) Getting By in America,*[94] *The Forgotten Americans: Thirty Million Working Poor in the Land of Opportunity,*[95] and *Making Work Pay: America After Welfare.*[96]

And what of education? Chester Finn argues that "[t]he shortcomings of American education" flow from "entrusting decisions to fifteen thousand local school boards" and from "mistaken ideas and beliefs (such as the view that boosting a child's self-esteem is more important than ensuring that he or she acquires intellectual skills and knowledge)."[97] Here the culprits are either governments or liberals. Finn does not consider the possibility that, through no fault of anyone in particular, American children are being educated to perpetuate a society—that is, modern capitalism—whose distinctive ways of continually making, constantly marketing, and ceaselessly buying may require what anthropologists such as Jules Henry, thinking especially of shopping impulses, might describe as a considerable measure of arrested development.[98]

Beyond specific policy realms, conservatives sometimes generalize. Thus Richard Viguerie observes in 1980 that "[c]ivil unrest, racial strife, a lost war in Vietnam, illegal drug use, soaring inflation, a declining business climate, attacks on the family, sex and pornography in the movies and on TV, a lack of presidential leadership, a weak U.S. military and a strong and aggressive Soviet military, are some examples of our major problems." Such difficulties dismay people of good will. Yet where do they come from? As Viguerie says, "Perhaps many of our personal and national problems have developed because we have forgotten to thank God for our blessings, our opportunities, our freedoms and our great country."[99] Leaving off the "perhaps," Jerry Falwell confidently sums up the Christian Right's idea that America's problems have theological rather than economic explanations. As he puts it, "I believe that Satan himself is the primary force behind every modern [liberal] movement to destroy the children."[100]

Forgiving Capitalists

These are not isolated cases of rightists letting capitalism off lightly. Because liberals advocate government regulation of business and industry, conservatives argue that capitalists should not be hampered because of problems caused less by CEOs than by liberals, bureaucrats, personal immorality, and so forth. Thus Wilhelm Ropke notes that although "degenerate aspects of our economic system" occasionally appear, "the foundation" of that system is sound and should not be made "the scapegoat for the political sins of our generation."[101] Or, as Jesse Helms contends, "The system [capitalism] is excellent; the primary fault lies with politicians and legislators and bureaucrats and judges in high places who have manhandled, not only the system, but the very meaning of freedom itself."[102] In which case, "[i]t is not the economic system that needs changing. The changes must be made in the allegiances and sense of values of men ... [say, by] deepening the sense of individual responsibility."[103]

William Donohue restates the point. Critics claim that capitalism abounds with "greed and narcissism," he says. "But the sleaze on Wall Street that has been so apparent in recent years," he continues, "and the profiteering that former government insiders traffic in so casually, is more a function of a culture gone wild with irresponsibility [liberalism] than a reflection of market economics."[104] Irving Kristol seconds this thought by treating capitalism as an ideal. To this end he argues that the system will work well if capitalists will seek profits according to "the pursuit of self-interest rightly understood."[105] Pessimists might regard this advice as tantamount to saying that capitalism will prosper if, at crucial moments, the people who practice it will not behave like real capitalists. Nevertheless, Rush Limbaugh is even more upbeat than Kristol. "We are told," he says, "that there is an inequitable distribution of food and other products under capitalism. Wrong. That's not the problem. The world's biggest problem is the unequal distribution of capitalism. If there were capitalism everywhere, you wouldn't have food shortages."[106]

Corporations

The message projected by conservatives is that something called capitalism promotes prosperity whereas capitalists in real life, whom we need not examine closely, may display faults without demonstrating any defect in the system.[107] In their overall praise for capitalism, whose private property presumably stands as a bulwark against potential governmental tyranny over civil society, devotees like

Limbaugh might agree that this sort of enterprise is epitomized in corporations that appear on the historical stage as joint stock companies of limited liability. But what are these entities like? What do they do in the real world from day to day?

Political scientist Charles Lindblom studied the financial resources of such corporations, their ability to create novel products, their capacity for building new factories and closing old ones, their influence on mass media entities via ownership and advertising, and their lobbying for low taxes and few environmental regulations. He observed that corporations are artificial entities rather than natural creatures, that they enjoy many legal rights of individuals even though they are collectivities, that they wield a measure of influence not available to most citizens, and that they therefore do not fit easily into theories of democracy that relate mainly to ordinary people and their political activities.[108]

In short, Lindblom showed that corporations do many things, some of them worrisome. But this complex behavior rarely appears in right-wing writings.[109] Instead, economic conservatives claim that people use the resources they own to make goods and services that they buy and sell in the marketplace. In this model, describing corporate activity is unnecessary. After all, say the Friedmans, "the existence of the modern corporation does not alter matters," because the "corporation is merely an intermediary between its owners—the stockholders—and ... resources other than the stockholders' capital, the services of which it purchases."[110] Robert Hesson wields the same abstract notion of corporations as shareholders writ large, and he argues that corporations are not created by law but arise from voluntary associations of citizens who are recognized by government when they together exercise their natural rights to produce, buy, and sell in free markets.[111]

Like economic conservatives, social conservatives say little about corporations. One may sense this when they discuss "mediating institutions" of family, neighborhood, and religion, which stand between individuals and the state. In conservative eyes, these intermediaries enable citizens to associate voluntarily and pool their resources to confront government agencies, which, driven by bureaucratic impulses, may oppress citizens unless checked by countervailing power.

Well, yes. But by size, shape, and location, corporations look very much like collective entities standing somewhere between individuals and their government. So why don't conservatives see them there? Well, real corporations are not as accessible to ordinary citizens as they are to people who can afford to buy stocks; their "members" include workers who can be downsized and outsourced if management decides to discard them; and their "neighbors" may feel compelled to reduce local taxes for companies that threaten to move elsewhere. It follows that conservatives will not assign corporations to the category of "mediating institutions." To do so would suggest that they deserve attention for promoting freedom, whereas to look at what they actually do might suggest that capitalism is not always as friendly to freedom as conservatives want us to believe.

Accordingly, right-wingers tend to skip over corporations when they highlight problematic aspects of American life. William Bennett, for example, says that children should know more than they are taught today about American history, the importance of families, and the dangers of drug abuse.[112] He does not insist that they will learn more about business lobbyists in Washington or, say, the role of American companies in globalization.[113] John Ankerberg notes that television is dominated by corporate networks, major newsmagazines, and "a handful of newspaper chains," which together control "roughly 97 percent of the information the average American gets." Ankerberg hopes we will agree that such corporations often make odious products. But he attributes those less to a diligent pursuit of profits than to media corporations being "controlled by a very narrow group of people who are determined to push us" into a world order characterized by liberalism and humanism.[114]

Advertising

While praising capitalism but not looking too closely at its corporate actors, conservatives also treat advertising briefly or not at all. Businesspeople advertise their wares because, among other reasons, science and technology enable modern factories to produce mountains of goods that must be sold. To justify this exercise in communication, which often takes place between small people and large organizations, one must assume that citizens respond to ads because of their own desires—what economists call "endogenous demand"—rather than from a disposition inspired by ads. In other words, to regard advertisers as benign, one must, logically speaking, regard individuals as capable of resisting the highly emotional messages that advertisers project in the hope of persuading shoppers to buy whatever products the system generates.

Along these lines, consumers appear in right-wing talk more as the progeny of Adam Smith than as the patients of Sigmund Freud, even while conservatives refrain from seriously studying how real advertisements might affect real people. Thus Milton and Rose Friedman argue that consumers are not "led by the nose by advertising." They will, instead, refuse to buy what they do not want, such as, in the late 1950s, Edsel cars. Therefore, say the Friedmans, businessmen who understand this fact of capitalist life know that it is "more sensible to appeal to the real wants or desires of consumers than to try to manufacture artificial wants or desires."[115]

This argument underlies Ronald Nash's defense of "planned obsolescence." Professors of marketing understand that producers try to induce consumers to buy redesigned products that look slightly different from old but serviceable things they already own. Thus advertising describes later versions of tennis racquets and wristwatches as better than earlier models. Nash argues that no persuasion operates here, since consumers will buy a spruced-up product only because they truly desire things that are new and improved.[116] The same claim, that purchases are made voluntarily, can be used to assess children's behavior. For example, Chester Finn argues in favor of allowing entrepreneurs to show television programs in schools in return for a right to run commercials during those programs. Advertising on television is hardly unusual, says Finn. "It's part of the world we inhabit, and nobody is forcing anyone to buy. . . . I've yet to meet a teenager who can be forced to heed a television commercial."[117]

Such high regard for how people decide what to buy assumes that shoppers exercise rationality that can resist powerful commercial messages. This is what Michael Novak has in mind when he argues that, just as we trust "the ordinary wisdom of plain human beings on juries, in the voting booth, and in the development of public dialogue," so, too, "a wise society trusts individuals to spend their hard-earned dollars as they judge best."[118] Or, as George Roche says, "consumers are quite capable of applying their own decision-making process in the market."[119]

The Dependence Effect

Since many ads rely on enchantment,[120] there is a sense in which, when conservatives talk about consumers, they are promoting an upbeat view of people's capacity for reason.[121] Alternatively, economist John Kenneth Galbraith argues that people who produce things and services use advertisements to stimulate citizens to buy. It follows, according to Galbraith, that there is a "dependence effect" between supply and demand in the economy, where consumers are at least somewhat dependent on producers in the sense that they will buy not just on personal impulse but sometimes because producers' ads evoke in them desire.[122] Galbraith did not attempt to measure precisely the extent of this dependence. But commercial sponsors, who constantly investigate consumer motivations, certainly believe that large sums paid for marketing are worth spending.[123]

Nevertheless, conservatives little discuss what ads do to Americans because they reject Galbraith's contention that producers exercise power over consumers.[124] Instead, they assume that no matter how large business entities may become, even the biggest of them must serve the interests of consumers who are separately weak but, while constituting the public at large, together wield sovereign power over markets. In this view, when producers compete against one another via ads, consumers can choose to buy only what they want and only at prices that satisfy them. Where that is the case, the bottom line is that producers, as a class, will serve everyone's interests, brought as if by an invisible hand to do so because doing otherwise—manufacturing the wrong item or offering it for sale at too high a price—would risk declining sales and bankruptcy.[125]

The doctrine of consumer sovereignty suggests a democratic implication that conservatives in their populist mode particularly admire. Thus modern rightists argue that shopping enables every citizen, richer or poorer, to participate in controlling the market, to the point where it will produce what pleases everyone. As John Tower says, "There is no democracy like the democracy of the market place. When a consumer spends a dollar, he is, in effect, casting a ballot; a ballot that determines what goods and services American business will produce."[126] And, as George Roche assures us, "Everybody (including children) can and does 'vote,' and every dollar counts."[127] Or, as Irving Kristol says, the market is thoroughly "democratic—one dollar, one vote. A civilization shaped by market transactions is a civilization responsive to the ... appetites, preferences, and aspirations of common people."[128]

Creative Destruction

Beyond slighting consumer behavior, conservatives also slight the creative destruction that capitalism engenders. Fueled by science and managerial imagination, individuals and firms are constantly upgrading yesterday's techniques and products, thereby undermining the value of old products, work locations, machinery, skills, and social arrangements. Conservatives usually write as if this process does not significantly affect society. Thus Jerry Falwell lists five "major problems" that have "political consequences." These include abortion, homosexuality, pornography, humanism, and "the fractured family."[129] They do *not* include advertising, computerization, downsizing, outsourcing, and globalization, all of which some scholars see as vehicles of creative destruction and agents of personal, social, and ecological disorder. The oversight here is similar to that of Robert Bork, when he argues that the "destruction of [moral] standards" in "American popular culture" is caused by "the liberal view of human nature."[130] Nothing in the charge cites lifestyle changes driven by the existence of, say, cars, movies, shopping malls, superstores, television, fast foods, jet planes, computers, mobile phones, and iPods, all produced and promoted by entrepreneurs.

On the other hand, conservatives may remark on the potency of creative destruction but downplay its destructive power. Friedrich Hayek, for example, observes that "the usefulness of some trade or special skill is [occasionally] changed by ... some invention which greatly benefits the rest of society." He concludes, though, that society should not subsidize the work of people whom progress relegates to redundancy because doing so would penalize those capable of providing new goods and services to all.[131] Milton and Rose Friedman agree that gains outweigh losses during periods of economic growth. As they note, nineteenth-century government officials decided not to subsidize hand weaving but to encourage the introduction of power looms into British textile factories, which turned out to be a "temporarily harsh but ultimately beneficent policy of letting market forces work."[132]

Michael Cox and Richard Alm build on such reasoning to argue that the unpredictable and confusing process of economic change—which they call a "churn"—cannot go forward without temporary job losses. These are tolerable, though, because "the churn ... allows companies to carve away inefficiency, keeps firms competitive, spawns new technologies, and delivers new products into the marketplace." All this "has made the United States a wealthy nation."[133] Or, as Michael Novak says, we should appreciate America's "robber barons" more than we do. "No elite on earth has been without its victims, but," he claims, "not all have equally liberated and enriched the many."[134]

Thomas Friedman praises globalization for promoting creative destruction everywhere. He insists, however, that every country must be willing to "shoot its wounded," by which he means abandoning business firms that cannot compete. In this New Age version of the old maxim that one cannot make omelets without breaking eggs, Friedman argues that a country seeking long-term economic success should provide workers who "fall behind" with a social safety net, although the net should not be too "cushy."[135] Newt Gingrich is equally enthusiastic about keeping pace with creative destruction. In his words, in our "bright future," children "will accept as a given that whatever job they do at twenty may not exist when they are fifty. They will invite and enjoy constant change."[136]

In general, the tilt in how conservatives relate to creative destruction reflects an emphasis on people as consumers rather than as producers. Right-wingers praise economic growth for generating products that consumers buy, from better farm machinery to refrigerators to mechanical transportation to miracle drugs to television, computers, and more. But they say little about men and women living together not as buyers but as sellers, who may suffer major damage—which economists sometimes describe blandly as "transition costs" or "externalities"—in times of economic growth. For example, Gingrich may speak of how producers should upgrade their skills to exploit new economic situations. But exactly who will pay to retrain workers, and who will help families to relocate, and how citizens will maintain personal relations and long-standing values during a lifetime of constant and sometimes shocking dislocations, he does not say.[137]

The Conservative Mind

So how do conservatives close ranks in public? Our first observation, in Chapter Four, was that, despite not always agreeing on what has gone wrong, say, in Iraq, and on what should be done to improve matters, and especially despite differences of opinion between social and economic conservatives concerning the advisability of government activism, right-wingers of every sort join forces to reject people they define as enemies. In addition to socialists and communists, and those the Right used to call "fellow travelers," these enemies are now called members of the new class, counterculturalists, multiculturalists, humanists, relativists, activist judges, tenured radicals, feminists, coercive utopians, Hollywood producers, the cultural Left, elitist intellectuals, and liberals by any other name.

Having noted a conservative campaign against guilty parties, we observed that rightists resent various men and women whom they regard as dominant in American life and responsible for much that is deplorable in it. This resentment is to some extent rooted in a process of creative destruction that has downgraded old skills and values, and that has undermined the status of people committed to them. It can also be sparked, however, by what Max Weber described as disenchantment. Like their neighbors, right-wingers live in a modern world that admires rational achievements of science, technology, and administration. Nevertheless, they are committed to a considerable measure of what Weber called enchantment in the realms of religious and economic thought. Moreover, they believe that national life will improve vastly if more Americans will espouse what conservatives believe is true about God and free markets.

In our analysis, the conservative commitment to Truth in religious and economic thought does not require much explication. The basic principles that right-wingers promote on both counts are fairly straightforward and, for some people, easily grasped by faith. What takes longer to explain is how conservatives make their case more attractive by not relating much to a good deal of information and speculation that is available in modern fields of knowledge. Such omissions we noted in regard to the origins of human life, the lessons of the Reformation, the condition of real families, the nature of scientific communities, the behavior of capitalists, what goes on in corporations, the influence of advertising, and the impact of creative destruction. Each omission is important separately but, on all of them together, there hangs a tale.

The Good Society

Let us stipulate: The minimal presence in right-wing talk of some topics highlights more visible items that tell us where conservatives think America has been, what the country is doing now, and how its leaders and citizens should proceed. In this tale, however, the partisan selection of oversights is especially striking if and when conservative claims are compared with those advanced by many political scientists, economists, sociologists, historians, anthropologists, psychologists, and other people who make it their business to investigate real-world phenomena such as families, race relations, corporations, and marketing.

Of course conservatives heed some social science findings. But as we have seen, they prefer to argue (1) that what is wrong with America today has more to do with principles than with great historical trends (neglected) and (2) that troublesome times are more a consequence of holding the wrong convictions than the outcome of what many scholars say they know about how people adjust to social and economic institutions (also neglected). Paul Weyrich assumed this sort of oversight was justified when he insisted in 1982 that he and his compatriots, building on grassroots enthusiasm sparked by Barry Goldwater's 1964 presidential campaign, saw more clearly than older conservatives, such as William Buckley Jr. and Russell Kirk, the commanding political importance of stressing what are now called cultural or value issues.[138]

We may restate this last point. Both conservatives and their critics fret about many aspects of modernity. Who in America, after all, can be happy about high divorce rates, persistent poverty, children who fail in school, neighborhoods that decline, outsourcing of good jobs to people overseas, Main Streets that languish, the impact of money on American politics, widespread substance abuse, environmental deterioration, media sensationalism, and more? Accordingly, the difference between conservatives and their critics is not that the former worry about such matters while the latter do not. The difference lies in how the two groups assign blame and propose treatment for whatever conditions worry them most.

Thus when conservatives complain about ethical laxity rather than institutional repercussions, they are expressing a faith that, despite how various cases might sometimes suggest otherwise, values decisively shape society today. On this score, many rightists believe in an essential Truth, a Truth that lies somewhere behind a world of scholarly research that, by conservative lights, does not always look in the right places. Or, to use another metaphor, there comes into play here a kind of gestalt switch, where conservatives tend to highlight principles rather than social processes in a way that not so much denies as does not play up what many scholars, working professionally, say they see in the world.[139]

The Primacy of Values

On such matters, not every conservative writer agrees with all others. Nevertheless, the emphasis on values, rather than on processes or institutions, turns up again and again. For example, James Hefley claims that "[w]hen a people cease to be good, they soon cease to be free. As Burke propounded, 'Men are qualified for civil liberties in exact proportion to their disposition to put moral chains on their own appetites.'"[140] That is, what really promotes freedom is not, say, checks and balances in government, or a social safety net, but that men will be virtuous.

John Ankerberg and John Weldon apparently agree with Hefley when they say that "[w]e teach that religious values are good but simultaneously undermine their influence in society. Liberal social elements, such as the ACLU, work to prohibit religion and protect pornography and [then] we wonder why we have a problem with child molestation, rape and other forms of violence against women."[141] In this scenario, sex crimes are caused more by the bad attitudes of liberals than by the bad behavior of sex offenders who, according to sociologists and psychologists, may be driven by personal pathology or pernicious circumstances.

A similar concern for precepts more than context appears when Edward Rowe notes that "Marx was an environmental determinist, whereas Christ was a spiritual determinist.... In recent years men have sought to establish a 'Great Society' through political reform and welfare state practices. The effort failed because greatness is impossible apart from goodness."[142] In this view, little can be gained from acquiring knowledge of how to build more effective institutions. Instead, the importance of personal morality is nailed home by George Roche. "As a historian," he says, "I find an extraordinary connection between moral behavior and a prosperous life." America, he continues, has combined freedom with "a deeply religious understanding of life. The result has been an explosion of invention and capital investment that has made us rich." Thus, "We owe our prosperity to our *goodness*."[143] That is, America owes its prosperity not to a fortunate geopolitical location, not to a far-flung internal marketplace, not to its wealth of natural resources, not to a temperate climate, not to sensible political institutions, and not to the fact that Euro-Americans seized the country from those people who inhabited it in the first place.

Faith and Disillusion

The bottom line here is that to slight the importance of scientific findings is to heighten a commitment to enchantment, is to press on with what conservatives know in their hearts is true, is to rely on powerful convictions to the point of assuming that, in a contest between political ideas, one must stipulate a verdict and only later, or perhaps never, conduct a trial. The opposite view is summed up by historian Daniel Boorstin, who speaks for the Enlightenment and modern scientists when he remarks that "[n]owadays, everybody tells us that what we need is more belief, a stronger and deeper and more encompassing faith." This is not true, says Boorstin. Rather, "[w]hat we need first and now is to disillusion ourselves.... We suffer primarily not from our vices or our weaknesses, but from our illusions. We are haunted, not by reality, but by those images we have put in place of reality. To discover our illusions will not solve the problems of our world.... But it ... will liberate us and sharpen our vision. It will clear away the fog so we can face the world we share with all mankind."[144]

Chapter Six
Stories

Clues to the next step in right-wing talk come from Allan Bloom, professor of political philosophy at the University of Chicago, from George Roche, president of Hillsdale College, Michigan, and from William Bennett, fellow at the Heritage Foundation.[1] Unlike Daniel Boorstin, these men praise neither the Enlightenment, science, nor disillusionment. Bloom, for example, claims that philosophy should promote enchantment in modern life because men need myths to live by. "Reason has become a prejudice with us," he says;[2] therefore, it is time to return to powerful truths that reside in great books of insight and revelation. In his words, "a life based on the Book," by which Bloom means the Bible, provides "access to the real nature of things."[3]

Roche agrees and insists that the West will be saved by "a poetic, figurative analysis that touches the wellsprings of the earth and of men's hearts." We need, he says, "men and values of mythic and heroic proportion. America once had such a myth—such a dream, such a vision of themselves."[4] It must be taught again, especially with the help of stories about, say, Socrates, David and Jonathan, the Good Samaritan, Joan of Arc, the Boston Tea Party, the Declaration of Independence, Nathan Hale, Harriet Tubman, the Gettysburg Address, the Little Engine that Could, the Wright brothers, Anne Frank, the landing at Normandy, and Martin Luther King Jr. Stories like these are collected by William Bennett in *The Book of Virtues: A Treasury of Great Moral Stories* (1993) and in *The Spirit of America: Words of Advice from the Founders in Stories, Letters, Poems, and Speeches* (1997).[5]

What Bloom, Roche, and Bennett demonstrate is that conservatives not only reject Boorstin's recommendation for challenging old images across the board but believe they can sponsor Truth by telling stories that project some of those same images. This is the conviction we will explore now. What we will see is that when their preference for storytelling translates into practice, conservatives enjoy a striking advantage in politics today.

Storytelling

Stories work well in public debate. They help convince citizens to join parties; they help party members work together; they help voters decide to support this or that candidate; they help officials choose among policy alternatives; they help leaders and pundits seem credible when they appear on television. As media experts say, stories "frame" reality so as to evoke particular images and emotional responses.[6] In which case, when partisans debate public policy, whoever offers the most appealing stories is likely to defeat whoever has few or no stories to tell. Television has little patience with those who recite statistics, or with scholars who parse what Robert Browning called "learning's crabbed text."[7] Whoever wants to sway voters and win elections must lead with an entertaining story.[8]

Yet who is likely to excel at storytelling? According to Weber, the world of enchantment is a world that cannot be explained mathematically and scientifically, a world that uses a leavening of stories to help us make sense of things we cannot see or, when seen, we cannot comprehend. This explains why people like Allan Bloom, who praise myths, often search for them in premodern writings, where they find riveting stories about, say, the curiosity of Pandora, the wrath of Achilles, the faith of Job, the courage of Daniel, the wisdom of Solomon, and the treachery of Judas.

In Weber's scheme, however, the premodern world not only generates stories but also requires them. After all, when science cannot speak, only enchanted understandings can explicate things that are crucial to our existence but seem mysterious in origin and operation. Thus to make sense of what they could not fathom otherwise, the ancients told stories of gods, angels, demons, elves, witches, prophets, saints, wise men, and fools. And thus priests, ministers, rabbis, and imams still rise in their pulpits to recall sacred tales and draw from them current inferences.

From all this it follows that, just as premodern people told stories to expound what they regarded as important truths,[9] people who rely on enchantment today will use stories to express their Truth. It is not surprising then that, as we have seen, American conservatives prefer timely tales. The superstar on this score was Ronald Reagan. His chief talent was for turning ideas into stories, and he did this by telling anecdotes—little stories—that lined up to illustrate larger truths.[10] Furthermore, he was particularly adept at combining disparate conservative ideas and making them look like interlocking elements of a national saga, a modern sort of Pilgrim's Progress where individuals work hard, live virtuously, and receive just rewards.

The Conservative Story

Because Reagan could talk as poignantly as Norman Rockwell painted, his small stories seem to evoke an overarching tale from the Right. Formally, however, there was no such tale, and there still is none, because no hallowed scripture unites American conservatives as some texts—like the *Communist Manifesto* or *Mein Kampf*—unite other ideological communities. There are, instead, smaller stories that appear here and there in conservative talk coming from Reagan and other right-wingers ranging from Patrick Buchanan to George Will, from William Kristol to David Horowitz, from Rush Limbaugh to Sean Hannity, from Rick Santorum to Gertrude Himmelfarb, from Thomas Sowell to Dinesh D'Souza, from Newt Gingrich to Roger Kimball, from Mike Huckabee to Lindsey Graham.

Such men and women do not all tell exactly the same stories. In that sense, conservatism is a mood rather than a catechism. But what holds their stories together, in the largest sense and for the most part, is a backdrop of historical stipulations and ethical ideals we touched on in Chapter One when we noted the six-point credenda of the *National Review* (1955) and the five principles that appear in the *Contract with America* (1994). Such framework expressions warn against the tyranny of large government, the perfidy of socialism, and the treachery of liberal culture, and they praise commitment to what right-wingers call personal responsibility and economic opportunity. Similar or complementary principles appear in other conservative publications.[11] Furthermore, this broad understanding of American "exceptionalism" is backed up by a host of small stories, anecdotes, homilies, chronicles, models, parables, and historical interpretations. Some of these we have seen and will not rehearse now. They are about central planning, good intentions, human nature, private property, minimum wages, mediating institutions, single mothers, nihilism, overweening governments, Western culture, rational discrimination, multiculturalism, bumbling bureaucrats, radical professors, humanism, the lower class, affirmative action, Tax Day, bourgeois families, slippery slopes, relativism, and more.

The Larger Tale

Now, when smaller conservative stories are told, they suggest a larger tale—which scholars might call a "meta-narrative"—along the following lines. The highest goal for any society is *freedom*. Freedom requires establishing an appropriate sort of *politics,* where *power* must be authorized, exercised, and tamed. In politics, democratic institutions encourage citizens to practice *self-government* and safeguard their *rights* against the potential *tyranny* of public authorities. The Declaration describes the rights that are at stake, and the Constitution provides *checks and balances* so that American governments will maintain rather than violate those rights.

Citizens also pursue freedom in the *economy,* where *efficiency* is generated in *markets* via making and selling, getting, and spending. In economic life, private *property* and commercial *competition* foster centers of financial and organizational strength that help citizens to forestall political tyranny. Here is a *mediating function.* Moreover, the *division of labor* in such an economy facilitates scientific and technological *innovation,* which over time leads to *progress*—for example, mechanical reapers, skyscrapers, penicillin, and computers. Furthermore, progress leads to *economic growth,* and growth provides so many goods as to permit distributing them to an ever widening circle of ordinary citizens.

And finally, Americans seek freedom in *society,* in a realm of decisions and activities that should be free from unnecessary government interference. Here is an arena that especially encourages the exercise of *morality.* In this realm, people can make the right decisions in life and those decisions will count as virtuous to the extent they are freely chosen rather than imposed by other people. Additionally, in this realm citizens may exercise *personal responsibility* for themselves and their dependents; they can voluntarily join other Americans in religious, charitable, and civic associations; and they are at liberty to build loving and supportive *families.*

To such propositions about politics, economics, and society, conservatives often add that good performance in all three realms depends on *religion* and *entrepreneurship.* Thus conservatives talk about how only theism rather than, say, humanism or relativism can provide firm standards for decent behavior everywhere.[12] On this score, politicians are encouraged to incorporate *values* into their public policies, say, on the issue of abortion; businessmen are encouraged to incorporate *values* into their competitive behavior, say, by making wholesome movies; and citizens are encouraged to incorporate *values* into their lives, say, by working hard to stay off welfare. Some conservatives argue that a Judeo-Christian ethic can provide the necessary values. Others make the case more neutrally, claiming that people who are religious or traditional, regardless of denomination, are inclined to behave better than those who doubt that God exists.[13]

As for entrepreneurship, early theories of capitalism emphasized abstinence as the capitalist's unique contribution to productivity, as if capitalists saved money for investments by postponing consumption.[14] It came to pass, though, that some wealthy people ceased to abstain in this sense, in which case the profits they received could no longer be regarded as reflecting sacrifice on their part. Accordingly, conservatives adopted the notion that what generates large economic rewards to particular people today—say, Bill Gates—is not abstinence but ingenuity, creativity, and perseverance. The *entrepreneur* thus becomes, and commendably so, a key figure in capitalist progress.[15] Indeed, for conservatives like George Gilder, the entrepreneur is a hero of modern economic life.[16]

Optimism and Simplicity

Having a narrative framework or principled vision, backed up by smaller stories, is a step toward success in political debate. But content is also important, and therefore rightists pump up their stories with frequent expressions of optimism, in which case, by implication, those who oppose conservatism may seem anxious and gloomy. This happens when, for example, Emmett Tyrrell[17] describes modern conservatives as more cheerful than earlier right-wingers such as Richard Weaver or James Burnham, both of whom feared a decline of the West.[18] On that score, optimism became an arrow in the populist quiver carried by conservatives especially after the Goldwater campaign of 1964.[19]

This is why Jeffrey Bell argues that we do not need liberal elites in government telling everyone what to do because, as he says, ordinary people can "make economic decisions affecting their lives."[20] Along similar lines, Lawrence Kudlow says that optimists, by whom he means conservatives, "believe in ordinary people. Pessimists are people who believe in elites and governments."[21] The inclination to optimism explains why Jerry Pournelle says that "[t]he only limit to human expansion is nerve; for man does not live on a limited planet."[22] Or, as Ronald Reagan showcased optimism in his 1984 campaign slogan, "It's Morning Again in America."

No less important than optimism, conservatives insist, is the simple wisdom their vision embodies. On that note, they flatter audiences by suggesting that ordinary people can easily grasp plain truths about the world and are therefore competent to judge how society should act. As Clyde Wilson claims, "All the great men of the world have been great because of their capacity for profound simplicity. And great issues are simple ones." Therefore, "a little simplification such as is posed by the New Right is just what we need.... We need to return to a simple republican form of government."[23] Or, as Dick Armey declares, "The problem with our public education system is very simple: too often it is run by people more concerned with protecting the system than serving the public. The solution is even simpler: break this monopoly of power, give parents the power to choose where and how their children will be taught."[24]

In the words of Phyllis Schlafly, "[T]here are simple solutions for most of the problems that confront our country today. Barry Goldwater is the man who can cut through the egghead complexities in Foggy Bottom and solve these problems for us."[25] Martin Gross similarly favors simplicity. Like Alexander boldly slicing through a pesky Gordian knot, he advocates streamlining Congress by eliminating half of all congressional committees, chairmen, and staff members, and he suggests reducing the budgets of federal agencies by firing at least 20 percent of the attorneys, scientists, mathematicians, engineers, accountants, and other professionals who work in those agencies.[26] Rus Walton offers an equally uncluttered response to feminists. "Women should have the right to control their own lives," he says. "And, in a word, they do. That word is 'no.' That's all it takes. Less than three percent of abortions are performed because of rape or incest."[27]

Neglecting Science

Optimism and simplicity *are there*. That is, they appear in the conservative vision and enhance its attractiveness. Significantly, though, science *is not there*. We observed this absence in Chapter Five, but now we can see that the oversight is conspicuous because the rise of science—from Copernicus to Galileo to Newton to Faraday to Darwin to Pasteur to Curie to Einstein to Fleming to Watson and Crick and to many remarkable people in between—is one of history's great stories. As Isaac Asimov said, "No one can really feel at home in the modern world and judge the nature of its problems—and the possible solutions to those problems—unless one has some intelligent notion of what science is up to. Furthermore, initiation into the magnificent world of science brings great esthetic satisfaction, inspiration to youth, fulfillment of the desire to know, and a deeper appreciation of the wonderful potentialities and achievements of the human mind."[28]

Probably conservatives, who love stories in general, neglect that of science because doing otherwise might draw attention and commitment away from things they regard as cardinally important. For example, the religious Right cannot be much interested in promoting science because people who practice it are likely to undermine many sorts of enchantment.[29] Accordingly, scientists must be resisted politically over issues such as stem cell research and evolution, and they must be confronted intellectually over issues such as biblical criticism and the anthropology of religion.

On the other hand, we should not expect social conservatives, apart from the religious Right, to extol science either. After all, many sociologists, economists, political scientists, historians, and psychologists are likely to challenge right-wing beliefs about crime, poverty, welfare, family life, public schools, race relations, and more. Moreover, even if social science research results were occasionally to endorse conservative propositions concerning such matters, few conservatives would want to acknowledge that Science, rather than Truth, should specify which possible solutions to public policy problems are worth debating in America.[30]

Furthermore, economic conservatives will dwell little on science because a key part of what Max Weber wrote about it is incompatible with a widely entertained right-wing sentiment. In sociological terms, Weber describes scientific work as driven by a sense of vocation.[31] By this he means that scientists are impelled not just to make a living but even more by an intense desire to discover something no one knew in the past. In this sense, scientists are animated by the intrinsic worth of their work, much as artists must paint or sculpt, as writers are driven to compose,[32] as physicians seek to heal the sick, as ministers are inspired to counsel parishioners, and as soldiers feel honor bound to defend their countries.

All this may be so, but Weber's concept of vocation clashes with right-wing notions of human nature that portray people as inspired not by vocation but by hope of personal gain. As we have seen, many conservatives emphasize what they call economic rationality, which they describe as put into play by an acquisitive human nature that gets channeled by markets into a search for profits. In this view, progress comes from capitalists and not scientists, from people intent on acquiring money rather than from people seeking knowledge for its own sake. That is the assumption that prompts Jesse Helms to complain that "[n]ot everyone has a firm grasp of the obvious fact that the profit motive has been responsible for much of the progress our nation has made. This is the difference between America's mass production and comforts and conveniences, and the primitive tribal conditions in the Australian Outback."[33] But where are scientists and their vocations in this vision?

Similarly, Ronald Nash claims that "[c]apitalism has enormously raised the level of the masses. It has wiped out whole areas of poverty. It has greatly reduced infant mortality, and made it possible to cure disease and prolong life."[34] Such accomplishments are remarkable. But were they produced by capitalists, or by scientists, or by some combination of both? Nash does not say. Dinesh D'Souza offers a similar vision. As he says, "[T]he capitalist has this over the politician and the clergyman: he has in practice done more to raise the standard of living of the poor than all the government and church programs in history. Using techniques of high-yield agriculture, multinational corporations such as Monsanto and the Archer Daniels Midland Company have fed more hungry people than all the state-sponsored and clergy-operated soup kitchens combined."[35] Well, yes. But who discovered the "techniques of high-yield agriculture"?

Plausible History

The conservative narrative projects two powerful pluses of optimism and simplicity, and it enjoys one powerful minus, so to speak, on science. But beyond that, many of its smaller stories refer to history and events, or trends, that presumably brought us to where we are now. These stories contribute to conservatism's rhetorical power, but we should note that they reverberate in debate not because they are historically valid but because they seem morally plausible, not because they are accurate but because some people think they demonstrate the truth about human affairs.

To recognize this reality is *not* to suggest that conservative stories can *never* be true, or that those who tell such stories are fabricating evidence they *know* to be false. It is to observe, instead, that right-wingers often pursue Truth rather than Precision—the essence rather than the details—so that their stories will establish and maintain a useful resonance between those who tell and those who hear, between those who lead and those who supply votes and money to generate conservative influence in America today.

Not surprisingly in this regard, Ronald Reagan's career was typically conservative. The stories he told about, say, welfare queens and his wartime service were not particularly true. But they worked for seeming to illustrate plain verities that some in his audiences wanted to believe, and only critics questioned the accuracy of what he said. We should expect, then, that other conservatives, intent on delivering important messages, will from time to time promote historical references that are useful but inaccurate.

Take European history. Jude Wanniski, who admires Rome for maintaining a trading area stretching from England to Egypt, suggests that imperial law and order in that area were so attractive that "[u]nder the Caesars, the Empire expanded not by conquest but by liberation."[36] Vercingetorix, Cleopatra, and Queen Boudicca, to say nothing of the Judeans, would have disagreed. With equal imprecision, Milton Friedman insists that history suggests "that capitalism is a necessary condition for political freedom."[37] In other words, forget about Athens, where democracy first flourished.

American history fares little better. "The Americans," says Jesse Helms, who admires tradition, "fought [the Revolution] to reclaim their traditional rights as Englishmen."[38] But that is not true, because in 1776 the Americans, having understood that English rights did not authorize them to defy king and Parliament, wrote the Declaration of Independence to show that their revolution flowed from natural rights rather than tradition. Or see Mark Anthony, enthusiastic about capitalism, who explains that the Founders built a government to preserve John Locke's goals of "life, liberty and property."[39] The Founding was surely a defining American moment. Anthony does not notice, though, that Jefferson wrote into the Declaration of Independence, and the Continental Congress affirmed, that American government would *not* endorse Locke's vision but would protect men's natural rights to "life, liberty, and the pursuit of happiness."[40] Or, for the immediate past, Brannon Howse reminds us of such television programs as *Leave It to Beaver, Father Knows Best, I Love Lucy,* and *Ozzie and Harriet.* "That," says Howse, "is how the 1950s really were."[41] Really.

The George W. Bush Version

Small stories, anecdotes, propositions, and omissions like these add up to a larger conservative vision, in the sense of forming a backdrop of oft-repeated references and benchmarks that enable audiences to read between the lines when conservatives talk and thereby understand what sort of reality the speakers have in mind. Such small items are available for recollection, for example, to help viewers sense, approximately, where President George W. Bush stood, in principle, when in his first inaugural address he declared,

> We have a place, all of us, in a long story—a story we continue, but whose end we will not see. It is the story of a new world that became a friend and liberator of the old, a story of a slave-holding society that became a servant of freedom, the story of a power that went into the world to protect but not possess, to defend but not to conquer. It is the American story—a story of flawed and fallible people, united across the generations by grand and enduring ideals. The grandest of these ideals is an unfolding promise that everyone belongs, that everyone deserves a chance, that no insignificant person was ever born. Americans are called to enact this promise in our lives and in our laws. And though our nation has sometimes halted, and sometimes delayed, we must follow no other course. Through much of the last century, America's faith in freedom and democracy was a rock in a raging sea. Now it is a seed upon the wind, taking root in many nations. Our democratic faith is more than the creed of our country, it is the inborn hope of our humanity, an ideal we carry but do not own, a trust we bear and pass along.... While many of our citizens prosper, others doubt the promise, even the justice, of our own country. The ambitions of some Americans are limited by failing schools and hidden prejudice and the circumstances of their birth.... We do not accept this, and we will not allow it. Our unity, our union, is the serious work of leaders and citizens in every generation. And this is my solemn pledge: I will work to build a single nation of justice and opportunity. I know this is in our reach because we are guided by a power larger than ourselves who creates us equal in His image.[42]

The Liberal Story

There is, then, a conservative narrative. Parts of it suffer from inaccuracy—which, to be fair, may also accompany partisanship from the Left—and its parameters are difficult to describe precisely. But its overall thrust is promoted constantly, by preachers, think tankers, politicians, journalists, and activists, via models, anecdotes, recollections, chronicles, and homilies, and with optimism, simplicity, patriotism, and a host of other endearing qualities.

There is, however, no comparable liberal story. Why not? In Weberian terms, the people who apply reason to modern life will reject stories that conveyed enchantment for many years. This is what happened when Charles Darwin published *On the Origin of Species* (1859) and thereby denied the biblical story of Creation. We should expect, then, that science will undermine important traditional stories. But the civic outcome of this process is perhaps greater than we might anticipate. And that is because when an old story is repudiated, it will not always be replaced with a new tale. Not, at least, by people who, as Weber described them, hope to substitute mathematical equations for mystical explanations as the fount of insight and understanding.[43]

This shortfall has serious political consequences because, in a way, conservatives and liberals have lined up on different sides of the story divide. Thus there is a sense in which to be rational according to Weber is to be liberal according to today's political lexicon. That does not mean that every, or even any, liberal is completely rational. But it does mean that, analytically speaking, to be liberal, as opposed to being conservative, is to tend to believe in a world without stories.[44]

FDR and JFK

This explains why, when confronted by a social problem, liberals are likely to say, as Franklin Roosevelt did during the Great Depression, let's apply some policy option to this problem. If it works, fine. If it doesn't, let's try something else. In the president's words, "The country needs ... and demands bold, persistent experimentation. It is common sense to take a method and try it: If it fails, admit it frankly and try another. But above all, try something. The millions who are in want will not stand by silently forever while the things to satisfy their needs are within easy reach."[45]

Roosevelt was not alone. For example, the same indifference to stories characterized John F. Kennedy's approach to problem solving. Thus he proclaimed at Yale University in 1962 that "[m]ythology distracts us everywhere—in government as in business, in politics as in economics, in foreign affairs as in domestic affairs.... What is at stake in our economic decisions ... is not some grand warfare of rival ideologies which will sweep the country with passion, but the practical management of a modern economy. What we need is not labels and clichés but more basic discussion of the sophisticated and technical questions involved in keeping a great economic machinery moving ahead.... These are ... problems ... [that] cannot be solved by incantations from the forgotten past."[46]

Pragmatism

Philosophically speaking, one can call this liberal approach to public policy "pragmatic." And if times are bad, as during the Depression, many citizens may vote for candidates who endorse liberalism. But to speak so matter-of-factly does not suggest a persuasive narrative and may fail to inspire.[47] Consequently, in times that lack urgency, liberal pragmatism may evoke little political commitment.

Furthermore, small capacity for inspiring will not be overcome by a tendency to praise, on behalf of multiculturalism, so many stories simultaneously as to encourage critics to conclude that liberals believe in nothing at all.[48]

It follows that, having either no story or too many tales, liberals are, to some extent, setting themselves up for failure in politics. As advocates of disenchantment, there is a sense in which they—not as individuals but as a collective persona—really don't believe in anything. This means, however, that when voters look at the political "horse race" in search of a nag with whom they can identify, it is as if liberals don't have one running. Moreover, given their propensity for science, rationalism, and secularism, we should not expect them to invent a horse on the spot. They may know they need a horse. But to make one and believe in it would be, for them, almost a contradiction in terms.

In other words, liberals are people who, by their nature, do not usually have political horses—that is, cardinal stories.[49] Conservatives sense this, as when Ralph Reed describes Democrats as a "hodgepodge of special interests ranging from gays, labor unions, and feminists to trial lawyers," in which case "modern liberalism is torn by the loud demands of its contending factions and no longer presents a coherent philosophy."[50] The problem for Democrats, or liberals, then, is that they offer no philosophy, or narrative, analogous to that advanced by conservatives such as Allan Bloom, who proclaims confidently that "in simple, rational speech that is immediately comprehensible and powerfully persuasive ... America tells one story: the unbroken, ineluctable progress of freedom and equality."[51] An African American, outsourced former autoworker in Detroit might wonder: unbroken? ineluctable? Yet if Democrats don't have horses, to continue the metaphor, it is not clear how, except for virtuosos like Bill Clinton and, perhaps, Barack Obama, liberals in modern politics can succeed against people who own a thoroughbred.[52]

Stories of Freedom

We have arrived at a vital generalization forecast in previous chapters. Within a framework of modern history, it suggests that conservatives tend to promote a large story and reinforce it with many smaller stories, whereas liberals have neither a large story nor the temperament to produce small ones that would make a large tale seem plausible.[53] One serious result of the imbalance, to which we shall return, is that many citizens, who learn from mass media outlets much of what they believe about partisan politics, regard the Republican Party as a champion of admirable values even while, according to public opinion polls, the Democratic Party does not seem to stand for anything in particular. There are, however, less obvious consequences to the mismatch, and some of those are worth noting here. What they show is that the centrality of freedom in conservative stories is more problematic than it might first appear.

Contradictions

To begin with, liberals, or progressives, or critics of conservatism by any other name, will insist that, for all its powerful storytelling, conservatives often say one thing and do another. But if that is the case, say critics, why should anyone regard right-wingers as men and women of principle who, if elected, will practice what they preach?

It is not difficult to press this attack because, as we noted in Chapter Four, some conservative ideas do clash with others. For example, but generally speaking, people on the right admire economic upheaval but complain that support for traditional values is collapsing; they champion the states as laboratories of democracy but favor a constitutional amendment to forbid local officials from marrying gay couples; they urge everyone to behave patriotically, but they oppose a military draft even in time of war; they accuse the new class of persuading voters to make "mistakes," but they assume that commercial advertisements will not have the same effect; they insist that the federal government is inherently stupid,[54] but they say counterculturalists should have endorsed Washington's decision to wage war in Vietnam; they say the rule of law is crucial to civilization, but they favored revealing Bill Clinton's secret grand jury testimony about Monica Lewinsky.

Furthermore, conservatives encourage college students to study "great books," but they commend a market that pays business students more than philosophers on graduation; they believe that bourgeois values should temper business practices but that government should sell corporations permission to pollute the environment; they claim that children are too young to make prudent decisions about sex but can choose correctly between evolution and creationism; they believe that everyone has a right to opt for whatever religion he or she wants but that the same he or she should be penalized for picking the wrong gender.

Unhampered Freedom

The inevitability of these tensions will become clear if we will consider how conservatives place "freedom" very attractively at the center of their stories about where America has been, where it is now, and where it should go. Recall, for example, Allan Bloom saying that the history of the country is no more nor less than the majestic unfolding of freedom and equality, an adjunct of freedom. The same contention runs through books like M. Stanton Evans's *The Theme Is Freedom* (1994)[55] and Dick Armey's *The Freedom Revolution* (1995).[56]

In light of that emphasis, policy juxtapositions like those above seem contradictory mainly when conservatives define freedom as an absence of governmental activism, in which case, presumably, the less government, the better for everyone. Right-wing examples of this approach abound. Thus Barry Goldwater contends that "[t]hroughout history, government has proved to be the chief instrument for thwarting man's liberty."[57] Thus Marvin Olasky claims that freedom is "the opportunity to work and worship without government restraint."[58] Thus Phil Kent says that "people are only as free as the government to which they give power allows them to be."[59] Thus Walter Williams proclaims that "[i]n free societies, the only legitimate function of government is to preserve and protect the rights of individuals."[60] And thus William Simon argues that "freedom is difficult to understand because it isn't a *presence* but an *absence*—an absence of governmental restraint."[61]

If right-wingers were to entertain *only* an ideal of negative freedom, they should not praise personal responsibility while recommending government censorship of pornography. Similarly, it would be inconsistent for them to endorse religious freedom and promote public school prayers, or to admire Walmart for selling profitable goods but call for "tort reform" to restrain lawyers from charging fees that clients are willing to pay. However, these apparent contradictions, and others like them, shrink or disappear entirely when we consider that conservatives also offer a second definition of freedom.

Bounded Freedom

Yes, some conservatives see less government as more freedom. But others, harkening back to, say, John Winthrop in colonial Massachusetts, regard freedom as the opportunity to do not what one wants but the right thing.[62] And this second, bounded definition of freedom permits the conservative movement as a whole to exercise ideological flexibility, for it permits some people on the right to assume that constraints may be necessary to help men and women do what they should do anyway.[63]

Not surprisingly, the concept of bounded freedom is often promoted by rightists who hope Americans will accept guidelines from Christianity. Thus Rus Walton, who regards America as a Christian nation, says that "[t]he foundation of freedom is self-government and the foundation of self-government is self-control.... In fact, true freedom is a dynamic balance (self-imposed) of rights and responsibilities; for each right there is generally a corresponding and co-equal responsibility."[64] As Daniel Flynn restates this point, "With freedom comes responsibility. Religion [Christianity] informs that responsibility. 'Thus, while the law permits the Americans to do what they please,' Tocqueville observed, 'religion prevents them from conceiving, and forbids them to commit, what is rash or unjust.'"[65]

To this end, Roy Moore observes that Americans cherish "the pursuit of happiness." But he adds that freedom to pursue happiness should not be taken to mean that men and women are free to be gay, because "[y]ou can't be happy unless you follow God's law and if you follow God's law you can't help but be happy."[66] Calvin Beisner fortifies Johnson's proposition by recalling that "St. Augustine insisted that true freedom is something deeper than mere immunity to forced servitude to others.... It is one's ability to live as he was created to live, to walk in righteousness according to the law of God." Freedom, he continues, is "liberty to do what is right, not the license to do whatever we wish."[67]

The Idea Market

Where theology encourages conservatives to combat "license," it seems to them reasonable to demand governmental regulation, as when religious rightists urge legislators to forbid same-sex marriages and what they call "abortion on demand." But other conservatives, more philosophically than theologically minded, may also hold freedom to be an ideal set of circumstances that should yield to rules enforcing virtue as conservatives define it.

The Clash of Values

For example, right-wingers speak clearly about the need to defend social and cultural values. "There is no such thing," they say, "as a self-regulating market in morals."[68] Accordingly, we cannot let everyone choose whichever personal practices and ethical principles he or she might prefer if, at the same time, we want to maintain a decent and stable society. In this view, some standards of behavior—say, support for patriotism, equal rights, voluntary contracts, and "bourgeois values"—have over time demonstrated that they are at the core of what America is in the best sense. And therefore those standards must be cherished and enforced because they will permit Americans, as in previous generations, to live together peacefully and prosperously.

Edmund Burke would have warned that any other course will dissipate the wisdom that people store up over ages and violate the "social contract" that binds together past, present, and future members of any society.[69] And Alexis de Tocqueville would have noted that to adopt new practices and principles indiscriminately will undermine those "habits of the heart" that keep civilized men and women from barbarism.[70] The prescription for such deterioration and chaos, of course, conservatives today attribute to liberals, humanists, relativists, counterculturalists, multiculturalists, nihilists, and the like.

In short, American conservatives may praise changes of pace and style that accompany creative destruction in economic life. However, many of them also insist that commitment to an ideal society should forbid a comparable measure of, in effect, creative destruction in social and cultural affairs. This is the meaning of William Donohue arguing that "[t]here is a legitimate public interest in seeing to it that the behaviors that appeal to the worst in us, that is, behaviors that are debasing to the human spirit, do not flourish unencumbered by law." Thus if "morally responsible individuals form the basis of a free society, then it is morally irresponsible to lift legal prohibitions against acts that constitute and induce morally irresponsible behavior."[71]

The same sentiments underlie Irving Kristol's proposals for censorship of pornography. "The basic psychological fact about pornography and obscenity," he says, "is that it appeals to and provokes a kind of sexual regression." And that is why it must be banned. "What is at stake is civilization and humanity, nothing else."[72] Similarly, Myron Magnet criticizes the *New York Times* for merely noting, rather than condemning, the way state courts have affirmed the evolution of same-sex relations in America. "Such a view," says Magnet, "allows one to endorse change without responsibly discussing what its consequences might be or, more fundamentally, whether it is right or wrong."[73]

The Importance of Mill

There is nothing remarkable about conservatives' arguing that freedom should attach to convictions and acts they admire. After all, rightists claim they know which values and lifestyles reflect what is True. They are therefore unlikely to praise laws that permit their neighbors to choose *other* values and *other* lifestyles, which are obviously False.[74] What is noteworthy, though, is the way the second conservative view of freedom sets even secular conservatives on a collision course with many scholars in America's colleges and universities. The gravity of this confrontation appears when right-wingers explain their reluctance to innovate, and their occasional support for government regulations, as a critique of John Stuart Mill's famous essay *On Liberty* (1859).

The first problem with *On Liberty,* say conservatives, is that in it Mill recommends an open marketplace for ideas because he believes that traditions and habits of mind can be tested, and sometimes replaced, only by new ideas coming from people who are at least somewhat unconventional. For describing how a marketplace for ideas should work, and for arguing in favor of what might emerge from competition between different concepts, *On Liberty* became a leading text, in the English-speaking world, about how forward-looking men and women, by their willingness to consider novel ideas and explanations, can promote improvements in human life. In this sense, Mill's justification of open-ended intellectual liberty is virtually an "icon of modernity,"[75] almost an epitome of the scientific outlook, or that frame of mind that Weber called disenchanted. As such, it is a major inspiration for academic research and scholarly debate.

The Gresham Problem

Yet by conservative lights, Mill's recommendation for intellectual combat, if implemented, may produce social and cultural disaster starting from the fact, as remarked by conservatives, that when ideas compete, the "best" do not always win. Thus Robert Bork complains that "[t]he winner in the marketplace [of ideas] is not always, or perhaps even usually, the superior product. The economic marketplace penalizes bad decisions. The intellectual and cultural 'marketplace'—in which the ideas of politics, the humanities, and most of the social sciences, and popular entertainment are offered—imposes few or no penalties for being wrong."[76] Roger Kimball agrees. "It is a melancholy truth," he says, "that good arguments often prevail over better ones, and that very bad arguments sometimes gain a virtual monopoly in the court of public sentiment."[77] Irving Kristol is equally pessimistic. "In a free market," he notes with regret, "Gresham's Law can work for books or theater as efficiently as it does for coinage—driving out the good, establishing the debased. The cultural market in the United States today is being preempted by dirty books, dirty movies, dirty theater."[78]

But which propositions will succumb to competition? Mill thought that many precepts in nineteenth-century England were inadequate relics of earlier Christian traditions and explanations. Thus he argues that much of what constitutes Christianity, going back to St. Paul and other church fathers, was "one sided and incomplete." Even when original Christian teachings took shape, says Mill, practical men supplemented them with Greek and Roman ideas, especially concerning "obligation to the public."[79] Therefore, after praising "secular standards" as necessary additions to Christian principles and practices, Mill goes on to insist that "[i]t can do truth no service to blink the fact . . . that a large portion of the noblest and most valuable moral teaching has been the work, not only of men who did not know, but of men who knew and rejected, the Christian faith."[80]

Unswerving Ethics

Now obviously, people who claim that Judeo-Christian ethics can generate social moderation, economic growth, personal happiness, and political stability cannot abide the notion that, in the name of a marketplace for ideas, those ethics should be constantly challenged and possibly replaced, as Mill recommended. This explains why Gertrude Himmelfarb charges that Mill elevated the "absolute principle of liberty," that is, the intellectual marketplace, to such importance that he invalidated "all those other principles—history, custom, law, interest, opinion, religion—which have traditionally served to support particular liberties."[81] What she means is that one cannot reject this or that ethical proposition without unsettling the sum total of moral commitments that sustain liberties like racial equality, freedom of religion, the right to trial by jury, and so forth.[82]

Roger Kimball makes a similar argument in Burkean terms. "The tradition that Mill opposed," he says, "celebrated custom, prejudice, and established morality precisely because they had prevailed and given good service through the vicissitudes of time and change; their longevity was an important token of their worthiness. It was in this sense ... that Edmund Burke extolled prejudice, writing that 'prejudice renders a man's virtue his habit.... Through just prejudice, his duty becomes a part of his nature.'"[83] Again, the lesson is that one cannot safely poke out a few bricks from the pedestal of sentiment, habit, and principle that supports commendable social practices in the real world.

In sum, these conservatives challenge Mill's marketplace for ideas because in Weberian terms, it dispels mystery while they prefer enchantment, which may justify what Burke described as useful prejudices. But that challenge brings the same conservatives into conflict, in principle at least, with people in higher education who praise the marketplace of ideas as an ethical ideal that informs their investigations into political, social, and economic activities. The tension on this score is especially severe to the extent that outspoken right-wingers, intent on persuading voters, winning elections, and setting public policy, incorporate into their advocacy elements of rhetorical style and substance such as those we have considered. The alternative ideal of scholarly research animated more by Millian expectations is summed up, although not intentionally, by professor David Myers: "My concern ... is ... with assembling an accurate picture of reality. In doing so, I rely much less on compelling stories than on research findings. As an experimental social psychologist ... I'm not much persuaded by anecdotes, testimonials, or inspirational pronouncements.... The truth of human experience, I believe, is better discerned by surveys that faithfully represent the population and control for complicating factors, and by careful experiments."[84]

Public and Private

Conservatives have a second reason for rejecting Mill's market for ideas. To maintain social stability, says Mill, it may be necessary to enforce some standards of public behavior. Nevertheless, he continues, we should maximize liberty by differentiating between public and private acts, and by permitting citizens to decide how to perform the latter. This is justified because we know that, in the perpetual contest of ideas, today's standards may eventually seem unsatisfactory and worth revising. It follows that where those standards are likely someday to fall from favor, we should even now leave citizens free to reject them privately. Government can afford to overlook the occasionally eccentric behavior of such people because if it will cause harm, only they will be hurt.

On this score Mill, writing more than 150 years ago, is somewhat in tune with conservatives who today define freedom as an absence of government restraint. Yet as Gertrude Himmelfarb points out, Mill's case for a right to be personally unconventional hinges on his distinction between private and public or, in another formulation of the same thing, on his claim that some acts are "self-regarding" and others are "other-regarding." In the real world, however, this distinction is often untenable, she says, because apparently personal practices and opinions may eventually influence the shape of social standards and behavior.[85]

One example of such a spillover effect comes when the consumption of pornography, which starts as a private preference, can over time become so routine and unremarkable as to undermine traditional restraints on violence and sex in public forums such as television, theater, and cinema. Another might be when large numbers of people decide privately in favor of divorce. Such decisions to unhitch, according to Phillip Johnson, legitimize the easy breakup of marriages in general, with severe consequences for children across the country.[86] William Dannemeyer sums up what is at stake here when he discusses homosexuality, an apparently private choice. In truth, he says, the personal practice of same-sex relations will eventually be carried into the public square and will there break down traditional standards and moral expectations, in which case it must be limited or prohibited "in order to establish [or maintain] a sense of order and decency in our society, to reconnect us with our normative past."[87]

Order and Progress

A long-standing dilemma spurs the conservative fusion of public and private acts. Wherever people live, some will belong to the "party of order" and others will make up a "party of progress." In the larger scheme of things, every society needs to balance these two forces, lest order forestall progress or progress foment disorder. Surely that consideration animated the Founders when they wrote the Constitution. But because social circumstances vary, no one knows for sure how, as a general rule, to create and maintain such balances in difference times and places. And therefore people on either side of the ledger in any particular country, driven by personal inclinations, will tend to favor not balance but what they, rather than their adversaries, want to achieve in public life.

Robert Bork, for example, notes that Enlightenment philosophers, and writers of books such as *On Liberty,* generously promoted individual liberty. But they assumed, he says, "that order was not a serious problem and could be left, pretty much, to take care of itself."[88] Bork disagrees because, in his view, repeated instances of unconventional micro behavior can generate dangerous macro consequences. Yet where that is so, someone must accept responsibility for ensuring that these consequences, perhaps unintended by those who act "privately," do not erode the ethical foundations of society. To this end, Bork strongly believes that government, to prevent those foundations from crumbling, should encourage or compel conformity in a wide range of personal activities.

Here the party of order is speaking, and Gertrude Himmelfarb is Bork's ally there when she asks, "Why is it proper for the government to prohibit insalubrious foods but not sadistic movies, to control the pollution of the environment but not of the culture, to prevent racial segregation but not moral degradation?"[89] Mill, she says, unfortunately "made it possible, and plausible ... to think that smog and insecticides are perilous enough to call for restrictions on liberty, but that pornography and obscenity are not; or that the Surgeon General can properly compel cigarette packages to carry a warning declaring them hazardous to health, but that the Attorney General cannot authorize a label on obscene recordings declaring them deleterious to the soul. As one wit has said," according to Himmelfarb, "it is now permissible for a performer to masturbate on the stage, but only if he or she is paid the minimum wage."[90]

The Counterestablishment

In previous chapters, I noted evidence that challenges various right-wing propositions. Some Americans find such evidence plausible, and liberals deploy much of it in political debate. Furthermore, tensions in and between conservative stories are likely to persist. But in the showdown between conservatives and liberals today, neither evidence, for whatever it is worth, nor contradictions, even if they seem serious, will save liberals from having to confront a conservative ace that Sidney Blumenthal calls the "counterestablishment."[91]

The rationale for this entity appeared when in the 1970s, right-wingers decided to seriously confront what they regarded as a liberal lock on intellectual life.[92] "What we desperately need in America today," said William Simon, "is a powerful counterintelligentsia that will issue ... challenges" to "new class opinion."[93] To this end, conservatives decided to fund right-wing think tanks like the American Enterprise Institute, the Heritage Foundation, the Manhattan Institute for Policy Research, the Hoover Institution, and the Cato Institute, and they sought to identify and sponsor university scholars of a conservative bent, say at Stanford, Harvard, the University of Chicago, and George Mason University.

As Simon explained, capitalists are not morally obliged to help pay for institutions that criticize capitalism. Instead, he continued, successful businesspeople should provide for "the non-egalitarian [conservative] scholars and writers in our society who today work largely alone in the face of overwhelming indifference or hostility. They must be given grants, grants, and more grants in exchange for books, books, and more books."[94]

Flooding the Market

The books Simon called for—and articles, conferences, press releases, talk show appearances, retreats, and more—were needed to compete against what conservatives saw as a preponderance of liberal entries in the marketplace of ideas. To this end, when Simon finished his term as secretary of the Treasury under President Gerald Ford, he became president of the John M. Olin Foundation, which supported, among other beneficiaries, the Manhattan Institute, William Buckley Jr.'s *Firing Line* television program, Phyllis Schlafly's Eagle Forum, the *National Interest,* the *New Criterion,* William Bennett at the Heritage Foundation, Dinesh D'Souza, Irving Kristol, and Robert Bork at the American Enterprise Institute, Allan Bloom as a director of the John M. Olin Center for Inquiry into the Theory and Practice of Democracy at the University of Chicago, Paul Craig Roberts at the Institute for Political Economy, Walter E. Williams, John M. Olin distinguished professor of economics at George Mason University, and, at Harvard University, Harvey Mansfield's Program on Constitutional Government and Samuel Huntington, director of the John M. Olin Institute for Strategic Studies.

Thirty years later, the conservative counterestablishment is firmly in place and generously funded. From New York to California, it includes hundreds of think tanks and public policy institutes, some already noted above but also the Hudson Institute, the Intercollegiate Studies Institute, the National Center for Policy Analysis, the Ethics and Public Policy Center, the Rutherford Institute,[95] Judicial Watch, the Federalist Society for Law and Public Policy Studies, and more. In addition, conservative donors extend financial support to thousands of right-wing activists, publicists, pundits, and scholars, some appearing in journals and newspapers such as the *National Review,* the *New Criterion,* the *National Interest, Commentary, Policy Review,* the *American Spectator,* the *Washington Times,* and the *Weekly Standard.*

These entities and individuals generate a massive flow of conservative ideas and proposals—in books, in magazines, in op-ed articles, in talk shows, in congressional testimony, in conferences, and so forth—all made possible by contributions from foundations, corporations, membership fees, subscriptions, and direct mail solicitations adding up over the past twenty years to substantially more than $1 billion.[96] Conservative foundations alone, for example, distributed grants totaling $254 million in support of right-wing projects during 1999–2001.[97] The chronology and players in this saga are described elsewhere, so we need not repeat here what appears there.[98] But some aspects of the new establishment are worth noting.

Hawking the Truth

We have seen that conservatives hold fast to what they believe is True. Thus when Richard Neuhaus writes about challenging what he regards as mistaken ideas in modern debate, he says that "[f]ortunately, there are still institutions, laws, traditions, and what Tocqueville called 'habits of the heart' that succeed, some of the time, in holding us back from the abyss in actual life. But all of these are perilously weak if they cannot be defended by public argument that lays claim to being the *truth* of the matter."[99] The same assumption that one can know the Truth underlies Roger Kimball's view of European culture, which he describes as based on "faith in the liberating power of truth," such as when the Gospel of St. John tells us that "[y]ou shall know the truth and the truth shall set you free." It follows, in Kimball's view, that Nietzsche is the great villain of modern philosophy for arguing that absolute truth is a chimera.[100] On the contrary, some things are valid for all time, in which case Brannon Howse can ask, "Does our country really need more change away from the traditions and moral absolutes that made it so great? Is change the answer, or does our nation just need restoration?"[101]

In these circumstances, when conservatives speak publicly their aim may be more to expound a bundle of axioms than to establish a series of facts. The result is that many conservative writings, generously and steadily funded, are more like advertisements than intellectual projects, that is, are more likely to start from a conclusion than to go looking for it. After all, when patrons are paying the bill, conservative authors understand they are expected to express opinions that those patrons entertain and want to promote. In this sense, the counterestablishment consists of sponsors and products, where the sponsor knows which ideas he or she wants to sell, and where his or her investment inspires a product that will be faithful to the intent, packaged attractively, and marketed energetically.[102]

On the other hand, rather than comparing them to advertisements, one may think of many conservative writings as similar to legal briefs. In those documents, an advocate pleads the best case available to his or her client rather than trying to figure out what he or she did and what it means. It is not surprising, then, that conservative books such as Richard J. Herrnstein and Charles Murray's *The Bell Curve: Intelligence and Class Structure in American Life* (1994)[103] and Terry Eastland's *Ending Affirmative Action: The Case for Colorblind Justice* (1997)[104] project a systematic and sustained argument for only one point of view, from the right, of whatever issue they examine.

The Rise of Footnotes

We can restate this point in still different terms. Conservatives like to use anecdotes to strengthen the case they are making, and we saw in Chapter Three that these anecdotes are often unaccompanied by footnotes. Tactically, this is like offering advertisements that cannot be refuted because the source of their claims cannot be checked. Yet where the counterestablishment operates today, it sponsors many publications that *can* be cited. These include, for example, books from Regnery Publishers,[105] Arlington House, and Encounter Books, articles from the *National Review,* the *Wall Street Journal,* and the *Weekly Standard,* and occasional reports from places like Americans for Tax Reform, Accuracy in Academia, the National Center for Policy Analysis, and the Competitive Enterprise Institute. Consequently, apart from telling anecdotes that can or cannot be confirmed, conservative writings are increasingly punctuated with footnotes whose presence suggests that some conservatives, in scholarly fashion, try to validate their claims by reference to supposedly impartial sources.[106]

Books of this sort may sound persuasive. In truth, though, their reasoning is often circular. Liberals tend to cite academic works in which, after testing, some ideas may replace others from time to time. But because many footnotes in conservative writings are based on right-wing sources, themselves usually sponsored by the counterestablishment,[107] there is a sense in which conservatives wind up quoting mainly one another, a chorus of people who are certain of their convictions rather than interested in evidence of other possibilities. Few surprises flow from such consistency, because right-wing writers are unlikely to cite and concede validity to, say, the findings of scientists who insist that Washington should ratify the Kyoto Treaty on global warming.[108]

Idea Marketing

In sum, conservatives since the 1960s created a host of policy organizations because they were determined to promote their stories. Then they created stories that people in those organizations told repeatedly, in a wide array of forums, some of which they also created. Yet the result of this process was probably unanticipated. We can see this by returning to what John Stuart Mill hoped for when he recommended, in *On Liberty,* a kind of contest whereby people might propose new ideas, test some hypotheses against others, advance understanding, reject venerable certainties, and improve society.

In fact, Mill thought beyond *whether* ideas should compete with one another. Thus he also considered *how* that competition might unfold properly. In this connection, he cautioned that "the free expression of all opinions should be ... temperate" and should "not pass the bounds of fair discussion." In the interest of "truth and justice," he added, such discussion should not entail "invective" or "sarcasm," nor should it refer to "personality." To that effect, one must not "stigmatize those who hold the contrary opinion as bad and immoral men."[109]

In Victorian times, Mill hoped for courteous debate. But the real problem posed by right-wing marketing is not that, as we have seen, conservatives sometimes say that liberals hate America, or that liberals resemble communists in their opinions and practices, or that liberals are people of generous intent but tiny understanding. On that score, we need not take Ann Coulter, David Horowitz, William Buckley Jr., Roger Kimball, Rush Limbaugh, and the like, in their sarcastic mode, as typical of all conservatives. The real problem lies deeper than occasional partisan exaggerations—some also appearing on the left—because there is, in a sense, perhaps something inherently intemperate in the way that William Simon's vision of a right-wing counterintelligentsia—producing books, books, and more books—has been realized.

What happened is suggested by a *Policy Review* article entitled "So You Want to Start a Think Tank." In it, John Andrews—president of the Independent Institute—says that "[i]dea marketing should be the constant litany of any policy entrepreneur.... The easy part is getting your message right [that is, paying authors to write books and essays].... It is necessary but not sufficient. The real test is getting your message out." To accomplish this, you must market, market, market. "Market your policy recommendations," says Andrews, "market the principles and values behind them, market the tangible publications and events your organization is producing. Market the think-tank concept itself. Then market your specific organization. And never stop marketing yourself and the other key individuals who personify the organization."[110]

A later article in the same journal describes how to promote ideas in "the community at large." To this end, says Heather Richardson—a governor of the Smith Richardson Foundation—there is "one important factor constant throughout—'agitprop' (short for 'agitation propaganda')." The Soviet term comes unexpectedly from an American conservative, but the intent is clear. Like Simon says, books should be sponsored and written. "They're not necessarily new, or original," says Richardson, "but often they take something that we all understand ... and create a new vocabulary for it." In addition, "empirical studies" should be published. "Because they come, at least ostensibly, without ideological bias," says Richardson, "empirical studies are often widely reported."[111] And the main thing, after all, *is* to get one's ideas widely reported because failure to do so was, in conservative eyes, the original barrier to right-wing political success.

Andrews and Richardson show us that what American conservatives say in the marketplace of ideas will be flogged energetically and effectively according to techniques developed in public relations and advertising. People at the Heritage Foundation and other right-wing policy organizations are entirely candid about their intent to do this.[112] Their books—and articles and op-ed pieces and press conferences and "background papers" and talk show patter and more—do not have to say very much new because Truth, like in-house commodities, is to rightists a known entity. As in public relations and advertising, what is important is the packaging, or the "spin," or, say, a "new vocabulary" describing something that, as Richardson says, we already "understand." That and, of course, constant repetition made possible by tenacious financing.

Temperance

Formally, no problem exists here because no laws forbid marketing of intellectual products. In practice, however, things are more complicated, because what started on a small scale, to correct a presumed imbalance, soon turned into an immense project for marketing ideas powerfully and continuously. Certainly Mill never intended this sort of promotion when he thought that, by placing ideas "temperately" in competition, men and women would increase their chances of understanding more of the world and how to live successfully in it.

For example, we know from the theory of monopolistic competition and its descendants that costly and sustained advertising can lend to some commercial products a competitive advantage. Is it temperate to introduce such a factor into the competition between ideas? John Locke's ideas were not marketed that way. Neither were those of Adam Smith, or Alexis de Tocqueville, or John Stuart Mill, or Charles Darwin, or Sigmund Freud, or Albert Einstein, or John Maynard Keynes. And neither are most of the books, research reports, and journal articles written by countless social and natural scientists today.

Scholarly precepts show what is at stake. In many realms of modern inquiry, say, in physics or history or psychology, the aspiration that animated Mill has been codified in practices adopted by scientific communities. There, ideas are formulated, reviewed, published, and discussed, not on the basis of marketing imperatives but within a framework of testing, whenever possible, and a commitment to vocational integrity. The process is imperfect, and sometimes distortions such as plagiarism, or reports based on false data, must be acknowledged and corrected. But it is a process that proceeds mainly according to standards of inquiry rather than the pursuit of victory, in which case participants expect an outcome that reflects the plausibility of hypotheses rather than the commanding presence of one party over another.

The Conservative Mind

In sum, from fear of drowning in strong currents of modernity, conservatives created an apparatus for marketing ideas that makes more political than scientific sense. Yet here is a final source of right-wing strength in public life for, by ignoring scientific etiquette in the realm of information, right-wingers gain an electoral advantage. This advantage can be understood in terms of what Hugh Heclo calls "closure," by which he means that, in some policy realms, due to unquenchable enthusiasm and indefatigable funding, the political system has lost some of its ability to close, that is, to "find a nonviolent decision-rule (by voting) for ending debate in favor of action."[113]

Heclo sees modern politics, heavily reliant on data and theories, as encouraging many people to collect information, to analyze issues, to join groups, to attend meetings and conferences, to publish their views, and to organize demonstrations. To empower such large numbers of people is a democratic plus. On the other hand, voting under such circumstances may do little to resolve differences of opinion because the losers may retain "experts" who, by deploying their own data and theories, will protest endlessly that the vote did not take adequate account of crucial facts and propositions. Here, a democratic capability can wither.

Applying Heclo's concept of closure to the way liberals challenge conservatives, one may conclude that no matter how much evidence critics will amass—from history, economics, sociology, political science, jurisprudence, biology, astronomy, literature, business administration, physics, anthropology, and more—they are unlikely to "disprove" any idea important to conservatives. This is because, as we noted, conservatives do not advance ideas to stimulate debate but start with received truths they then seek to present persuasively. Because this is so, books that conservatives write are not usually offered as tentative contributions to human understanding but as, in effect, elaborations of what are often updated versions of stories that need no dispassionate validation.

No Recantations

Yet here is the ultimate effect of an affluent counterestablishment. The like-minded advocates who staff that entity operate not in the sort of marketplace that the best sort of intellectuals recommend, where citizens are supposed to conduct a freewheeling debate, but in one that businessmen are most familiar with, where they have a product and aim to peddle it vigorously. Accordingly, no matter how objectively the worth of a conservative idea may be challenged, sponsors in places like the Sara Scaife Foundation, the Castle Rock Foundation (Coors), the Earhart Foundation, the Smith Richardson Foundation (Vicks), the Lynde and Harry Bradley Foundation, the Richard and Helen DeVos Foundation (Amway), and a host of major corporations will continue to allocate grants for new conservative works—books, articles, columns, magazines, conferences, retreats, talk shows, symposia, and more—which promote that same idea, more or less. Thus we continue to hear from right-wingers that the likelihood of global warming is greatly exaggerated[114] and that Social Security is set to implode.[115]

Such talk suggests that conservative sponsors are not much open to persuasion. By their lights, the claims they finance cannot be "disproved," as some ideas in intellectual markets occasionally are. Rather, members of the counterestablishment feel that the product they recommend is inherently desirable. Lost a battle? Tactical mishap. War going badly? Temporary setback. How to respond? Restore faith. What next? New campaign. Above all—from advocates of what Weber called enchantment—no recantations.[116]

Part III
Reality Checks

Chapter Seven
A Tale Against Tales

We have seen that rhetoric and faith combine to project a powerful right-wing view of what America was, is, and should be. In that process, small stories appear, merge, and culminate in ways we cannot describe precisely, in a sweeping narrative that works well, though not infallibly, in electoral politics. All of this, in effect, adds up to a conservative example of "the vision thing" that (1) George H. W. Bush labeled with an arresting phrase, that (2) he sensed was important in modern politics, and that (3) he regretted not being able to express passionately, eloquently, and authentically as a Republican candidate for president in 1988.

Alternatives

While reviewing these matters, I noted difficulties that strain some parts of the larger right-wing story. Consequently, readers may expect that, by way of conclusion, I will now offer a constructive alternative to it, that is, a substitute story that, in my opinion, advances propositions more accurate, useful, and/or virtuous than those I cannot recommend. In other words, if I am unenthusiastic about what is at hand, why not offer something better?

I have contended, however, that liberals do not tell stories in the same sense that conservatives do. Under the circumstances, if I would suggest now a counterstory to what I have described, it could not serve as a narrative capable of uniting liberals from any one place, time, or election, to another. And therefore, because I believe that modern liberals will not rally to any story—except perhaps momentarily and temporarily—I will refrain from proposing one here.[1]

Lessons

On the other hand, while refraining on that score, I believe that what we have seen so far suggests an important lesson. To distill it from right-wing talk, we should start from the fact that when conservatives are committed and skillful, they command resources that can add up to a message greater than the sum of its parts. This fact invites us, I think, to ask whether or not conservative ideas tell us something about storytelling as a vital political act. That is, in the totality of right-wing talk, is there something we can learn about stories in a general sense from seeing how some conservative tales, which flow from such talk, measure up against public events, which attest to reality?

To Focus on Stories

To learn from a relationship between right-wing stories and tangible events, one must begin by deciding which story to examine. To this end, we may safely assume that little insight would flow from focusing chiefly on current headlines and controversies. This is because behind immediate political issues—such as health care, economic recovery, illegal immigration, and catastrophic oil spills—electoral considerations encourage lawmakers, journalists, think tankers, and political activists to express shifting propositions tuned to short-term confrontations. As a result, current headlines and the debates they describe—for example, about the Tea Party movement—are likely to change as this book goes to press. In search of long-run insights, then, we should assume it will be most profitable to review a case where conservative ideas have already intersected with, and left their mark on, the real world.

One such case, lingering even as these lines are written, is the war in Iraq. To explore it is to consider how the Republican decision to go to war, and thereby begin to transform Arabian life into something more democratic, was, in some respects, seriously unrealistic. Consequently, the same exploration can—and here is the potential lesson—encourage wariness about the role of political stories in public life.

The Saga of 2004

The Iraq War figured dramatically in the 2004 presidential campaign. At that time, Republican politicians, activists, and pundits successfully broadcast to voters an image of Democrats as people who would not strongly prosecute the "War on Terror" in Baghdad or elsewhere. Senator John Kerry was, they said, fickle and erratic. Indeed, he was consistent about nothing but changing his mind.[2] The charge flowed easily from stories that right-wingers told about themselves wherein, as opposed to how they portrayed liberals as "skeptical," "ungodly," or even "nihilistic," leaders on the right, such as when President Bush appeared in a fighter pilot's flight suit in 2003, were clothed with fortitude, tenacity, decisiveness, optimism, simplicity, and commitment to the Truth.[3] The payoff was enormous. Even while the war dragged on, and even though Republicans in Congress had borrowed huge sums to finance it, President Bush won a popular majority and the electoral college in 2004 by campaigning on this theme, that Kerry waffled constantly on matters vital to America's very existence. The electoral consequences of so "framing" the party that made the New Deal and the Great Society—the party of Social Security, the Tennessee Valley Authority, the National Labor Relations Act, the Peace Corps, the Civil Rights Acts of 1964 and 1965, and Medicare—were summed up by two liberals in 2006 as follows: "Republicans continue to hold double-digit advantages over Democrats on the key attribute of 'know what they stand for' and fewer than four in 10 voters believe the Democratic Party has 'a clear set of policies for the country.' This trend . . . we call the 'identity gap.' . . . No identity translates into no character. No personal integrity. No vision worth fighting for. No domestic agenda. No national-security agenda. No basic understanding of the problems facing everyday citizens. No contest with the other side. No reason to vote for progressive candidates."[4]

The Original Expedition

The 2004 election campaign reminds us that, in general, conservatives are better than liberals at political storytelling. However, a story that wins an election does not necessarily describe a nation's circumstances accurately. Here was a war that George W. Bush and other right-wingers insisted was worth waging to protect America from implacable enemies and make the world a better place to live in. Yet this was also a war that did not go well, and that fact may suggest that modern citizens should exercise great caution toward political stories.

Alcibiades

That care is warranted on this score is an idea accompanying Western civilization since, in his *History of the Peloponnesian War* (c. 403 BCE), Thucydides described how Alcibiades talked the citizens of Athens into sending half of their empire's soldiers and sailors to besiege Syracuse. Subsequently, there ensued a disastrous series of battles in Sicily during 415–413 BCE, from which most of the Athenian fighters never came home.[5] When Thucydides reported on what had happened, the "demagogue" took his place in Western political thought as someone who, like Alcibiades, weaves an inspiring vision of rhetoric and sentiment that may enlist political support even while it does not provide adequate grounds for public policy.

With that history in mind, to use the Iraq war as a platform for discussing a possible case of modern demagoguery is to consider, in effect, a tale against tales. This tale suggests that some politicians, who might be wise or not, may tell a rousing story and get elected. Thus, as we shall see, Bush II's story about terrorism and Iraq was rhetorically powerful and could evoke great enthusiasm. The danger, however, is that such a narrative may propel candidates into office but not connect them, or their associates, with what they must know to govern well. That is, their story may be analogous to what Alcibiades said when he encouraged Athenians to mount the original Sicilian expedition.

Going to War

Some facts of this case are clear. On October 10, 2002, the House of Representatives voted 296–133 to authorize President Bush II to go to war against Iraq to protect the United States and enforce United Nations resolutions. House Republicans supported the authorization by a margin of 215–6; House Democrats opposed it, 126–81. A day later, the Senate approved the same authorization by a vote of 77–23. Republican senators voted in favor by a margin of 48–1; Democratic senators did the same, 29–21. The combined Republican vote was thus 263 for war and 7 against, while the combined Democratic vote was 90 for war and 147 against. The two authorizations were signed into law on October 16, 2002, and the president ordered American forces into Iraq on March 20, 2003.

Accordingly, the war in Iraq was mainly a Republican project, at a time when that party had become largely conservative. Certainly the decision to send troops into battle was a right-wing policy act. Nevertheless, it is not easy to know why the president and his colleagues decided to attack Iraq.[6] Most conservatives and liberals shared a willingness to confront communism during the Cold War. But when the two sides debated each other from one generation to another, the talk was, and still is, mainly about how to build a better society at home. Consequently, there has never been a distinctively conservative, or liberal, concept of how Americans should relate to countries other than their own. The Right has those who lean toward staying home, for example, Patrick Buchanan, and the Left has those who promote intervention abroad, for example, Lyndon Johnson and Bill Clinton.

In such circumstances, one cannot easily trace Bush II's foreign policy decisions to any standard conservative wisdom in that realm. Moreover, because confidential government documents are declassified only many years after current events, it is too early to discover who said what to whom and therefore to know on exactly what basis America went to war in 2003. Some writers are already trying to connect various dots,[7] but we must assume that time will reveal more than we know now. Furthermore, although Bush officials spoke very little in public about the importance of who controls Iraqi oil wells, it is hard to imagine that such a practical consideration had nothing to do with what happened.[8]

So the available evidence is not yet conclusive. Still, we can already say something about how the president and his colleagues justified the war, about the objectives they hoped the war would serve, and about the frame of mind that anticipated such an enterprise succeeding. On this score, even if the White House, the State Department, and the Department of Defense took into consideration material interests such as oil and geopolitical locations, there were also ideological factors, less tangible but maybe decisive, in the equation. This is especially so if we will look, like we did while exploring right-wing talk generally, at what supporters of the war said about it as a story, a narrative about America's role in world history, a tale about how America got to where it was in 2003 and what it should do after that.

The Setting

The story started taking shape because, between 1989 and 1991, the Berlin Wall fell and the Soviet Union collapsed. During the Cold War, a commitment to anticommunism helped social and economic conservatives work together politically, and it justified high defense spending that would help America resist efforts by communists to expand their sphere of influence. Since many liberals also opposed communism and supported large defense budgets, this period of confrontation provided Americans with a national vocation.[9] Then suddenly the enemy was gone and therefore the unifying mission also vanished.

Some thinkers on the right rose to this occasion by positing new enemies whose existence might justify a second round of national conviction and big budgets. There were no obvious dangers, but such people spoke as if there were. Thus Robert Kagan and William Kristol edited a collection of essays entitled *Present Dangers: Crisis and Opportunity in American Foreign and Defense Policy* (2000)[10] Other thinkers evoked images of rogue states and international terrorism, of cultural frictions and proliferating weapons of mass destruction. That was the significance of Samuel Huntington's book entitled *The Clash of Civilizations and the Remaking of World Order* (1996),[11] which predicted a violent confrontation between "the West" and "Islam."

In short, when the Cold War disappeared, some politicians, think tankers, pundits, and activists began to fashion a new rationale for high defense spending.

There was no agreement, however—not between Republicans and Democrats, and not within either of the two parties—on why, while no major wars threatened, Washington should continue to spend as before. Military budgets did not fall significantly. But that was due less to new visions than to the routine distribution of political pork, and Bush II was elected in 2000 without promising to promote any particular approach to foreign affairs.

All this changed on September 11, 2001. In a moment of acute national anxiety, the president and his advisers decided to respond militarily but also felt that a story explaining that response would help Americans make sense of the great confusion into which their lives had suddenly been thrown.[12] The requisite story, known since 2002 as the Bush Doctrine, emerged in time to authorize the invasion of Iraq. Apparently the White House turned for inspiration mainly to a vision already available in writings by various right-wingers who were known as, or associated with, the journalists, professors, and think tankers commonly called neoconservatives. Those people were not necessarily more perceptive than other foreign policy wonks at the time. But they had a post–Cold War narrative ready, and some of them were in positions from which they could influence the president's choice of terms.

Good and Evil

The basic assumption was that circumstances had thrust the country into a dangerous and protracted conflict with terrorism, which is practiced by people who promote evil. Thus only hours after Muslim hijackers flew passenger planes into the World Trade Center and the Pentagon, the president announced that America was embarked on a "war against terrorism,"[13] and soon afterward he explained that states that "sponsor" such terrorism constitute "an axis of evil" seeking "weapons of mass destruction" and threatening "the peace of the world."[14] Under American leadership, he added, the war against evil would last indefinitely. "Americans should not expect one battle," said the president, "but a lengthy campaign, unlike any other we have ever seen." The war, he continued, "will not end until every terrorist group of global reach has been found, stopped and defeated."[15]

There are important similarities between Bush's description of "terrorists" as "evil" and the Cold War project of anticommunism. Thus when Bush described a world inhabited by good and bad people, he echoed Ronald Reagan's 1983 declaration that the Soviet Union constituted an "evil empire" against which America must wage a war "between right and wrong and good and evil."[16] By renewing the Reaganite image of a dangerous and despicable adversary, Bush assured *all Americans* that they were pure and their cause was just. He thereby challenged them to adopt a new national vocation aimed at defending what they regarded as civilization. Moreover, talking about evil in world affairs sent a coded message to *religious Americans,* including many evangelicals, who once opposed "godless Communism." Now they could project their personal anxieties against a new scourge of immorality. And finally, by offering his vision especially to *people on the right,* Bush suggested that by working together against a new enemy, social and economic conservatives could continue to ignore the extent to which, as we noted in Chapter Four, their objectives of safeguarding traditional values and promoting economic innovation clashed.[17]

The Lack of Middle Ground

Bush's portrait of an implacable foe, intent on threatening America for years to come, enjoyed great rhetorical power. It obscured, however, as much as it illuminated, because it expressed little concern for middle-ground realities. As we saw in Chapter Two, right-wing talk has skipped over in-between options for many years, as when (1) conservatives defined economies as ruled either by "central planning" or by "free markets," when (2) they described governments as either "socialist" or "democratic," and when (3) they characterized American behavior as inspired either by "Judeo-Christian values" or by the "secular humanist worldview."

More recently, such bifurcation appeared when Bush II spoke of some people favoring "freedom," "justice," and "human dignity," whereas other people promote "fear," "cruelty," "tyranny," and "death."[18] Here was a dichotomy that largely ignored the opinion of those who believe that real-world situations may be so complex and ambiguous as to favor compromises that lie somewhere between the poles of freedom and autocracy. For example, reasoning in and around the middle of reality seems to have animated French and German leaders who advised Bush not to invade Iraq.[19]

In George W. Bush's story, the advice of such critics had no place in American deliberations because, as the president said repeatedly, people who were not *with* America were thereby *against* her. As he put it, "[E]very nation, in every region, now has a decision to make. Either you are with us, or you are with the terrorists."[20] Or, a little later, "Every nation has a choice to make. In this conflict, there is no neutral ground."[21] Such Manichaeism tends to overlook information that may be needed for making realistic assessments of existing conditions. Therefore critics will always suspect that, had the president and, say, the secretary of state, the national security adviser, and the secretary of defense paid more attention to middle-ground advice, American troops might never have entered Iraq.[22]

Preemptive War

The premise was that evil stalks the world and must be resisted. Yet if a war had to be fought and won, an appropriate strategy had to be fashioned and justified. And that meant that various presidential statements, each telling its own tale, contributed to a larger story that explained how America reached this point in history, how various nations and states accompany it there, and how Washington must orchestrate the moves of all these players so as to promote America's interests and, at the same time, enable people around the world to enjoy freedom and the good things of life.

The scheme started with readiness for preemptive war. As Lawrence Kaplan and William Kristol note approvingly, "The first element of the Bush Doctrine is a willingness to acknowledge that under certain circumstances, preemptive action will be required."[23] Or, in the words of the *National Security Strategy of the United States, 2002,* "as a matter of common sense and self-defense, America will act against ... emerging threats before they are fully formed."[24]

The new lexicon was sometimes vague on this point, but what Kaplan and Kristol called "preemptive" wars are actually what statesmen have long called "preventive" wars. A truly preemptive war, as defined for generations in the language of diplomacy, is justified when states confront immediate threats, in which case they are entitled to initiate a response rather than absorb a devastating first strike. This was probably the case in 1967, when the governments of Egypt, Syria, and Jordan massed their armies on Israel's borders and Jerusalem reacted, after fruitless diplomatic protests, by attacking those armies to remove the looming danger.

A preventive war, however, is something else. The president argued after 9/11 that modern life fosters threats that are not imminent but are so dangerous that America cannot afford to refrain from acting until they materialize in battle. Such threats flow first from efforts made by "terrorists" and "rogue states" to acquire weapons of mass destruction and second from the intention of such people to employ those weapons, without warning, against the United States and other democratic societies. Thus the president said that "I will not stand by, as peril draws closer and closer. The United States will not permit the world's most dangerous regimes to threaten us with the world's most destructive weapons."[25] Moreover, "If we wait for threats to fully materialize, we will have waited too long."[26] Or, in the case of Iraq, "Saddam Hussein ... continues to develop weapons of mass destruction. The first time we may be completely certain he has a nuclear weapon is when, God forbid, he uses one. We owe it to all our citizens to do everything in our power to prevent that day from coming."[27]

In effect, the argument was that containment will not work against irrational regimes, détente cannot be pursued successfully with rulers who scorn compromise, and deterrence is useless against suicide bombers.[28] Accordingly, Bush II and his advisers thought they should replace a foreign policy axiom familiar to America since World War II with an anticipatory strategy that took into account new dangers. As the *National Security Strategy* said, "Legal scholars and international jurists . . . conditioned the legitimacy of preemption on the existence of an imminent threat—most often a visible mobilization of armies, navies, and air forces preparing to attack. We must adapt the concept of imminent threat to the capabilities and objectives of today's adversaries. Rogue states and terrorists do not seek to attack us using conventional means." Therefore, "To forestall or prevent such hostile acts by our adversaries, the United States will, if necessary, act preemptively."[29]

Regime Change

The logic may sound compelling. But the project that Bush's doctrine called "preemption" was actually a "preventive war," and commitment to that sort of war is an invitation to error. To strike before danger materializes, a commander must rely on intelligence estimates—sometimes speculative, often equivocal, and always disputable—about enemy capabilities and intentions rather than on patent facts, such as that on December 7, 1941, Japanese carrier forces attacked an American fleet at Pearl Harbor. Consequently, Washington went to war in 2003 because the Bush administration believed, or so it said, that Saddam Hussein had weapons of mass destruction. American soldiers then discovered that he had none.[30]

The difficulties did not stop there, because the Bush Doctrine avowed that America would not only destroy any regime it regarded as dangerous but would remain on the ground to rearrange public life where that regime had ruled. Here was a second part of the Bush story on foreign affairs, the commitment to "regime change." In the new logic, this commitment seemed necessary because if "present dangers" are described apocalyptically, it is not enough to forestall them temporarily. Such dangers—for example, that weapons of mass destruction might fall into unreliable hands—had to be prevented from arising in the future by installing a democratic regime that would detest terrorism inherently and pursue its international interests peacefully.[31]

As the president said in February 2003, in anticipation of the war he started one month later: "The United States has no intention of determining the precise form of Iraq's new government. That choice belongs to the Iraqi people. Yet, we will ensure that one brutal dictator is not replaced by another. All Iraqis must have a voice in the new government, and all citizens must have their rights protected."[32] In short, Iraqis could have any government they might want so long as it would work, in principle, like America's.

The Domino Effect

Regime change in Iraq was intended to prevent future dangers from materializing there. From the outset, however, the enthusiasm for replacing Saddam Hussein with elected officials had wider implications, because Washington promised that dethroning an Arab tyrant would beget a democratic domino effect. In this view, establishing democracy in Iraq would reverberate throughout the Middle East, encouraging other Arabs to press their rulers to abandon authoritarian devices, embrace openness, and establish representative institutions. As the president said, "A liberated Iraq can show the power of freedom to transform that vital region, by bringing hope and progress into the lives of millions. . . . A new regime in Iraq would serve as a dramatic and inspiring example of freedom for other nations in the region."[33]

Lawrence Kaplan and William Kristol spoke more explicitly. What they called "liberal democratic rule" in Iraq could lead, they said, to liberalization in Iran, Saudi Arabia, Qatar, Morocco, and Jordan.[34] Such projections encouraged them to believe in 2003 that "far from destabilizing the region, the replacement of Saddam Hussein would, over time, allow for greater stability."[35] Similarly inspired, the president flew to the USS *Abraham Lincoln* off the coast of California and announced from the deck of that aircraft carrier on May 1, 2003, that major "combat operations in Iraq have ended. In the battle of Iraq, the United States and our allies have prevailed."[36]

Encumbrances

Well, not exactly. Beyond Iraq, authoritarian dominoes still stand. Furthermore, it is clear that Bush II severely miscalculated America's capacity for rearranging life even in Iraq.[37] Probably he did so because of misleading assumptions made in talk most familiar to him. On this score, we saw in Chapter Two that conservatives tend to think in terms of *individualism*, as if America is composed of citizens who act morally and economically on their own, to the point where each is *personally responsible* for his or her degree of virtue and success in life. But as we also saw, this view discounts or ignores what many diplomats and scholars believe, which is that historical, sociological, religious, economic, and political *conditions*, sometimes shared, in fact influence almost all individuals, to the point where such *encumbrances* may be difficult for even energetic and well-motivated people to overcome.[38]

By assuming individualism, the president's story portrayed Iraqis as autonomous persons rather than as Middle Easterners living together fortuitously and sometimes uneasily within state borders fixed in 1922 by (1) British imperialists seeking access to oil fields and (2) local potentates sharing few or no social or political interests. Thus the Bush Doctrine said nothing about Shi'ites, Sunnis, Kurds, and lesser Iraqi groups based on sect, ethnicity, tribes, and extended families.[39] Consequently it ignored inherited anxieties and animosities that encumber such people and shape their intentions and expectations. Instead it stipulated that those who were ruled by Saddam Hussein wanted above all freedom rather than, say, revenge, salvation, honor, family solidarity, personal safety, glory, or power over others.

To dramatize this last point, the president insisted that "[m]en and women in every culture need liberty like they need food and water and air. Everywhere that freedom arrives, humanity rejoices."[40] Similarly, the president announced that "[h]uman cultures can be vastly different. Yet the human heart desires the same good things, everywhere on Earth.... [Thus] freedom and democracy will always and everywhere have greater appeal than the slogans of hatred and the tactics of error."[41] Or, on another occasion, "We will prevail because the desire to live in freedom is embedded in the soul of every man, woman and child on this Earth."[42] Supporters of the president said much the same thing. William Bennett, for example, asserted confidently that "mankind" has a "universal interest in life, liberty, and the pursuit of happiness."[43] And Michael Novak insisted that the "hunger" for liberty "is universal, even when it is latent, for the preconditions for it slumber in every human breast."[44]

Munich and Vietnam

In other words, the president's story, like some elements of right-wing talk we noted in previous contexts, was weak on sociology and, for example, ignored the teaching of psychologists who claim, based on empirical research, that some people prefer the certainties of authoritarianism to the ambiguities of freedom.[45] Still, one might have expected Bush II to suspect that regime change in Baghdad would not proceed smoothly. After all, Bush I stopped the Gulf War in 1991 without entering Iraq to overthrow Saddam Hussein. And as Richard Cheney, secretary of defense at that time, said, no one knew what sort of government—Sunni? Shi'ite? Kurdish? Ba'athist?—to install in Hussein's place, in which case "it would have been a mistake for us to get bogged down in the quagmire inside Iraq."[46]

This early Cheney sounds prescient today. But Bush II built his doctrine on a school of thought in modern conservatism that regards recent history, and especially the Vietnam War, as demonstrating no reason for Washington policy makers to expect getting stuck in Iraq or anyplace else. This historiography starts by highlighting what happened in Munich in 1938, where Prime Minister Neville Chamberlain of Great Britain is said to have "appeased" Adolf Hitler by permitting his takeover of the Sudetenland to stand without challenge.

The lesson of Munich, in this view, is that if Chamberlain had threatened Hitler with hostilities, the German chancellor would have backed down and World War II would not have occurred. Ergo, democrats must deal with dictators, tyrants, and terrorists early and firmly, so as to prevent greater dangers and damage in the long run. Thus Robert Kagan describes Munich as a policy that "proved disastrous for Britain and France. . . . [The] Second World War that resulted from this failure of European strategy and diplomacy all but destroyed European nations as global powers."[47] The president picked up the refrain. "In this century," he said, "when evil men plot chemical, biological and nuclear terror, a policy of appeasement could bring destruction of a kind never before seen on this earth."[48]

As stated, the lesson of Munich seems unequivocal. But to some Americans, the prescription for quick and violent confrontation is not always valid. Thus it could be argued that when Washington tried to apply the lesson of Munich in Vietnam, the attempt failed. The national policy of containing Moscow and Beijing called for Washington to draw a line against communist expansion by fighting limited wars to reduce the likelihood of wider conflicts breaking out later. On those grounds, even American officials who were not particularly right-wing thought they should resist a left-wing insurgency dedicated to seizing power in South Vietnam. Yet after years of heavy fighting there, President Lyndon Johnson and his advisers, much of the Democratic Party, and many of the people who voted for Richard Nixon in 1968, had had enough. Evidently they concluded that sending to Vietnam outside forces from a faraway land who did not speak the local language, who were ignorant of local customs, who could not distinguish friend from foe, who had to ally themselves to local autocrats, and who were regarded by many Vietnamese as colonial agents, could not succeed.[49]

Looking at Vietnam this way suggests that trying to play midwife to democracy elsewhere in the Third World may trap American soldiers in similar quagmires. That is why Bush I hesitated.[50] However, his son's record reads as if such a possibility never threatened the present war in Iraq, and perhaps that is because Bush II lived in a conversation where many right-wingers have long argued that America failed in Vietnam not because the war was unwinnable but because liberals did not seek victory there boldly or zealously enough.

On this score Richard Viguerie charges that "[l]iberal politicians lost a war in Vietnam they wouldn't let America mobilize to win."[51] Similarly, David Horowitz complains that liberal members of Congress blocked economic and military aid that would have enabled South Vietnam to successfully repel the 1974 attack against it by North Vietnam.[52] That failure to extend American aid still angers Robert Bork. Thus he declares that "[t]he subsequent fate of the South Vietnamese people ought to convince anyone that the war should have been fought and won."[53]

American Preeminence

Blaming failure in Vietnam on liberals may have led some conservatives, including the president, to assume that since a war in Southeast Asia had been winnable, there was no reason to believe that a war in the Middle East, properly waged this time, would not go well. There were, however, additional reasons why the Bush administration may have thought that a military occupation dedicated to regime change was more feasible than it turned out to be. These have to do with what Kaplan and Kristol call "American preeminence," which they regard as the third pillar of the Bush Doctrine.[54] Here there came into play assumptions about why America, armed after 1989 more heavily than the next dozen militarized countries in the world,[55] was so strong and, no less important, so wise that, whatever course her commanders might choose, it would trump resistance.

National Responsibilities

One part of the preeminence equation defined America as so great a power that Washington, regardless of how other countries might protest, must assume a dominant role in maintaining order in the world. The idea was that while great disparities in military spending obtain between nations, lesser powers like Russia and the European Union will hold back from supporting American initiatives and thereby leave Washington with no alternative to taking the lead in eliminating extraordinary dangers, such as nuclear proliferation, that threaten everyone. Under these circumstances, a strategy of preeminence assumed that world order might collapse if America did not act firmly, sometimes even unilaterally.

Conservative talk was pivotal here, because many right-wing Americans have long regarded their country as endowed with special qualities and unique responsibilities. Sometimes the Declaration of Independence is recalled, with its stirring message that America believes all men are created equal; sometimes the Judeo-Christian tradition is praised for inspiring family values, individual liberties, and toleration; and sometimes free markets and private property are extolled for facilitating creativity and resistance to tyranny. All these presumably excellent parts of the American experience stood behind William Bennett when he called upon Bush II to "summon Americans to meet their great destiny as a people."[56] And all were present when the president declared that "the United States is guided by the conviction that all nations have important responsibilities. Nations that enjoy freedom [America] must actively fight terror. Nations that depend on international stability [America] must help prevent the spread of weapons of mass destruction."[57]

America the Good

Well, yes. But when America exercises great "responsibilities" unilaterally, critics may charge that leasing foreign bases, stationing soldiers abroad, practicing gunboat diplomacy, and launching occasional invasions, amount to acts of imperialism.[58] The president and his supporters insisted this was not so because, they said, the interests that America pursues are shared by everyone in the world, except for tyrants and terrorists. "This is not," the president said, "just America's fight. And what is at stake is not just America's freedom. This is the world's fight. This is civilization's fight. This is the fight of all who believe in progress and pluralism, tolerance and freedom."[59] Alternatively, "We come to Iraq," said the president, "with respect for its citizens, for their great civilization and for the religious faiths they practice. We have no ambition in Iraq, except to remove a threat and restore control of that country to its own people."[60] Moreover, "The United States has no right, no desire and no intention to impose our form of government on anyone else. That is one of the main differences between us and our enemies. They seek to impose and expand an empire of oppression.... Our aim is to build and preserve a community of free and independent nations."[61]

Other conservatives endorse this story. Terms such as "imperium" or "hegemon," says James Caesar, "do not describe the kind of enterprise in which the nation is engaged, which is not directly to rule others, but to maintain a civilized world order and allow the benefits of free government to become known."[62] We "are not," says Charles Krauthammer, "just any hegemon. We run a uniquely benign imperium. This is not mere self-congratulation; it is a fact manifest in the way others welcome our power."[63] America, says William Bennett, "is *not* interested in territorial conquest, subjugation of others, or world domination. Behind our attempt to advance American ideals abroad has been the belief that basic rights are inalienable, universal, God-given, and therefore all people, wherever they may be, are deserving of them."[64] In fact, say Lawrence Kaplan and William Kristol, "unlike past imperial powers, if the United States has created a Pax Americana, it is not built on colonial conquest or economic aggrandizement.... Rather, what upholds today's world order is America's benevolent influence—nurtured, to be sure, by American power, but also by emulation and the recognition around the world that American ideals are genuinely universal."[65]

Hating America

In some respects, the story was beautiful and inspiring. Incorporated into Bush II's reelection campaign, it helped him win a second term in 2004. But if America serves only universal goals, and if Washington stands ready to help Iraqis achieve such aims in public life, why were so many Iraqis killing each other and the

American soldiers who came to their land only to promote peace and justice? That is, why did the "insurgents" surge?

One way to answer this question is to note that, as usual in conservative talk, the vision of a benevolent American colossus missed the strength of encumbrances. That is, it skipped over the impact of local circumstances, habits, traditions, memories, aspirations, apprehensions, and expectations. The world is not full of Americans; foreigners do not always aspire to whatever Americans admire; some people around the world suffer from the creative destruction that America promotes;[66] and for Washington to assume that countries with their own histories, stories, and destinies hunger to establish American-style institutions is, in many cases, unrealistic.

Nevertheless, the Bush Doctrine ignored encumbrances. First, the attack on America evoked disbelief. After September 11, George W. Bush sounded genuinely puzzled. "Americans are asking," he said, "why do they hate us?"[67] Or, "[H]ow do I respond when I see that in some Islamic countries there is vitriolic hatred for America? I'll tell you how I respond: I'm amazed. I'm amazed that there is such misunderstanding of what our country is about, that people would hate us. I am, I am—like most Americans, I just can't believe it. Because I know how good we are."[68]

Second, the president claimed that those who attacked his country hated it not because of what America has done but because of what it is. "They hate our freedoms," he said, "our freedom of religion, our freedom of speech, our freedom to vote and assemble and disagree with each other."[69] Or, as Michael Ledeen explained, "The tyrants' hatred of America is not the result of any given American policy. It is our existence, not our actions, that threaten them, because our existence inspires their people to desire different rulers in a different kind of polity."[70]

This point was robustly patriotic. But it did not explain where "terrorists" and "tyrants" come from if we assume, as some conservatives do, that America is good and everyone wants to be like Americans. Right-wing talk proceeds as if, driven by a love of freedom, all people are similarly motivated. In such circumstances, if there are people whose aspirations differ from those of the rest, there must be something peculiar about the former. Accordingly, in riffs around the Bush Doctrine, Middle East tyrants and terrorists seemed to be not just deviant but even defective human beings because, for no good reason, they espoused a murderous form of Islam that set them apart from hundreds of millions of moderate Muslims around the world.[71]

In this view, the enemy was a disembodied activity called "terrorism," which had no encumbrances; this activity was promoted by people called "terrorists," who had not explained why they are violent; and the attack came from the Middle East, which had no local history worth taking into account.[72] That being the president's take on what happened, it is no wonder he was surprised that nineteen Arabs might hate America enough to fly planes into the Twin Towers and the Pentagon. To say nothing of "insurgents" in Iraq who might be similarly motivated, and who blow up Americans and neighbors and sometimes themselves.

Costs

Conservative talk underlay the war on evil, the inclination to preemption (which is actually prevention), the eagerness for regime change, and the insistence on preeminence. Together, these ideas impelled the Bush II administration, by invading Iraq, to make some of the worst foreign policy errors in American history. In the realm of diplomacy, long-standing allies such as France, Germany, Italy, Spain, Japan, and moderate Arab states were partially or entirely alienated; avowed adversaries such as Iran, Syria, North Korea, Hamas, and Hezbollah were emboldened; and potential terrorists flocked to Iraq to gain training and experience.[73] Moreover, vital American resources, such as military personal, equipment, and national morale, were lavished on this project to the point where one estimate put just financial costs of the war—including direct expenditures, care for injured veterans, replenishment of military hardware, and loss of earning power, but not including increased oil prices or destruction of life and property in Iraq—at more than $3 trillion *if* American troops were withdrawn by 2010.[74]

Reflections

At a minimum, Bush II's doctrine demonstrates that nations should check very carefully before using any particular story to justify their choice of public policies. Here is a lesson that is especially important because in recent years, and in a "television age" wherein the "framing" engendered by storytelling is vital to public communications, stories have contributed greatly to electoral success. Of course, political parties and activists want to win. Who doesn't? But when candidates offer an attractive story, voters should keep in mind that it may lead the country astray, in which case they should be ready, if necessary, to seek more realistic candidates.[75] To this end, caution may be warranted by general reflections on perversity, morality, reality, liberty, tenacity, and tragedy.

Perversity

Right-wingers say that most public projects, except for those maintaining defense and civil order, cannot improve life in America. They justify this conviction, as we saw in Chapter One, with arguments about perversity, jeopardy, and futility. When warning against governmental action, they claim that a host of unpredictable conditions, bureaucratic ignorance, human nature, or some divine plan must thwart even the good intentions of elected officials and government agencies. This will happen, in their view, after any publicly organized effort to, say, renew cities, ease poverty, diminish racism, advance minorities, empower women, increase employment, safeguard the environment, promote economic growth, and foster public goods. Thus they expound what they call the law of unintended consequences, and they promote the idea that progress, with perhaps rare exceptions, can flow only from individual efforts and personal virtue.

It follows that Bush II's recent story about preemptive war and regime change was strikingly optimistic even by conservative lights. The president and his advisers assumed that officials in the Central Intelligence Agency, the National Security Agency, the Federal Bureau of Investigation, and the National Security Council were able to discover whether Iraq was building weapons of mass destruction. Why were they sure of this if bureaucrats are, in principle, self-centered and incompetent?[76] In fact, the weapons were not there. Later the president sent American solders and civilian officials first to destroy and then to rebuild Iraq's government and public life. Why would he do this if, according to conservative talk, the people he sent would be incapable, as government employees, of fashioning and administering programs of social reconstruction even where, in America, they might be familiar with local customs, motivations, aspirations, and expectations?[77] So far the rebuilding of Iraq has failed.

Morality

Most probably, a determination to promote what conservatives regard as national morality overrode sensitivity to their predictions of perversity and in the White House spurred enthusiasm for going to war. Historians may attribute this enthusiasm to the shocking events of September 11, which drove many Americans to hunger for drastic responses. Beyond this immediate casus belli, however, some conservatives were likely to promote a latter-day version of the nineteenth-century doctrine of America's manifest destiny. For example, they might borrow the famous coda to George Kennan's call for a policy of containing the Soviet Union. Facing the possibility of nuclear apocalypse, Kennan declared in 1947 that Americans should be grateful to God, who "has made their entire security as a nation dependent on their pulling themselves together and accepting the responsibilities of moral and political leadership that history plainly intended them to bear."[78]

To survive the challenge, Kennan recommended restraining Moscow from without, avoiding direct war with the Soviet Union, and waiting for internal power struggles to disable dictatorship in the Kremlin. But conservatives talked, after the Cold War, more impetuously than Kennan did about Washington's global role. And their willingness to go beyond his caution flowed from a conviction that Vietnam could have been "won" militarily by America but was "lost" on some motivational plane because liberal politicians in Washington, demoralized by decadent "new class" people and "counterculturalists," were insufficiently daring and resolute.[79]

What eventually became important as an operative principle for some conservatives, and especially for neoconservatives, was that this postulate suggested to them another. The second held that after the Vietnam War, Washington suffered from defeatism in that many government officials, including some serving Bush I, believed that fighting in Southeast Asia revealed limitations on America's ability to influence events in other countries. It followed, according to advocates of preventive wars, regime change and preeminence, that this defeatism constituted a sort of "Vietnam syndrome" that America should overcome in order to do what it must to keep the world safe for everyone.[80] As Bush II said, "[W]e began [after September 11] to think less of the goods we can accumulate, and more about the good we can do." Under the circumstances the president continued, like Kennan, that "[w]e've been offered a unique opportunity, and we must not let this moment pass."[81]

Reality

But did not encumbrances threaten strategic plans? That is, did not Washington promote a story line that overlooked what many diplomats, historians, and ordinary people believe happened in Vietnam and was likely to happen again, under local circumstances, in Iraq? Surely Bush II and his colleagues failed to study the natives.[82]

What may have been even more dangerous was that, with considerable passion and sincerity, some Bush people permitted what they regarded as Truth to override what other people saw as Reality. Here again, conservative talk helps us to understand what happened. We have seen how conservatives are not troubled if their stories—like Ronald Reagan's homily about the "welfare queen"—are somewhat inaccurate, because the same stories may be useful for conveying an "essential" truth. This sort of truth inspired Bush II when he said, after September 11, that "[w]e've come to know truths that we will never question: evil is real, and it must be opposed."[83] It also helped him to avoid dwelling on encumbrances because, as he said when announcing the Bush Doctrine, "[d]ifferent circumstances require different methods, but not different moralities. Moral truth is the same in every culture, in every time, and in every place."[84]

The stakes were prodigious. By fixing on what it regarded as Truth, the White House could discount reality in favor of imposing its vision on what might appear to some people as abiding obstacles to conviction and imagination. Testimony to this delusion appeared after reality started to bite back. Reporter Ron Suskind interviewed a White House aide in the summer of 2002 and later wrote that "[t]he aide said that guys like me were 'in what we [White House staffers] call the reality-based community,' which he defined as people who 'believe that solutions emerge from your judicious study of discernible reality.' I nodded and murmured something about enlightenment principles and empiricism. He cut me off. 'That's not the way the world really works anymore,' he continued. 'We're an empire now, and when we act, we create our own reality.... We're history's actors ... and you, all of you, will be left to just study what we do."[85]

Liberty

Even a critic might regard as magnificent a story that could persuade a voting majority of Americans to believe after September 11 that they could overcome reality. In truth, it *was* magnificent, because the Bush Doctrine built on a powerful conservative vision promoted over many years and centering on the growth of "freedom," or "liberty," in American history. We met one version of this story when we noted how Allan Bloom, among others, saw freedom as the defining characteristic of American life.[86]

The same story inspired at least four decades of right-wing talk, from Barry M. Goldwater to George W. Bush. Thus in his 1964 speech accepting the Republican Party's nomination for president, Senator Goldwater mentioned "freedom," "free," and "liberty"—and derivatives such as "liberties," "liberated," "freedom's light," and "liberation"—forty-three times, including his ultimate declaration that "[e]xtremism in the defense of liberty is no vice."[87] The same emphasis appeared in Bush II's second inaugural address in 2005. On that occasion, the president mentioned "freedom," "liberty," and "free" forty-nine times in a seventeen-minute speech.[88]

To keep this vision on stage and up front, Bush II referred to it frequently. Thus he said that "[t]he story of America is the story of expanding liberty: an ever-widening circle, constantly growing to reach further and include more. Our nation's founding commitment is still our deepest commitment: in our world, and here at home, we will extend the frontiers of freedom."[89] As American soldiers fought to extend those frontiers in Iraq, Bush II proclaimed that "those who serve today are taking their rightful place among the greatest generations that have worn our nation's uniform. When the history of this period is written, the liberation of Afghanistan and the liberation of Iraq will be remembered as great turning points in the story of freedom."[90]

Relying not just on repetition, the president buttressed his story with a claim of divinity. Thus he explained that "[t]he road of Providence is uneven and unpredictable—yet we know where it leads: It leads to freedom."[91] Or, in summing up, "I believe that America is called to lead the cause of freedom in a new century. I believe that millions in the Middle East plead in silence for their liberty. I believe that given the chance they will embrace the most honorable form of government ever devised by man. I believe all these things because freedom is not America's gift to the world, it is the Almighty God's gift to every man and woman in the world."[92] To highlight the point he wanted to make, Bush II named the war in Afghanistan "Operation Enduring Freedom," and he called the war in Iraq "Operation Iraqi Freedom."

Tenacity

The Bush II story about terrorism, evil, preemptive war, democracy, military preeminence, and freedom, with its specific marshalling of various right-wing propositions, led to a massive misallocation of soldiers, equipment, money, emotional energy, and national reputation. Once this reality is sufficiently recognized, America will leave Iraq as it left Vietnam. But the new Alcibiades and his disciples are not likely to renounce their story and apologize. Politics rarely works that way, and neither will the network of right-wing advocates that operates as a tenacious "counterestablishment."

We can safely predict, then, that even after the war is over, "closure," in the sense of a national decision to put the matter aside, will not occur. Well-funded conservative thinkers—in places like the Heritage Foundation, the American Enterprise Institute, the Hudson Institute, the Hoover Institution, and the Manhattan Institute, and in various talk shows, seminars, newspapers, journals, and magazines—will continue to promote the original story, more or less.[93] They will argue that the overall concept was valid, even if some of its details could have been implemented more effectively.[94] And they will claim that any turmoil and suffering that might accompany or follow the extrication should be charged to critics—that is, to liberals—for undermining national resolve and causing Washington to withdraw American soldiers from Iraq before giving them enough time to win there. Recriminations will rule the day.[95]

Tragedy

As for other Americans, their job is to see past polemics. Citizens occupy democracy's smallest office and, by voting, control the rest. From that office, they are obliged, I think, to try to do well by heeding history's great lessons.[96] And one of those, as we have just seen, is that some political stories, which may be attractive but also unrealistic, must be avoided because, if they will become guides to political action, dreadful outcomes will ensue.[97]

This is, in fact, precisely the lesson taught by wise Greeks who knew men like Alcibiades, and who wrote tragic plays—such as *Agamemnon, Oedipus the King, The Orestian Trilogy,* and *The Trojan Women*—to warn, more than 2,000 years ago, that if men and women do not behave reasonably, they will suffer terrible consequences.[98] Those plays had two messages. First, that citizens rarely learn from previous errors, either personal or political, in their lives or in history. Second, that the same citizens therefore tend to err again, hence the reckless Sicilian Expedition that for some of the playwrights took place on their watch.

Aeschylus, Sophocles, and Euripides hoped that their audiences, after seeing tragic stories performed on stage, would learn from them to avoid choosing leaders who would produce disasters in real life. For critics of the war in Iraq, this message has long been clear. For them, every American voter is personally responsible, no matter how inspiring the tale, for rejecting candidates of any affiliation who promote a political story that recommends more of the calamitous overreaching that Greek playwrights knew as hubris.[99]

A Left-Wing Tale?

So much for Bush II's story. But what will come next? In 2006, Geoffrey Nunberg concluded that "[s]ince the late 1960s, "the right's appeals have rested on a collection of overlapping stories about the currents of contemporary American life—stories that illustrate declining patriotism and moral standards, the out-of-touch media and the self-righteous liberal elite, the feminization of public life, minorities demanding special privileges and unwilling to assimilate to American culture and language, growing crime and lenient judges, ludicrous restrictions on permissible speech, disrespect for religious faith, a swollen government that intrudes officiously in private life, and arching over all of them, an America divided into two nations by different values, culture, and lifestyle. With occasional exceptions like Bill Clinton's 1992 campaign, Democrats and liberals have not offered compelling narratives that could compete with those."[100]

In 2007, Drew Westen agreed with Nunberg. The Left, he said, "has no brand, no counterbrand, no master narrative, no counternarrative. It has no shared terms or 'talking points' for its leaders to repeat until they are part of our political lexicon. Instead, every Democrat who runs for office, every Democrat who offers commentaries on television or radio, every Democrat who even talks with friends at the water cooler, has to reinvent what it means to be a Democrat, using his or her own words and concepts."[101]

Yet the right-wing vision that we have considered, and that so impressed commentators like Nunberg and Westen, apparently succumbed to liberal talk in the election of 2008. Thus during the winning campaign of Barack Obama and Joseph Biden, liberals seemingly described the world and our circumstances in a way that, more than before, would enable them to confront conservatives and Republicans successfully in the realm of storytelling. That is, liberals found their narrative. But did they really?

The Obama Story

This point is worth holding clearly in mind. The world of right-wing talk suggests that political conservatives have for several decades enjoyed an advantage over liberals in the realm of storytelling. That did not mean, however, that they would win every election during those decades, and it does not mean that, if they will display narrative virtuosity into the future, they will win every election yet to come. Rather, as we saw in Chapter Six, Democrats such as Franklin Roosevelt, who are more *pragmatic* than traditional, may win elections when, as in 1932, hard times undermine the power of otherwise appealing narratives. Or Democrats such as Bill Clinton, blessed with *charisma,* may win elections when, as in 1992 and 1996, their Republican opponents seem less charming and adept.

All these things being so, gaining an electoral victory does not necessarily prove that what one said during the campaign amounted to a winning vision. And therefore we cannot know yet whether the liberal, Democratic victory that Obama and Biden achieved was a unique performance or an indication of how Democrats will campaign successfully from now on. For one thing, economic turmoil late in the 2008 campaign may have persuaded, on pragmatic grounds, a decisive number of voters to see Republican candidates John McCain and Sarah Palin as associated, via the party of Bush II, with that turmoil and to vote against them. Here may be evidence of a one-shot affair.

Moreover, Barack Obama is unquestionably charismatic. Tall, energetic, handsome, well-spoken, endowed with a great smile—he is, image-wise, the equal of what Bill Clinton used to be and maybe even more so. Yet where that is the case, like Clinton in 2000, Obama's electoral flair may be based so largely on personal talent that it will not help other Democrats. For example, in off-year elections during 2009, the president endorsed, and even campaigned for, Jon Corzine and Creigh Deeds, Democratic gubernatorial candidates in New Jersey and Virginia, respectively. Nevertheless, both were defeated. Similarly, Democrat Martha Oakley, although supported by the president, lost to Republican Scott Brown in a special senatorial election held in Massachusetts early in 2010.

And finally, in terms of storytelling per se, one may plausibly claim that Obama did not fashion a vision capable of serving other liberals in the future. It may be, instead, that the new president, with considerable poise and wit, and by highlighting his special odyssey in life, in effect made himself, rather than cardinal principles, the central story of the 2008 campaign.[102] Yet if that is what happened, we must wait to see if that story can be adapted somehow to fit Democrats across the board once Obama is no longer a candidate for public office.

The Bottom Line

In sum, here is a bottom line. We should not conclude, from the evidence so far, that liberals closed the storytelling gap in 2008. We might more realistically assume that Barack Obama and other Democrats benefited from some measure of national weariness caused by an ongoing war, to say nothing of a disastrous economy. In those terms, it appears that a majority of voters decided they would no longer endorse Bush II's story even if they did not necessarily unite around any other tale. Concerning the Iraq war, then, President Obama will seek to extricate America from it just as President Nixon, after his election in 1968, moved to wind down the Vietnam War.

Unfortunately, however, the new Administration will probably learn, as Aeschylus, Sophocles, and Euripides knew long ago, that wars are easier to start an to finish. On Iraq, that seems clear. Moreover, as I write these lines the president has just relieved General Stanley McChrystal of his command in Afghanistan. There, too, a bottom line is clear, because everyone in Washington now knows, whether or not they admit it publically, that finishing the war in Afghanistan—a project that George W. Bush called "Operation Enduring Freedom"—will be no less difficult than completing the mission in Iraq.

Notes

Introduction

1. See Linda Bilmes and Joseph L. Stiglitz, *The Three Trillion Dollar War: The True Cost of the Iraq Conflict* (New York: Norton, 2008).

2. Prediction is risky. Michael Lienesch, *Redeeming America: Piety and Politics in the New Christian Right* (Chapel Hill: University of North Carolina Press, 1993), correctly predicted that Christian rightists would rebound after their disarray in the late 1980s. John Micklethwait and Adrian Wooldridge, *The Right Nation: Conservative Power in America* (New York: Penguin, 2004), wrongly predicted long-term Republican dominance after 2004.

3. In favor, Kevin P. Phillips, *The Emerging Republican Majority* (New Rochelle, NY: Arlington House, 1969); against, Thomas Byrne Edsall and Mary D. Edsall, *Chain Reaction: The Impact of Race, Rights, and Taxes on American Politics* (New York: Norton, 1991). The southern strategy is not always explicit but sometimes rests on winks and nods. For example, on August 3, 1980, Ronald Reagan touched off his presidential campaign with a speech at the Nashoba County Fair, held near Philadelphia, Mississippi, in an area where three civil rights workers were murdered in the summer of 1964. In that speech, coded to match certain local sentiments, the Republican standard-bearer assured his local audience of 15,000 mainly white people that "I believe in state's rights.... And if I do get the job I'm looking for, I'm going to devote myself to trying to ... restore to the states and local communities those functions which properly belong there." See http://neshobademocrat.com/main.asp?SectionID=2&SubSectionID=297&ArticleID=15599&TM=60417.67.

4. My description of right-wing talk leaves aside the nuanced preferences of philosophical conservatives such as Leo Strauss, Eric Voeglin, and Hadley Arkes. It considers instead what is said, with less theoretical elegance but great historical impact, by America's political conservatives. These practical activists, while inspiring citizens to vote for candidates on the right, usually ignore Strauss and his peers in their books, articles, speeches, sermons, and talk show patter.

5. Larry M. Bartels, *Unequal Democracy: The Political Economy of the New Gilded Age* (Princeton, NJ: Princeton University Press, 2008).

6. On that script, see political scientist George C. Edwards III, *Governing by Campaigning: The Politics of the Bush Presidency* (New York: Pearson Longman, 2007); linguist Geoffrey Nunberg, *Talking Right: How Conservatives Turned Liberalism into a Tax-Raising, Latte-Drinking, Sushi-Eating, Volvo-Driving,* New York Times*–Reading, Body-Piercing, Hollywood-Loving, Left-Wing Freak Show* (New York: PublicAffairs, 2006); columnist Frank Rich, *The Greatest Story Ever Sold: The Decline and Fall of Truth from 9/11 to Katrina* (New York: Penguin, 2007); and newspaper editor Fred Barnes, *Rebel-in-Chief: Inside the Bold and Controversial Presidency of George W. Bush* (New York: Crown Forum, 2006).

7. Some scholars say that such talk helps conservatives "set" part of "the agenda" of public debate in America, and they hold that right-wing terms may "frame" the way many Americans perceive various social conditions as problematic or not and capable or not of being improved with or without government action. For example, see Nunberg, *Talking Right*; George Lakoff, *Whose Freedom? The Battle Over America's Most Important Idea* (New York: Farrar, Straus, and Giroux, 2006); and Drew Westen, *The Political Brain: The Role of Emotion in Deciding the Fate of the Nation* (New York: PublicAffairs, 2007). In this book, I will say little about agenda setting or framing. I will assume, because right-wing candidates have won many elections in recent decades, that right-wing talk impacts powerfully on American public life. But only empirical tests can measure accurately, if at all, the extent of that impact. For example, see James N. Druckman, "Political Preference Formation: Competition, Deliberation, and the (Ir)relevance of Framing Effects," *American Political Science Review* (November 2004): 671–686.

8. For example, see Sara Diamond, *Roads to Dominion: Right-Wing Movements and Political Power in the United States* (New York: Guilford, 1995); Thomas Ferguson and Joel Rogers, *Right Turn: The Decline of the Democrats and the Future of American Politics* (New York: Hill and Wang, 1986); Jerome L. Himmelstein, *To the Right: The Transformation of American Conservatism* (Berkeley: University of California Press, 1990); Gary Dorrien, *The Neoconservative Mind: Politics, Culture and the War of Ideology* (Philadelphia: Temple University Press, 1993); Dan T. Carter, *The Politics of Rage: George Wallace, the Origins of the New Conservatism, and the Transformation of American Politics* (Baton Rouge: Louisiana State University Press, 1995); Mary C. Brennan, *Turning Right in the Sixties: The Conservative Capture of the GOP* (Chapel Hill: University of North Carolina Press, 1995); Dan Baltz and Ronald Brownstein, *Storming the Gates: Protest Politics and the Republican Revival* (Boston: Little, Brown, 1995); Godfrey Hodgson, *The World Turned Right Side Up: A History of the Conservative Ascendancy in America* (Boston: Houghton Mifflin, 1996); Mark Gerson, *The Neoconservative Vision: From the Cold War to the Culture Wars* (Lanham, MD: Madison Books, 1996); Michael Lind, *Up from Conservatism: Why the Right Is Wrong for America* (New York: Simon & Schuster, 1997); Amy E. Ansell, *Unraveling the Right: The New Conservatism in American Thought and Politics* (Boulder, CO: Westview, 1998); Lee Edwards, *The Conservative Revolution: The Movement that Remade America* (New York: Free Press, 1999); Jonathan M. Schoenwald, *A Time for Choosing: The Rise of Modern American Conservatism* (New York: Oxford University Press, 2001); Lisa McGirr, *Suburban Warriors: The Origins of the New American Right* (Princeton, NJ: Princeton University Press, 2001); Kevin M. Kruse, *White Flight: Atlanta and the Making of Modern Conservatism* (Princeton, NJ: Princeton University Press, 2005); Jacob Heilbrunn, *They Knew They Were Right: The*

Rise of the Neoconservatives (New York: Doubleday, 2006); Paul Pierson and Theda Skocpol, eds., *The Transformation of American Politics: Activist Government and the Rise of Conservatism* (Princeton, NJ: Princeton University Press, 2007); Donald Critchlow, *The Conservative Ascendancy: How the GOP Right Made Political History* (Cambridge, MA: Harvard University Press, 2007); Kevin Mattson, *Rebels All!: A Short History of the Conservative Mind in Postwar America* (New Brunswick, NJ: Rutgers University, 2008); Rick Perlstein, *Nixonland: The Rise of a President and the Fracturing of America* (New York: Scribners, 2008); Bruce Shulman and Julian E. Zelizer, eds., *Rightward Bound: Making America Conservative in the 1970s* (Cambridge, MA: Harvard University Press, 2008); Sean Wilentz, *The Age of Reagan: A History, 1974–2008* (New York: Harper, 2008); and Donald Critchlow and Nancy MacLean, eds., *The American Conservative Movement: 1945 to the Present* (Lanham, MD: Rowman & Littlefield, 2009).

9. Russell Kirk, *The Conservative Mind, from Burke to Santayana* (Chicago: Regnery, 1953).

10. Some words about methodology are warranted here. In this project, I will cite several hundred books—mostly written between 1950 and 2010—that explore what conservatives believe. Most of the people who wrote those books see themselves as conservative. But they do not subscribe to an official set of qualifications for that title. Therefore, my sources in toto amount to a forest with many trees, and the best way to characterize that forest is to let some of the trees speak for themselves. In such a strategy, two dangers reside. First, I may quote short passages accurately but not do justice to conservative authors who write comprehensively about large matters of great importance. Danger on this score may be called the "snippet challenge." Readers should notice, however, that the sources I cite, even though I do so only briefly, represent a wide range of conservatives, from activists to scholars, from urban intellectuals to small-town ministers, from politicians to talk show hosts. This spectrum demonstrates, I think, that different kinds of conservatives tend to make arguments similarly, and that is the message I wish to convey. Second, I have something to say. The danger there is that I will quote only right-wing men and women whose words confirm my agenda. Call this the "foregone conclusion challenge." I concede that this danger exists, as if, were I to choose other sources, I might reveal a sort of conservatism more plausible than what I will describe. Nevertheless, the array of authors I cite is broad, and it includes politicians such as Ronald Reagan and George W. Bush, clerics such as Jerry Falwell and James Dobson, think tankers from the American Enterprise Institute and the Heritage Foundation, and journalists associated with, say, the *National Review*, the *Weekly Standard*, and *Fox News*. Given that these people are regarded as mainstream advocates for right-wing propositions—I will quote Ann Coulter only sparingly—I hope that my analysis of their views will represent accurately the universe of terms, aspirations, and expectations within which conservatives operate politically.

11. These thinkers and interpreters are acclaimed in Edwin J. Feulner Jr., ed., *Leadership for America: The Principles of Conservatism* (Dallas: Spence, 2000). See also the authors whose writings are excerpted in Chilton Williamson Jr., ed., *The Conservative Bookshelf: Essential Works that Impact Today's Conservative Thinkers* (New York: Citadel, 2004).

12. One may speculate on whether modern American conservatives are truly "conservative" in some generic sense of how that term is applied to the works of people like Edmund Burke and Michael Oakeshott. (See the discussion in Ray Nichols, "'Conservatism' and 'the Right' in America: Ideological Conflict, Categories and Language," *Journal of Political Ideologies* [October 1997]: 239–257, and Carl T. Bogus, "Rescuing Burke,"

Missouri Law Review [Spring 2007]: 387–476.) Right-wingers such as Ronald Reagan, Newt Gingrich, Irving Kristol, and Rush Limbaugh will not always seem "conservative" according to that test. It follows that some scholars might regard such partisans as not deserving the conservative label. I will not take sides on this issue.

13. Westen, *The Political Brain,* p. 169.

14. Frank Rich, "The Up-or-Down Vote on Obama's Presidency," *New York Times,* March 7, 2010, p. WK10.

15. In political analysis, short-term impressions can mislead. Thus Garry Dorrien, who is a first-rate scholar, writes in 1998 that "[t]he high water mark for neoconservatism as a distinctive political movement has surely passed. Neoconservatives are unlikely to regain the political influence and power they attained during Reagan's presidency. The dissolution of the Soviet Union has stripped neoconservatism of its unifying enemy and ended the world-historical phase of politicization by which the movement was principally defined." See Garry Dorrien, "Inventing an American Conservatism: the Neoconservative Episode," in *Unraveling the Right: The New Conservatism in American Thought and Politics,* ed. Amy E. Ansell (Boulder, CO: Westview, 2001), p. 64. Then came September 11, 2001—which Dorrien could not have predicted—after which, as we shall see in Chapter Seven, neoconservatives helped to fashion the rationale for America's going to war against Iraq.

16. Intense media hype accompanied the Obama-Biden campaign. But by historical benchmarks a different perspective emerges. For example, one may compare what happened in 2008 with recent Democratic presidential victories that are not considered remarkable. Obama and Biden received 365 electoral votes. But in 1992, Bill Clinton and Al Gore received 370 electoral votes, and in 1996, they received 379. (Clinton and Gore's popular vote totals are difficult to compare with that of Obama and Biden, because third-party candidate Ross Perot took 19 percent of the popular vote in 1992 and 9 percent in 1996.) Conservatives cling to this point. Thus Charles Krauthammer, "The Myth of '08, Demolished," *Washington Post,* November 6, 2009, p. A23: "A uniquely charismatic candidate was running at a time of deep war weariness, with an intensely unpopular Republican president, against a politically incompetent opponent, amid the greatest financial collapse since the Great Depression. And he [Obama] still won by only seven points [in the popular vote]."

Chapter One

1. For complications that arise when trying to define conservatism, see David Y. Allen, "Modern Conservatism: The Problem of Definition," *Review of Politics* (October 1981): 582–604. See also Charles Dunn and J. David Woodward, "The Problem of Defining Conservatism," in *The Conservative Tradition in America* (Lanham, MD: Rowman & Littlefield, 1996), pp. 21–43.

2. In other words, one must analyze conservative ideas as an intellectual historian rather than as a quantitative social scientist. This imperative is discussed in David Ricci, "Political Science and Conservative Ideas: The American Case," *History of Political Ideologies* (June 2009): 165–167. That standard methodologies cannot grasp conservative ideas is noted by William Connolly, "The Evangelical-Capitalist Resonance Machine," *Political Theory* (December 2005): 870.

3. People commonly known as conservatives have expounded different versions of

this story. In writings about conservatism, variations of these sorts are sometimes used to justify speaking about the Old Right, the New Right, the Populist Right, the Christian Right, social conservatives, economic conservatives, libertarians, paleoconservatives, neoconservatives, international realists, and more. (A brief overview of such groups is available in George H. Nash, "The Uneasy Future of Conservatism," in *The Future of Conservatism: Conflict and Consensus in the Post-Reagan Era,* ed. Charles W. Dunn [Wilmington, DE: Intercollegiate Studies Institute, 2007], pp. 1–19.) Such labels suggest static group commitments. Events in the real world, however—like the war in Iraq and the subprime mortgage crisis—press in to the point where from any once-stipulated conservative faction, such as those originally called neoconservatives, some people will eventually diverge and find new allies. When that happens, continuing to use the old labels is likely to obscure the shared elements that help us to understand why certain people, despite their disagreements here and there, are known, and should be known, as conservatives.

4. On the political importance of narratives, see Rogers M. Smith, *Stories of Peoplehood: The Politics and Morals of Political Membership* (New York: Cambridge University Press, 2003); Howard Gardner, *Changing Minds: The Art and Science of Changing Our Own and Other People's Minds* (Cambridge, MA: Harvard University Press, 2004); and Evan Cornog, *The Power and the Story: How the Crafted Presidential Narrative Has Determined Political Success from George Washington to George W. Bush* (New York: Penguin, 2004).

5. These propositions appear in "The Magazine's Credenda," *National Review,* November 19, 1955, p. 6.

6. Newt Gingrich and Dick Armey, *Contract with America* (New York: Times Books), p. 4.

7. For example, see Frank S. Meyer, "Conservatism," in *Left, Right and Center: Essays on Liberalism and Conservatism in the United States,* ed. Robert A. Goldwin (Chicago: Rand McNally, 1966), pp. 5–8, which lists seven conservative "articles of belief" that include (A) faith in a "moral order based on ontological foundations," (B) an emphasis on the individual person, (C) an inclination to antiutopianism, (D) an insistence on a limited state, (E) a preference for a "free economic system," (F) support for "the Constitution of the United States as originally conceived," and (G) a commitment to opposing "Communism" as a threat to "the very existence of Western civilization and the United States." See also Richard A. Viguerie, *The New Right: We're Ready to Lead* (Falls Church, VA: Viguerie Company, 1980), p. 11: "[A] conservative believes in six basic things: (1) a moral order, based on God; (2) the individual as the center of political and social action; (3) limited government; (4) a free as contrasted to a planned society; (5) the Constitution of the United States, as originally conceived by the Founding Fathers; and (6) the recognition of Communism as an unchanging enemy of the Free World." Similar lists appear when conservatives describe the beliefs that inspire them to pursue lives of public service. See Tom DeLay, *No Retreat, No Surrender: One American's Fight* (New York: Sentinel, 2007), esp. pp. 99–100, and Edwin J. Feulner, *Getting America Right: The True Conservative Values Our Nation Needs Today* (New York: Three Rivers Press, 2007), pp. 2–3.

8. Russell Kirk, *The Conservative Mind, from Burke to Santayana* (Chicago: Regnery, 1953); James Burnham, *The Suicide of the West: An Essay on the Meaning and Destiny of Liberalism* (New York: John Day, 1964); and Richard Weaver, *Ideas Have Consequences* (orig. 1948; Chicago: University of Chicago Press, 1984).

9. Some of their works are excerpted in Jerry Z. Muller, ed., *Conservatism: An Anthology of Social and Political Thought from David Hume to the Present* (Princeton, NJ: Princeton University Press, 1997).

10. Many conservatives today support voter identity laws whereby, in some states, citizens must present a government-issued photo ID in order to vote. However, conservatives say that such laws are not designed to make voting by poor people difficult but to prevent voter fraud. Thus Judge Richard Poser, writing the Seventh Circuit Court of Appeals' decision in *William Crawford v. Marion County Election Board* (2007), upheld Indiana's voter identity law on the grounds that "[t]he purpose of the Indiana law is to reduce voting fraud, and voting fraud impairs the right of legitimate voters to vote by diluting their votes—dilution being recognized to be an impairment of the right to vote" (USCA-02-C-0072-1-4-07). See the same argument in Newt Gingrich, *Winning the Future: A 21st Century Contract with America* (Washington, DC: Regnery, 2006), p. 99. (Posner's decision was upheld by the Supreme Court in 2008.)

11. Ben Kinchlow, "Transforming America from the Inside Out," in D. James Kennedy, Gary Bauer, John Ashcroft, et al., *Reclaiming America for Christ* (Fort Lauderdale, FL: Coral Ridge Ministries, 1996), p. 93.

12. Charles Colson, *A Dance with Deception: Revealing the Truth Behind the Headlines* (Dallas: Word, 1993), p. 16.

13. H. Edward Rowe, *Save America!* (Old Tappan, NJ: Fleming H. Revell Co., 1976), pp. 66–67. See also Jerry Falwell, *The New American Family* (Dallas: Word, 1992), p. 212: "If we are to rise up and take back this nation, we will need the power of God within us. Jesus Christ said, 'you shall know the truth, and the truth shall make you free' (John 8:32). When we are empowered by God's truth, nothing can stop us."

14. Barry Goldwater, *The Conscience of a Conservative* (Shepherdsville, KY: Victor), p. 3.

15. Frank S. Meyer, "Freedom, Tradition, Conservatism," in *What Is Conservatism?* ed. Frank S. Meyer (New York: Holt, Rinehart, and Winston, 1964), p. 12.

16. Jeffrey Hart, "Modern American Conservatism," in *The New Right Papers,* ed. Robert W. Whitaker (New York: St. Martin's Press, 1985), p. 34.

17. See Albert Hirschman, *The Rhetoric of Reaction: Perversity, Futility, Jeopardy* (Cambridge, MA: Harvard University Press, 1991).

18. Ibid., p. 9.

19. Milton and Rose Friedman, *Free to Choose: A Personal Statement* (orig. 1979; New York: Harcourt Brace, 1990), p. 53.

20. Edward Banfield, *The Unheavenly City Revisited* (Boston: Little, Brown, 1974), p. 149.

21. James Q. Wilson, foreword to *The Essential Neoconservative Reader,* ed. Mark Gerson (New York: Addison-Wesley, 1996), p. vii. See also Joshua Muravchik, who criticizes policy ideas advanced by what he calls the "New Left" in "The Cure Is Worse than the Disease," in *Second Thoughts: Former Radicals Look Back at the Sixties,* ed. Peter Collier and David Horowitz (New York: Madison Books, 1989), pp. 161–165.

22. For Wilson, see ibid. For Himmelfarb, see Gertrude Himmelfarb, *One Nation, Two Cultures* (New York: Knopf, 1999), p. 75.

23. Larry Burkett, *The Coming Economic Earthquake,* rev. ed. (Chicago: Moody, 1994), p. 63.

24. David Frum, *What's Right: The New Conservative Majority and the Remaking of America* (New York: Basic Books, 1996), p. 131.

25. See Irving Kristol, "Welfare: The Best of Intentions, the Worst of Results [1971]," in Irving Kristol, *Neoconservatism: The Autobiography of an Idea* (New York: Free Press, 1995), pp. 43–49.

26. Friedrich A. Hayek, *The Road to Serfdom* (Chicago: University of Chicago Press, 1957), p. 5.

27. Rush Limbaugh, *See, I Told You So* (New York: Pocket Books, 1993), p. 241.

28. Bill O'Reilly, *The No Spin Zone: Confrontations with the Powerful and Famous in America* (New York: Broadway Books, 2001), p. 125.

29. Marvin Olasky, *The Tragedy of American Compassion* (Washington, DC: Regnery, 1992). See especially pp. 101–113, where Olasky discusses seven principles he says can cure poverty but are promoted only in nongovernmental philanthropic agencies. These principles are affiliation, bonding, categorization, discernment, employment, freedom, and God.

30. Charles Murray, *Losing Ground: American Social Policy, 1950–1980* (New York: Basic Books, 1984), esp. pp. 146, 150–151, 175–176, 180–181.

31. Ibid., p. 23.

32. Ibid., pp. 227–228.

33. Michael Bauman, "The Dangerous Samaritans: How We Unintentionally Injure the Poor," in *Morality and the Marketplace,* ed. Michael Bauman (Hillsdale, MI: Hillsdale College Press, 1994), pp. 3–16.

34. Himmelfarb, *One Nation, Two Cultures,* p. 53.

35. George Gilder, *Wealth and Poverty* (New York: Basic Books, 1981), p. 122. Congress started phasing out AFDC in 1996.

36. Ibid., p. 115.

37. Ronald H. Nash, *Social Justice and the Christian Church* (Fenton, MI: Mott Media, 1983), p. 106.

38. Milton and Rose Friedman, *Free to Choose,* p. 237.

39. Ibid. Friedman and Friedman estimated that raising the minimum wage around 1990 would prevent the creation of 400,000 to 500,000 jobs. Alternatively, some economists have argued that increases in the minimum wage for, say, fast food workers have either no effect or a positive impact on measured employment rates. See David E. Card and Alan Kruger, *Myth and Measurement: The New Economics of the Minimum Wage* (Princeton, NJ: Princeton University Press, 1997).

40. Banfield, *The Unheavenly City Revisited,* p. 118.

41. Jack Kemp, *An American Renaissance: A Strategy for the 1980s* (Lake Wylie, SC: Robert E. Hopper and Associates, 1979), pp. 41–42.

42. James Watt, *The Courage of a Conservative* (New York: Simon & Schuster, 1985), p. 68.

43. Viguerie, *The New Right,* pp. 221–222.

44. Holmes believed that Albany had a constitutional right to limit the work of New York bakers to sixty hours per week. For recent endorsement of the laissez-faire doctrine that Holmes criticized, see Rus Walton, *One Nation Under God* (Washington, DC: Third Century, 1975), p. 143: "Is not the minimum wage law a violation of the unalienable rights of those young people? You bet it is. Who are we—and who is Caesar—to tell them they cannot pump gas, or sweep floors, or carry parcels for less than so much an hour? That is a matter between the employee and the employer."

45. Mark Anthony, *Vanishing Republic: How Can We Save the American Dream?* (Altamonte Springs, FL: Encore, 1995), p. 342.

46. Himmelfarb, *One Nation, Two Cultures,* p. 55.

47. Carol Ianonne, "The Feminist Confusion," in Collier and Horowitz, eds., *Second Thoughts,* p. 150.

48. Gilder, *Wealth and Poverty,* p. 125

49. Robert Bork, *Slouching Towards Gomorrah: Modern Liberalism and American Decline* (New York: Regan, 1996), p. 193.

50. The ERA read as follows: "SECTION 1. Equality of rights under the law shall not be denied or abridged by the United States or any state on account of sex. SECTION 2. The Congress shall have power to enforce this article by appropriate legislation. SECTION 3. This amendment shall take effect two years after the date of ratification."

51. Phyllis Schlafly, *The Power of the Positive Woman* (New Rochelle, NY: Arlington House Publishers, 1977), pp. 68–119.

52. Jerry Falwell, *Listen, America!* (New York: Doubleday, 1980), pp. 150–151, and John W. Whitehead, *The Stealing of America* (Westchester, IL: Crossway, 1983), pp. 117–118. The biblical reference is to Ephesians 5:21–23.

53. Rosemary Thomson, *The Price of LIBerty* (Carol Stream, IL: Creation House, 1978), p. 83.

54. Hirschman, *The Rhetoric of Reaction,* p. 81.

55. William F. Buckley Jr., *Inveighing We Will Go* (New York: Berkley, 1972), p. 38.

56. George Charles Roche, III, *The Bewildered Society* (Hillsdale, Michigan: Hillsdale College Press, 1974), p. 213.

57. M. Stanton Evans, *Clear and Present Dangers: A Conservative View of America's Government* (New York: Harcourt, Brace, Jovanovich, 1975), p. 389.

58. Donald Lambro, *The Conscience of a Young Conservative* (New Rochelle, NY: Arlington House, 1976), p. 89.

59. Walton, *One Nation Under God,* p. 186. Walton is quoting Henry Hazlitt here.

60. Harold Brown, *The Reconstruction of the Republic* (Milford, MI: Mott Media, 1981), p. 169.

61. Jesse Helms, *When Free Men Shall Stand* (Grand Rapids, MI: Zondervan, 1976), p. 67.

62. Ronald Reagan, *Abortion and the Conscience of the Nation* (New York: Thomas Nelson, 1984), p. 18.

63. The essay by Koop, who served as Reagan's surgeon general, is reprinted in ibid., pp. 41–73.

64. William Dannemeyer, *Shadow in the Land: Homosexuality in America* (San Francisco: Ignatius, 1989), p. 218.

65. William A. Donohue, *The New Freedom: Individualism and Collectivism in the Social Lives of Americans* (New Brunswick, NJ: Transaction, 1990), p. 99.

66. Barry M. Goldwater, "Acceptance Speech," in Barry M. Goldwater, *Where I Stand* (New York: McGraw-Hill, 1964), p. 16.

67. Milton Friedman, *Capitalism and Freedom* (Chicago: University of Chicago Press, 1962), p. 13.

68. George Roche, *America By the Throat: The Stranglehold of Federal Bureaucracy* (Hillsdale, MI: Hillsdale College Press, 1985), p. 57.

69. Michael Novak, *Free Persons and the Common Good* (Lanham, MD: Madison Books, 1989), p. 37.

70. Robert H. Bork, *The Tempting of America: The Political Seduction of the Law* (New York: Touchstone, 1991), p. 341.

71. Joshua Muravchik, "An Anti-Communist Manifesto," in Collier and Horowitz, eds., *Second Thoughts*, p. 228.

72. Hayek expounds this point repeatedly. A good example is Hayek, *The Road to Serfdom*, p. xiv.

73. Nash, *Social Justice and the Christian Church*, pp. 103–104.

74. William E. Simon, *A Time for Truth* (New York: Berkley, 1978), pp. 34–36.

75. Brannon S. Howse, *Reclaiming a Nation at Risk: the Battle for Your Faith, Family, and Freedoms* (Chandler, AZ: Bridgestone Multimedia Group, 1995), pp. 223–224.

76. Rowe, *Save America!* p. 42.

77. Inattention to middle-ground possibilities is described as "binary" thinking in Linda Kintz, *Between Jesus and the Market: The Emotions that Matter in Right-Wing America* (Durham, NC: Duke University Press, 1997), esp. pp. 179–186.

78. Reagan, *Abortion and the Conscience of the Nation*, p. 34.

79. Hirschman, *The Rhetoric of Reaction*, p. 43.

80. Goldwater, *The Conscience of a Conservative*, p. 11. See also William Murchison, *Reclaiming Morality in America* (Nashville: Nelson, 1994), pp. 11–12: "Morality, rightly understood, is *a set of propositions about human nature*: who we are, where we came from, where we are bound, how we ought to conduct ourselves on the journey.... If a particular action harmonizes with our nature, then such an action must be, in common parlance, *right*. An action at odds with that nature—one that is dangerous or harmful to it—is *wrong*. This means that morality is never arbitrary, never the result of individual or local perception. Its roots lie deep in our nature."

81. David Horowitz, *Hating Whitey and Other Progressive Causes* (Dallas: Spence, 1999), p. 285. George Orwell scoffed at conservative pessimists, such as James Burnham, who argued that human nature is fixed and that "human history is in fact one long tale of greed, robbery and oppression." If that were so, said Orwell, "why is it that we not only don't practice cannibalism any longer, but don't even want to?" From George Orwell, "As I Please" (1944), in *The Collected Essays, Journalism and Letters of George Orwell*, vol. 3, ed. Sonia Orwell and Ian Angus (New York: Harcourt, Brace and World, 1968), pp. 189–190.

82. Edward Banfield, *The Unheavenly City: The Nature and Future of Our Urban Crisis* (Boston: Little, Brown, 1970). This is the original version of the book cited in n. 20, above.

83. Roger Kimball, *Experiments Against Reality: The Fate of Culture in the Postmodern Age* (Chicago: Ivan Dee, 2000).

84. James Q. Wilson, "A New Approach to Welfare Reform: Humility," in *Backward and Upward: The New Conservative Writing*, ed. David Brooks (New York: Vintage, 1996), pp. 240–246.

85. Along these lines, Charles Colson believes that America's founders instituted checks and balances in government because they regarded men as "depraved." See Colson, *A Dance with Deception*, p. 141. See also Pat Robertson, *The New World Order* (Dallas: Word, 1991), p. 203: The Constitution assumes the "sinful nature of man" because, as Jeremiah said, "The heart of man is deceitful above all things, and desperately wicked; who can know it?" (Jeremiah 17:19).

86. Brown, *The Reconstruction of the Republic,* p. 92.

87. Thomas Lane, *The Breakdown of the Old Politics* (New Rochelle, NY: Arlington House, 1974), pp. 139–141.

88. See William F. Buckley Jr., *God and Man at Yale* (Chicago: Regnery, 1951), p. 51.

89. George Roche, *One By One: Preserving Values and Freedom in Heartland America* (Hillsdale, MI: Hillsdale College Press, 1990), p. 127.

90. Ronald H. Nash, *Poverty and Wealth: Why Socialism Doesn't Work* (Richardson, TX: Probe, 1986), p. 18.

91. See Friedman's classic *Capitalism and Freedom* (Chicago: University of Chicago Press, 1962).

92. See Simon, *A Time for Truth.*

93. Joseph Schumpeter, *Capitalism, Socialism, and Democracy,* 3rd ed. (New York: Harper & Row, 1962), pp. 81–86.

94. See Hayek, *The Road to Serfdom,* pp. 122–124.

95. Gilder, *Wealth and Poverty,* p. 237.

96. Richard J. Herrnstein and Charles Murray, *The Bell Curve: Intelligence and Class Structure in American Life* (New York: Free Press, 1994).

97. Dinesh D'Souza, *The End of Racism: Principles for a Multiracial Society* (New York: Free Press, 1995), esp. pp. 303–304, 442–444, 475–476.

98. Herrnstein and Murray, *The Bell Curve,* p. 475, recommends scrapping affirmative action programs and favoring African Americans in schooling and employment only if an individual of that group is as qualified as any other candidate. See also p. 523, where African Americans in the "underclass" are described as being in it "because of inherent shortcomings [genetic deficiencies] about which little can be done." Against the thesis that IQ is genetically determined, see James R. Flynn, *Where Have All the Liberals Gone?: Race, Class, and Ideals in America* (New York: Cambridge University Press, 2008), esp. pp. 68–111.

99. This approach informs George Gilder, *Men and Marriage* (Gretna, LA: Pelican, 1993).

100. Schlafly, *The Power of the Positive Woman,* pp. 37–38,

101. Midge Decter, *The New Chastity and Other Arguments Against Women's Liberation* (New York: Coward, McGann & Geoghegan, 1972), pp. 56–57, 124–125, 175.

102. James Burnham, *Suicide of the West: An Essay on the Meaning and Destiny of Liberalism* (New York: John Day, 1964), pp. 54, 69. See also Nash, *Social Justice and the Christian Church,* p. 114: "Conservatives think that liberals consistently overestimated mankind's propensities for good and thus became infatuated with the basic error of utopianism, namely, the perfectibility of man and the possibility of a perfect society."

103. William F. Buckley Jr., *Up From Liberalism,* 25th anniversary ed. (New York: Stein and Day, 1984), p. 35. See also Dinesh D'Souza, *Letters to a Young Conservative* (New York: Basic Books, 2005), p. 9: "At root, conservatives and liberals see the world so differently because they have two different conceptions of human nature. Liberals tend to believe in Rousseau's proposition that human nature is intrinsically good."

104. Rael and Erich Isaac, *The Coercive Utopians: Social Deception by America's Power Players* (Chicago: Regnery, 1983), p. 2. Isaac and Isaac recommend, instead, "a return to the stubborn wisdom of the founding fathers who knew that men are not, and could not be made perfect," p. 309.

105. Kimball, in *Experiments Against Reality,* pp. 177. Kimball is here quoting, with approval, James Fitzjames Stephen, one of Mill's nineteenth-century critics.

106. Irving Kristol, "Utopianism and American Politics [1971]," in Irving Kristol, *On the Democratic Idea in America* (New York: Harper & Row, 1972), p. 127–149.

107. David Horowitz, *The Art of Political War and Other Radical Pursuits* (Dallas: Spence, 2000), p. 56.

108. Jude Wanniski, *The Way the World Works* (New York: Touchstone, 1978), and Paul Craig Roberts, *The Supply-Side Revolution: An Insider's Account of Policymaking in Washington* (Cambridge, MA: Harvard University Press, 1984).

109. Against supply-side theories, see Robert H. Frank, *Luxury Fever: Money and Happiness in an Era of Excess* (Princeton, NJ: Princeton University Press, 1999), pp. 227–250.

110. See praise for supply-side economics and the Laffer Curve in Kemp, *An American Renaissance,* but esp. pp. 51–53, and in Bruce R. Bartlett, *Reaganomics: Supply Side Economics in Action* (Westport, CT: Arlington House, 1981).

111. Senator Daniel P. Moynihan (D-NY), "Reagan's Bankrupt Budget" (1983), in Daniel Moynihan, *Came the Revolution: Argument in the Reagan Era* (New York: Harcourt, Brace, Jovanovich, 1988), pp. 151–160, claims that Ronald Reagan knew before his tax cuts were enacted that they would cause budget deficits. However, according to Moynihan, the president regarded deficits not as a "vice" but as an "opportunity," because he knew they would grow so large as to force Congress to cut social programs favored by liberals.

112. The usefulness to conservatives of austerity compelled by supply-side tax cuts is explored by Theda Skocpol, *Boomerang: Clinton's Health Security Effort and the Turn against Government in U.S. Politics* (New York: Norton, 1996), esp. pp. 174–178. See also Mark A. Smith, "Economic Insecurity, Party Reputations, and the Republican Ascendancy," in *The Transformation of American Politics: Activist Government and the Rise of Conservatism,* ed. Paul Pierson and Theda Skocpol (Princeton, NJ: Princeton University Press, 2007), pp. 155–157: "While its status as an economic doctrine was a subject of skepticism, Reagan's supply-side economics achieved success as a political doctrine."

113. For generations, conservatives preached the virtues of balanced budgets. Thus Henry Hazlitt, in his *Economics in One Lesson,* 50th anniversary ed. (orig. 1946; San Francisco: Laissez Faire, 1996), p. 4, criticizes Keynesian economics for its puckish motto that "In the long run we are all dead." Hazlitt insists instead that the consequences—now and later—of deficit spending to support Keynesian social programs can be devastating. Some conservatives still insist on balanced budgets. See Richard A. Viguerie, *Conservatives Betrayed: How Big Government Republicans Hijacked the Conservative Cause and Sold Out Their Supporters* (Los Angeles: Bonus, 2006).

114. Newt Gingrich, "Why Balancing the Budget Is Vital," in *Window of Opportunity: A Blueprint for the Future* (New York: Tom Doherty Enterprises, 1984), pp. 184–197.

115. Gingrich and Armey, *Contract with America,* pp. 23–24, 26–28, 31–32.

116. Newt Gingrich, *Lessons Learned the Hard Way* (New York: HarperCollins, 1998), p. 25. See also Lawrence Kudlow, *American Abundance: The New Economic and Moral Prosperity* (New York: Forbes, 1997), p. xix: "What's more, tax reduction is consistent with, even a necessary condition for, budget restraint. Just as in business, nothing reduces expenses and overhead faster than declining revenues and profits ... Show me a committed tax-cutter and I'll show you a shrinking government, at least as a share of GDP."

117. Paul Krugman, "Maestro of Chutzpah," *New York Times,* March 3, 2004, p. A23.

118. Sometimes the argument is summed up succinctly. For example, see D'Souza, *Letters to a Young Conservative,* p. 10: "I am a conservative, Chris, because I believe that conservatives have an accurate understanding of human nature and liberals do not. Since liberals have a wrong view of man, their policies are unlikely to achieve good results. Indeed, liberals programs frequently subvert liberal objectives."

119. In supply-side terms, the key law was titled "The Economic Growth and Tax Relief Reconciliation Act of 2001." Republicans in the House voted for it 210–0. Democrats in the House voted against it 153–28. Republicans in the Senate voted for it 45–2. Democrats in the Senate voted against it 31–12. The total vote was thus Republicans in favor 255–2 and Democrats opposed 184–40.

Chapter Two

1. Conservatives who promote the notion of intelligent design know that most scientists think it is false. They therefore insist that intelligent design—regardless of its small scientific merit—be given equal time with the theory of evolution in school classrooms. Against the notion of intelligent design, see Matt Young and Taner Edis, eds., *Why Intelligent Design Fails: A Scientific Critique of the New Creationism* (New Brunswick, NJ: Rutgers University Press, 2004), and John Brockman, ed., *Intelligent Thought: Science Versus the Intelligent Design Movement* (New York: Vintage, 2006).

2. Jerry Falwell, *The New American Family: The Rebirth of the American Dream* (Dallas: Word, 1992), p. 99.

3. See Randall Terry, *Operation Rescue* (Springdale, PA: Whitaker House, 1988), p. 75. This book's title is derived from Proverbs 24:11—"Rescue those who are unjustly sentenced to death; don't stand back and let them die."

4. Ibid., p. 90. The admonition is from Acts 5:29.

5. Robert P. Dugan Jr., "Why This Book?" in *The High Cost of Indifference: Can Christians Afford Not to Act?* ed. Richard Cizik (Ventura, CA: Regal, 1984), p. 11.

6. See Ralph Reed, *Politically Incorrect: The Emerging Faith Factor in American Politics* (Dallas: Word, 1994), p. 10.

7. D. James Kennedy, "Reclaiming America for Christ," in D. James Kennedy, Gary Bauer, John Ashcroft, et al., *Reclaiming America for Christ* (Fort Lauderdale, FL: Coral Ridge Ministries, 1996), p. 8.

8. Pat Robertson, *The New World Order* (Dallas: Word, 1991), p. 231.

9. See Neil Postman, *Amusing Ourselves to Death: Public Discourse in the Age of Show Business* (New York: Penguin, 1985), pp. 127–128.

10. Milton and Rose Friedman, *Free to Choose: A Personal Statement* (New York: Harcourt Brace, 1990), p. 51.

11. Ibid., p. 43.

12. Thomas Sowell, *Markets and Minorities* (New York: Basic Books, 1981), p. 35.

13. Jude Wanniski, *The Way the World Works* (New York: Touchstone, 1978), p. 97.

14. See Paul Craig Roberts, *The Supply-Side Revolution: An Insider's Account of Policymaking in Washington* (Cambridge, MA: Harvard University Press, 1984), p. 38: "[R]ising marginal tax rates discourage further work."

15. Wanniski does not claim to know. As he says, in his *The Way the World Works,* pp. 98–99, "It is the task of the political leader [not Wanniski] to determine point E [that is, the point on the Laffer Curve where, presumably, tax receipts and national production, both in the real world, are 'maximized']." See also William C. Mitchell and Randy T. Simmons, *Beyond Politics: Markets, Welfare, and the Failure of Bureaucracy* (Boulder, CO: Westview, 1994), p. 185: "One problem with the Laffer analysis is that careful analysts are just beginning to establish the 'exact' shape and position of the curve, and it appears there is not a single, determinate general curve. That fact, however, does not diminish the political uses of Laffer's theory."

16. Wanniski, *The Way the World Works,* p. 302. What does the word *reliable* mean in this context? It would be significant if Wanniski described the model as *valid,* but he does not.

17. Jude Wanniski, for example, wrote *The Way the World Works* (1978). But what he described in that book was not economic activity but his model of how people behave economically, in which case the book is not about the real world but about what that world would be like if people were to behave according to Wanniski's model. (In this sense, a more accurate title for the book would have been *The Way the World of Wanniski Works.*) The logic is the same as when Herman Kahn said that real Americans might recover quickly from nuclear war if after such a war they would behave as he assumed, in his book *On Thermonuclear War* (Princeton, NJ: Princeton University Press, 1960), that hypothetical Americans would behave. (In this light, Kahn's book should have been entitled *On Herman's Thermonuclear War.*)

18. Henry Hazlitt, "How the Price System Works," in *Economics in One Lesson* (1946; San Francisco: Laissez Faire, 1996), pp. 87–93.

19. Michael Novak, *The Spirit of Democratic Capitalism* (New York: Simon & Schuster, 1982), p. 14.

20. Ibid., p. 14.

21. Ronald H. Nash, *Poverty and Wealth: Why Socialism Doesn't Work* (Richardson, TX: Probe, 1986), pp. 47–53.

22. Paul H. Weaver, *The Suicidal Corporation* (New York: Touchstone, 1988), p. 253.

23. Richard A. Viguerie, *The Establishment vs. The People: Is a New Populist Revolt on the Way?* (Chicago: Regnery, 1983), p. 31.

24. James Q. Wilson, *Thinking About Crime,* rev. ed. (New York: Basic Books, 1983), p. 1. Two of the three "obvious" examples of human behavior that Wilson cites are not necessarily true, because (1) people do not always "shop around to find the best buy" and (2) they do not always "change jobs [and neighborhoods, colleagues, and friends] when the opportunity arises to earn more money for the same amount of effort."

25. Newt Gingrich, *Window of Opportunity: A Blueprint for the Future* (New York: Tom Doherty Enterprises, 1984), p. 167.

26. William E. Simon, *A Time for Action* (New York: Reader's Digest, 1980), p. 40.

27. Charles Murray, *Losing Ground: American Social Policy, 1950–1980* (New York: Basic Books, 1984), p. 156.

28. Ibid., p. 161. Murray apparently believes that people usually marry for economic reasons. Mark Anthony, *Vanishing Republic: How Can We Save the American Dream?* (Altamonte Springs, FL: Encore, 1995), p. 135, believes that child bearing, too, is economically determined. As he says, "Unfortunately, Health and Human Services Secretary,

Donna Shalala, disputes the contention that welfare mothers intentionally bear additional children in order to increase Uncle Sam's subsidy. What other reason *could* there be? Are we to believe that poor unwed mothers continue to become pregnant because they *enjoy* the experience of poverty-stricken, single parenthood? Of course not. They continue to bear children because the government subsidizes their procreation." Emphasis is in the original.

29. Anthony, *Vanishing Republic,* p. 204.

30. Gary S. Becker, *The Economics of Discrimination* (Chicago: University of Chicago Press, 1957). On Becker as a conservative, see Gary Becker, "Competition," in *Leadership For America: The Principles of Conservatism,* ed. Edwin J. Feulner Jr. (Dallas: Spence, 2000), pp. 275–289.

31. Thomas Sowell, *Race and Economics* (New York: David McKay, 1975), pp. 164, 171, and Sowell, *Markets and Minorities,* pp. 28–29.

32. Robert H. Bork, *Slouching Towards Gomorrah: Modern Liberalism and American Decline* (New York: Regan, 1996), p. 237.

33. Paul Craig Roberts and Lawrence M. Stratton, *The New Color Line: How Quotas and Privilege Destroy Democracy* (Washington, DC: Regnery, 1995), p. 88.

34. Dinesh D'Souza, *The End of Racism: Principles for a Multiracial Society* (New York: Free Press, 1995), pp. 277, 545.

35. Ibid., p. 545.

36. Ibid., pp. 278–287.

37. Ibid. What D'Souza calls "rational discrimination," some people might call "racial profiling."

38. Ibid., p. 91. (On pp. 92–93, D'Souza describes the treatment of slaves as awful.) Charles Dickens, who saw the real thing, would have regarded D'Souza's economic reasoning as naive. Coming in 1842 to Washington, D.C., from Richmond, Virginia, Dickens wrote a friend that "[t]hey [Southern whites] *will* ask you what you think of it [slavery], and *will* expatiate on slavery as if it were one of the greatest blessings of mankind. 'It's not,' said a hard-bad-looking fellow to me the other day, 'it's not the interest of a man to use his slaves ill. It's damned nonsense that you hear in England.'—I told him quietly that it was not a man's interest to get drunk, or to steal, or to game, or to indulge in any other vice, but he *did* indulge in it for all that." See Walter Dexter, ed., *The Letters of Charles Dickens,* vol. 1 (London: Nonesuch Press, 1938), pp. 409–410.

39. Friedman and Friedman, *Free to Choose,* p. 215. This passage implies that the desirable amount of balance should be calculated by economists rather than ecologists.

40. Rus Walton, *One Nation Under God* (Washington, DC: Third Century, 1975), p. 168. The "one person" here could be a liberal or an ecologist. See also Larry Burkett, *Whatever Happened to the American Dream?* p. 124: "Don't be duped by the activists who cry, 'We're destroying the world ecological balance.' There is no scientific evidence to support such a claim. However, there is a vast array of evidence to support the fact [i.e., indicate] that millions of future jobs are being destroyed by their ever-increasing attack on any industrialized expansion."

41. Aaron Wildavsky, "Richer Is Safer," *Public Interest* (Summer 1980): 23–39.

42. See Rael and Erich Isaac, *The Coercive Utopians: Social Deception by America's Power Players* (Chicago: Regnery, 1983), pp. 51, 310, who agree with Wildavsky's notion that "richer is safer." See also Newt Gingrich, *Winning the Future: A 21st Century Contract with America* (Washington, DC: Regnery, 2006), p. 169: "The greatest dangers

to biodiversity on the planet today are poor people cutting down tropical forests for money and killing endangered species for meat. Wealthy people can afford to protect the forests and protect endangered species."

43. See Julian L. Simon, *The Ultimate Resource* (Princeton, NJ: Princeton University Press, 1981), pp. 16–50.

44. Simon's calculations in ibid., passim—such as his figures showing that cultivated acreage and agricultural output have grown in modern times—are presented without reference to parallel figures on increasing pollution and environmental degradation, such as the accumulation of pesticides, the loss of topsoil, and the destruction of rain forests.

45. Wildavsky makes this connection in "Richer Is Safer," p. 35, when he says that because "whatever happens [ecologically] will be unexpected.... [R]esilience [wealth] will afford better protection than anticipation [legislation now]." See also Dinesh D'Souza, *The Virtue of Prosperity: Finding Values in an Age of Techno-Affluence* (New York: Free Press, 2000), p. 47: "[O]ne of the great benefits of wealth and technology [dollars and science] is that they give us the resources and the knowledge to preserve our forests, our rivers, and our wildlife."

46. George Gilder, *The Spirit of Enterprise* (New York: Simon & Schuster, 1984), pp. 74–91.

47. R. Emmett Tyrrell Jr., *The Liberal Crack-Up* (New York: Simon & Schuster, 1984), p. 82. In support of the market fix, see also William Simon, *A Time for Truth* (New York: Berkley, 1978), pp. 81–92, but esp. p. 81: "[T]he intelligent Republican free enterpriser knows exactly how to solve the energy crisis. He knows he should deregulate the tortured productive system; drop price controls, destructive bans, and crippling subsidies; and let exploration and production rip with the profit motive as guide, allowing prices to find their true market level."

48. Simon, *The Ultimate Resource*, p. 71 (emphasis supplied).

49. Ibid., p. 56 (emphasis supplied). See also David Frum, *How We Got Here: The '70s, The Decade that Brought You Modern Life—For Better or Worse* (New York: Basic Books, 2000), p. 161: "It was true that Africa immediately south of the Sahara [Mali, Ethiopia] ... suffered a terrible famine in 1974–1975. But as with most famines, people starved because of malign politics, rather than an absolute shortage of food.... More than sufficient stocks of food existed to save all the victims of crop failure if, and this was the crucial if, the governments of the starving did not impede the delivery of the food for reasons of their own."

50. Historians sometimes promote what they call the Cleopatra's Nose theory of historical causation. (See Daniel J. Boorstin, *Cleopatra's Nose: Essays on the Unexpected* [New York: Vintage, 1995], pp. ix–x.) This theory suggests that crucial events are often driven by, for instance, how Cleopatra's beauty captivated Mark Antony and what serious consequences that entailed. Social scientists are more familiar with chance occurrences being predicted by Murphy's Law, which states that *if* something *can* go wrong, it *will*.

51. William Bennett, *The Index of Leading Cultural Indicators: Facts and Figures on the State of American Society* (New York: Touchstone, 1994), p. 116. See also Patrick F. Fagan, *Why Religion Matters: The Impact of Religious Practice on Social Stability* (Washington, DC: Heritage Foundation, 1996).

52. Friedman and Friedman, *Free to Choose*, pp. 1–2 (emphasis is in the original).

53. Mitchell and Simmons, *Beyond Politics*, p. 43.

54. I refer here to most American conservatives after the Goldwater campaign of 1964. Earlier American conservatives, such as George Santayana, Russell Kirk, Richard Weaver, and Peter Viereck, were likely to endorse Burke's organic vision. On the earlier sort of American conservatism, see Allen Guttmann, *The Conservative Tradition in America* (New York: Oxford University Press, 1967).

55. Walton, *One Nation Under God,* p. xii.

56. Dick DeVos, *Rediscovering American Values: Foundations of Our Freedom for the 21st Century* (New York: Dutton, 1997), p. 292.

57. Simon, *A Time for Truth,* p. 237.

58. Irving Kristol, "What Is 'Social Justice'? [1976]," in Irving Kristol, *Neoconservatism: The Autobiography of an Idea* (New York: Free Press, 1995), p. 254.

59. Meyer, "Consensus and Divergence," in *What Is Conservatism?* ed. Frank Meyer (New York: Holt, Rinehart, and Winston, 1964), p. 230.

60. Barry Goldwater, "Acceptance Speech," in Goldwater, *Where I Stand* (New York: McGraw-Hill, 1964), pp. 14–15.

61. George Roche, *One by One: Preserving Values and Freedom in Heartland America* (Hillsdale, MI: Hillsdale College Press, 1990), pp. 14–16.

62. Lawrence Kudlow, *American Abundance: The New Economic and Moral Prosperity* (New York: Forbes, 1997), p. 172.

63. Harvey C. Mansfield Jr., *America's Constitutional Soul* (Baltimore: Johns Hopkins University Press, 1991), p. 86.

64. Alan Keyes, *Our Character, Our Future: Reclaiming America's Moral Destiny* (Grand Rapids, MI: Zondervan, 1996), p. 34.

65. Stuart Butler and Anna Kondratas, *Out of the Poverty Trap: A Conservative Strategy of Welfare Reform* (New York: Free Press, 1987), p. 56.

66. Reed, *Politically Incorrect,* p. 229.

67. David Horowitz, *The Art of Political War and Other Radical Pursuits* (Dallas: Spence, 2000), p. 37.

68. Rush Limbaugh, *The Way Things Ought to Be* (New York: Pocket Books, 1994), p. 207.

69. To this effect, conservatives may quote Harlan's dissent, which appears in *Plessy v. Ferguson,* 163 U.S. 537 (1896). (For example, see Terry Eastland, *Ending Affirmative Action: The Case for Colorblind Justice* [New York: Basic Books, 1997], pp. 27–28.) They do not publicize Harlan's explanation for why he favored "color-blind" justice. As Harlan said in the same dissent, "The white race deems itself to be the dominant race in this country. And so it is, in prestige, in achievements, in education, in wealth, and in power. So, I doubt not, it will continue to be for all time, if it remains true to its great heritage and holds fast to the principles of constitutional liberty." In other words, Harlan recommended applying "the principles of constitutional liberty" neutrally because he thought doing so would help whites to continue to dominate blacks socially and economically.

70. Right-wingers sometimes describe Martin Luther King Jr. as a great civil rights leader because, they say, he sought "color-blind" social justice in America. See Dinesh D'Souza, *What's So Great About America* (Washington, DC: Regnery, 2002), pp. 121–122; David Horowitz, *Hating Whitey and Other Progressive Causes* (Dallas: Spence, 1999), p. 69; and Lynne V. Cheney, *Telling the Truth: Why Our Culture and Our Country Have Stopped Making Sense—And What We Can Do About It* (New York: Touchstone, 1995), p. 138. This is a selective view of King, focused on his early opposition to de jure segregation—as in his "I Have a Dream Speech" in 1963—and overlooking his later

insistence, such as in Memphis where he was murdered, on affirmative action measures designed to overcome the results of de facto segregation.

71. On Johnson's speech as a turning point, see Stephan Thernstrom and Abigail Thernstrom, *America in Black and White: One Nation, Indivisible* (New York: Touchstone, 1999), p. 172; Eastland, *Ending Affirmative Action,* pp. 39–40; and Roberts and Stratton, *The New Color Line,* p. 101.

72. This historical evolution is outlined in Roberts and Stratton, "Progress Redefined," in *The New Color Line,* pp. 13–20.

73. Eastland, *Ending Affirmative Action,* p. 158.

74. Michael Sandel, "The Procedural Republic and the Unencumbered Self," *Political Theory* (February 1984): 81–96.

75. John Rawls, *A Theory of Justice: Original Edition* (1971; Cambridge, MA: Harvard University Press, 2005), pp. 118–194.

76. Sandel criticized Rawls as one sort of liberal against another, in an academic debate over the relative merits of what scholars then called "individualism" and "communitarianism." See Shlomo Avineri and Avner de Shalit, eds., *Communitarianism and Individualism* (Oxford: Oxford University Press, 1992).

77. This message underlies their entire book. See Richard J. Herrnstein and Charles Murray, *The Bell Curve: Intelligence and Class Structure in American Life* (New York: Free Press, 1994).

78. Ibid., p. 315.

79. Buckley, for example, grew up on a forty-seven-acre estate in Sharon, Connecticut, where governesses taught him to speak French and Spanish. On the governesses and other child-centered projects in the Buckley family, see John B. Judis, *William Buckley: Patron Saint of the Conservatives* (New York: Simon & Schuster, 1988), pp. 30–31. On what is likely to happen to children who inherit fewer advantages, see Annette Lareau, *Unequal Childhoods: Class, Race, and Family Life* (Berkeley: University of California Press, 2003).

80. William J. Bennett, *The De-Valuing of America: The Fight for Our Culture and Our Children* (New York: Summit, 1992), p. 145. He also recommends expelling drug addicts from school, p. 101.

81. Milton Friedman, *Capitalism and Freedom* (Chicago: University of Chicago Press, 1962), p. 13.

82. Nash, *Poverty and Wealth,* pp. 63–64.

83. George Roche, *America By the Throat: The Stranglehold of Federal Bureaucracy* (Hillsdale, MI: Hillsdale College Press, 1985), p. 74.

84. Limbaugh, *The Way Things Ought to Be,* p. 26.

85. Bork, *Slouching Towards Gommorah,* pp. 68, 80.

86. D'Souza, *The Virtue of Prosperity,* pp. 71–72. D'Souza did not foresee that, in 2005, Hurricane Katrina would kill some people in New Orleans because they owned not even a Hyundai in which to flee the city.

87. Fred Block, *Postindustrial Possibilities: A Critique of Economic Discourse* (Berkeley: University of California Press, 1990), p. 79.

88. Irving Kristol, "The Cultural Revolution and the Capitalist Future [1992]," in Kristol, *Neoconservatism,* p. 124. In contrast to Kristol's view, see the hypothetical case described in Tom Slee, *No One Makes You Shop at Wal-Mart: The Surprising Deceptions of Individual Choice* (Toronto: Between the Lines, 2006), pp. 201–202. A woman, Slee says, goes for a walk in the countryside and falls into an abandoned mineshaft from

which, on her own, she cannot escape. A day and a night pass before someone comes by and hears her cries for help. He offers to pull her up for $10,000 and sends down, for her signature, a contract to that effect. In real life, this exchange would be condemned as "exploitation" even though both sides "consent" to it.

89. Economists may overlook these. Thus Stanley Lebergott, *Pursuing Happiness: American Consumers in the Twentieth Century* (Princeton, NJ: Princeton University Press, 1993), pp. 32–33, argues that large income differentials translate into only small differences in the consumption of commodities such as food (e.g., the "top 15 percent of American families consumed not 15 percent of the nation's food, but 22 percent"). On the basis of such calculations, Lebergott says that consumption and not income is "the issue." (For a right-wing argument along these lines, see W. Michael Cox and Richard Alm, "You Are What You Spend," *New York Times,* February 10, 2008, "Week in Review," p. 14.) He thereby relegates to insignificance the fact that rich people acquire more income than poor people, whereupon saving part of that income adds up to acquiring wealth and the things that wealth can buy. For example, income gaps—and consequently wealth disparities—are very large between American blacks and whites. See Dalton Conley, *Being Black, Living in the Red: Race, Wealth and Social Policy in America* (Berkeley: University of California Press, 1999), pp. 156–157, but esp. p. 1: "If I could cite one statistic that inspired this book, it would be the following: in 1994, the median white family held assets worth more than seven times those of the median nonwhite family."

90. The influence of wealth-holders on policy-making is discussed in John. P. McCormick, "Contain the Wealthy and Patrol the Magistrates: Restoring Elite Accountability to Popular Government," *American Political Science Review* (May 2006): 147–163. See also Martin Gilens, "Inequality and Democratic Responsiveness," *Public Opinion Quarterly* (Special Issue, 2005): 778–796, and Nolan McCarty, Keith T. Poole, and Howard Rosenthal, *Polarized America: The Dance of Ideology and Unequal Riches* (Cambridge, MA: MIT Press, 2006).

91. Simon, *The Ultimate Resource,* pp. 270–271.

92. See Michael Walzer, *Spheres of Justice: A Defense of Pluralism and Equality* (New York: Basic Books, 1983).

93. For an example of single proposition analysis, see Friedman and Friedman, *Free to Choose,* p. 27: "The scientist seeking to advance the frontiers of his discipline, the missionary seeking to convert infidels to the true faith, the philanthropist seeking to bring comfort to the needy—all are pursuing their interests, as they see them, as they judge them by their own values." Walzer would argue that such people may have different vocations, different motivations, different values—that is, different standards of justice. For the Friedmans, they all act out of "self-interest."

94. On "blocked exchanges," see Walzer, *Spheres of Justice,* pp. 100–103.

95. Television particularly impairs our sense of which things should remain in separate spheres of real-life justice. Two classic studies of television's power on this score are Postman, *Amusing Ourselves to Death,* and Joshua Meyrowitz, *No Sense of Place: The Impact of Electronic Media on Social Behavior* (New York: Oxford University Press, 1985). Postman argues that television, in pursuit of ratings, emphasizes the entertainment value of activities that should provoke contemplation, and Meyrowitz argues that watching events on television robs us of the emotional messages and value judgments that emerge when people together experience various human undertakings in physical settings as different as factories, cemeteries, stadiums, theaters, churches, and battlefields.

96. For an example of political analysis that rejects individualism and emphasizes the commanding power of groups and organizations such as realtors and homeowners, chambers of commerce, professional and scientific societies, industrial associations, labor unions, and more, see Frances Fox Piven and Richard A. Cloward, *The Breaking of the American Social Compact* (New York: New Press, 1997), esp. pp. 277–281.

97. Milton and Rose Friedman, *Tyranny of the Status Quo* (New York: Harcourt Brace Jovanovich, 1984), p. 121.

98. Kristol, "Business and the 'New Class' [1975]," in Kristol, *Neoconservatism,* p. 208.

99. See Irving Kristol, "Pornography, Obscenity, and the Case for Censorship [1971]," in Irving Kristol, *On the Democratic Idea in America* (New York: Harper & Row, 1972), pp. 31–47.

100. Newt Gingrich, *To Renew America* (New York: HarperCollins, 1995), p. 8.

101. Melvyn Krauss, *How Nations Grow Rich: The Case for Free Trade* (New York: Oxford University Press, 1997), p. 53.

102. This incident is recalled when the "Marines' Hymn" says that "[f]rom the halls of Montezuma [Mexico] to the shores of Tripoli [Libya], we fight our country's battles in the air, on land, and sea."

103. Wanniski, *The Way the World Works,* p. 67.

104. Patrick J. Buchanan, *The Death of the West: How Dying Populations and Immigrant Invasions Imperil Our Country and Our Civilization* (New York: St. Martin's Press, 2002), pp. 38–39.

105. See also Simon, *The Ultimate Resource.* Simon relies on economic rather than scientific reasoning to argue that it doesn't matter how many people live on the earth. The more people there will be, the more their technology will pollute. But, as Simon says, the economist "asks about the *optimal* level of pollution. How much cleanliness are we willing to pay for?" p. 129 (emphasis supplied). Here is an approach that rejects the notion that there are ecological red lines, discovered by science, that should not be crossed by human preferences.

106. For example, conservatives are likely to praise Adam Smith's *The Wealth of Nations* (1776) as offering, in their view, an accurate analysis of market-driven behavior by individuals. But right-wing books say little or nothing about patterns of human behavior displayed by many people together and explored by, for example, Gustave LeBon, *The Crowd: A Study of the Popular Mind* (1895; New York: Macmillan, 1938); Robert Michels, *Political Parties: A Sociological Study of the Oligarchical Tendencies of Modern Democracy* (1914; New York: Collier, 1962); Sigmund Freud, *Group Psychology and the Analysis of the Ego* (New York: Boni and Liveright, 1920); Jules Henry, *Culture Against Man* (New York: Vintage, 1963); John Kenneth Galbraith, *The Affluent Society* (New York: Mentor, 1958); Mancur Olson, *The Logic of Collective Action: Public Goods and the Theory of Groups* (Cambridge, MA: Harvard University Press, 1965); Tibor Scitovsky, *The Joyless Economy: An Inquiry Into Human Satisfaction and Consumer Dissatisfaction* (New York: Oxford University Press, 1976); Fred Hirsch, *The Social Limits to Growth* (Cambridge, MA: Harvard University Press, 1978); Paul Wachtel, *The Poverty of Affluence: A Psychological Portrait of the American Way of Life* (New York: Free Press, 1988); Barry Schwartz, *The Costs of Living: How Market Freedom Erodes the Best Things in Life* (New York: Norton, 1994); Juliet Schor, *Do Americans Shop Too Much?* (Boston: Beacon, 2000); Robert J. Shiller, *Irrational Exuberance* (Princeton, NJ: Princeton University Press, 2000); David Myers, *The American Paradox: Spiritual Hunger in an Age of Plenty*

(New Haven, CT: Yale University Press, 2001); Robert Lane, *The Loss of Happiness in Market Democracies* (New Haven, CT: Yale University Press, 2001).

107. Tom Rose, *Economics: Principles and Policy From a Christian Perspective* (Milford, MI: Mott Media).

108. Tom Rose, *Economics: The American Economy from a Christian Perspective* (Mercer, PA: American Enterprise).

109. On macro and micro, see also Gertrude Himmelfarb, *One Nation, Two Cultures* (New York: Knopf, 1999), p. 79: "In denigrating the state, we ... risk attenuating the idea of citizenship." Himmelfarb makes this point because she concedes, uneasily, that conservatives do often denigrate the state, in which case between doing that and aspiring to vibrant citizenship there are serious trade-offs. But Himmelfarb does not examine those trade-offs, and they can be analyzed adequately only by exploring the relationship between macro procedures (the state) *and* micro routines (individualism).

110. Friedman, *Capitalism and Freedom,* pp. 13–14.

111. Nash, *Poverty and Wealth,* p. 14.

112. Roche, *One by One,* p. 135.

113. Kristol, "Capitalism, Socialism, and Nihilism [1973]," in Kristol, *Neoconservatism,* p. 97. He continues in order to explain that environmentalists and "the consumer protection movement" want to remake society according to their lights, instead of accepting "the kind of civilization that common men create when they are given the power, which a market economy does uniquely give them, to shape the world in which they wish to live," pp. 97–98. There again is the image of a macroeconomy—the world—shaped by "common men" via individual trades and exchanges, without reference to group actors such as nations, tribes, unions, corporations, churches, political parties, and more.

114. For example, Roger E. Meiners and Roger LeRoy Miller, *Gridlock in Government: How to Break the Stagnation of America* (Washington, DC: Free Congress Foundation, 1992), p. 67: "[John F.] Kennedy was off the mark; what he should have said [in his inaugural address] was: *Ask not what your country can do for you or what you can do for your country. Do what is best for you and your family and the rest will take care of itself*" (emphasis is in the original). Robert Heilbroner and William Milberg, *The Crisis of Vision in Modern Economic Thought* (New York: Cambridge University Press, 1995), pp. 64–67, explores the failure of economists to explain fully how macroeconomics and microeconomics are linked. See also Schwartz, *The Paradox of Choice.* Schwartz criticizes right-wing thinking about the desirability of creating ever-larger "free markets" (macro life). Thus he explains, as a psychologist and on the basis of research into human behavior (micro life), that "the fact that *some* choice is good doesn't necessarily mean that *more* choice is better," p. 3. In fact, says Schwartz, people feel overwhelmed when they are confronted by too many choices, such as when on a local supermarket's shelves they see 285 kinds of cookies, 116 kinds of skin cream, 175 salad dressings, and 64 kinds of barbecue sauce, pp. 9–10.

Chapter Three

1. Russell Kirk, foreword to R. Q. Armington and William D. Ellis, *More: The Rediscovery of American Common Sense* (Chicago: Regnery, 1984), p. 10.

2. Rus Walton, *One Nation Under God* (Washington: DC: Third Century, 1975), p. 204.

3. Grover G. Norquist, *Rock the House* (Ft. Lauderdale, FL: VYTIS, 1995), p. 46.

4. David Horowitz, *The Politics of Bad Faith: the Radical Assault on America's Future* (New York: Touchstone, 1998), pp. 17–18.

5. Dick Armey, *The Freedom Revolution* (Washington, DC: Regnery, 1995), p. 89.

6. Bill O'Reilly, *The No Spin Zone: Confrontations with the Powerful and Famous in America* (New York: Broadway, 2001), p. 110.

7. Larry Burkett, *The Coming Economic Earthquake,* rev. ed. (Chicago: Moody, 1994), p. 25.

8. George Roche, *A World Without Heroes: The Modern Tragedy* (Hillsdale, MI: Hillsdale College Press, 1987), p. 62.

9. John Ankerberg, "The Battle for the Heart and Mind of America," in Hal Lindsey, John Ankerberg, Henry Morris, Chuck Missler, Don McAlvany, *Steeling the Mind of America,* ed. Bill Perkins (Green Forest, AR: New Leaf, 1995), p. 18.

10. William J. Bennett, *The De-Valuing of America: The Fight for Our Culture and Our Children* (New York: Summit, 1992), p. 12.

11. Steve Forbes, "The Moral Basis of a Free Society," *Policy Review* (November–December 1997): 23. He then tells several anecdotes, one about an eighteen-year-old girl giving birth in the powder room at a senior prom, then throwing the child away in a plastic bag before returning to the dance floor, and another about a fifteen-year-old boy sold "by his mother to a drug dealer to cover a $1,000 cocaine debt."

12. The prevalence of anecdotes in right-wing writings on families is noted by Sara Diamond, *Not By Politics Alone: The Enduring Influence of the Christian Right* (New York: Guilford, 1998), pp. 117–120.

13. This story appears in Garry Wills, *Reagan's America* (New York: Penguin, 1988), pp. 199–210.

14. For criticism of Reagan's stories, see Mark Green and Gail MacColl, *There He Goes Again: Ronald Reagan's Reign of Error* (New York: Pantheon, 1983).

15. See Wills, *Reagan's America,* p. 458: "When I asked a group of American businessmen assembled abroad what they thought of Reagan's claim to have photographed the death camps, they supported the President for expressing a 'higher truth' of concern for the persecuted. Heads nodded when one executive's wife said, 'Even Jesus spoke in parables.'" For conservative confirmation of this point, see Dinesh D'Souza, *Ronald Reagan: How an Ordinary Man Became an Extraordinary Leader* (New York: Touchstone, 1997), p. 53: Reagan's "stories were 'morality tales,' and the particular incident at hand was only an illustration of a broader theme. As he [Reagan] saw it, just because this or that particular detail might be erroneous did not mean that the moral of the story was invalid."

16. For a morality tale of this sort, see also Michael Tanner, "Ending Welfare as We Know It," in *Toward Liberty: The Idea that Is Changing the World,* ed. David Boaz (Washington, DC: Cato Institute, 2002), p. 114: "It [government welfare] is a system in which illiterate homeless people with mental illnesses are handed 17-page forms to fill out, women nine months pregnant are told to verify their pregnancies, a woman who is raped is told she is ineligible for benefits because she can't list the baby's father on the required form."

17. Midge Decter, *Liberal Parents, Radical Children* (New York: Coward, McCann & Geoghegan, 1975), p. 37.

18. Milton and Rose Friedman, *Tyranny of the Status Quo* (New York: Harcourt, Brace, Jovanovich, 1984), p. 164.

19. Armey, *The Freedom Revolution,* p. 245.

20. Limbaugh, *See, I Told You So* (New York: Pocket Books, 1993), p. 189.

21. Phyllis Schlafly and Chester Ward, *The Gravediggers* (Alton, IL: Pere Marquette Press, 1964), p. 42.

22. John Ankerberg and John Weldon, *The Myth of Safe Sex: The Devastating Consequences of Violating God's Plan* (Chicago: Moody, 1993), p. 44.

23. Irving Kristol, "Human Nature and Social Reform," in *The Essential Neoconservative Reader,* ed. Mark Gerson (New York: Addison-Wesley, 1996), p. 210.

24. Patrick J. Buchanan, *The Death of the West: How Dying Populations and Immigrant Invasions Imperil Our Country and Our Civilization* (New York: St. Martin's Press, 2002), p. 183.

25. William A. Donohue, *The New Freedom: Individualism and Collectivism in the Social Lives of Americans* (New Brunswick, NJ: Transaction, 1990), p. 236.

26. Bennett, *The De-Valuing of America,* pp. 204–205.

27. Roche, *A World Without Heroes,* p. 57.

28. Jerry Falwell, *The New American Family* (Dallas: Word, 1992), p. 96.

29. Ronald Reagan, *Abortion and the Conscience of the Nation* (New York: Thomas Nelson, 1984), p. 35.

30. Harold O. J. Brown, *The Reconstruction of the Republic* (Milford, MI: Mott Media, 1981), p. 221.

31. Randall A. Terry, *Operation Rescue* (Springdale, PA: Whitaker House, 1988), p. 20.

32. John W. Whitehead, *The Stealing of America* (Westchester, IL: Crossway, 1983), p. 50.

33. Michael Medved, *Hollywood vs. America* (New York: Harper Perennial, 1992), p. 41.

34. Irving Kristol, *Two Cheers for Capitalism* (New York: Mentor, 1978), p. 128.

35. Gertrude Himmelfarb, *On Looking into the Abyss: Untimely Thoughts on Culture and Society* (New York: Knopf, 1994), p. 104.

36. Pat Buchanan, *Conservative Votes, Liberal Victories: Why the Right Has Failed* (New York: Quadrangle, 1975), p. 30.

37. Jude Wanniski, *The Way the World Works* (New York: Touchstone, 1978), p. 94.

38. Irving Kristol, "Utopianism: Ancient and Modern [1973]," in Irving Kristol, ed., *Neoconservatism: The Autobiography of an Idea* (New York: Free Press, 1995), p. 194.

39. On what might be called "rat race" discontent, see psychologist Tim Kasser, *The High Price of Materialism* (Cambridge, MA: MIT Press, 2002), esp. p. 43: "Before Silicon Graphics, [Jim] Clark [founder of Netscape] said a fortune of $10 million would make him happy; before Netscape, $100 million; before Healtheon, a billion; now, he told [Michael] Lewis, 'Once I have more money than Larry Ellison, I'll be satisfied.' Ellison, the founder of the software company Oracle, is worth $13 billion."

40. George F. Will, *Restoration: Congress, Term Limits, and the Recovery of Deliberate Democracy* (New York: Free Press, 1996), p. 9.

41. Some survey findings that relate to this decline are described in Gary Orren, "Fall from Grace: The Public's Loss of Faith in Government," in *Why People Don't Trust*

Government, ed. Joseph S. Nye Jr., Philip D. Zelnikow, and David C. King (Cambridge, MA: Harvard University Press, 1997), pp. 77–107.

42. Myron Magnet, *The Dream and the Nightmare: The Sixties Legacy to the Underclass* (New York: William Morrow, 1993), p. 167.

43. Armey, *The Freedom Revolution,* p. 242.

44. Friedman and Friedman, *Tyranny of the Status Quo,* p. 133.

45. Bennett, *The De-Valuing of America,* p. 55.

46. William Bennett, *Our Children, Our Country* (New York: Touchstone, 1988), pp. 61–62.

47. Armey, *The Freedom Revolution,* p. 195.

48. When conservatives say that school expenditures do not match educational performance, they tend to cite overall, or average, figures for many schools and many children. This means that various sorts of expenditures are lumped together, including what it costs to hire inner-city guards who contribute to security but not reading proficiency. This tack is taken by, for example, Chester E. Finn Jr., *We Must Take Charge: Our Schools and Our Future* (New York: Free Press, 1991), pp. 36–37. Alternatively, Jonathan Kozol claims that when specific rather than average expenditures are considered, it is clear that some schools, mostly private or suburban, outspend inner-city public schools, provide better plant and instructional facilities, conduct smaller classes, and send a higher percentage of their seniors to colleges and universities. See Jonathan Kozol, *Savage Inequalities: Children in America's Schools* (New York: Crown, 1991).

49. Falwell, *The New American Family,* p. 80.

50. William Dannemeyer, *Shadow in the Land: Homosexuality in America* (San Francisco: Ignatius, 1989), p. 158.

51. Ankerberg, "The Battle for the Heart and Mind of America," p. 24.

52. Donohue, *The New Freedom,* p. 112.

53. This is the major message in Medved, *Hollywood vs. America.*

54. Burkett, *Whatever Happened to the American Dream?* p. 259.

55. Brown, *The Reconstruction of the Republic,* p. 132.

56. Ankerberg and Weldon, *The Myth of Safe Sex,* p. 23.

57. Thomas A. Lane, *The Breakdown of the Old Politics* (New Rochelle, NY: Arlington House, 1974), pp. 179–180.

58. Against multiculturalism, see Dinesh D'Souza, *Illiberal Education: The Politics of Race and Sex on Campus* (New York: Vintage, 1992), and Allan Bloom, *The Closing of the American Mind: How Higher Education Has Failed Democracy and Impoverished the Souls of Today's Students* (New York: Touchstone, 1987).

59. Aaron Wildavsky, "Richer Is Safer," *Public Interest* (Summer 1980): 23–39.

60. Armey, *The Freedom Revolution,* pp. 214–215.

61. See Thomas Byrne Edsall and Mary D. Edsall, *Chain Reaction: The Impact of Race, Rights, and Taxes on American Politics* (New York: Norton, 1991); Dan T. Carter, *The Politics of Rage: George Wallace, the Origins of the New Conservatism, and the Transformation of American Politics* (Baton Rouge: Louisiana State University, 1995); and Kevin M. Kruse, *White Flight: Atlanta and the Making of Modern Conservatism* (Princeton, NJ: Princeton University Press, 2007).

62. *Report of the National Advisory Commission on Civil Disorders* (New York: Bantam, 1968), p. 203.

63. See Jeffrey Bell, *Populism and Elitism: Politics in the Age of Equality* (Washington, DC: Regnery, 1992), p. 131: "One milestone [to what Bell calls 'powerful political and

journalistic elites' accepting left-wing views of American society] was appointment of the Kerner Commission on urban rioting, which was to assign the blame for the riots to 'white racism'—in effect, to American culture as a whole." See also Stephan Thernstrom, Fred Siegel, and Robert Woodson Sr., *The Kerner Commission Report and the Failed Legacy of Liberal Social Policy* (Washington, DC: Heritage Foundation, 1998), Heritage Lectures, no. 619.

64. Charles Murray, *Losing Ground: American Social Policy, 1950–1980* (New York: Basic Books, 1984), p. 32.

65. Stephan Thernstrom and Abigail Thernstrom, *America in Black and White: One Nation, Indivisible* (New York: Touchstone, 1999).

66. Ibid., pp. 204–213.

67. Lane, *The Breakdown of the Old Politics*, p. 118.

68. David Horowitz, *Hating Whitey and Other Progressive Causes* (Dallas: Spence, 1999), pp. 38–39.

69. Dinesh D'Souza, *The End of Racism: Principles for a Multiracial Society* (New York: Free Press, 1995), p. 208.

70. Dinesh D'Souza, *What's So Great About America* (Washington, DC: Regnery, 2002), p. 118. Thus classical racism is expressed by such people as Joseph Arthur de Gobineau, Friedrich Nietzsche, Richard Wagner, and, of course, Adolf Hitler. D'Souza mentions these four in *The End of Racism*, p. 63.

71. D'Souza, *The End of Racism*, p. 27. The full definition sets a high threshold. See ibid., p. 28: "In order to be a racist, you must first believe in the existence of biologically distinguishable groups or races. Second, you must rank these races in terms of superiority and inferiority. Third, you must hold these rankings to be intrinsic or innate. Finally, you typically seek to use them as the basis for discrimination, segregation, or the denial of rights extended to other human beings." On such grounds, Americans who resemble television's Archie Bunker are not sufficiently rigorous in their thinking to be judged "racist."

72. Thernstrom and Thernstrom, *America in Black and White*, p. 500.

73. Limbaugh, *See, I Told You So*, pp. 272–273.

74. An argument to this effect runs through Michael K. Brown, Martin Carnoy, Elliott Currie, Troy Duster, David B. Oppenheimer, Marjorie M. Schultz, and David Wellman, *Whitewashing Race: The Myth of a Color-Blind Society* (Berkeley: University of California Press, 2003).

75. Robert W. Whitaker, foreword to *The New Right Papers*, ed. Robert W. Whitaker (New York: St. Martin's Press, 1985), pp. ix–xi. The same reasoning informs Thernstrom and Thernstrom, *America in Black and White*, p. 500. Kruse, *White Flight*, describes the political impact of this idea during recent decades in and around Atlanta.

76. For example, Marvin Olasky, *Compassionate Conservatism: What It Is, What It Does, and How It Can Transform America* (New York: Free Press, 2000), passim.

77. Consequently, Thernstrom and Thernstrom, *America in Black and White*, pp. 420–422, recommend that most African-American students will enroll in second- and third-tier colleges and universities. For similar reasons, Linda Chavez, *An Unlikely Conservative: The Transformation of an Ex-Liberal (Or, How I Became the Most Hated Hispanic in America)* (New York: Basic Books, 2002), pp. 54–86, opposes affirmative action for Hispanics.

78. Edward C. Banfield, *The Unheavenly City Revisited* (Boston: Little, Brown, 1974),

p. 56. This is a reprint, with some additional introductory material, of *The Unheavenly City: The Nature and Future of Our Urban Crisis* (Boston: Little, Brown, 1970).

79. Ibid., pp. 61–62.

80. Ibid., p. 63.

81. A classic example of the liberal view appears in William Ryan, *Blaming the Victim* (New York: Pantheon, 1971).

82. D'Souza, *The End of Racism,* p. 260. When D'Souza writes about crime (for example, pp. 260–267), he means violent crimes such as robbery, murder, rape, and aggravated assault, all covered in Uniform Crime Reports published by the Federal Bureau of Investigation. The same is true for Thernstrom and Thernstrom, *America in Black and White,* pp. 258–285, and for James Q. Wilson and Richard J. Herrnstein, *Crime and Human Nature* (New York: Simon & Schuster, 1985), passim, but esp. pp. 22–23, 31–33. This means that conservatives tend to leave out of their work acts not appearing in the Uniform Crime Reports, that is, white-collar crimes including embezzlement, food adulteration, environmental pollution, bribery, price fixing, stock market swindles, and various kinds of fraud. Such crimes, as in the savings-and-loan scandal and cases such as Enron and WorldCom and Bernard Madoff's Ponzi scheme, are more likely to be committed by people who are not poor and therefore more likely to be white than black. In fact, white-collar crimes are nationwide more costly, and generate more violence, such as workplace and pollution deaths, than what are commonly known as violent crimes. For information and opinions on crimes missing from the conservative view, see Jeffrey Reiman, *The Rich Get Richer and the Poor Get Prison: Ideology, Crime, and Criminal Justice,* 4th ed. (Boston: Allyn and Bacon, 1995), and Katherine Beckett and Theodore Sasson, *The Politics of Injustice: Crime and Punishment in America* (Thousand Oaks, CA: Sage, 2004).

83. See Thernstrom and Thernstrom, *America in Black and White,* pp. 232–285, 348–422.

84. George Gilder, *Wealth and Poverty* (New York: Basic Books, 1981), pp. 90–93.

85. D'Souza, *The End of Racism,* esp. pp. 245–287.

86. The complaints listed here appear in books by Dinesh D'Souza, Charles Murray, George Gilder, Stephan and Abigail Thernstrom, Thomas Sowell, Gertrude Himmelfarb, and Richard Brookhiser.

87. Thernstrom and Thernstrom, *America in Black and White,* p. 223.

88. See ibid., p. 387, and Terry Eastland, *Ending Affirmative Action: The Case for Colorblind Justice* (New York: Basic Books, 1997), p. 87. The argument is rejected by Beverly Daniel Tatum, *"Why Are Black Kids Sitting Together in the Cafeteria?": A Psychologist Explains the Development of Racial Identity,* rev. ed. (New York: Basic Books, 2003).

89. D'Souza, *Illiberal Education,* pp. 240–241.

90. D'Souza, *The End of Racism,* pp. 286–287.

91. Ibid., p. 287.

92. Nathan Glazer praises Irving Kristol for using almost no footnotes in his voluminous writings. As Glazer says, "This is a style that has powerfully advanced certain ideas. More cautious and modulated statements would never have gotten so far. The ideas have, on the whole, been right and have contributed significantly to making the world of ideas in the 1990s radically different from that in the 1950s and 1960s." See Glazer, "A Man Without Footnotes," in *The Neoconservative Imagination: Essays in Honor of*

Irving Kristol, ed. Christopher DeMuth and William Kristol (Washington, DC: American Enterprise Institute, 1995), p. 11. At stake here are considerations going back to Plato, who warned that rhetorical techniques deployed by men known as sophists might be so effective as to enable well-crafted arguments to triumph over true ideas advanced by opponents less skilled in debate. Glazer isn't worried about that happening in Kristol's case because he thinks Kristol has, "on the whole, been right," by which he means correct.

93. Various reverse sequences—concerning poverty, inequality, education, welfare, and religiosity—appear in Arthur C. Brooks, *Who Really Cares: The Surprising Truth About Compassionate Conservatism: America's Charity Divide—Who Gives, Who Doesn't, and Why It Matters* (New York: Basic Books, 2006).

94. Robert H. Bork, *The Tempting of America: The Political Seduction of the Law* (New York: Touchstone, 1991), pp. 136–137.

95. Banfield, *The Unheavenly City Revisited,* p. 97.

96. Rush Limbaugh, *The Way Things Ought to Be* (New York: Pocket Books, 1994), p. 255.

97. Buchanan, *Conservative Votes, Liberal Victories,* p. 43.

98. Paul Craig Roberts, *The Supply-Side Revolution: An Insider's Account of Policymaking in Washington* (Cambridge, MA: Harvard University Press, 1984), p. 53.

99. Joshua Muravchik, "An Anti-Communist Manifesto," in *Second Thoughts: Former Radicals Look Back at the Sixties,* ed. Peter Collier and David Horowitz (New York: Madison Books, 1989), p. 229.

100. Rael and Erich Isaac, *The Coercive Utopians: Social Deception by America's Power Players* (Chicago: Regnery, 1983), p. 3.

101. Phil Kent, *The Dark Side of Liberalism: Unchaining the Truth* (Augusta, GA: Harbor House, 2003), p. 115.

102. Limbaugh, *The Way Things Ought to Be,* p. 118.

103. Bob Grant, *Let's Be Heard* (New York: Pocket Books, 1996), p. 224.

104. William Simon, "A Tribute to Irving Kristol," in DeMuth and Kristol, *The Neoconservative Imagination,* p. 86.

105. R. Emmett Tyrrell, introduction to *Orthodoxy: The American Spectator's 20th Anniversary Anthology,* ed. Emmett Tyrrell (New York: Harper & Row, 1987), p. ix.

106. Norman Podhoretz, "Second Thoughts: A Generational Perspective," in Collier and Horowitz, eds., *Second Thoughts,* p. 193.

107. Robert H. Bork, *Slouching Towards Gomorrah: Modern Liberalism and American Decline* (New York: Regan, 1996), p. 17.

108. Donohue, *The New Freedom,* p. 175.

109. The last three in this list are from M. Stanton Evans, *Clear and Present Dangers: A Conservative View of America's Government* (New York: Harcourt, Brace, Jovanovich, 1975), p. 2.

110. In his *Reason to Believe* (New York: Touchstone, 1995), former New York governor Mario Cuomo, an obvious liberal, criticizes at length Newt Gingrich and Dick Armey, *Contract with America* (New York: Times Books, 1994). I think few readers will find in Cuomo's book evidence that its author hates America. See also Dan Savage, *Skipping Towards Gomorrah: The Seven Deadly Sins and the Pursuit of Happiness in America* (New York: Plume, 2003), p. 263: "I'm a patriot. [Savage is also a Democrat, sex-advice columnist, and gay man.] On September 11, I didn't blame America; I blamed bin Laden. And while I may love this country for different reasons from the scolds and virtucrats, I do love this country. I love the separation of church and state, for starters;

I love the First Amendment; I love the 'pursuit of happiness' stuff in the Declaration of Independence—and I've always loved New York City."

111. Ann Coulter, *Slander: Liberal Lies About the American Right* (New York: Crown, 2002), pp. 5–6.

112. Ann Coulter, *Treason: Liberal Treachery from the Cold War to the War on Terrorism* (New York: Crown Forum, 2003), p. 203.

113. Ibid., p. 16 (emphasis supplied).

114. John W. Kingdon, *Agendas, Alternatives, and Public Policies,* 2nd ed. (New York: HarperCollins, 1995).

115. For example, Charles Murray, in *Losing Ground* (1984) argues that welfare payments are the chief cause of poor women's bearing children but preferring not to marry. Alternatively, Frank Levy, *Dollars and Dreams: The Changing American Income Distribution* (New York: Norton, 1988), pp. 189–190, describes how, from the mid-1960s to 1984, the number of single-mother families rose even while welfare payments were worth less and less in inflation-adjusted dollars. He concludes that it was not those dollars but a growing shortage of family-sustaining jobs for poor men that led to more single-mother families. That is, the real cause of immiseration was not welfare but a sputtering economic system [private property, free enterprise, globalization] that Murray does not blame.

116. See William J. Bennett, *The Index of Leading Cultural Indicators: Facts and Figures on the State of American Society* (New York: Touchstone, 1994), which ignores economic and environmental indices but describes crime and out-of-wedlock births as if both are caused entirely by bad character and weak volition.

117. Banfield, *The Unheavenly City Revisited,* p. 79.

118. Thernstrom and Thernstrom, *America in Black and White,* p. 256.

119. D'Souza, *What's So Great About America,* pp. 129–130.

120. D'Souza, *The End of Racism,* p. 436.

Chapter Four

1. Observers often note these tensions. Thus Peter Steinfels, *The Neo-Conservatives: The Men Who Are Changing America's Politics* (New York: Simon & Schuster, 1979), pp. 102–105; Alan Crawford, *Thunder on the Right: The "New Right" and the Politics of Resentment* (New York: Pantheon, 1980), pp. 220–224; and Godfrey Hodgson, *The World Turned Right Side Up: A History of the Conservative Ascendancy in America* (New York: Houghton Mifflin, 1996), pp. 312–315. See also Ray Nichols, "'Conservatism' and 'The Right' in America: Ideological Conflict, Categories and Language," *Journal of Political Ideologies* (October 1997): 239–257.

2. Therefore, American conservatives have a more difficult job of advocacy than old-time rightists like Edmund Burke. Burke could criticize revolutionaries in France while he, in England, wanted to preserve a social system of ranks and values dominated by landed aristocrats who rarely innovated. But conservatives in America must divert attention from the fact that they are not criticizing but defending the greatest revolutionaries of our age, the entrepreneurs and corporations who—unlike Burke's aristocrats—are constantly altering the conditions of American life, the people most responsible for unremitting social flux and the painful side of "creative destruction."

3. Problematic results caused by such innovations are discussed in Daniel Bell, *The Cultural Contradictions of Capitalism* (New York: Basic Books, 1976).

4. For example, Barry Bluestone and Bennett Harrison, introduction to *The Deindustrialization of America: Plant Closings, Community Abandonment, and the Dismantling of Basic Industry* (New York: Basic Books, 1982), pp. 3–21.

5. Harold O. J. Brown, *The Reconstruction of the Republic* (Milford, Michigan: Mott Media, 1981), p. 55.

6. Irving Kristol, "Utopianism, Ancient and Modern [1973]," in Irving Kristol, *Neoconservatism: The Autobiography of an Idea* (New York: Free Press, 1995), p. 195.

7. Thomas Fleming, "Old Rights and the New Right," in *The New Right Papers*, ed. Robert Whitaker (New York: St. Martin's Press, 1982), p. 200.

8. For a contribution of some traditionalists to this equation, with their suggestion of civil disobedience against Supreme Court decisions that sanction abortions, see essays by Robert H. Bork, Russell Hittinger, Hadley Arkes, Charles Colson, and Robert P. George in *The End of Democracy? The Celebrated "First Things" Debate with Arguments Pro and Con and "The Anatomy of a Controversy" by Richard John Neuhaus*, ed. Mitchell S. Muncy (Dallas: Spence, 1997), pp. 10–62.

9. Norman Mailer, *Why Are We At War?* (New York: Random House, 2003), p. 46.

10. Matthew 19:24.

11. The argument in this paragraph comes from Rus Walton, *One Nation Under God* (Washington, DC: Third Century, 1975). The quoted phrases are from pp. 137–138.

12. Walton uses this argument throughout ibid. See also M. Stanton Evans, *The Theme Is Freedom: Religion, Politics, and the American Tradition* (Washington, DC: Regnery, 1994), which interprets Western history as the unfolding of a Christianity that, by opposing pagan animism, freed men and women to exploit the world of nature via open and competitive markets.

13. Ronald H. Nash, *Poverty and Wealth: Why Socialism Doesn't Work* (Richardson, TX: Probe Books, 1986), p. 68.

14. Lawrence Kudlow, *American Abundance: The New Economic and Moral Prosperity* (New York: Forbes, 1997), p. 179.

15. Michael Novak, *The Spirit of Democratic Capitalism* (New York: Simon & Schuster, 1982), p. 121. Novak assumes that the "Judeo-Christian tradition" provides shared values that inspire Americans to behave well while pursuing personal gain. Alvin J. Schmidt agrees. See his *The Menace of Multiculturalism: Trojan Horse in America* (Westport, CT: Praeger, 1997), p. 8, note 7. See also Roberta Combs, "Historic Judeo-Christian Principles," in *Why I Am a Reagan Conservative*, ed. Michael K. Deaver (New York: HarperCollins, 2005), pp. 181–182.

16. George Roche, *A World Without Heroes: The Modern Tragedy* (Hillsdale, MI: Hillsdale College Press, 1987), p. 66.

17. Milton and Rose Friedman, *Free to Choose: A Personal Statement* (New York: Harcourt Brace, 1990), pp. 20–21.

18. George Gilder, *Wealth and Poverty* (New York: Basic Books, 1981), p. 68.

19. Robert H. Bork, *The Tempting of America: The Political Seduction of the Law* (New York: Touchstone, 1991), p. 95.

20. William J. Bennett, *The Index of Leading Social Indicators: Facts and Figures on the State of American Society* (New York: Touchstone, 1994), pp. 10–12.

21. For criticism of corporate power in the world, see David C. Korten, *When Corporations Rule the World* (West Hartford, CT: Kumarian Press, 1995); William Greider, *One World, Ready or Not: The Manic Logic of Global Capitalism* (New York: Touchstone,

1997); and Noreena Hertz, *The Silent Takeover: Global Capitalism and the Death of Democracy* (New York: Free Press, 2001).

22. For commentary on how advertising can overwhelm commendable instincts, see Susan Linn, *Consuming Kids: The Hostile Takeover of Childhood* (New York: New Press, 2004). See esp. pp. 38–39, where Linn discusses how merchants use ads to excite children about consumer products and then tell parents they are free to say no when their children ask for another toy or slice of pizza. Linn notes how saying no repeatedly to children may prevent parents from establishing the healthy ties of support, sympathy, confidence, and trust they would like to maintain with those children.

23. Richard John Neuhaus and Peter Berger, *To Empower People: The Role of Mediating Structures in Public Policy* (Washington, DC: American Enterprise Institute, 1977), p. 2.

24. Ibid.

25. Ibid., p. 3.

26. William J. Bennett, *The De-Valuing of America: The Fight for Our Culture and Our Children* (New York: Summit, 1992), p. 36.

27. Nash, *Poverty and Wealth,* p. 182.

28. Robert H. Bork, *Slouching Towards Gomorrah: Modern Liberalism and American Decline* (New York: Regan, 1996), pp. 328–329.

29. Stuart M. Butler and Anna Kondratas, *Out of the Poverty Trap: A Conservative Strategy of Welfare Reform* (New York: Free Press, 1987), p. 71.

30. Richard John Neuhaus and Peter Berger, "From *To Empower People: The Role of Mediating Structures in Public Policy,*" in *The Essential Conservative Reader,* ed. Mark Gerson (New York: Addison-Wesley, 1996), p. 216.

31. Jerry Falwell, *The New American Family* (Dallas: Word, 1992); Rick Santorum, *It Takes a Family: Conservatism and the Common Good* (Wilmington, DE: ISI, 2005); and Rebecca Hagelin, *Home Invasion: Protecting Your Family in a Culture That's Gone Stark Raving Mad* (Nashville: Nelson Current, 2005).

32. On the ability of work to shape the meaning of private life, see Richard Sennett, *The Corrosion of Character: The Personal Consequences of Work in the New Capitalism* (New York: Norton, 1998). See also William Julius Wilson, *When Work Disappears: The World of the New Urban Poor* (New York: Vintage, 1996).

33. For example, Bork, *Slouching Towards Gomorrah,* pp. 328–329, leaves unions out of his discussion of mediating institutions. When they do write about unions, conservative writers are mainly critical of them. (See Reed Larson, *Stranglehold: How Union Bosses Have Hijacked Our Government* [Ottawa, IL: Jameson, 1999], which recommends enacting state laws to make union organizing difficult.) Rightists may claim that organized workers insist on receiving a share of business income that is larger than what their productivity is worth to employers. (For example, James D. Gwartney and Richard L. Stroup, *What Everyone Should Know About Economics and Prosperity* [Midland, MI: Mackinac Center, 1993], p. 15.) This claim is challenged by scholars who hold that the share of a corporation's income that will go to workers rather than employers reflects not relative degrees of productivity but who controls how corporate profits are divided among stockholders, management, and workers. On this point, see Lucien Bebchuk, "The Growth of Executive Pay," *Oxford Review of Economic Policy* (Summer 2005): 282–303.

34. One early attempt at bridging was called "fusionism," which Frank Meyer defined as "reason operating within tradition." See his "Freedom, Tradition, Conservatism," in

What Is Conservatism? ed. Frank S. Meyer (New York: Holt, Rinehart, and Winston, 1964), p. 11. In the same volume, Stephen J. Tonsor showed that only mysticism can reconcile the two. See his "The Conservative Search for Identity," in ibid., p. 135: "Not only singular personalities, but history itself by slow conjunction unites the opposites which men so often find in contradiction. Providence, which has its own purposes, disposes, and wise men conform themselves to a world whose ordering was only partially theirs.... [Indeed] it is only through historical understanding, through action, and finally through faith in God's Providence that the reconciliation of opposites becomes possible."

35. Garry Wills, *Confessions of a Conservative* (New York: Doubleday, 1979), p. 55.

36. This point is variously phrased by conservatives. For example, see Grover G. Norquist, *Rock the House* (Fort Lauderdale, FL: VYTIS, 1995), p. 71: "The reason the Christian Right and the economic conservatives are not at each other's throats is that they both fit comfortably into the 'Leave Us Alone' coalition."

37. This denunciation appears in, among other places, "The Magazine's Credenda," *National Review*, November 19, 1955, p. 6.

38. While making this statement, Fierce was director of strategic planning for the Republican National Committee. He is quoted in Dan Baltz and Ronald Brownstein, *Storming the Gates: Protest Politics and the Republican Revival* (Boston: Little, Brown, 1996), p. 15.

39. James G. Watt, *The Courage of a Conservative* (New York: Simon & Schuster, 1985), p. 17.

40. Jack Kemp, *An American Renaissance: A Strategy for the 1980s* (Lake Wylie, SC: Robert E. Hopper and Associates, 1979), p. 2.

41. Thomas A. Lane, *The Breakdown of the Old Politics*, (New Rochelle, NY: Arlington House, 1974), p. 104. Against the Court, see also George F. Will, *The Woven Figure: Conservatism and America's Fabric, 1994–1997* (New York: Scribner, 1997), p. 49. Here, Will describes how Melissa Drexler, age eighteen, went to the women's restroom, gave birth, tossed the baby into a trash bin, where he expired, returned to her high school prom, and danced the night away. Will then asks, "Who taught Ms. Drexler to think, or not think, in a way that caused her to regard her newborn baby as disposable trash? Many people and things, no doubt.... However, foremost among the moral tutors who prepared Ms. Drexler to act as she did is the Supreme Court." By which, apparently, Will means that the Court's decision legalizing abortions in *Roe v. Wade* (1973) encouraged Drexler to throw away her baby.

42. Dick Armey, *The Freedom Revolution* (Washington, DC: Regnery, 1995), p. 316.

43. Bennett, *The De-Valuing of America*, p. 11.

44. From his first inaugural address, "Let Us Begin an Era of National Renewal," *New York Times*, January 21, 1981, p. B1.

45. Marvin Olasky, *Compassionate Conservatism: What It Is, What It Does, and How It Can Transform America* (New York: Free Press, 2000), p. 190.

46. Donald Lambro, *The Conscience of a Young Conservative* (New Rochelle, NY: Arlington House, 1976), p. 50. See also William P. Hoar, *Handouts and Pickpockets: Our Government Gone Berserk* (Lafayette, LA: Huntington House, 1996), pp. 15, 105: "Whatever the state possesses must come from the productive sector.... Individuals produce wealth; governments pilfer it."

47. Gilder, *Wealth and Poverty*, p. 45.

48. George Roche, *One by One: Preserving Values and Freedom in Heartland America* (Hillsdale, MI: Hillsdale College Press, 1990), p. 26.

49. Rush Limbaugh, *See, I Told You So* (New York: Pocket Books, 1993), p. 136.

50. Dinesh D'Souza, *The Virtue of Prosperity: Finding Values in an Age of Techno-Affluence* (New York: Free Press, 2000), p. 231.

51. Formally, Keynes insisted that economic growth is stimulated more by demand than by supply. On how Keynesianism was challenged by free market enthusiasts in America, see Mark Blyth, *Great Transformations: Economic Ideas and Institutional Change in the Twentieth Century* (New York: Cambridge University Press, 2002), esp. Chapter 5, "Disembedding Liberalism in the United States," pp. 152–201.

52. Larry Burkett, *The Coming Economic Earthquake*, rev. ed. (Chicago: Moody, 1994), p. 19.

53. Bob Grant, *Let's Be Heard* (New York: Pocket Books, 1996), p. 130.

54. Barry Goldwater, *The Conscience of a Conservative* (Shepherdsville, KY: Victor, 1960), p. 60.

55. William E. Simon, *A Time for Truth* (New York: Berkley, 1978), p. 98.

56. Armey, *The Freedom Revolution*, p. 18.

57. Anthony, *Vanishing Republic: How Can We Save the American Dream?* (Altamonte Springs, FL: Encore, 1995), p. 20.

58. Kent, *The Dark Side of Liberalism: Unchaining the Truth* (Augusta, GA: Harbor House, 2003), p. 112.

59. Jerry Falwell, *Listen, America!* (New York: Doubleday, 1980), p. 75, and Falwell, *The New American Family*, p. 111.

60. Limbaugh, *See, I Told You So*, p. 67.

61. Norquist, *Rock the House*, p. 36.

62. Jesse Helms, *When Free Men Shall Stand* (Grand Rapids, MI: Zondervan, 1976), p. 47.

63. Charlotte A. Twight, *Dependent on D.C.: The Rise of Federal Control Over the Lives of Ordinary Americans* (New York: Palgrave, 2002), p. 209.

64. Hoar, *Handouts and Pickpockets*, p. 166. James L. Payne, *The Culture of Spending: Why Congress Lives Beyond Our Means* (San Francisco: ICI, 1991), pp. 185–186, estimates that overhead costs amount to 65 cents for each tax dollar collected. (For example, if $1 billion is collected, the country also spent $650 million to collect it.) These costs, according to Payne, include the cost of running the IRS, enforcement costs, compliance costs, evasion costs, and emotional and moral costs.

65. For example, Midge Dector, *The New Chastity and Other Arguments Against Women's Liberation* (New York: Coward, McGann, and Geoghegan, 1972), and Harvey Mansfield, *Manliness* (New Haven, CT: Yale University Press, 2006).

66. Gingrich and Armey, *Contract with America*, p. 86. See also p. 15: "Burdensome government regulations stifle wages, economic growth levels are frustratingly below the post–World War II norm.... The result is that middle-class families are making their first home purchase later in life, scrambling to pay college tuition, and putting a second earner [the wife] in the market not to support the household but to support the cost of government."

67. Ralph Reed, *Politically Incorrect: The Emerging Faith Factor in American Politics* (Dallas: Word, 1994), p. 227.

68. Pat Robertson, *The New World Order* (Dallas: Word, 1991), p. 238.

69. Such costs are discussed in Elizabeth Warren, *The Two Income Trap: Why Middle-Class Mothers and Fathers Are Going Broke* (New York: Basic Books, 2003). See also Nancy Folbre, *The Invisible Heart: Economics and Family Values* (New York: New Press, 2001), and Ann Crittenden, *The Price of Motherhood: Why the Most Important Job in the World is Still the Least Valued* (New York: Metropolitan, 2001).

70. See Friedman and Friedman, *Free to Choose,* p. 142: "The members of the new class are in general among the highest paid persons in the community. And for many among them, preaching equality and promoting or administering the resulting legislation has proved an effective means of achieving such high incomes. All of us find it easy to identify our own welfare with the welfare of the community."

71. Irving Kristol, "Business and the New Class [1975]," in Kristol, *Neoconservatism,* p. 207.

72. Irving Kristol, "Corporate Capitalism in America [1975]," ibid., p. 221.

73. Charles Murray, *Losing Ground: American Social Policy, 1950–1980* (New York: Basic Books, 1984), p. 42.

74. Ibid., p. 43.

75. Bork, *The Tempting of America,* pp. 8, 18, et passim. Bork's original intent thesis is refuted by Supreme Court Justice David Souter, "Harvard Commencement Address" (May 27, 2010), at www.harvard.edu/gazette/story/2010/05/text-of-justice-david-souters-speech/.

76. Marvin Olasky, *The Tragedy of American Compassion* (Washington, DC: Regnery, 1992), esp. pp. 143–149.

77. Rael Isaac and Erich Isaac, *The Coercive Utopians: Social Deception by America's Power Players* (Chicago: Regnery, 1983), pp. 4–5.

78. John Ankerberg and John Weldon, *The Myth of Safe Sex: The Devastating Consequences of Violating God's Plan* (Chicago: Moody, 1993), p. 91.

79. William A. Donohue, *The Politics of the American Civil Liberties Union* (New Brunswick, NJ: Transaction, 1985), p. 327. See pp. 327–346, on the ACLU as a new class organization.

80. What sociologists might describe as a new class does not resemble what conservatives have in mind. For example, see Alvin Gouldner, *The Future of the Intellectuals and the Rise of the New Class: A Frame of Reference, Theses, Conjectures, Arguments, and an Historical Perspective on the Role of Intellectuals and Intelligentsia in the International Class Context of the Modern Era* (New York: Seabury, 1979).

81. Jeane Kirkpatrick, "Politics and the New Class," in *The New Class?* ed. B. Bruce-Briggs (New Brunswick, NJ: Transaction, 1979), p. 33.

82. On the role played in conservative politics by the new class concept, see Barbara Ehrenreich, *Fear of Falling: The Inner Life of the Middle Class* (New York: Pantheon, 1990), pp. 144–195. Lisa McGirr, *Suburban Warriors: The Origins of the New American Right* (Princeton, NJ: Princeton University Press, 2001), pp. 164–168, describes different sorts of conservatives attacking a common enemy. See also Paul Waldman, *Being Right Is Not Enough: What Progressives Must Learn from Conservative Success* (New York: John Wiley and Sons, 2006). After observing that factions on the right often disagree (p. 18), Waldman offers the following (p. 19): "What progressives should learn from Norquist [Grover Norquist, head of Americans for Tax Reform, who holds in Washington weekly strategy sessions on Wednesday mornings for right-wing activists, journalists, elected officials, and bureaucrats] isn't just the power of organization and coordination, as important as they are. More vital is the warrior spirit that animates Norquist and his allies.

They may sometimes believe that some Republican politician is or isn't their friend, but they never forget for an instant who their enemy is."

83. Bork, *Slouching Towards Gomorrah,* p. 51.

84. James Q. Wilson, *Thinking About Crime,* rev. ed. (New York: Basic Books, 1983), pp. 237–240.

85. Robert H. Bork, "Culture and Kristol," in *The Neoconservative Imagination: Essays in Honor of Irving Kristol,* ed. Christopher DeMuth and William Kristol (Washington, DC: American Enterprise Institute, 1995), p. 136.

86. Gertrude Himmelfarb, *The De-Moralization of Society: From Victorian Virtues to Modern Values* (New York: Vintage, 1995), esp. p. 224.

87. Charles Colson, *A Dance with Deception: Revealing the Truth Behind the Headlines* (Dallas: Word, 1993), pp. 17–18.

88. Richard A. Viguerie, *The New Right: We're Ready to Lead* (Falls Church, VA: Viguerie Company, 1980), p. 12.

89. James Burnham, *Suicide of the West: An Essay on the Meaning and Destiny of Liberalism* (New York: John Day, 1964), passim.

90. David Lebedoff, *The New Elite: The Death of Democracy* (New York: Franklin Watts, 1981), passim.

91. David Frum, *Dead Right* (New York: Basic Books, 1994), p. 5.

92. Gertrude Himmelfarb, *On Looking Into the Abyss: Untimely Thoughts on Culture and Society* (New York: Knopf, 1994), pp. 74–75.

93. Books by adults who inspired the counterculture include Herbert Marcuse, *One Dimensional Man: Studies in the Ideology of Advanced Industrial Society* (Boston: Beacon, 1962); Theodore Roszak, *The Making of a Counterculture: Reflections on the Technocratic Society and Its Youthful Opposition* (New York: Doubleday, 1969); Charles Reich, *The Greening of America* (New York: Random House, 1970); and Robert M. Pirseg, *Zen and the Art of Motorcycle Maintenance: An Inquiry into Values* (New York: Bantam, 1974).

94. The Woodstock music festival took place on a farm near Bethel, New York, August 15–17, 1969. For a conservative who links Woodstock to Clinton, see Reed, "Clinton Agonistes: Woodstock Goes to the White House," in *Politically Incorrect,* pp. 203–220.

95. Patrick J. Buchanan, *The Death of the West: How Dying Populations and Immigrant Invasions Imperil Our Country and Our Civilization* (New York: St. Martin's Press, 2002), pp. 11–49.

96. The quoted phrases in this paragraph are from Chuck Colson and Jack Eckerd, *Why America Doesn't Work* (Dallas: Word, 1991), pp. 3–47. Alternatively, see anthropologist Marvin Harris, *America Now: The Anthropology of a Changing Culture* (New York: Simon & Schuster, 1981). Harris says, in effect, that "nothing works" in America because of how capitalism [not liberalism or atheism or nihilism] has evolved beyond what it used to be. Accordingly, "when people change their way of making a living, unintended consequences are likely to be felt in a broad range of customs and institutions," pp. 11–12.

97. The verse is from Judges 17:6. The accusation comes from Falwell, *Listen, America!* p. 61, who complains that the 1970s were, culturally speaking, an extension of the 1960s.

98. All quotations in this paragraph come from Donohue, *The New Freedom,* pp. 39–59.

99. Harvey C. Mansfield Jr., *America's Constitutional Soul* (Baltimore: Johns Hopkins University Press, 1991), p. 23. In the light of Mansfield's enthusiasm for what he describes as Reagan's overthrow of counterculture values, one can appreciate how shocked conservatives were later by the apparently retrograde election of Bill Clinton, who, according to Buchanan, *The Death of the West,* p. 94, was a "paragon of the Woodstock generation."

100. Gertrude Himmelfarb, *One Nation, Two Cultures* (New York: Knopf, 1999), p. 18. Promoting persuasive correlations is the tactic here.

101. Newt Gingrich, *Window of Opportunity: A Blueprint for the Future* (New York: Tom Dougherty, 1984), pp. 56–57.

102. Burton Yale Pines, *Back to Basics: The Traditional Movement that Is Sweeping Grass-Roots America* (New York: William Morrow, 1982), pp. 25–27.

103. See Midge Decter, "A Letter to the Young (and to their parents) [1975]," in Gerson, ed., *The Essential Neoconservative Reader,* pp. 64–75. See also the essays in Midge Decter, *Liberal Parents, Radical Children* (New York: Coward, McCann, and Geoghegan, 1975).

104. Decter, *Liberal Parents, Radical Children,* p. 27.

105. Ibid., p. 31.

106. Ibid., p. 36.

107. Irving Kristol, "Countercultures [1994]," in Kristol, *Neoconservatism,* p. 136 (the emphasis is Kristol's).

108. Samuel P. Huntington, *American Politics: The Promise of Disharmony* (Cambridge, MA: Harvard University Press, 1981).

109. Ibid., p. 178.

110. Ibid., p. 214.

111. Conservatives also criticize multiculturalism in grade schools. For example, James C. Hefley, *Textbooks On Trial* (Wheaton, IL: SP Publications, 1976), and Mel and Norma Gabler, *What Are They Teaching Our Children?* (Wheaton, IL: Victor, 1985).

112. Francis J. Beckworth and Michael E. Bauman, eds., *Are You Politically Correct? Debating America's Cultural Standards* (Buffalo, NY: Prometheus, 1993), p. 11.

113. Roger Kimball, *Tenured Radicals: How Politics Has Corrupted Our Higher Education* (New York: HarperPerennial, 1990), p. 1.

114. Ibid., p. 201.

115. Dinesh D'Souza, *Illiberal Education: the Politics of Race and Sex on Campus* (New York: Vintage, 1992), p. 85.

116. Allan Bloom, *The Closing of the American Mind* (New York: Touchstone, 1987), p. 64.

117. Ibid., passim, argued at length in favor of placing "great books" at the center of university education.

118. Bennett, *The De-Valuing of America.*

119. D'Souza, *Illiberal Education.*

120. Kimball, *Tenured Radicals,* p. xiii. The quotation is from Matthew Arnold, *Culture and Anarchy* (1869; New Haven, CT: Yale University Press, 1996), p. 4. Citing Arnold on this point is a conservative staple. Thus Myron Magnet, *The Dream and the Nightmare: The Sixties' Legacy to the Underclass* (New York: William Morrow, 1993), p. 197, and William Bennett, *To Reclaim a Legacy: A Report on the Humanities in Higher Education* (Washington, DC: National Endowment for the Humanities, 1984),

p. 3. Neither Kimball nor the others explains who will decide what is "best" and on what grounds. If they could ask Arnold (1822–1888) that question, they might find his Victorian answer unsatisfactory.

121. Bloom, *The Closing of the American Mind,* p. 64.

122. William F. Buckley Jr., "Yale and Her Alumni," in *God and Man at Yale* (Chicago: Regnery, 1951), pp. 114–135. A similar argument is made in John Howard, "The Responsibility of College Trustees," *Policy Review* (Summer 1977): 71–79.

123. The message of Buckley's *God and Man at Yale* was that "new knowledge" in fields such as philosophy and economics might constitute not understanding but error, in which case Buckley concluded that those who pay the bills should intervene. For a 1941 case of such intervention, see "Appendix: How Bertrand Russell Was Prevented from Teaching at the College of the City of New York," in Bertrand Russell, *Why I Am Not a Christian,* ed. Paul Edwards (New York: Simon & Schuster, 1957), pp. 207–259.

124. Schmidt: *The Menace of Multiculturalism,* p. 3.

125. Grant, *Let's Be Heard,* p. 41. See also Daniel J. Flynn, *Why the Left Hates America: Exposing the Lies that Have Obscured Our Nation's Greatness* (Roseville, CA: Forum, 2002), p. 9: "Looking out America's window on the world beyond Western civilization ... [i]n Africa, one finds widespread female genital mutilation, race-based slavery, extreme poverty, land expropriation campaigns aimed at whites, and a paucity of rights. Democracy is absent from the entire Arab world. While self-government is nonexistent, one finds conversion by the sword, so-called honor killings, public enthusiasm for terrorism, and the veil in abundance. Parts of Asia boast dowry killings, forced abortions, and imprisonment for rape victims. Cultural sensitivity should not require us to don cultural blindfolds to ... [what happens] beyond our borders."

126. Kimball, *Tenured Radicals,* p. 206.

127. Flynn, *Why the Left Hates America,* p. 69.

128. Ibid., pp. 147–183.

129. Schmidt, *The Menace of Multiculturalism,* pp. 33–41.

130. Buchanan, *The Death of the West,* p. 58, and David Horowitz, *Hating Whitey and Other Progressive Causes* (Dallas: Spence, 1999), p. 10.

131. Flynn, *Why the Left Hates America,* p. 61.

132. O'Reilly, *The No Spin Zone: Confrontations with the Powerful and Famous in America* (New York: Broadway, 2001), p. 11. There is no footnote for this anecdote.

133. Colson, *A Dance with Deception,* p. 39.

134. James Q. Wilson, *The Moral Sense* (New York: Free Press, 1993), pp. 4–5.

135. Bloom, *The Closing of the American Mind,* p. 25.

136. Lofton, "The Media Attack on the Religious Right," in Howard Phillips, Paul Weyrich, Albion Knight, John Lofton, Richard Viguerie, Morton Blackwell, *The New Right at Harvard* (Vienna, VA: Conservative Caucus, 1983), pp. 84–86.

137. Dinesh D'Souza, *The End of Racism: Principles for a Multiracial Society* (New York: Free Press, 1995), p. 117.

138. Ibid., p. 155.

139. Ibid., p. 527.

140. James Hefley, *America—One Nation Under God* (Wheaton, IL: SP, 1975), pp. 2–83.

141. H. Edward Rowe, *Save America!* (Old Tappan, NJ: Fleming H. Revell, 1976), pp. 43–44.

142. Samuel Blumenfeld, "The Whole Language/OBE Fraud," in D. James Kennedy,

Gary Bauer, John Ashcroft, et al., *Reclaiming America for Christ* (Fort Lauderdale, FL: Coral Ridge Ministries, 1996), p. 192

143. Phyllis Schlafly, *The Power of the Positive Woman* (New Rochelle, NY: Arlington House, 1977), pp. 144–145.

144. John Ankerberg, "The Battle for the Heart and Mind of America," in Hal Lindsey, John Ankerberg, Henry Morris, Chuck Missler, Don McAlvany, *Steeling the Mind of America,* ed. Bill Perkins (Green Forest, AR: New Leaf, 1995), pp. 12–14.

145. Walton, *One Nation Under God,* p. 107. The reference is to Judges 17:6 or Judges 21:25.

146. Hefley, *America—One Nation Under God,* p. 39.

147. Ben Kinchlow, "Transforming America From the Inside Out," in Kennedy, Bauer, and Ashcroft, *Reclaiming American for Christ,* p. 92. The source of this anecdote is not indicated.

148. This because it is dominated by liberals. See Tammy Bruce, *The New American Revolution: How You Can Fight the Tyranny of the Left's Cultural and Moral Decay* (New York: William Morrow, 2005), and Kevin McCullough, *Musclehead Revolution: Overturning Liberalism with Commonsense Thinking* (New York: Harvest, 2006).

149. Joseph Schumpeter, *Capitalism, Socialism and Democracy,* 3rd. ed. (New York: Harper & Row, 1950), pp. 81–86.

150. Irving Kristol, "The Cultural Revolution and the Capitalist Future [1992]," in Kristol, *Neoconservatism,* p. 127: "It is not ... the economics [creative destruction] of capitalism that is our fundamental, unmanageable problem. That problem today is located in the culture of our society ... [in] an aggressive animus [by liberals] against the bourgeois society that is organically associated with our market economy." See also Ben Shapiro, *Porn Generation: How Social Liberalism Is Corrupting Our Future* (Washington, DC: Regnery, 2005), p. 10, and Dinesh D'Souza, *The Enemy at Home: The Cultural Left and Its Responsibility for 9/11* (New York: Doubleday, 2007), pp. 20–21.

151. On the missing commitment, see Colson, *A Dance with Deception,* p. 57: "When black students, women students, or Latino students refuse to even read the works of other people, what they are saying is that each group has its own truths—that there is no single, overarching, universal truth. But Christianity makes the bold claim that it is an overarching, universal truth—the truth about ultimate reality." See a similar view in Tammy Bruce, *The Death of Right and Wrong: Exposing the Left's Assault on Our Culture and Values* (New York: Three Rivers, 2003), p. 24: "The Left Elite's 'values' are ... that they have no values. Theirs is the standard of no standard. My friends on the Left even ask, What's the danger of a morally relative culture? After all, they argue, everything *is* relative."

152. Ernest van den Haag, "The Desolation of Reality," in *The Ambiguous Legacy of the Enlightenment,* ed. William A. Rusher (Lanham, MD: University Press of America, 1995), p. 77.

153. Thomas M. Nies, "Ethics and the Marketplace," in *Morality in the Marketplace,* ed. Michael Bauman (Hillsdale, MI: Hillsdale College Press, 1994), p. 60.

154. Michael Medved, *Hollywood vs. America* (New York: HarperPerennial, 1992), p. 89.

155. Falwell, *The New American Family,* p. 78.

156. John W. Whitehead, *The Stealing of America* (Westchester, IL: Crossway, 1983), p. 96.

157. Scott M. Huse, *The Collapse of Evolution,* 2nd ed. (Grand Rapids, MI: Baker

Book House, 1993), p. 125. See also D. James Kennedy, with Jerry Newcombe, *What If America Were a Christian Nation Again?* (Nashville: Nelson, 2003), p. 64: "Some eleven thousand courses are now being taught in American colleges about ethics, mostly by psychologists or academics, and virtually all of them are relativists. They are trying to do the impossible—teach morality without certainty and ethics without absolutes. It cannot be done, and the more classes they teach, the worse the situation."

158. This is the main theme in Richard Brookhiser, *The Way of the WASP: How It Made America, and How It Can Save It, So to Speak* (New York: Free Press, 1991). It also pervades Himmelfarb, *One Nation, Two Cultures.*

159. For example, see Frum, *Dead Right,* p. 96: "What are the bourgeois virtues anyway? The paramount ones are thrift, prudence, sobriety, fidelity, and orderliness.... They are the virtues that settled America ... and they are the virtues whose ebbing conservatives mourn." See also Kristol, "The Cultural Revolution and the Capitalist Future," p. 127: "[The bourgeois] virtues ... include a willingness to work hard to improve one's condition, a respect for law, an appreciation of the merits of deferred gratification, a deference toward traditional religions, a concern for family and community, and so on."

160. Newt Gingrich, *To Renew America* (New York: HarperCollins, 1995), p. 30: "The counterculture began to repudiate middle-class values—even though the creators of that counterculture were clearly middle class themselves."

161. Bork, *Slouching Towards Gomorrah,* p. 7: Universities, churches, foundations, the national press, Hollywood, parts of the Democratic Party and the judiciary are "institutions controlled by people [the new class] who view the world from a common perspective, a perspective not generally shared by the public at large." See also R. Emmett Tyrrell Jr., *The Liberal Crack-Up* (New York: Simon & Schuster, 1992), p. 33: "New Age Liberalism was in essence nothing more complicated or noble than a running argument with life as it was led by normal Americans.... [Liberals of the New Age] were out to bust up the joint, to make the bourgeoisie squeal."

162. Thus Congressman Henry J. Hyde, "The Importance of Transcendent Moral Values," in Deaver, ed., *Why I Am a Reagan Conservative,* p. 59: "I'm ... a conservative because I'm a great believer in the people and their wisdom.... I would much rather be ruled by the first two hundred names in the DuPage County phone book than by the faculty of the University of Chicago, intelligent as they may be. I believe there is an inherent sense of justice in the people." On the other hand, conservatives sometimes scorn choices made by the sum total of ordinary Americans—that is, "the people." This happened in 1997–1998 when opinion polls showed that a majority of Americans did not believe Bill Clinton should be impeached. At that point, William Bennett, *The Death of Outrage: Bill Clinton and the Assault on American Ideals* (New York: Free Press, 1998), found the president's continuing popularity outrageous.

Chapter Five

1. For example, James Q. Wilson, foreword to *The Essential Neoconservative Reader,* ed. Mark Gerson (New York: Addison-Wesley, 1996), p. ix: "What I am most struck by among my friends [the neoconservatives] ... is that they have great sympathy for and often take their cues from the general and settled convictions of the average American."

2. Jacob S. Hacker and Paul Pierson, *Off Center: The Republican Revolution and*

the Erosion of American Democracy (New Haven, CT: Yale University Press, 2006), pp. 15–18.

3. The complexity of investigating the conservatism-liberalism spectrum of citizens and voters is discussed and some of the latest social science theories and findings concerning that spectrum are described in Pietro S. Nivola and David W. Brady, eds., *Red and Blue Nation? Characteristics and Causes of America's Polarized Politics* (Washington, DC: Brookings Institution, 2006).

4. The point is made by James W. Ceaser, "Four Heads and One Hearth: The Modern Conservative Movement," in *The Future of Conservatism: Conflict and Consensus in the Post-Reagan Era,* ed. Charles W. Dunn (Wilmington, DE: ISI, 2007), p. 21: "I have heard it said humorously that contemporary American conservatism, known to be fraught with many serious internal tensions, is held together by two self-evident truths: [Congresswoman] Nancy Pelosi and [Senator] Barbara Boxer. If... these personal references are discarded, the general point still remains. Much of the unity that is found among conservatives today stems from their shared antipathy to liberalism, which serves as the common heart that beats in the breast of the conservative movement. Were liberalism ... to cease to exist tomorrow, conservatism as we know it would begin to break apart on the next day."

5. For example, William Buckley Jr. defines modern American conservatism as "a spirit of resistance to the twentieth century" in his "Did You Ever See a Dream Walking?" in *Keeping the Tablets: Modern American Conservative Thought,* ed. William F. Buckley and Charles R. Kessler (New York: Harper & Row, 1988), p. 33.

6. On resentment among modern American conservatives, see Jean Hardisty, *Mobilizing Resentment: Conservative Resurgence from the John Birch Society to the Promise Keepers* (Boston: Beacon, 1999). See also Lisa McGirr, *Suburban Warriors: The Origins of the New American Right* (Princeton, NJ: Princeton University Press, 2001), pp. 61–163.

7. Kevin Phillips, *The Emerging Republican Majority* (New Rochelle, NY: Arlington House, 1969), recommends that the Republican Party exploit resentment, especially in the South and in the Southwest. In a *Human Events* interview about his book, Phillips observes that "what you have [among potential Republican voters] is a social conservatism, I think, in the sense that the role of government in taxing the many for the benefit of the few—whether they be rich or poor—has gone too far. You've got a resentment of the expanding role of government in everyday life, a resentment of the attempts of certain aspects of the liberal community to make government into an all-powerful social planning establishment and regulatory body." This quotation appears in Sara Diamond, *Roads to Dominion: Right-Wing Movements and Political Power in the United States* (New York: Guilford, 1995), p. 115.

8. Burton Yale Pines, *Back to Basics: The Traditional Movement that Is Sweeping Grass-Roots America* (New York: William Morrow, 1982), p. 18. See also Tim LaHaye, "Help! We've Been Robbed!" in *Faith of Our Founding Fathers: A Comprehensive Study of America's Christian Foundations* (Green Forest, AR: Master, 1990), pp. 1–15.

9. Ralph Reed, *Politically Incorrect: The Emerging Faith Factor in American Politics* (Dallas: Word, 1994), p. 18.

10. James Q. Wilson, *The Moral Sense* (New York: Free Press, 1993), pp. viii, x, 12–13.

11. Terry Eastland, *Ending Affirmative Action: The Case for Colorblind Justice* (New York: Basic Books, 1997), p. 87.

12. Donald Lambro, *The Conscience of a Young Conservative* (New Rochelle, NY: Arlington House, 1976), p. 9.

13. Pat Buchanan, *Conservative Votes, Liberal Victories: Why the Right Has Failed* (New York: Quadrangle, 1975), p. 44.

14. Charles Murray, *Losing Ground: American Social Policy, 1950–1980* (New York: Basic Books, 1984), p. 146.

15. Clyde Wilson, "Citizens or Subjects?" in *The New Right Papers,* ed. Robert W. Whitaker (New York: St. Martin's Press, 1985), pp. 112–117.

16. See Daniel Bell, ed., *The Radical Right* (Garden City, NY: Doubleday, 1963), pp. 1–38, 87–134.

17. On this topic, see Joseph Schumpeter, *Capitalism, Socialism, and Democracy,* 3rd ed. (New York: Harper & Row, 1950), pp. 81–86.

18. There are subtleties at work here that anger those who feel downgraded. For example, see Donald E. Wildmon, *The Home Invaders* (Wheaton, IL: SP, 1986). Wildmon, then executive director of the National Federation for Decency, complains that Hollywood is flooding America with movies and television programs that belittle Christians and Christian values. Among many examples, he notes the *Saturday Night Live* episode that "featured Ethel, a Christian waitress whose favorite expression was 'The Lord works in mysterious ways.' At first, Ethel was told that her fiance had married another woman. Then she was told that her house had been destroyed, her mother and brother killed, and that she had only one week to live. Each time, Ethel responded 'That's all right. I should have expected it. The Lord works in mysterious ways.' The sketch suggested," says Wildman, "that Christians are unintelligent parrots and their God is cruel," pp. 67–68.

19. See Hardisty, *Mobilizing Resentment,* p. 10: "The negative effect of economic restructuring has caused large numbers of working and middle-class people to feel resentful and insecure. Such feelings are fertile ground for right-wing populism."

20. Irving Kristol, "The Shaking of the Foundations [1968]," in *On the Democratic Idea in America* (New York: Harper & Row, 1972), pp. 28–29.

21. Samuel T. Francis, "MESSAGE FROM MARs: The Social Politics of the New Right," in Whitaker, ed., *The New Right Papers,* p. 69.

22. Rush Limbaugh, *The Way Things Ought to Be* (New York: Pocket Books, 1993), p. 177.

23. On disenchantment, see Max Weber, "Science as a Vocation" (1922), in *From Max Weber: Essays in Sociology,* ed. H. H. Gerth and C. Wright Mills (New York: Oxford University Press, 1946), p. 155: "The fate of our times is characterized by rationalization and intellectualization and, above all, by the 'disenchantment of the world.'" See also p. 139.

24. For a classic scholarly description of the Enlightenment, see Peter Gay, *The Enlightenment: An Interpretation, Vol. II: The Science of Freedom* (New York: Knopf, 1969), p. 27: "The advance of knowledge ... [during the Enlightenment] meant the advance of reason. In the course of the eighteenth century, the world, at least the world of the literate, was being emptied of mystery. Pseudo science was giving way to science, credence in the miraculous intervention of divine forces was being corroded by the acid of skepticism and overpowered by scientific cosmology." For alternative characterizations of the Enlightenment, see Dorinda Outram, *The Enlightenment* (New York: Cambridge University Press, 1995).

25. See George Ritzer, *The McDonaldization of Society* (Thousand Oaks, CA: Pine Forge, 2000), esp. pp. 132–133.

26. The problem has many names. Against "secular humanism," see James Watt, *The Courage of a Conservative* (New York: Simon & Schuster, 1985), pp. 112–113. Against "situational ethics," see Rus Walton, *One Nation Under God* (Washington, DC: Third Century, 1975), p. 107. Against "nominalism," see Richard M. Weaver, *Ideas Have Consequences* (1948; Chicago: University of Chicago, 1984), pp. 3–6. Against "subjectivism," see Jerry Falwell, *The New American Family* (Dallas: Word, 1992), pp. 58–59. Against "presentism," see George Roche, *A World Without Heroes: The Modern Tragedy* (Hillsdale, MI: Hillsdale College Press, 1987), p. 86. Against "cultural relativism," see Wilson, *The Moral Sense,* p. 46. By whatever name, the problem is summed up in Chuck Colson and Jack Eckerd, *Why America Doesn't Work* (Dallas: Word, 1991), pp. 67–68: "Another legacy of the sixties [the counterculture] is a refusal to acknowledge any standards."

27. For example, Randall A. Terry, *Operation Rescue* (Springdale, PA: Whitaker House, 1988), passim, which recommends picketing and demonstrations outside abortion clinics.

28. Allan Bloom, *The Closing of the American Mind: How Higher Education Has Failed Democracy and Impoverished the Souls of Today's Students* (New York: Touchstone, 1987), expresses this fear.

29. The moral qualities of Western civilization are praised in Daniel J. Flynn, *Why the Left Hates America: Exposing the Lies that Have Obscured Our Nation's Greatness* (Roseville, CA: Forum, 2002), esp. pp. 9–11, 34–37. See also Alvin J. Schmidt, *The Menace of Multiculturalism: Trojan Horse in America* (Westport, CT: Praeger, 1997), pp. 33–41, and Patrick J. Buchanan, *The Death of the West: How Dying Populations and Immigrant Invasions Imperil Our Country and Our Civilization* (New York: St. Martin's Press, 2002), passim.

30. Harold O. J. Brown, *The Reconstruction of the Republic* (Milford, MI: Mott Media, 1981), p. 36.

31. Ibid., pp. 227–228.

32. For an example of what right-wingers are likely to resent, see Richard Rorty, *Objectivity, Relativism, and Truth: Philosophical Papers* (New York: Cambridge University Press, 1991), p. 193: "The encouragement of light-mindedness [Rorty's postmodern recipe for taking little interest in metaphysics and epistemology] about traditional philosophical topics serves the same purposes as does the encouragement of light-mindedness about traditional theological topics. Like the rise of large market economies, the increase in literacy, the proliferation of artistic genres, and the insouciant pluralism of contemporary culture, such philosophical superficiality and light-mindedness helps along *the disenchantment of the world.*" Emphasis supplied.

33. Stephen Carter, *The Culture of Disbelief: How American Law and Politics Trivialize Religious Devotion* (New York: Anchor, 1994), p. 24. Carter is not necessarily conservative on nonreligious issues.

34. William A. Donohue, *The New Freedom: Individualism and Collectivism in the Social Lives of Americans* (New Brunswick, NJ: Transaction, 1990), pp. 186–187, praises transcendental morality for helping people to resist evil. He illustrates the point with a query from philosopher Leon Kolakowski: "To put it crudely, shall we say that the difference between a vegetarian and a cannibal is just a matter of taste?"

35. Watt, *The Courage of a Conservative,* pp. 109–110. On the two "theories," see also Mel and Norma Gabler, *What Are They Teaching Our Children?* (Wheaton, IL:

Victor, 1985), p. 133: "Evolution and creation really are hypotheses, though we shall use the term 'theory' to describe both."

36. As in Walton, *One Nation Under God,* p. 115: "[E]ither drop the theory of evolution from the classroom, or give the story of creation equal time and equal weight."

37. Watt, *The Courage of a Conservative,* pp. 109–110.

38. This approach characterizes books like Caryl Matrisciana and Roger Oakland, *The Evolution Conspiracy* (Eugene, OR: Harvest House, 1991); Jonathan D. Sarfati, *Refuting Evolution: A Handbook for Students, Parents, and Teachers Countering the Latest Arguments for Evolution* (Green Forest, AR: Master, 1999); and Bruce Bickel and Stan Jantz, *Creation & Evolution 101: A Guide to Science and the Bible in Plain Language* (Eugene, OR: Harvest House, 2001).

39. Scott M. Huse, *The Collapse of Evolution* (Grand Rapids, MI: Baker, 1997), p. 54.

40. For the complete argument that America's Founders wanted to keep the state out of religion but also leave people of faith free to promote religious values in the public square, see David Barton, *The Myth of Separation: What Is the Correct Relationship Between Church and State?* (Aledo, TX: WallBuilder, 1989), and Dee Wampler, *The Myth of Separation Between Church and State,* 2nd ed. (Enumclaw, WA: WinePress, 2004).

41. See Falwell, *The New American Family,* p. 218: "Above all, give your support only to those candidates for office who are clearly and vocally committed to the Judeo-Christian values on which this nation was founded." See also John Warwick Montgomery, *The Shaping of America* (Minneapolis: Bethany Fellowship, 1976), p. 187: "What do you suppose the effect on the Supreme Court's abortion decision would have been if at least five committed Christian judges had been sitting on the bench?"

42. Carter, *The Culture of Disbelief,* p. 230: "What is needed, then, is a willingness to *listen,* not because the speaker has *the right voice* but because the speaker has *the right to speak.*" (A similar argument for placing Christmas symbols in public places, as if doing so would be a legitimate expression of free speech, is made by John Gibson, *The War On Christmas: How the Liberal Plot to Ban the Sacred Christian Holiday Is Worse than You Thought* [New York: Sentinel, 2005], pp. 161–163.) It sounds harmless to recommend that everyone should merely listen. However, the principle of separating churches and states assumes that if people have a right to propose religion-based policies—say, a national ban on gay marriages—then sooner or later something of what they propose may be enacted into law, in which case that law will seek to impose religious conformity precisely as the Founders hoped to avoid.

43. Jefferson's first reference to separation of church and state appears in "Letter to Danbury Baptist Association," January 1, 1802, in *Writings of Thomas Jefferson,* Monticello edition (Washington, DC: Thomas Jefferson Memorial Association, 1904–1905), vol. 16, pp. 281–282.

44. An exception was Edward Banfield, who taught me in graduate school. Banfield used to say that organizing society around markets is preferable to organizing it around piety, since dollar compromises are possible but differences of opinion over sacred values preclude concessions and are likely to provoke bloodshed. On this score, he used to quote Samuel Johnson (1709–1784) to the effect that a man is never so innocently employed as when he is making money.

45. Other effects may be regarded as exceptions. See Reed, *Politically Incorrect,* p. 55: "Every religion has fringe or criminal elements who commit horrible acts in the mistaken

name of their God. But those persons—the rioting Hindu in India or the violent Jew on the West Bank—are aberrations rather than exemplars of their religion."

46. John Wright, "God & Government: Restoring the Standard," in D. James Kennedy, Gary Bauer, John Ashcroft, et al., *Reclaiming American for Christ* (Fort Lauderdale, FL: Coral Ridge Ministries, 1996), p. 104.

47. Reed, *Politically Incorrect,* p. 7.

48. For some of the story, see Stephen Haynes, *Noah's Curse: The Biblical Justification of American Slavery* (New York: Oxford University Press, 2002). On the Southern Baptist Convention's eventual turn away from segregation, see Mark Newman, *Getting Right with God: Southern Baptists and Desegregation, 1945–1995* (Tuscaloosa: University of Alabama Press, 2001).

49. On how the Founders tried to keep religious dangers from spilling over into public life, see Jon Meacham, *American Gospel: God, the Founding Fathers, and the Making of a Nation* (New York: Random House, 2006), esp. pp. 3–113. For an argument that the Founders were more committed to religious principles than Meacham describes, see Newt Gingrich, *Winning the Future: A 21st Century Contract with America* (Washington, DC: Regnery, 2006), pp. 43–56. Gingrich says that "[t]he Bill of Rights was designed to protect freedom *of* religion not freedom *from* religion," p. 50. It follows that the Supreme Court should permit school boards to prescribe voluntary prayers in public schools.

50. Jerry Falwell, *Listen, America!* (Garden City, NY: Doubleday, 1980), pp. 23–124.

51. Falwell, *The New American Family,* pp. 31, 69–74.

52. Phyllis Schlafly, *The Power of the Positive Woman* (New Rochelle, NY: Arlington House, 1977), p. 59.

53. Donohue, *The New Freedom,* p. 151. David Frum, *Dead Right* (New York: Basic Books, 1994), p. 196, lists bourgeois virtues as including "thrift, diligence, prudence, sobriety, fidelity, and orderliness."

54. A challenge to this view of family history appears in Stephanie Coontz, *The Way We Never Were: American Families and the Nostalgia Trap* (New York: Basic Books, 1992).

55. Donohue, *The New Freedom,* p. 149. The same conference is criticized for slighting traditional families in Midge Decter, "Family," in Edwin J. Feulner Jr., *Leadership in America: The Principles of Conservatism* (Dallas: Spence, 2000), p. 112.

56. Ed Gillespie and Bob Schellhas, eds., *Contract with America: The Bold Plan by Rep. Newt Gingrich, Rep. Dick Armey and the House Republicans to Change the Nation* (New York: Times, 1994), esp. pp. 79–90.

57. Stuart M. Butler and Anna Kondratas, *Out of the Poverty Trap: A Conservative Strategy of Welfare Reform* (New York: Free Press, 1987), pp. 151–159.

58. Bryce J. Christensen, *Utopia Against the Family: The Problems and Politics of the American Family* (San Francisco: Ignatius, 1990), passim.

59. Donohue, *The New Freedom,* pp. 231–236.

60. William J. Bennett, *The Broken Hearth: Reversing the Moral Collapse of the American Family* (New York: Broadway, 2003), esp. pp. 180–183.

61. Rick Santorum, *It Takes a Family: Conservatism and the Common Good* (Wilmington, DE: ISI, 2005).

62. For Santorum's discussion of how to promote Putnam's social capital, see ibid., pp. 54–72.

63. In his *Bowling Alone: The Collapse and Revival of American Community*

(New York: Simon & Schuster, 2000), p. 283, Putnam estimates that "electronic entertainment—above all, television," accounts for "perhaps 25 percent of the [post–World War II] decline" in "civic engagement and social capital."

64. Johnson, foreword to Phillip E. Johnson, *The Right Questions: Truth, Meaning and Public Debate* (Downers Grove, IL: Intervarsity Press, 2002), p. 11.

65. Huse, *The Collapse of Evolution,* p. 3.

66. Johnson, *The Right Questions,* p. 70.

67. James Burnham, *Suicide of the West: An Essay on the Meaning and Destiny of Liberalism* (New York: John Day, 1964), p. 75.

68. Karl Popper, *The Logic of Scientific Discovery* (1936; New York: Routledge, 1992).

69. Thomas S. Kuhn , *The Structure of Scientific Revolutions,* 3rd ed. (1962; Chicago: University of Chicago Press, 1996).

70. The election of Republican majorities in the Senate and House in 1994 encouraged right-wing Republicans to challenge scientific findings—on global warming, on evolution, on stem cell research, and more—that might shape government policy. What happened is described in Chris Mooney, *The Republican War on Science,* rev. ed. (New York: Basic Books, 2005), pp. 65–76.

71. William F. Buckley Jr., *Up from Liberalism* (New York: Stein & Day, 1984), p. 142.

72. George F. Will, *Restoration: Congress, Term Limits, and the Recovery of Deliberative Democracy* (New York: Free Press, 1996), p. 141. For an alternative view, see Harold Meyerson, "The Speaker in Charge," *Washington Post,* August 1, 2007, p. A17, where Speaker of the House Nancy Pelosi (D-CA) anticipates Republican arguments concerning the Iraq War: "The plural of anecdote is not data.... I'm very concerned they'll pass off anecdotal successes as progress in Iraq."

73. John Ashcroft, *On My Honor: The Beliefs that Shape My Life* (Nashville: Thomas Nelson, 2001), pp. 128–129.

74. Thus the story, probably not historically accurate, that Galileo, after publicly denying in 1633 the heliocentric theory of Copernicus, muttered under his breath that, regardless of his audible orthodoxy, the earth *does* move.

75. David G. Myers, *The American Paradox: Spiritual Hunger in an Age of Plenty* (New Haven, CT: Yale University Press, 2000), p. xiii.

76. Robert H. Nelson, *Economics as Religion: From Samuelson to Chicago and Beyond* (University Park: Pennsylvania State University Press, 2001), and Duncan K. Foley, *Adam's Fallacy: A Guide to Economic Theology* (Cambridge, MA: Harvard University Press, 2006).

77. Harvey Cox, "The Market as God," *Atlantic Monthly,* March 1999, p. 18.

78. George Charles Roche, *The Bewildered Society* (Hillsdale, MI: Hillsdale College Press, 1974), p. 253.

79. The point is made in Irving Kristol, "Capitalism, Socialism, and Nihilism [1973]," in Irving Kristol, *Neoconservatism: The Autobiography of an Idea* (New York: Free Press, 1995), pp. 94–95: "One of the keystones of modern economic thought is that it is impossible to have an *a priori* knowledge of what constitutes happiness for other people; that such knowledge is incorporated in an individual's 'utility schedule'; and [that] this knowledge, in turn, is revealed by the choices the individual makes in a free market."

80. Dinesh D'Souza, *The Virtue of Prosperity: Finding Values in an Age of Techno-Affluence* (New York: Free Press, 2000), p. 108.

81. George Gilder, *Wealth and Poverty* (New York: Basic Books, 1981), p. 63.

82. Quoted in John Ord Tipple, *Crisis of the American Dream: A History of American Social Thought, 1920–1940* (New York: Pegasus, 1968), pp. 136–137.

83. See especially Milton Friedman, *Capitalism and Freedom* (Chicago: University of Chicago Press, 1962).

84. See Jude Wanniski, *The Way the World Works* (New York: Touchstone, 1978).

85. See Michael Novak, *The Spirit of Democratic Capitalism* (New York: Simon & Schuster, 1982).

86. See George Gilder, *The Spirit of Enterprise* (New York: Simon & Schuster, 1984).

87. Tammy Bruce, *The Death of Right and Wrong: Exposing the Left's Assault on Our Culture and Values* (New York: Three Rivers, 2003), p. 232.

88. John Ankerberg and John Weldon, *The Myth of Safe Sex: The Devastating Consequences of Violating God's Plan* (Chicago: Moody, 1993), p. 94

89. Ibid., p. 95.

90. For the claim that mass media organizations behave badly because left-wingers dominate media management circles, see Bruce, *The Death of Right and Wrong,* pp. 229–260. For an alternative view, see James T. Hamilton, *Channeling Violence: The Economic Market for Violent Television Programming* (Princeton, NJ: Princeton University Press, 2000).

91. George Hansen, *To Harass Our People: The IRS and Government Abuse of Power* (Washington, DC: Positive Publications, 1984), p. 167.

92. Pines, *Back to Basics,* p. 82.

93. Butler and Kondratas, *Out of the Poverty Trap,* p. 227.

94. Barbara Ehrenreich, *Nickled and Dimed: On (Not) Getting By in America* (New York: Metropolitan Books, 2001). See also Katherine S. Neuman, *No Shame in My Game: The Working Poor in the Inner City* (New York: Knopf and the Russell Sage Foundation, 1999).

95. John E. Schwartz and Thomas J. Volgy, *The Forgotten Americans: Thirty Million Working Poor in the Land of Opportunity* (New York: Norton, 1993).

96. Robert Kuttner, ed., *Making Work Pay: America After Welfare* (New York: New Press, 2002), esp. p. 25: "According to a 'Job Gap' report published by the Northwest Policy Center at the University of Washington, the state's living wage, defined as the amount that allows a family to meet basic needs without resorting to public assistance, is $11.07 an hour for a single adult and $14.75 for a single adult with two children. According to the Northwest Policy Center, 37 percent of the jobs in the state pay less than the former and 73 percent pay less than the latter."

97. Chester E. Finn, *We Must Take Charge: Our Schools and Our Future* (New York: Free Press, 1991), p. xiv.

98. On America replicating itself, see Jules Henry, *Culture Against Man* (New York: Vintage, 1963), p. 48: "In order for our economy to continue in its present form people must learn [in school and at home] to be fuzzy-minded and impulsive, for if they were clear-headed and deliberate they would rarely put their hands in their pockets; or, if they did, they would leave them there. If we were all logicians the economy could not survive, and herein lies a terrifying paradox; for in order to exist economically as we are we must try by might and main to remain stupid."

99. Richard A. Viguerie, *The New Right: We're Ready to Lead* (Falls Church, VA: Viguerie Company, 1980), pp. 171–172.

100. Falwell, *The New American Family,* p. 117.

101. Wilhelm Ropke, *Economics of the Free Society* (1937; Chicago: Regnery, 1963), pp. 231–232, 250–251.

102. Jesse Helms, *When Free Men Shall Stand* (Grand Rapids, MI: Zondervan, 1976), p. 77.

103. Ibid., pp. 32–33.

104. Donohue, *The New Freedom,* p. 224.

105. Irving Kristol, "Horatio Alger and Profits," in Irving Kristol, *Two Cheers for Capitalism* (New York: Mentor, 1978), p. 80.

106. Rush Limbaugh, *The Way Things Ought to Be* (New York: Pocket Books, 1994), p. 48.

107. Alternatively, some of the ways in which capitalists falter morally in the real world are described in books such as Paul Blumberg, *The Predatory Society: Deception in the American Marketplace* (New York: Oxford University Press, 1989), and Ralph Estes, *Tyranny of the Bottom Line: Why Corporations Make Good People Do Bad Things* (San Francisco: Berrett-Koehler, 1996).

108. Charles E. Lindblom, *Politics and Markets: The World's Political Economic Systems* (New York: Basic Books, 1977), p. 356: "The large private corporation [by size, wealth, and power] fits oddly into democratic theory and vision. Indeed, it does not fit."

109. Furthermore, conservatives condemned Lindblom's book at length. See the essays in Robert Hesson, ed., *Does Big Business Rule America? Critical Commentaries on Charles E. Lindblom's 'Politics and Markets'* (Washington, DC: Ethics and Public Policy Center, 1981).

110. Milton and Rose Friedman, *Free to Choose: A Personal Statement* (1979; New York: Harcourt Brace, 1990), p. 20.

111. Robert Hesson, *In Defense of the Corporation* (Stanford, CA: Hoover Institution Press, 1979), pp. 3–46. See esp. p. 46, where Hesson says that "anyone who proposes to deny or destroy the rights of a corporation is really attacking individual rights."

112. William J. Bennett, *Our Children and Our Country* (New York: Touchstone, 1988), passim.

113. On corporations acting badly in global markets, see John Perkins, *Confessions of an Economic Hit Man* (San Francisco: Berrett-Koehler, 2004). On a corporation trying to do business there virtuously but succeeding only partially, see Karl Schoenberger, *Levi's Children: Coming to Terms With Human Rights in the Global Marketplace* (New York: Atlantic Monthly Press, 2000). The reference is to Levi Strauss & Company.

114. John Ankerberg, "The Battle for the Heart and Mind of America," in Hal Lindsay, John Ankerberg, Henry Morris, Chuck Missler, Don McAlvany, *Steeling the Mind of America,* ed. Bill Perkins (Green Forest, AR: New Leaf, 1995), p. 25.

115. Friedman and Friedman, *Free to Choose,* p. 224. Alternatively, one may argue that modern economies thrive only when producers provoke endless desires rather than fulfill natural needs, which are, after all, limited. For example, see William Leach, *Land of Desire: Merchants, Power, and the Rise of a New American Culture* (New York: Vintage, 1993).

116. Ronald H. Nash, *Social Justice and the Christian Church* (Fenton, MI: Mott Media, 1983), p. 128.

117. Finn, *We Must Take Charge,* p. 198. For a less reassuring view of how ads affect children, see Susan Linn, *Consuming Kids: Protecting our Children from the Onslaught of Marketing and Advertising* (New York: Anchor, 2005), esp. pp. 95–104, on marketing

fattening foods to children, and pp. 157–174, on marketing alcohol and tobacco to children.

118. Novak, *The Spirit of Democratic Capitalism,* p. 107.

119. Roche, *The Bewildered Society,* p. 255.

120. See Sut Jhally, "Advertising as Religion: The Dialectic of Technology and Magic," in *Cultural Politics in America,* ed. Ian Angus and Sut Jhally (New York: Routledge, 1989), pp. 221–224.

121. On reason yielding to marketing assaults, see Naomi Wolf, *The Beauty Myth: How Images of Beauty Are Used Against Women* (New York: Anchor, 1992), and Juliet Schor, *The Overspent American: Upscaling, Downshifting, and the New Consumer* (New York: Basic Books, 1998).

122. Galbraith, "The Dependence Effect," in *The Affluent Society* (1958; New York: Mentor, 1963), pp. 124–130.

123. For an indication of how much producers believe it pays for them to market even ordinary commodities possessing no unique qualities—what advertisers call "parity items"—see Walter LaFeber, *Michael Jordan and the New Global Capitalism* (New York: Norton, 1999), p. 107: "Michael Jordan's $20-million endorsement fee [for Nike shoes] was higher than the combined yearly payrolls of the Indonesian plants that made the [Nike] shoes."

124. For example, Irving Kristol, "Business and the New Class [1975]," in Kristol, *Neoconservatism,* p. 216: "John Kenneth Galbraith's notion that the large corporation simply manipulates its market through the power of advertising and fixes the price level with sovereign authority is a wild exaggeration."

125. This sort of reasoning can be found in Roche, *The Bewildered Society,* p. 265; Ropke, *Economics of the Free Society,* p. 237; John Chamberlain, *The Roots of Capitalism* (Indianapolis: Liberty, 1959), p. 221; and G. Warren Nutter, *Political Economy and Freedom: A Collection of Essays* (Indianapolis: Liberty, 1983), p. 24.

126. John G. Tower, *A Program for Conservatives* (New York: MacFadden-Bartell, 1962), p. 13.

127. George Roche, *One By One: Preserving Values and Freedom in Heartland America* (Hillsdale, MI: Hillsdale College Press, 1990), p. 195.

128. Irving Kristol, "Business and the 'New Class' [1975]," in Kristol, *Neoconservatism,* p. 208. Conservatives do not always claim that "common people" can exercise independence of mind. For example, Stephen Powers, David J. Rothman, and Stanley Rothman, *Hollywood's America: Social and Political Themes in Motion Pictures* (Boulder, CO: Westview, 1996), passim, complains that moviegoers are duped by liberal moviemakers into watching bad films even though, according to the theory of consumer sovereignty, citizens are capable of deciding what they want and have chosen to see those films rather than pay for entertainment that Powers, Rothman, and Rothman regard as more wholesome.

129. Falwell, *Listen, America!* pp. 253–254.

130. Bork, *Slouching Towards Gomorrah,* pp. 139–140.

131. Friedrich Hayek, *The Road to Serfdom* (Chicago: University of Chicago Press, 1957), pp. 122–130.

132. Friedman and Friedman, *Free to Choose,* pp. 63–64. The Friedmans do not describe how English government officials, like those they praise, enforced laissez-faire marketing rules in India and caused perhaps 5 million deaths there in 1877–1878. See Mike Davis, "Victoria's Ghosts," in *Late Victorian Holocausts: El Nino Famines and the*

Making of the Third World (New York: Verso, 2001), pp. 25–59, on famine striking India late in the 1870s. At that time, Britain's colonial government insisted on free trade and, instead of keeping food in India, encouraged exports of grain from there to the United Kingdom in the belief that profits in world markets would somehow finance an adequate diet for poor Indians.

133. W. Michael Cox and Richard Alm, *Myths of Rich and Poor: Why We're Better Off than We Think* (New York: Basic Books, 1999), pp. 111, 132–137.

134. Novak, *The Spirit of Democratic Capitalism,* p. 27. Along these lines, see also Burton W. Folsom, *The Myth of the Robber Barons,* 3rd ed. (Herndon, VA: Young America's Foundation, 1987, 1991, 1996).

135. Thomas L. Friedman, *The Lexus and the Olive Tree* (New York: Anchor, 2000), pp. 11, 235–238, 446, 449.

136. Newt Gingrich, *Window of Opportunity: A Blueprint for the Future* (New York: Tom Doherty Enterprises, 1984), pp. 18–19, 168–169.

137. The issue of dislocations is discussed in Louis Uchitelle, *The Disposable American: Layoffs and Their Consequences* (New York: Knopf, 2006), esp. pp. 178–204. See also Richard Sennett, *The Corrosion of Character: The Personal Consequences of Work in the New Capitalism* (New York: Norton, 1998).

138. Paul M. Weyrich, "Blue Collar or Blue Blood: The New Right Compared With the Old Right," in Whitaker, ed., *The New Right Papers,* pp. 52–53.

139. For scholarly inquiry into social processes, emphasizing especially the way real markets can fail to promote human happiness, see psychologist Barry Schwartz, *The Costs of Living: How Market Freedom Erodes the Best Things in Life* (New York: Norton, 1994), and psychologist David Myers, *The American Paradox: Spiritual Hunger in an Age of Plenty* (New Haven, CT: Yale University Press, 2000).

140. James C. Hefley, *America: One Nation Under God* (Wheaton, IL: SP, 1975), p. 34.

141. Ankerberg and Weldon, *The Myth of Safe Sex,* p. 46.

142. H. Edward Rowe, *Save America!* (Old Tappan, NJ: Fleming H. Revell, 1976), pp. 100, 113.

143. Roche, *One by One,* p. 58. See also James Q. Wilson, foreword to *The Essential Neoconservative Reader,* p. ix: "And perhaps most important of all, neoconservatives embrace the American conviction that many of the central problems of our society arise out of a want of good character and human virtue." See also Mike Huckabee, *Character Is the Issue: How People with Integrity Can Revolutionize America* (Nashville: Broadman and Holman, 1997).

144. Daniel Boorstin, *The Image: A Guide to Pseudo-Events in America* (New York: Harper, 1962), p. 6.

Chapter Six

1. Allan Bloom died in 1992; George Roche retired from Hillsdale College in 1999; William Bennett is still affiliated with the Heritage Foundation.

2. Allan Bloom, *The Closing of the American Mind: How Higher Education Has Failed Democracy and Impoverished the Souls of Today's Students* (New York: Touchstone, 1987), p. 253.

3. Ibid., p. 60, but also pp. 38, 197, 264–265.

4. George Roche, *The Bewildered Society* (Hillsdale, MI: Hillsdale College Press, 1974), pp. 330–331.

5. William J. Bennett, ed., *The Book of Virtues* (New York: Touchstone, 1993), and William J. Bennett, ed., *The Spirit of America* (New York: Touchstone, 1997).

6. On framing, see George Lakoff, *Don't Think of an Elephant: Know Your Values and Frame the Debate* (White River, VT: Chelsea Green, 2004). There is space in this chapter only to discuss stories. But framing sometimes aims at encapsulating a *story* in short *phrases,* so that when each such phrase is repeated, via mass media or word of mouth, it evokes particular images by triggering emotional reactions to the vocabulary itself. Conservatives are outstanding practitioners of framing in this sense, and we can see the evocative results when they talk about "abortion on demand," "the media elite," "tenured radicals," "reverse discrimination," "colorblind justice," "big government," "tort reform," "the right to work," "tax relief," "the death tax," "voluntary school prayer," "victims' rights," "individual responsibility," "the war on terror," "Operation Iraqi Freedom," and "death panels."

7. Robert Browning, "The Grammarian's Funeral," in *The Complete Works of Robert Browning* (Athens: Ohio University, 1996), p. 132.

8. See Neil Postman, *Entertaining Ourselves to Death: Public Discourse in the Age of Show Business* (New York: Penguin, 1986), on how television demands that all aspects of public life be presented in an entertaining way. A later version of a similar thesis infuses Todd Gitlin, *Media Unlimited: How the Torrent of Images and Sounds Overwhelms Our Lives* (New York: Henry Holt, 2003).

9. The quintessential conservative Edmund Burke championed this practice. He charged that people who overthrew the French monarchy in 1789 never understood the importance of stories in public life. As he put it, "[N]ow [in revolutionary France] all is to be changed. All the pleasing illusions [stories, traditions] which made power gentle and obedience liberal ... are to be dissolved by this new conquering empire of light and reason. All the decent drapery [stories, traditions] of life is to be rudely torn off.... On this scheme of things, a king is but a man, a queen is but a woman; a woman is but an animal, and an animal not of the highest order.... The murder of a king, or a queen, or a bishop, or a father, are only common homicide.... Nothing is left which engages the affections on the part of the commonwealth." See Edmund Burke, *Reflections on the Revolution in France* (New York: Liberal Arts, 1955), p. 87. The distinction that Weber drew between those who promote enchantment and those who do not can be seen in the historical juxtaposition of Burke and Denis Diderot during the Enlightenment. Burke praised inspiring stories about kings, queens, and bishops, and Diderot coined the famous epigram "Man will never be free until the last [enchanted] king is strangled in the entrails of the last [enchanted] priest."

10. Reagan's talent for telling stories is the main theme in Paul D. Erickson, *Reagan Speaks: The Making of an American Myth* (New York: New York University Press, 1985). See Haynes Johnson, *Sleepwalking Through History: America in the Reagan Years* (New York: Anchor, 1991), pp. 59–60, for two stories, neither true but both inspiring, that Reagan told in numerous speeches throughout his political career. The first is about a mysterious speaker in Philadelphia's Independence Hall who persuaded America's Founding Fathers to sign the Declaration of Independence in 1776 and then disappeared; the second is about an American bomber pilot in World War II who stayed in his falling plane to comfort a gunner who was trapped in one of its ball turrets and could not parachute to safety.

11. See the examples in Chapter One, note 7. For additional credo statements, see Myron Magnet, *The Dream and the Nightmare: The Sixties' Legacy to the Underclass* (New York: William Morrow, 1993), p. 227, and Rush Limbaugh, *The Way Things Ought to Be* (New York: Pocket Books, 1994), pp. 2–3.

12. See Michael Novak, *The Spirit of Democratic Capitalism* (New York: Simon & Schuster, 1982), pp. 56–57: "Democratic capitalism is not a 'free enterprise system' alone. It cannot thrive apart from the moral culture that nourishes the virtues and values on which its existence depends."

13. For example, Pat Fagan, *Why Religion Matters: The Impact of Religious Practice on Social Stability* (Washington, DC: Heritage Foundation, 1996).

14. On rewards to capitalists for abstinence, see Adam Smith, *An Inquiry into the Nature and Causes of the Wealth of Nations* (1776; New York: Modern Library, 1937), p. 321, and Nassau Senior, *An Outline of the Science of Political Economy* (1836; London: G. Allen & Unwin, 1951), p. 58.

15. See William H. Peterson, "Privatization: The Rediscovery of Entrepreneurship," in *Private Cures for Public Ills: The Promise of Privatization,* ed. Lawrence W. Reed (Irvington-on-Hudson, New York: The Foundation for Economic Education, 1996), p. 17: Entrepreneurship "is the risk-assuming organization and management of an enterprise. It is the very-present fourth and most indispensable factor of production beyond the other three of land, labor, and capital.... It is the sine qua non of freedom and free enterprise, of what Adam Smith called 'the wealth of nations,' of the manifestation of his famous 'invisible hand' in action—of self-interest harnessed to the public interest, the common good."

16. See George Gilder, *Wealth and Poverty* (New York: Basic, 1981), passim, and George Gilder, *The Spirit of Enterprise* (New York: Simon and Schuster, 1984), passim.

17. R. Emmett Tyrrell Jr., *The Conservative Crack-Up* (New York: Simon & Schuster, 1992), pp. 32–33.

18. See Richard Weaver, *Ideas Have Consequences* (1948; Chicago: University of Chicago Press, 1984), and James Burnham, *Suicide of the West: An Essay on the Meaning and Destiny of Liberalism* (New York: John Day, 1964).

19. In Chapter Two we saw that conservatism is somewhat pessimistic for being animated by notions of perversity, jeopardy, and futility. In conservative talk, however, pessimism and optimism can be reconciled when right-wingers refer to the mercy of God and/or the prosperity that free markets will presumably generate. For example, Stephen J. Tonsor, "The Conservative Search for Identity," in Frank S. Meyer, *What Is Conservatism?* (New York: Holt, Rinehart, and Winston, 1964), p. 135: "Although [Lord Acton and de Tocqueville] both were pessimistic about human nature, both were optimists largely because of their belief in a benevolent Providence. Acton said, 'Christ is risen on the world and fails not.' Tocqueville wrote, 'I cannot believe that the Creator made man to leave him in an endless struggle with the intellectual wretchedness that surrounds us.'"

20. Jeffrey Bell, *Populism and Elitism: Politics in the Age of Equality* (Washington, DC: Regnery, 1992), p. 14.

21. Lawrence Kudlow, *American Abundance: The New Economic and Moral Prosperity* (New York: Forbes, 1997), p. 15.

22. Jerry Pournelle, preface to Newt Gingrich, *Window of Opportunity: A Blueprint for the Future* (New York: Tom Doherty Enterprises, 1984), p. xiii.

23. Clyde N. Wilson, "Citizens or Subjects?" in *The New Right Papers,* ed. Robert W. Whitaker (New York: St. Martin's Press, 1985), p. 126.

24. Dick Armey, *The Freedom Revolution* (Washington, DC: Regnery, 1995), p. 193.

25. Phyllis Schlafly, *A Choice Not an Echo* (Alton, IL: Pere Marquette Press, 1964), p. 83.

26. Martin L. Gross, *The Government Racket: Washington Waste From A to Z* (New York: Bantam, 1992), pp. 51, 63.

27. Rus Walton, *One Nation Under God* (Washington, DC: Third Century, 1975), p. 93. On simplicity, see also Grover G. Norquist, *Rock the House* (Fort Lauderdale, FL: VYTIS, 1995), p. 47: "[T]he conservative solution to crime—putting violent offenders in prison for longer periods of time—works, is cost-effective, and is easily understood by anyone who has not graduated from Yale Law School." See also Brink Lindsey, "Free Trade from the Bottom Up," in *Toward Liberty: The Idea that Is Changing the World*, ed. David Boaz (Washington, DC: Cato Institute, 2002), p. 309: "The case for free trade at home can be embellished with all kinds of technical complexities, but in the end it boils down to *common sense*.... The benefits of free trade are the benefits of larger free markets."

28. Isaac Asimov, *The Intelligent Man's Guide to Science*, vol. 1 (New York: Basic Books, 1960), p. 20.

29. The general problem for the religious Right is implicit in John Gribbin, *The Scientists: A History of Science Told Through the Lives of Its Greatest Inventors* (New York: Random House, 2004), p. xix, when Gribbin says that "human life turned out to be no different from any other kind of life on Earth. As the work of Charles Darwin and Alfred Wallace established in the nineteenth century, all you need to make human beings out of amoebas is the process of evolution by natural selection, and plenty of time." Or, Newton's laws led to "the realization that the world works on essentially mechanical principles that can be understood by human beings, and is not run in accordance with magic or the whims of capricious gods," p. 187.

30. Thus Bryce J. Christensen, *Utopia Against the Family: The Problems and Politics of the American Family* (San Francisco: Ignatius, 1990), p. 2: "Any plausible definition of modern life must give pride of place to science as the source of the theories and technology which have made it easy to forget the Fall and its consequences."

31. See his "Science as a Vocation," (1922), in *From Max Weber: Essays in Sociology*, ed. H. H. Gerth and C. Wright Mills (New York: Oxford University Press, 1946), esp. pp. 134–137.

32. Thus Franz Kafka, says one of his biographers, "was a writer. Not a man who wrote, but one to whom writing was the only form of being, the only means of defying death in life. The difference involves fundamentals: the radical distinction between genius and talent, among others, but above all the approach to writing as a holy vocation, a sacred service rather than a means to many ends, a way of life as sternly self-contained as the daily Talmud study of Kafka's legendary sainted ancestors on his mother's side." See Ernest Pawel, *The Nightmare of Reason: A Life of Franz Kafka* (New York: Noonday Press, 1992), p. 97.

33. Jesse Helms, *When Free Men Shall Stand* (Grand Rapids, MI: Zondervan, 1976), pp. 35–37.

34. Ronald H. Nash, *Poverty and Wealth: Why Socialism Doesn't Work* (Richardson, TX: Probe, 1986), p. 76.

35. Dinesh D'Souza, *The Virtue of Prosperity: Finding Values in an Age of Techno-Affluence* (New York: Free Press, 2000), p. 240.

36. Jude Wanniski, *The Way the World Works* (New York: Touchstone, 1978), p. 31.

37. Milton Friedman, *Capitalism and Freedom* (Chicago: University of Chicago Press, 1962), p. 10.

38. Helms, *When Free Men Shall Stand,* p. 22.

39. Mark Anthony, *Vanishing Republic: How Can We Save the American Dream* (Altamonte Springs, FL: Encore, 1995), p. 86.

40. On the ends of government according to Locke, see *The Second Treatise* (1690) in *Locke's Two Treatises of Government,* ed. Peter Laslett (Cambridge: Cambridge University Press, 1960), Chapter Nine, pp. 368–371.

41. Brannon S. Howse, *Reclaiming a Nation At Risk* (Chandler, AZ: Bridgestone Multimedia Group, 1995), p. 53.

42. See http://georgewbush-whitehouse.archives.gov/news/print/inaugural-address.html, accessed May 29, 2009.

43. This hope is summed up in the aphorism attributed to the great physicist Sir William Thompson, Lord Kelvin, who declared in 1883 that "[w]hen you can measure what you are speaking about and express it in numbers, you know something about it; but when you cannot measure, when you cannot express it in numbers, your knowledge is of a meager and unsatisfactory kind." Since 1929 an abbreviated version of these words has appeared on the outer wall of the Social Science Research Building at the University of Chicago.

44. The missing stories are noted by Drew Westen, *The Political Brain: The Role of Emotion in Deciding the Fate of the Nation* (New York: PublicAffairs, 2007). Westen offers a prescription for future liberal success: "It means abandoning traditional Democratic laundry lists, with each special interest putting its 'issue' in the bag.... It means selecting and nurturing candidates ... who can tell compelling [progressive] stories about who they are and what they believe that will provide their fellow citizens with hope and inspiration," pp. 419–420.

45. From Roosevelt's campaign speech at Oglethorp University in Atlanta on May 22, 1932, excerpted in Howard Zinn, ed., *New Deal Thought* (Indianapolis: Bobbs-Merrill, 1966), p. 83.

46. "Text of President Kennedy's Commencement Address to Yale's Graduating Class," *New York Times,* June 12, 1962, p. 20.

47. See Burnham, *Suicide of the West,* p. 291: "Men become willing to endure, sacrifice and die for God, family, king, honor, [and] country, from a sense of absolute duty or an exalted vision of the meaning of history.... It is precisely these ideals and institutions that liberalism has criticized, attacked and in part overthrown as superstitious, archaic, reactionary and irrational." Weber recognized the same loss. See his "Science as a Vocation," p. 155: "The fate of our times is characterized by rationalization and intellectualization and, above all, by the 'disenchantment of the world.' Precisely the ultimate and most sublime values have retreated from public life either into the transcendental realm of mystic life or into the brotherliness of direct and personal human relations. It is not accidental that our greatest art is intimate and not monumental, nor is it accidental that today only within the smallest and intimate circles, in personal human situations, ... that something is pulsating that corresponds to the prophetic *pneuma* [spirit], which in former times swept through ... great communities like a firebrand, welding them together."

48. See Roger Kimball, *Tenured Radicals: How Politics Has Corrupted Our Higher*

Education (New York: HarperPerennial, 1990), p. 156: "Looming behind all Professor [Stanley] Fish's startling denials and rhetorical antics is a single large claim [of postmodernism] about the nature of truth. In brief, there isn't any." See also Lynne Cheney, *Telling the Truth: A Report on the State of the Humanities in Higher Education* (Washington, DC: National Endowment for the Humanities, 1992), p. 7: "An increasingly influential view [among professors] is that there is no truth to tell: What we think of as truth is merely a cultural construct, serving to empower some and oppress others."

49. One empirical indication that liberals do little storytelling appears in Larry M. Bartels, *Unequal Democracy: The Political Economy of the New Gilded Age* (Princeton, NJ: Princeton University Press, 2008), pp. 66–72. Bartels cites figures showing that in the second half of the twentieth century, the Democratic Party presidential vote declined among voters without college degrees and increased among voters with college degrees. This vote pattern suggests that people who tend to assess the world via science rather than tradition are more likely to vote for liberal candidates and projects. Another indication of likely enthusiasm for cardinal stories is religiosity. On the recent tendency of "religious traditionalists" to support Republican rather than Democratic candidates, see Geoffrey Layman, *The Great Divide: Religious and Cultural Conflict in American Party Politics* (New York: Columbia University Press, 2001), esp. pp. 168–204.

50. Ralph Reed, *Active Faith: How Christians Are Changing the Soul of American Politics* (New York: Free Press, 1996), p. 75.

51. Bloom, *The Closing of the American Mind,* p. 55. See also George W. Bush, "President's Remarks at the 2004 Republican National Convention," September 2, 2004: "The story of America is the story of expanding liberty: an ever-widening circle, constantly growing to reach further and include more." These remarks come from www.whitehouse.gov/news/releases/2004/09/print/20040902-2html, accessed January 16, 2007.

52. Without discussing political horse races, Thomas Frank, *What's the Matter with Kansas? How the Conservatives Won the Heart of America* (New York: Metropolitan, 2004), argues that many people in Kansas identify so strongly with the conservative story of cultural war in America that, in the absence of a liberal counterstory, they vote against their economic interests.

53. I do not mean to suggest that all liberals lack rhetorical talent and that none is capable of telling stories. Franklin Roosevelt described America in thrall to "economic royalists," John Kennedy called on Americans to serve their country rather than wait for it to serve them, and Mario Cuomo spoke movingly of his immigrant father's working hard in a new land to support his family. But isolated stories, no matter how rhetorically powerful by themselves, are not necessarily the foundation blocks for an overall and sustained narrative.

54. Readers will recall the maxim of Dick Armey: "The market is rational and the government is dumb." See Chapter Four, note 42.

55. M. Stanton Evans, *The Theme Is Freedom: Religion, Politics, and the American Tradition* (Washington, DC: Regnery, 1994).

56. Armey, *The Freedom Revolution.* Conservatives may also claim that, especially due to New Deal programs and other liberal projects, American politicians have reduced freedom. For example, see James Bovard, *Freedom in Chains: The Rise of the State and the Demise of the Citizen* (New York: St. Martin's Press, 1999).

57. Barry Goldwater, *The Conscience of a Conservative* (Shepherdsville, KY: Victor, 1960), p. 16.

58. Marvin Olasky, *The Tragedy of American Compassion* (Washington, DC: Regnery, 1992), p. 111.

59. Phil Kent, *The Dark Side of Liberalism: Unchaining the Truth* (Augusta, GA: Harbor House, 2003), p. 114.

60. Walter E. Williams, *All It Takes Is Guts: A Minority View* (Washington, DC: Regnery, 1987), p. 83.

61. William E. Simon, *A Time for Truth* (New York: Berkley, 1978), p. 21.

62. See John Winthrop, "Little Speech" (1645), in *Puritan Political Ideas: 1558–1794,* ed. Edmund S. Morgan (Indianapolis: Bobbs-Merrill, 1965), pp. 136–142, and esp. pp. 138–139: "There is a twofold liberty, natural (I mean as our nature is now corrupt) and civil or federal. The first is common to man with beasts and other creatures. By this, man, as he stands in relation to man simply, hath liberty to do what he lists; it is a liberty to evil as well as to good.... The other kind of liberty I call civil or federal, it may also be termed moral, in reference to the covenant between God and man, in the moral law, and the politic covenants and constitutions, amongst men themselves. This liberty is the proper end and object of authority, and cannot subsist without it; and it is a liberty to that only which is good, just, and honest." For an update on Winthrop, see D. James Kennedy, "Liberty or License," in *What If America Were a Christian Nation Again?* (New York: Thomas Nelson, 2003), pp. 55–70.

63. In Eric Foner, "Conservative Freedom," in *The Story of American Freedom* (New York: Norton, 1998), pp. 307–332, the two approaches to freedom are described as coexisting uneasily.

64. Walton, *One Nation Under God,* pp. 51–52.

65. Daniel J. Flynn, *Why the Left Hates America: Exposing the Lies that Have Obscured Our Nation's Greatness* (Roseville, CA: Forum, 2002), pp. 206–207.

66. Moore, "God & Government: Restoring the Standard," in D. James Kennedy, Gary Bauer, John Ashcraft, et al., *Reclaiming America for Christ* (Fort Lauderdale, FL: Coral Ridge Ministries, 1996), pp. 113–114.

67. E. Calvin Beisner, "Stewardship in a Free Society," in *Morality and the Marketplace,* ed. Michael Bauman (Hillsdale, MI: Hillsdale College Press, 1994), pp. 20, 23. See also Bob Dole, "A Legacy of Values, Not Just a Label," in *Why I Am a Reagan Conservative,* ed. Michael K. Deaver (New York: HarperCollins, 2005), p. 11: "Liberty ... should never be confused with license. Conservatives have no monopoly on virtue. Yet if we are true to our stated beliefs, we will take exceptions to a popular culture that all too often peddles trash for cash."

68. Steven Hayward, "Broken Cities: Liberalism's Urban Legacy," *Policy Review* (March–April 1998): 20. Here, Hayward approvingly quotes from Fred Siegel, *The Future Once Happened Here: New York. D.C., L.A., and the Fate of America's Big Cities* (New York: Free Press, 1997).

69. Burke, *Reflections on the Revolution in France,* p. 110.

70. Alexis de Tocqueville, *Democracy in America* (New York: Doubleday Anchor, 1969), p. 287.

71. William A. Donohue, *The New Freedom: Individualism and Collectivism in the Social Lives of Americans* (New Brunswick, NJ: Transaction, 1990), p. 210.

72. Irving Kristol, "Pornography, Obscenity, and the Case for Censorship [1971]," in Irving Kristol, *On the Democratic Idea in America* (New York: Harper & Row, 1972), pp. 38–39.

73. Magnet, *The Dream and the Nightmare,* pp. 136–137.

74. For example, William J. Bennett, "Truth," in *Leadership for America: The Principles of Conservatism*, ed. Edwin J. Feulner Jr. (Dallas: Spence, 2000), pp. 152–155, but esp. 153: "The invocation of 'tolerance' can be genuinely harmful when it becomes a euphemism for moral exhaustion and an indifferent neutrality toward moral truth."

75. The phrase is from Gertrude Himmelfarb, "Liberty: One Very Simple Principle?" in *On Looking into the Abyss: Untimely Thoughts on Culture and Society* (New York: Knopf, 1994), p. 75.

76. Robert H. Bork, *Slouching Towards Gomorrah: Modern Liberalism and American Decline* (New York: Regan, 1996), p. 334. Readers will notice that in this passage, Bork does not say which qualities define a "bad decision." Apparently if Brand X *commodity* is widely purchased, the item is not "wrong" but good. But if Brand X *idea* is widely espoused—in effect, intellectually "purchased"—it may be "bad" or at least not necessarily "the superior product." Why the idea is not morally equal to the commodity, Bork does not say.

77. Roger Kimball, "James Fitzjames Stephen v. John Stuart Mill," in *Experiments Against Reality: The Fate of Culture in the Postmodern Age* (Chicago: Ivan Dee, 2000), p. 159.

78. Kristol, "Pornography, Obscenity, and the Case for Censorship," pp. 45–46.

79. John Stuart Mill, *On Liberty* (1859; New York: Liberal Arts Press, 1956), pp. 9–61.

80. Ibid., pp. 62–63.

81. Himmelfarb, "Liberty: One Very Simple Principle?" p. 104.

82. Here is a conservative warning against jeopardy.

83. Kimball, "James Fitzjames Stephen v. John Stuart Mill," p. 167.

84. David G. Myers, *The American Paradox: Spiritual Hunger in an Age of Plenty* (New Haven, CT: Yale University Press, 2000), p. xiii.

85. Her argument along these lines appears in Himmelfarb, "Liberty: One Very Simple Principle?" esp. pp. 83–98. See also William J. Bennett, *The Broken Hearth: Reversing the Moral Collapse of the American Family* (New York: Broadway, 2003), p. 4: "It is fashionable these days to say and believe that matters like divorce, illegitimacy, cohabitation, and single-parenting are 'private' matters that are not the business of the wider community. To which I would respond: There are few matters of more profound *public* consequence than the condition of marriage and families. Most of our social pathologies—crime, imprisonment rates, welfare, educational underachievement, alcohol and drug abuse, suicide, depression, sexually transmitted diseases—are manifestations, direct and indirect, of the crack-up of the modern American family."

86. Phillip E. Johnson, *The Right Questions: Truth, Meaning and Public Debate* (Downers Grove, IL: Intervarsity, 2002), p. 29.

87. William Dannemeyer, *Shadow in the Land: Homosexuality in America* (San Francisco: Ignatius, 1989), p. 221. See also Ben Shapiro, *Porn Generation: How Social Liberalism Is Corrupting Our Future* (Washington, DC: Regnery, 2005), pp. 181–182: "Libertarians and social liberals would have us believe that ... we should allow opponents of traditional morality to live life their way, without consequences. This ignores the fact that these [their] actions are social, not individual.... Tolerance of all behavior leads to societal immorality, and societal approval of immoral personal behavior has vast externalities. Just as a manufacturing plant that produces toxic waste may affect others by poisoning a river, so too may the immoral among us affect others by poisoning the culture."

88. Bork, *Slouching Towards Gomorrah,* p. 63.

89. Himmelfarb, "Liberty: One Very Simple Principle?" p. 96.

90. Ibid., p. 98.

91. See Sidney Blumenthal, *The Rise of the Counterestablishment: From Conservative Ideology to Political Power* (New York: Times Books, 1986).

92. Important parts of the story are told in John J. Miller, *A Gift of Freedom: How the John M. Olin Foundation Changed America* (San Francisco: Encounter, 2005).

93. Simon, *A Time for Truth,* p. 239.

94. Ibid., p. 247. In the same time frame, see also Patrick J. Buchanan, *Conservative Votes, Liberal Victories: Why the Right Has Failed* (New York: Quadrangle, 1975), p. 46: "Businessmen sit upon the boards of trustees of most of the nation's private colleges. They are the alumni who make the large annual donations. They should link future contributions to a non-negotiable demand that capitalism be given due process in the department of economics, that the role of the businessman in American life be given fair treatment in the department of history."

95. The Rutherford Institute, headed by John W. Whitehead, paid for much of the sexual harassment lawsuit brought by Paula Jones against President Bill Clinton. See Joe Conason and Gene Lyons, *The Hunting of the President: The Ten-Year Campaign to Destroy Bill and Hillary Clinton* (New York: St. Martin's Press, 2001), pp. 319–321.

96. One estimate, based on annual reports published by the twenty largest conservative think tanks, concludes that during the 1990s, those twenty institutes would spend more than $1 billion. See *$1 Billion for Ideas: Conservative Think Tanks in the 1990s* (Washington, DC: National Committee for Responsive Philanthropy, 1999).

97. *Axis of Ideology: Conservative Foundations and Public Policy* (Washington, DC: National Committee for Responsive Philanthropy, 2004), p. 17.

98. See John Saloma III, *Ominous Politics: The New Conservative Labyrinth* (New York: Hill and Wang, 1984). See also Paul Gottfried and Thomas Fleming, *The Conservative Movement* (Boston: Twayne, 1988), pp. 59–76; Jerome L. Himmelstein, *To the Right: The Transformation of American Conservatism* (Berkeley: University of California Press, 1990), pp. 129–164; and Jean Stefanic and Richard Delgado, *No Mercy: How Conservative Think Tanks and Foundations Changed America's Social Agenda* (Philadelphia: Temple University Press, 1998).

99. Richard John Neuhaus, *America Against Itself: Moral Vision and the Public Order* (South Bend, IN: Notre Dame University Press, 1992), p. 182.

100. Kimball, *Experiments Against Reality,* p. 5. His essay, "The Legacy of Friedrich Nietzche," is at pp. 189–213.

101. Howse, *Reclaiming a Nation At Risk,* p. xv.

102. We are looking at an advertisement in this sense when Melvyn Krauss, author of *How Nations Grow Rich: The Case for Free Trade* (New York: Oxford University Press, 1997), thanks both the John Olin Foundation and the Manhattan Institute for their help and support, pp. ix–x. These are not the sort of sponsors that will give Krauss another grant or stipend if he expresses ideas with which they disagree. See also Stephan Thernstrom and Abigail Thernstrom, *America in Black and White: One Nation, Indivisible* (New York: Touchstone, 1999), whose authors acknowledge research funding from the Olin Foundation, the Bradley Foundation, the Smith Richardson Foundation, the Earhart Foundation, and the Carthage Foundation, p. 5.

103. Richard J. Herrnstein and Charles Murray, *The Bell Curve: Intelligence and Class Structure in American Life* (New York: Free Press, 1994).

104. Terry Eastland, *Ending Affirmative Action: The Case for Colorblind Justice* (New York: Basic Books, 1997).

105. Regnery helped to almost derail the Democratic presidential campaign in 2004 by publishing John E. O'Neill and Jerome R. Corsi, *Unfit for Command: Swift Boat Veterans Speak Out Against John Kerry* (Washington, DC: Regnery, 2004).

106. A related process of borrowing authority is sometimes expressed in blurbs that appear on book covers. On this score, see some of the cover blurbs for Wanniski's *The Way the World Works.* For example, "The best economic primer since Adam Smith" (Irving Kristol). Or, "In all honesty, I believe it is the best book on economics ever written" (Arthur Laffer). Or, "Could do for the Republican Party what Marx's Manifesto did for communism ... [though] unlike Marx, Wanniski is easy reading" (Malcolm S. Forbes Jr.). See also the blurbs for David Horowitz, *Hating Whitey and Other Progressive Causes* (Dallas: Spence, 1999). For example, "No one picks apart the pretensions of the civil rights crowd quite the way Horowitz does" (Fred Barnes). "This is a raw and courageous book that turns over some rocks and shows what is crawling underneath. It reveals the ugly reality behind the pretty and politically correct words and visions of our time" (Thomas Sowell).

107. Here are some examples. Dinesh D'Souza, *The Virtue of Prosperity: Finding Values in an Age of Techno-Affluence* (New York: Free Press, 2000), p. 76: "Poverty, understood as the absence of food, clothing, and shelter, is no longer a significant problem in America." To support this conclusion, D'Souza, a fellow at the American Enterprise Institute, cites figures supplied by Peter Huber, a fellow at the Manhattan Institute. Anthony, *Vanishing Republic,* p. 301, predicts what will happen if Congress enacts President Clinton's proposals for more unemployment benefits and health care reform: "Research from the National Center for Policy Analysis indicates 1.4 fewer million jobs will be created, and total wages in the economy will be $483 billion lower over the next five years." The NCPA is a conservative think tank located in Dallas and Washington, D.C. See also William P. Hoar, *Handouts and Pickpockets: Our Government Gone Berserk* (Lafayette, LA: Huntington House, 1996), p. 155: "A cabaret in Los Angeles ... was forced to close its shower stall on stage for strippers, not for violating decency standards but because, under the demands of the Americans with Disabilities Act, the shower stall was not accessible if a stripper in a wheelchair was to be hired." The source for this anecdote is an article from the *American Spectator.*

108. Conservative books that reject the findings of mainstream environmentalists and ecologists include Dixy Lee Ray, *Environmental Overkill: Whatever Happened to Common Sense?* (Washington, DC: Regnery, 1993); Ronald Bailey, ed., *The True State of the Planet* (New York: Free Press, 1995); Thomas Gale Moore, *Climate of Fear: Why We Shouldn't Worry About Global Warming* (Washington, DC: Cato Institute, 1998); Peter Huber, *Hard Green: Saving the Environment from the Environmentalists* (New York: Basic Books, 1999); Ronald Bailey, ed., *Global Warming and Other Eco-Myths: How the Environmental Movement Uses False Science to Scare Us to Death* (Roseville, CA: Forum, 2002); and Richard Stroup, *Eco-nomics: What Everyone Should Know About Economics and the Environment* (Washington, DC: Cato Institute, 2003).

109. All these terms appear in Mill, *On Liberty,* pp. 64–66.

110. John K. Andrews Jr., "So You Want to Start a Think Tank: A Battlefield Report from the States," *Policy Review* (Summer 1989): 64. *Policy Review* in 1989 was published by the Heritage Foundation. Since 2001 it has been published by the Hoover Institution.

111. Heather S. Richardson, "The Politics of Virtue: A Strategy for Transforming the Culture," *Policy Review* (Fall 1991): 21. This article is adapted from a talk that Richardson gave at the Heritage Foundation.

112. David Ricci, *The Transformation of American Politics: The New Washington and the Rise of Think Tanks* (New Haven, CT: Yale University Press, 1993), esp. pp. 166–171, describes how conservative think tanks in the 1970s and 1980s, led by the Heritage Foundation, moved increasingly toward marketing their public policy ideas. For a recent description of this project by Heritage's president, see Edwin J. Feulner Jr., introduction to Feulner, ed., *Leadership for America,* p. xxiii: "For years we have set the standard among think tanks for marketing our research, and as we approached our twenty-fifth anniversary, we resolved to take that work to a new level. This led us to create our Center for Media and Public Policy. It operates on the same basic principle that has always guided our marketing: We produce ideas, and the news media are one of our 'customer segments.' If we expect to 'sell' our ideas in that market, we had better focus on the needs and interests of journalists and stop grousing about their biases."

113. Hugh Heclo, "Issue Networks and the Executive Establishment," in *The New American Political System,* ed. Anthony King (Washington, DC: American Enterprise Institute, 1978), p. 121.

114. Conservative resistance to scientific findings on the dangers of global warming is examined in Ross Gelbspan, *The Heat Is On: The Climate Crisis, the Cover Up, the Prescription* (Cambridge, MA: Perseus, 1998), esp. pp. 15–83. One technique in this campaign is for self-interested sponsors to subsidize publications—such as *World Climate Report*—that are not refereed impartially by scientific peers, after which other right-wing publications and congressional testimony can cite such in-house "sources" as apparent proof that scientific opinion is divided on whether global warming is coming and on whether, if it does come, the results will be ecologically harmful.

115. For example, Marshall N. Carter and William G. Shipman, *Promises to Keep: Saving Social Security's Dream* (Washington, DC: Regnery, 1996), and Peter J. Ferrara and Michael Tanner, *A New Deal for Social Security* (Washington, DC: Cato Institute, 1998).

116. See Tom DeLay, *No Retreat, No Surrender: One American's Fight* (New York: Sentinel, 2007), p. 179: "I remain undaunted because I believe that my conservative values arise from Scripture, from the counsel of the Founding Fathers, and from the wisdom of the American experience. This is why I say, 'No retreat, No surrender.' Not to liberal tyranny. Not to the politics of personal destruction. Not to the lies of the leftist political machine. I am a Christian, a conservative, and a man deeply in love with his country. This is who I am. Here is where I stand. No retreat. No surrender." DeLay, nicknamed "The Hammer," served as a Republican congressman from Texas between 1984 and 2006.

Chapter Seven

1. For alternative stories, see Rogers M. Smith, *Stories of Peoplehood: The Politics and Morals of Political Membership* (New York: Cambridge University Press, 2003), esp. pp. 186–212; George Lakoff, *Whose Freedom: The Battle over America's Most Important Idea* (New York: Farrar, Straus, and Giroux, 2006), pp. 243–266; and Todd Gitlin, *The*

Bulldozer and the Big Tent: Blind Republicans, Lame Democrats, and the Recovery of American Ideals (New York: Wiley, 2007), pp. 238–249.

2. On Kerry as inconsistent and irresolute, see David N. Bossie, *The Many Faces of John Kerry: Why This Massachusetts Liberal Is Wrong for America* (Nashville: WND, 2003).

3. Bush II supporters portray him positively in, for example, David Frum, *The Right Man: The Surprise Presidency of George W. Bush* (New York: Random House, 2003), and Fred Barnes, *Rebel-in-Chief: Inside the Bold and Controversial Presidency of George W. Bush* (New York: Crown Forum, 2006). Frank Rich, *The Greatest Story Ever Sold: The Decline and Fall of Truth from 9/11 to Katrina* (New York: Penguin, 2006), is much more critical.

4. See John Halpin and Ruy Teixeira, "The Politics of Definition: The Real Third Way (Part I)." Parts I–IV of this report are available at http://makethemaccountable.com/articles/The_Politics_of_Definition.htm.

5. On Alcibiades and the battle for Syracuse, see Thucydides, *History of the Peloponnesian War* (c. 403 BCE; New York: Oxford University Press, 1960), Books 6–8, pp. 274–388. I am indebted to Anne Norton, "The Sicilian Expedition," in *Leo Strauss and the Politics of American Empire* (New Haven, CT: Yale University Press, 2004), pp. 181–200, for a discussion comparing recent events and the Peloponnesian War.

6. Part of what stymies contemporary observers on this score appears when Bob Woodward, *Bush at War* (New York: Simon & Schuster, 2002), pp. 145–146, recounts Bush II telling him that "I'm the commander—see, I don't need to explain—I do not need to explain why I say things. That's the interesting thing about being president. Maybe somebody needs to explain to me why they say something, but I don't feel like I owe anybody an explanation." So in a way there were no explanations for why America went to war. On the other hand, the president and his associates have offered so many explanations as to make it difficult to judge which was for them decisive. Thus Stephen Kinzer, *Overthrow: America's Century of Regime Change from Hawaii to Iraq* (New York: Times, 2006), p. 285, concludes that "President Bush and the handful of advisers with whom he conceived and launched this war explained their motives in a contradictory series of statements that changed as the war proceeded. Each had a particular set of motives, some declared and others left unsaid. The fact that there is so much debate and uncertainty about these motives makes the Iraq war unique in American history. It is the only conflict Americans ever fought without truly knowing why."

7. For example, George Packer, *The Assassin's Gate: America in Iraq* (New York: Farrar, Straus, and Giroux, 2005); Michael R. Gordon and Bernard E. Trainer, *Cobra II: The Inside Story of the Invasion and Occupation of Iraq* (New York: Pantheon, 2006); Mark Danner and Frank Rich, *The Secret Way to War: The Downing Street Memo and the Iraq War's Buried History* (New York: New York Review, 2006); James Fallows, *Blind into Baghdad: America's War in Iraq* (New York: Vintage, 2006); Peter W. Galbraith, *The End of Iraq: How American Incompetence Created a War Without End* (New York: Simon & Schuster, 2006); and Thomas E. Ricks, *Fiasco: The American Military Adventure in Iraq* (New York: Penguin, 2006).

8. On the importance of Persian Gulf oil to America, see Clyde Prestowitz, *Rogue Nation: American Unilateralism and the Failure of Good Intentions* (New York: Basic Books, 2004), pp. 81–109; Paul Roberts, *The End of Oil: On the Edge of a Perilous World* (Boston: Houghton Mifflin, 2004); and Antonia Juhasz, *The Tyranny of Oil: The World's*

Most Powerful Industry—And What We Must Do to Stop It (New York: William Morrow, 2008).

9. The phrase "national vocation" is from Ronald Steel, *Temptations of a Superpower* (Cambridge, MA: Harvard University Press, 1995), p. 1.

10. Robert Kagan and William Kristol, eds., *Present Dangers: Crisis and Opportunity in American Foreign and Defense Policy* (San Francisco: Encounter, 2000). Paul Wolfowitz, William Bennett, Donald Kagan, Richard Perle, Peter Rodman, and Elliot Abrams all wrote essays for *Present Dangers.*

11. Samuel Huntington, *The Clash of Civilizations and the Remaking of World Order* (New York: Simon & Schuster, 1996).

12. The shock that Bush responded to in 2003 was emotional and symbolic. The assumption that additional acts of terrorist violence would match the original devastation is challenged by John Mueller, *Overblown: How Politicians and the Terrorism Industry Inflate National Security Threats, and Why We Believe Them* (New York: Free Press, 2006), p. 13: "Even with the September 11 attacks included in the count . . . the number of Americans killed by international terrorism since the late 1960s (which is when the State Department began its accounting) is about the same as the number killed over the same period by lightning, or by accident-causing deer, or by severe allergic reactions to peanuts."

13. "Statement by the President in His Address to the Nation," September 11, 2001, www.whitehouse.gov/news/releases/2001/09/print/20010911-16.html, accessed January 16, 2007.

14. "President Delivers State of the Union Address," January 29, 2002, www.whitehouse.gov/news/releases/2002/01/print/20020129-11.html, accessed January 16, 2007.

15. "Address to a Joint Session of Congress and the American People," September 20, 2001, www.whitehouse.gov/news/releases/2001/09/print/20010920-8.html, accessed January 16, 2007. Or, as Robert Kagan and William Kristol say in their *Present Dangers,* p. 21: "Given the dangers we know currently exist, and given the certainty that unknown perils await us over the horizon, there can be no respite from this burden."

16. Ronald Reagan, "Remarks at the Annual Convention of the National Association of Evangelicals, Orlando, Florida, March 8, 1983," in *Speaking My Mind: Selected Speeches* (New York: Simon & Schuster, 1989), pp. 168–180, but esp. p. 179 on an "evil empire" and "the struggle between right and wrong and good and evil."

17. The way Bush's notion of a war on evil helps to pinpoint the putative enemies of conservatism is summed up in the title of Sean Hannity, *Deliver Us from Evil: Defeating Terrorism, Despotism, and Liberalism* (New York: HarperCollins, 2004).

18. See "Address to a Joint Session of Congress and the American People," September 20, 2001. See also "President Delivers State of the Union Address," January 29, 2002.

19. Similar warnings about complexity underlay the speech by Senator Robert Byrd (D-VA) against the 2002 congressional resolution authorizing the president to use force in Iraq. See Robert C. Byrd, *Losing America: Confronting a Reckless and Arrogant Presidency* (New York: Norton, 2004), pp. 230–235.

20. "Address to a Joint Session of Congress and the American People," September 20, 2001.

21. "Presidential Address to the Nation," October 7, 2001, in which Bush II announced the start of military strikes in Afghanistan, www.whitehouse.gov/news/releases/2001/10/print/20011007-8.html, accessed January 16, 2007. The same

exclusion of middle ground occurs in David Frum and Richard Perle, *An End to Evil: How to Win the War on Terror* (New York: Random House, 2003), p. 9: "For us, terrorism remains the great evil of our time, and the war against this evil, our generation's great cause.... There is no middle way for Americans: It is victory or holocaust." Arthur Miller confronted in McCarthyism an earlier version of this right-wing aversion to middle-ground positions and addressed it in *The Crucible* (1953), his drama about witch-hunting in colonial America. According to Miller, Deputy Governor Danforth defends the Salem, Massachusetts, trial court with these words: "But you [Francis Nurse] must understand, sir, that a person is either with this court or he must be counted against it, there be no road between. This is a sharp time, now, a precise time—we live, no longer in the dusky afternoon when evil mixed itself with good and befuddled the world. Now, by God's grace, the shining sun is up, and them that fear not light will surely praise it." Arthur Miller, "The Crucible," in *The Portable Arthur Miller*, rev. ed., ed. Christopher Bigby (New York: Penguin, 2003), Act Three, p. 209.

22. Some middle-ground advice was deflected by "killing the messenger." Robert Kagan, for example, argues that members of the European Union decided after the Cold War to reduce military spending and opt out of power politics on the world stage. It followed, in his view, that criticism on the subject of Iraq by French and German officials was designed to serve their small-minded interests rather than a larger truth known to Americans. See Robert Kagan, *Of Paradise and Power: America and Europe in the New World Order* (New York: Knopf, 2003), pp. 3–42, but esp. pp. 10–11, 29–32, 38, 40.

23. Lawrence F. Kaplan and William Kristol, *The War Over Iraq: Saddam's Tyranny and America's Mission* (San Francisco: Encounter, 2003), p. 79.

24. *National Security Strategy of the United States, 2002* (Washington, DC: White House, 2002), p. 2. The *National Security Strategy of the United States* is a statement of the president's foreign policy intentions. The 2002 version was released by the White House in September of that year.

25. "President Delivers State of the Union Address," January 29, 2002.

26. "President Bush Delivers Graduation Speech at West Point," June 1, 2002, www.whitehouse.gov/news/releases/2002/06/print/20020601-3.html, accessed January 16, 2007.

27. "President's Remarks at the United Nations General Assembly," September 12, 2002, www.whitehouse.gov/news/releases/2002/09/print/20020912-1.html, accessed January 16, 2007.

28. "President Bush Delivers Graduation Speech at West Point," June 1, 2002: "Deterrence—the promise of massive retaliation against nations—means nothing against shadowy terrorist networks with no nation or citizens to defend. Containment is not possible when unbalanced dictators with weapons of mass destruction can deliver those weapons on missiles or secretly provide them to terrorist allies." See also "President's Remarks at the 2004 Republican National Convention," September 2, 2004: "Do I forget the lessons of September the 11th and take the word of a madman, or do I take action to defend our country? Faced with that choice, I will defend America every time." (These remarks are available at www.whitehouse.gov/news/releases/2004/09/print/20040902-2.html, accessed January 16, 2007.)

29. *National Security Strategy of the United States, 2002*, p. 15.

30. Thus Secretary of State Colin Powell was trapped by uncertain intelligence estimates when, before the preventive American assault on Iraq, he addressed the UN Security Council on February 5, 2003. After describing at length how Iraq was armed

with weapons of mass destruction, Powell declared that "[m]y colleagues, every statement I make today is backed up by sources, solid sources. These are not assertions. What we are giving you are facts and conclusions based on solid intelligence." (These remarks are available at www.state.gov/secretary/former/powell/remarks/2003/17300.htm, accessed February 1, 2007.) What Powell described as "solid intelligence" is deconstructed in John Prados, *Hoodwinked: The Documents That Reveal How Bush Sold Us a War* (New York: New Press, 2004), esp. pp. 199–255.

31. See Kaplan and Kristol, *The War Over Iraq*, p. 95: "The second tenet of the Bush Doctrine is regime change—that is, the recognition that the United States cannot really coexist peacefully with governments that seek to develop weapons of mass destruction, threaten their neighbors, and brutalize their own citizens."

32. "President Discusses the Future of Iraq," February 26, 2003, www.whitehouse.gov/news/release/2003/02/print/20030226-11.html, accessed October 6, 2007.

33. Ibid.

34. Kaplan and Kristol, *The War Over Iraq*, p. 99.

35. Ibid., p. 97. See also William Kristol's testimony to the Senate Foreign Relations Committee on February 7, 2002: "A friendly, free, and oil-producing Iraq would leave Iran isolated and Syria cowed; the Palestinians more willing to negotiate seriously with Israel; and Saudi Arabia with less leverage over policy makers here and in Europe. Removing Saddam Hussein and his henchmen from power presents a genuine opportunity—one President Bush sees clearly—to transform the political landscape of the Middle East." This testimony is available at www.newamericancentury.org/defense-20020207.htm, accessed October 6, 2007.

36. "President Bush Announces Major Combat Operations in Iraq Have Ended," May 1, 2003, www.whitehouse.gov/news/releases/2003/05/print/20030501-15.html, accessed January 16, 2007. For a conservative description of this event, see Bill Sammon, *Misunderestimated: The President Battles Terrorism, Media Bias, and the Bush Haters* (New York: Regan, 2004), pp. 255–269.

37. Neither Bush II nor his advisers gave serious thought to how a government would be established and how Iraq would be run after deposing Saddam Hussein. Much of the story is told in Ricks, *Fiasco*, pp. 58–148.

38. For an example of the individualist assumption, see William J. Bennett, *Why We Fight: Moral Clarity and the War on Terrorism* (New York: Doubleday, 2002), p. 74: "[T]he best way to understand others is to assume that they are as fully responsible for their own behavior as we are for ours." Susanne Hoeber Rudolph, "The Imperialism of Categories: Situating Knowledge in a Globalizing World," *Perspectives on Politics* (March 2005): 5–14, reminds us that many Americans and not just conservatives tend to view the world in terms of individualism. They assume that, morally, people are in some sense equal, in which case their encumbrances should not be considered a decisive factor in political life. An example of this assumption would be the Declaration of Independence, which asserts that all men (individuals) have natural rights (which should supersede historical encumbrances), including the right to liberty.

39. On the other hand, conservatives may describe Iraqis as encumbered in ways they are not. For example, David Brooks, "A More Humble Hawk: Crisis of Confidence," in *The Right War?: The Conservative Debate on Iraq*, ed. Gary Rosen (New York: Cambridge University Press, 2005), p. 64: "Once the political process [in Iraq] moves ahead, nationalism will work in our favor, as Iraqis seek to become the leading reformers in the Arab world." Brooks supports here the democratic domino theory without, apparently,

noticing that a *lack* of commitment to Iraqi nationalism characterizes the country's Shi'ites, Sunnis, and Kurds.

40. "President Bush Announces Major Combat Operations in Iraq Have Ended," May 1, 2003.

41. "President Discusses the Future of Iraq," February 26, 2003.

42. "President Commemorates 60th Anniversary of V-J Day," August 30, 2005, www.whitehouse.gov/news/releases/2005/08/print/20050830-1.html, accessed January 16, 2007.

43. William J. Bennett, "Morality, Character, and American Foreign Policy," in Kagan and Kristol, *Present Dangers,* p. 304.

44. Michael Novak, *The Universal Hunger for Liberty: Why the Clash of Civilizations Is Not Inevitable* (New York: Basic Books, 2004), p. xiii.

45. Classic works in this vein are Erich Fromm, *Escape from Freedom,* (New York: Farrar & Rinehart, 1941), and T. W. Adorno, et al., *The Authoritarian Personality* (New York: Harper, 1950). Later research on personality and political outlook is surveyed in John T. Jost, Jack Glaser, Arie W. Kruglanski, and Frank J. Sullaway, "Political Conservatism as Motivated Social Cognition," *Psychological Bulletin* 129 (May 2003): 339–375, which cites 256 articles or books that touch on the motivation thesis.

46. Richard Cheney, "The Gulf War: A First Assessment" at the 1991 Soref Symposium of the Washington Institute for Near East Policy in Washington, D.C., www.washingtoninstitute.org/print.php?template+CO7&CID+55, accessed October 6, 2007.

47. Kagan, *Of Paradise and Power,* pp. 15–16.

48. "President Says Saddam Hussein Must Leave Iraq Within 48 Hours," March 17, 2003, www.whitehouse.gov/news/releases/ 2003/03/print/20030317-7.html, accessed January 16, 2007. See also Hannity, *Deliver Us from Evil,* pp. 47–53, where Hannity criticizes what Chamberlain did at Munich and claims that American liberals want to deal with Osama bin Laden and Saddam Hussein by repeating Chamberlain's policy of appeasement.

49. A reminder of what happened is Robert S. MacNamara, *In Retrospect: The Tragedy and Lessons of Vietnam* (New York: Vintage, 1996), pp. 321–323. Former Secretary of Defense (1961–1968) MacNamara lists "eleven major causes for our disaster in Vietnam," including overestimating the Vietnamese desire for "freedom and democracy," underestimating the "limitations of modern, high-technology military equipment, forces, and doctrine in confronting unconventional" fighters, and knowing little or nothing of "the history, culture, and politics of the people in the area, and the personalities and habits of their leaders."

50. Bush I seems to have shared a Reagan-era conviction that America should not promote democracy too energetically in most third-world countries. See George H. W. Bush and Brent Scowcroft, *A World Transformed* (New York: Knopf, 1998), pp. 488–492, where Bush and Scowcroft say they are opposed to the "breakup of the Iraqi state."

51. Richard A. Viguerie, *The New Right: We're Ready to Lead* (Falls Church, VA: Viguerie Company, 1980), p. 7.

52. David Horowitz, *Hating Whitey and Other Progressive Causes* (Dallas: Spence, 1999), p. 203.

53. Robert H. Bork, *Slouching Towards Gomorrah: Modern Liberalism and American Decline* (New York: Regan, 1996), p. 19.

54. Kaplan and Kristol, *The War Over Iraq,* p. 112.

55. For 2002, the year when Washington was planning to go to war, annual defense budgets were as follows: United States, $348 billion; China, $51 billion; France, $40 billion; Japan, $39 billion; United Kingdom, $38 billion; Germany, $33 billion; Italy, $25 billion; Saudi Arabia, $18 billion; India, $13 billion; South Korea, $13 billion; Israel, $9 billion; Brazil, $9 billion; Australia, $9 billion. See *The Military Balance 2004–2005* (London: International Institute for Strategic Studies, 2004), pp. 353–358.

56. Bennett, "Morality, Character and American Foreign Policy," in Kagan and Kristol, *Present Dangers,* p. 301.

57. *National Security Strategy of the United States, 2002,* p. 3.

58. This is the general theme of books that argue that American leaders have recently relied too much on force instead of diplomacy, trade, and other avenues to international compromise and the pursuit of shared interests. See, for example, Andrew Bacevich, *The New American Militarism: How Americans Are Seduced by War* (New York: Oxford University Press, 2005), and Chalmers Johnson, *The Sorrows of Empire: Militarism, Secrecy, and the End of the Republic* (New York: Owl, 2005).

59. "Address to a Joint Session of Congress and the American People," September 20, 2001.

60. "President Bush Addresses the Nation," March 19, 2003, www.whitehouse.gov/news/releases/2003/03/print/20030319-17.html, accessed January 16, 2007.

61. "State of the Union Address," February 2, 2005, www.whitehouse.gov/news/releases/2005/02/print/20050202-11.html, accessed January 16, 2007.

62. James W. Caesar, "The Great Divide: American Internationalism and Its Opponents," in Kagan and Kristol, *Present Dangers,* p. 41.

63. See Charles Krauthammer, "The Bush Doctrine," *Weekly Standard,* June 4, 2001. Quoted in Bacevich, *The New American Militarism,* p. 83.

64. Bennett, "Morality, Character and American Foreign Policy," in Kagan and Kristol, *Present Dangers,* p. 294.

65. Kaplan and Kristol, *The War Over Iraq,* p. 119.

66. For criticism of foreigners who resist creative destruction, see Michael A. Ledeen, *The War Against the Terror Masters: Why It Happened. Where We Are Now. How We'll Win.* (New York: St. Martin's Press, 2003), p. 212: "Creative destruction is our middle name, both within our own society and abroad. We tear down the old order every day, from business to science, literature, art, architecture, and cinema to politics and the law. Our enemies have always hated this whirlwind of energy and creativity, which menaces their traditions (whatever they may be) and shames them for their inability to keep pace. Seeing America undo traditional societies, they fear us, for they do not wish to be undone.... They must attack us in order to survive, just as we must destroy them to advance our historic mission."

67. "Address to a Joint Session of Congress and the American People," September 20, 2001.

68. "President Holds Prime Time News Conference," October 11, 2001, www.whitehouse.gov/news/releases/2001/10/print/20011001-7.html, accessed December 10, 2010.

69. "Address to a Joint Session of Congress and the American People," September 20, 2001.

70. Ledeen, *The War Against the Terror Masters,* p. 153.

71. The president referred to this form of Islam not as a particular response to authoritarianism, fundamentalism, colonialism, imperialism, and modernization, but

simply as a "radical ideology of hate." See "President's Remarks at the 2004 Republican National Convention," September 2, 2004.

72. Even after two years of war in Iraq, George W. Bush asserted that "in fact, we're not facing a series of grievances that can be soothed and addressed. We're facing a radical ideology with unalterable objectives: to enslave whole nations and intimidate the world. No act of ours invited the rage of the killers—and no concession, bribe or act of appeasement would change or limit their plans for murder." Bush is quoted in Louise Richardson, *What Terrorists Want: Understanding the Enemy, Containing the Threat* (New York: Random House, 2006), p. 196. See also Frum and Perle, *An End to Evil,* p. 48: "Where does this hatred come from? The United States has made mistakes in the Middle East, as it has elsewhere in the world. But a hatred as all-consuming and self-destructive as the hatred encountered in radical Islam tells us much more about those who hate than about the one who is hated."

73. Madeleine Albright, "Iraq: The Unintended Consequences," in *The Mighty and the Almighty: Reflections on America, God, and World Affairs* (New York: HarperCollins, 2006), pp. 165–183, attributes failures in Iraq to the Bush administration's ignorance of "the complexities created by history and religion."

74. This financial estimate comes from Linda Bilmes and Joseph E. Stiglitz, *The Three Trillion Dollar War: The True Cost of the Iraq Conflict* (New York: Norton, 2008). Additional costs are discussed in Francis Fox Piven, *The War at Home: The Domestic Costs of Bush's Militarism* (New York: New Press, 2004).

75. This does not mean that "realistic" candidates must avoid promoting narratives. Conservatives may be accused of dangerous storytelling because they tend to tell stories. Liberals usually avoid such charges because they are more practical than visionary. Nevertheless, liberals may be faulted not for telling the wrong stories but for not telling stories at all. This is because if they try to lead without evoking some of the zeal that powerful stories can inspire, shared commitments to support common endeavors may not emerge. Recognition of this dilemma is not new. Thus Proverbs 29:18 already warns that "[w]here there is no vision, the people perish." And I Corinthians 14:8 asks, "[I]f the trumpet give an uncertain sound, who shall prepare himself for the battle?" (See also the quotations in note 47, Chapter Six.) Such long-standing truisms suggest—and this is food for serious thought—why, although Democrats controlled the White House and dominated both houses of Congress in 2009–2010, they were unable, operating mainly as pragmatists, to enact a government option in American health care.

76. The incompetence of government agencies is presumed especially by libertarians in the conservative camp. For example, P. J. Rourke, "The Right to Do as You Please and Take the Consequences" [1993], in *Toward Liberty: The Idea that is Changing the World,* ed. David Boaz (Washington, DC: Cato Institute, 2002), p. 423: "We have a group of incredibly silly people in the [Clinton] White House right now, people who think government works. Or that government would work if you got some really bright young kids from Yale to run it."

77. Hurricane Katrina struck after Bush II went to war. But the bureaucratic incompetence of the Federal Emergency Management Agency in New Orleans was to be expected, according to conservative predictions. Thus it did not surprise Arkansas Governor Mike Huckabee, *From Hope to Higher Ground: 12 STOPs to Restoring America's Greatness* (New York: Center Street, 2007), p. 15: "As government [FEMA] failed, its people [Arkansas' volunteers] did not."

78. See George F. Kennan Jr., "The Sources of Soviet Conduct," *Foreign Affairs* (July

1947): 582. The passage is quoted approvingly by William Kristol and Robert Kagan, "National Interest and Global Responsibility," in Kagan and Kristol, eds., *Present Dangers,* p. 24. See also Norman Podhoretz, "World War IV: How It Started, What It Means, and Why We Have to Win," in Rosen, ed., *The Right War,* p. 169, where Podhoretz calls on Americans to accept once again what he calls "the responsibilities of moral and political leadership that history 'plainly intended' us to bear."

79. Feulner, *Getting America Right,* pp. 174–176. Kennan himself regarded America's campaign in Vietnam as an enormous policy error. See "The Statement and Testimony of the Honorable George F. Kennan," in *The Vietnam Hearings,* introduction by Senator J. William Fulbright (New York: Vintage, 1966), pp. 107–166, but esp. p. 108.

80. The Vietnam syndrome is discussed by Stefan A. Halper and Jonathan Clarke, *America Alone: The Neoconservatives and the Global Order* (New York: Cambridge University Press, 2004), pp. 30–31.

81. "President Delivers State of the Union Address," January 29, 2002.

82. See Galbraith, *The End of Iraq.* Galbraith tells of a meeting held shortly before the Iraq war started, in which three prominent Iraqis met with Bush II: "As the three described what they thought would be the political situation after Saddam's fall, they talked about Sunnis and Shiites. It became apparent to them that the president was unfamiliar with these terms." And so, "two months before he ordered U.S. troops into the country, the president of the United States did not appear to know about the division among Iraqis that has defined the country's history and politics." Accordingly, he "could not have anticipated U.S. troops being caught in the middle of a civil war between two religious sects that he did not know existed," p. 83. Further on, Galbraith remarks that "[t]he most durable [administration] preconception was that there was a single Iraq," p. 98. To that effect, he quotes Condoleezza Rice, then national security adviser, who in August 2004 declared publicly that "[w]hat has been impressive to me so far is that Iraqis—whether Kurds or Shia or Sunni or the many other ethnic groups in Iraq—have demonstrated that they really want to live as one in a unified Iraq," p. 99. We cannot be certain that Rice believed that or said it only as part of a White House effort to sell the president's policy to skeptics. However, a similar slighting of encumbrances appeared in Deputy Secretary of Defense Paul Wolfowitz's testimony to Congress on February 27, 2003, when he insisted that peacekeeping after the Iraq war would be less costly than in Bosnia. See Committee on the Budget, House of Representatives, *Department of Defense Budget Priorities for Fiscal Year 2004* (Washington, DC: Government Printing Office, 2003) p. 9: "[P]eacekeeping requirements in Iraq might be much lower than our historical experience in the Balkans suggest [*sic*]. There has been none of the record in Iraq of ethnic militias fighting one another that produced so much bloodshed and permanent scars in Bosnia, along with a continuing requirement for large peacekeeping forces to separate those militias." This proposition, while predicting modest budgetary outlays after preliminary fighting, ignores the fact, obvious to many diplomats, scholars, and journalists, that ethnic militias in Bosnia appeared *after* President Josip Tito of Yugoslavia died and his country broke up. In which case similar militias would appear in Iraq *after* Saddam Hussein would be deposed and unable to continue suppressing ethnic tensions in Iraq.

83. "President Delivers State of the Union Address," January 29, 2002.

84. "President Bush Delivers Graduation Speech at West Point," June 1, 2002. Social conservatives are especially likely to agree with Bush on this point of principle. See Jerry Falwell, *The New American Family* (Dallas: Word, 1992), p. 196: "Times change; values do not."

85. Ron Suskind, "Without a Doubt," *New York Times Magazine*, October 17, 2004, pp. 50–51. The emphasis on "enlightenment principles and empiricism" suggests that Max Weber would have regarded Suskind as "disenchanted."

86. See Chapter Six, in the text above note 49: "America tells one story: the unbroken, ineluctable progress of freedom and equality." After the failure of some European governments to support America's war in Iraq, Grover Norquist adapts this story appropriately. See his "America is Freedom," in *Why I Am a Reagan Conservative*, ed. Michael K. Deaver (New York: HarperCollins, 2005), p. 89: "For our constitution declares that all men and women have the God-given right to liberty. What we protect in America is deserved by all the people on the planet. Except maybe the French."

87. This acceptance speech is reprinted in Barry Goldwater, *Where I Stand* (New York: McGraw-Hill, 1964), pp. 9–17. The quoted words are on p. 16.

88. "President Sworn-in to a Second Term," January 20, 2005, www.whitehouse.gov/news/release/2005/01/print/20050120-1.html, accessed August 4, 2005.

89. "President's Remarks at the 2004 Republican National Convention," September 2, 2004.

90. "President Addresses the Nation, Discusses Iraq, War on Terror," June 28, 2005, www.whitehouse.gov/news/releases/2005/06/print/20050628-7.html, accessed January 16, 2007.

91. "State of the Union Address," February 2, 2005.

92. "President's Remarks at the 2004 Republican National Convention," September 2, 2004.

93. For example, Tony Blankley, *The West's Last Chance: Will We Win the Clash of Civilizations?* (Washington, DC: Regnery, 2005). Blankley is the editorial page editor of the *Washington Times*.

94. Perhaps they will take their cue from Condoleezza Rice, who as secretary of state on March 31, 2006, said that "I know we've made tactical errors—thousands of them, I'm sure. This could have gone that way or that could have gone this way. But when you look back in history, what will be judged is did you make the right strategic decision [to overthrow the dangerous dictator, Saddam Hussein]. And if you spend all of your time trying to judge this tactical issue or that tactical issue, I think you miss the larger sweep." See "Remarks at BBC Today—Chatham House Lecture," at www.state.gov.secretary/rm/2006/63969.htm, accessed August 19, 2007.

95. For example, against liberals: Dinesh D'Souza, *The Enemy at Home: The Cultural Left and Its Responsibility for 9/11* (New York: Doubleday, 2007). Conservatives will sometimes quarrel among themselves. Thus against Bush II's Iraq war, see Patrick J. Buchanan, *Where the Right Went Wrong: How Neoconservatives Subverted the Reagan Revolution and Hijacked the Bush Presidency* (New York: Thomas Dunne, 2004), and Francis Fukuyama, *America at the Crossroads: Democracy, Power, and the Neoconservative Legacy* (New Haven, CT: Yale University Press, 2006).

96. I have promoted that obligation in David M. Ricci, *Good Citizenship in America* (Cambridge: Cambridge University Press, 2004).

97. Humanists are more likely than social scientists to focus on powerful stories and their likely consequences. Thus Barry Unsworth, *The Song of Kings* (New York: Norton, 2004), tells an instructive version of the story of Iphigeneia at Aulis, where Odysseus helps to spin a tale that will persuade Agamemnon to sacrifice his daughter and thereby placate Zeus, who will then moderate the force of the sea wind and thus enable the Greek fleet to sail from Aulis to Troy, where Odysseus hopes to win fame and fortune by making

war. As Odysseus remarks (p. 296), in the contest between stories that men tell, "it is the stories told by the strong, the songs of the kings, that are believed in the end." Yet we know now how the story advising Agamemnon to placate Zeus eventually destroyed the Greek king, who believed the story, sacrificed Iphigeneia, and, upon returning home after the war, was killed in retaliation by her mother, Clytaemnestra.

98. This lesson is absent, and no Greek tragedies are excerpted, in William Bennett, ed., *The Book of Virtues: A Treasury of Great Moral Stories* (New York: Touchstone, 1993).

99. See Michael Isikoff and David Corn, *Hubris: The Inside Story of Spin, Scandal and the Selling of the Iraq War* (New York: Crown, 2006). The real hubris was not exaggeration in justifying a war but going to war under the circumstances. With regard to somewhat similar circumstances, Senator J. William Fulbright (D-AR) criticized President Lyndon Johnson and his administration for prosecuting what Fulbright regarded as a disastrous war in Vietnam. See William Fulbright, *The Arrogance of Power* (New York: Vintage, 1967), p. 3: "Power confuses itself with virtue and tends also to take itself for omnipotence. Once imbued with the idea of a mission, a great nation easily assumes that it has the means as well as the duty to do God's work." In which case, nations sometimes attempt more than they should try. As Fulbright remarks, "I am reminded of the three Boy Scouts who reported to their scoutmaster that as their good deed for the day they had helped an old lady to cross the street. 'That's fine,' said the scoutmaster, 'but why did it take three of you?' 'Well,' they explained, 'she didn't want to go,'" p. 12.

100. Geoffrey Nunberg, *Talking Right: How Conservatives Turned Liberalism into A Tax-Raising, Latte-Drinking, Sushi-Eating, Volvo-Driving,* New York Times*–Reading, Body-Piercing, Hollywood-Loving, Left-Wing Freak Show* (New York: PublicAffairs, 2006), p. 35.

101. Drew Westen, *The Political Brain: The Role of Emotion in Deciding the Fate of the Nation* (New York: PublicAffairs, 2007), p. 169.

102. For example, see Thomas Friedman, "The Fat Lady Has Sung," *New York Times,* February 21, 2010, p. WK8: "[T]he thing that baffles me about Mr. Obama is how a politician who speaks so well, and is trying to do so many worthy things, can't come up with a clear, simple, repeatable narrative to explain this politics." See also Richard Cohen, "President Obama's Enigmatic Intellectualism," *Washington Post* June 22, 2010, p. A19; "It can seem that at the heart of Barack Obama's foreign policy is no heart at all. It consists instead of a series of challenges—of problems that need fixing, not wrongs that need to be righted. As Winston Churchill once said of a certain pudding, Obama's approach to foreign affairs lacks theme. So, it seems does the man himself." On Obama's narrative weakness, see also Frank Rich, "The Up-or-Down Vote on Obama's Presidency," *New York Times,* March 7, 2010, p. WK10.

Index

abortion, 19, 22, 29, 212n41; anecdotes, 56, 59; and declining birthrates, 94; and disenchantment, 109; and the new class, 93–94; and personal responsibility, 42, 136
Abraham Lincoln (U.S. navy vessel), 168
abstinence, sexual, 58
Accuracy in Academia, 152
advertising, 123–125; and children, 124; of conservative policies, 152–154; and enchantment, 124–125
affirmative action, 24; and personal responsibility, 41–42, 42, 43; and perversity, 68, 69; and resentment, 106
Afghanistan War, costs, 27
African Americans, 70; IQ (intelligence quotient), 24, 44; in poverty, 65–66, 69–71, 71–72, 76–77, 101; school performance, 69; and unemployment, 17, 36–37, 76; unwed mothers, 69
Africans, enslaved in America, 37, 99–100
Age of Reason (Wilentz), 185n8
agenda setting, 74–75
agitprop (agitation propaganda), 153
agriculture, 39
AIDS, and personal responsibility, 42
Alcibiades, 161–162
Allen, David Y., "Modern Conservatism," 186n1
Alm, Richard and W. Michael Cox, "You Are What You Spend," 200n89
America in Black and White (Thernstrom and Thernstrom), 66, 67, 69, 76–77, 199n70
America Now (Harris), 215n96
American Abundance (Kudlow), 193n116
American Civil Liberties Union (ACLU), 91, 114
American Conservative Movement, The (Critchlow and MacLean), 185n8
American Dream, 67, 87
American Enterprise Institute, 149, 178, 185n10
American Friends Service Committee, 91
American Gospel (Meacham), 224n49
American Paradox (Myers), 201n106
American Political Science Review, 200n90
American preeminence, 171–178; and benevolence, 172–173; and encumbered people, 173; and hatred of America, 173–174; and responsibility, 171–172
American Renaissance, An (Kemp), 193n110
American Spectator, 150
Americans for Democratic Action, 73
Americans for Tax Reform, 89, 152
Ames, Bruce N., 56
Amusing Ourselves to Death (Postman), 200n95
Amway, as think tank sponsor, 154
Andrews, John, "So You Want to Start a Think Tank," 153

anecdotes, 55–59, 74; and footnotes, 151–152; on relativism, 102; vs. scientific knowledge, 116; and style, 58–59
Ankerberg, John, 58, 63, 64, 91, 119, 129
Anna Karenina (Tolstoy), 98
Ansell, Amy E., *Unraveling the Right,* 184n8, 186n15
Anthony, Mark, 17, 89, 138; *Vanishing Republic,* 195n28
Antigone, 109
Anti-Saloon League, 113
Arched Daniels Midland Company, 137
Aristotle, 4
Arkes, Hadley, 183n4
Arlington House (publisher), 152
Armey, Dick, 61–62, 87, 89, 89–90, 90; *Freedom Revolution,* 142
Armey, Dick and Newt Gingrich, *Contract with America,* 12, 133
Arnold, Matthew, 13; *Culture and Anarchy,* 216n120
Arrogance of Power (Fulbright), 249n99
Ashcroft, John, 90, 116
Asian Americans, 76, 77
Asimov, Isaac, 136
Assassin's Gate (Packer), 240n7
Athens, Greece, 138
Augustine, Saint, 22, 144
authoritarians vs. libertarians, 86
axis of evil, 164

bailouts, corporate, 27, 48
Baltz, Dan and Ronald Brownstein, *Storming the Gates,* 184n8
Banfield, Edward, 14–15, 17, 76, 223n44; *The Unheavenly City,* 22, 68, 71–72
bank bailout, of 2008, 27
Barbary Coast pirates, 50
Barnes, Fred, *Rebel-in-Chief,* 184n6
Bartels, Larry M., *Unequal Democracy,* 184n5, 234n49
Bartlett, Bruce R., *Reaganomics,* 193n110
Barton, David, *The Myth of Separation,* 223n40
Bauman, Michael, 16
Bebchuk, Lucien, "The Growth of Executive Pay," 211n33
Beck, Glenn, 2
Becker, Gary, 36
Being Black, Living in the Red (Conley), 200n89
Being Right Is Not Enough (Waldman), 214n82
Beisner, Calvin, 144
Bell, Daniel, *The Cultural Contradictions of Capitalism,* 209n3
Bell, Jeffrey, *Populism and Elitism,* 205n63
Bell Curve, The (Murray and Herrnstein), 44, 151, 192n98
Bennett, William, 45, 56, 62, 84, 85, 90, 98, 104, 115, 123, 131, 169, 172; *The Book of Virtues,* 131; *The Index of Leading Cultural Indicators,* 209n116; *The Spirit of America,* 131; *Why We Fight,* 243n38
Berger, Peter, 85
Berlin Wall, fall of, 163
Bible, The: and marriage, 18; as moral guide, 23, 29, 59, 83–84, 101–102, 131; and Scopes trial, 21–22; secular view, 101, 146
Biden, Joe, 6, 6–7, 180, 186n16
Bill of Rights, 84
Bilmes, Linda and Joseph L. Stiglitz, *The Three Trillion Dollar War,* 183
birth control, 94
Blaming the Victim (Ryan), 207n78
Bloom, Allan, 4, 98, 131, 141, 142, 150, 177
Bluestone, Barry and Bennett Harrison, *The Deindustrialization of America,* 210n4
Blumenfeld, Samuel, 101
Blumenthal, Sidney, 149
Boaz, David, *Toward Liberty,* 203n16
Bodin, Jean, *Six Books of the Commonwealth,* 112
Bogus, Carl, T., "Rescuing Burke," 185n12
Bonhoeffer, Dietrich, 110–111
Book of Virtues, The (Bennett), 131
Boomerang (Skocpol), 193n112
Boorstin, Daniel, 129–130, 131
Bork, Robert, 4, 20, 36, 45, 71, 84–85, 85, 92, 92–93, 148–149, 170
Boston Tea Party, 131
bourgeois family, 114–115
Breaking of the American Social Compact, The (Piven and Cloward), 201n96
Brennan, Mary C., *Turning Right in the Sixties,* 184n8
Brookhiser, Richard, *The Way of the WASP,* 219n158

Brooks, Arthur C., *Who Really Cares?,* 208n93
Brooks, David, 92
Brown, Harold, 19, 23, 59, 64, 82, 109
Brown, Scott, 180
Brown v. Board of Education, 19, 42–43
Brownback, Sam, 90
Browning, Robert, 132
Brownstein, Ronald and Dan Baltz, *Storming the Gates,* 184n8
Bruce, Tammy, 119; *The Death of Right and Wrong,* 218n151
Bryan, William Jennings, 21–22
Buchanan, Pat, 3, 59, 104, 107, 133, 162; on the British Empire, 60–61; *The Death of the West,* 216n99; on liberal power, 72; on population growth, 50–51, 94
Buckley, William F., Jr., 2, 7, 25, 44, 86, 150, 153; on *Brown v. Board of Education,* 19; founds *National Review,* 12; on higher education, 98; on science, 116
budget, federal, 27
bureaucracies, 85
Burger King, 17
Burke, Edmund, 13, 14, 40–41, 85, 104, 108, 144, 147, 185n12, 209n2, 230n9
Burkett, Larry, 15, 63–64, 88; *Whatever Happened to the American Dream?,* 196n40
Burnham, James, 93; *Suicide of the West,* 233n47
Bush, George H. W., 12, 159, 169, 170; and "the vision thing," 159
Bush, George W., 26, 27, 44, 90, 161, 164, 165, 166, 185n10. *See also* Bush Doctrine; 2004 presidential election, 1–2, 160–161, 172–173; announces end of Iraq War, 168; inaugural address, 138–139
Bush Doctrine, 164, 166, 167, 169, 169–170, 171; and American preeminence, 171–178; and ignoring reality, 176–177
Butler, Stuart, 42, 85, 115
Byrd, Robert, *Losing America,* 241n19

Caesar, James, 172
Canadian healthcare system, 20
canon, the, 97–100
capitalism: in conservative script, 11, 20–21; democratic, 33; laissez-faire, 23–24, 31, 45–48, 48–51, 50; and progress, 81–82, 137; and selfishness, 82
capitalism, laissez-faire: and Christianity, 83–84; and corporations, 84–85; and creative destruction, 102–104; and enchantment. *See* enchantment, free market; and encumbered people, 117–118; and environmental pollution, 64–65; hypothetical nature of, 117–119
Carson, Rachel, 59
Carter, Dan. T., *The Politics of Rage,* 184n8
Carter, Jimmy, 115
Carter, Stephen, 110
Castle Rock Foundation, 154
Cato Institute, 149
cause and effect, 60–61, 75
censorship, 49, 145, 146–147, 149
Central Intelligence Agency (CIA), 175
ceteris paribus, 38–40, 117–118; in rhetoric, 75–76
Chain Reaction (Edsall and Edsall), 183, 205n61
Chamberlain, Neville, 169–170
Changing Minds (Gardner), 187n4
charity, private, 15–16, 68
charter schools, 62
Chavez, Linda, *An Unlikely Conservative,* 206n77
Cheney, Dick, 169
Cheney, Lynne V., *Telling the Truth,* 198n70
child care, 18
children, and advertising, 124
children, delinquent, 58
China: counterfeit products from, 50; purchase of petroleum, 51
Chomsky, Noam, 92
Christensen, Bryce, 115; *Utopia Against the Family,* 232n30
Christian Coalition, 29
Christian economics, 83–85; corporations and, 84–85
Christianity, and conservative vision of America, 53
Christians, evangelical, 13; and church and state, 29–30, 59, 60, 103, 104, 143; and feminism, 18; and fight against evil, 21–22, 165; and homosexuality, 29;

Christians, evangelical (continued): and religious enchantment. *See* enchantment, religious; view of human nature, 23–24
Chrysler Corporation bailout, 1980, 48
church, as mediating structure, 85
church and state, 29, 59, 60, 103, 112–113, 143
churn, the, 126
Civil Rights Act of 1964, 43
Clash of Civilizations and the Remaking of World Order (Huntington), 97, 163
class, new, of intellectuals, 90–94, 107; defining characteristic, 91–92, 92–93
class, social, 68–69; and poverty, 71–72
climate change, 37–38, 50–51, 152, 154; and corporations, 64–65, 85
Clinton, Bill, 27, 56, 94, 141, 162, 180; election, 186n16; and Monica Lewinsky, 142
Clinton, Hillary, 92
closure, 154–155, 178
Cloward, Richard A. and Frances Fox Piven, *The Breaking of the American Social Compact,* 201n96
Coercive Utopians (Isaac and Isaac), 186n42
Cold War, 162, 164; end of, 163–164; as unifying, 86–87, 163; and War on Terror, 164–165, 175–176
colonial America, 143
Color Purple, The (Walker), 98
Colson, Charles, 13, 93, 94–95, 100
Commentary, 150
communism, 20–21; as common enemy, 86–87; as evil, 164–165
Communist Manifesto (Marx and Engels), 133
communists, liberals as, 72–73
Compassionate Conservatism (Olasky), 206n76
Competitive Enterprise Institute, 152
Confessions of an Economic Hit Man (Perkins), 227n113
Conley, Dalton, *Being Black, Living in the Red,* 200n89
Connolly, William, "The Evangelical-Capitalist Resonance Machine," 186n2
Conscience of a Conservative, The (Goldwater), 13, 88–89
Conservatism (Muller), 188n9
"Conservatism and the Right in America" (Nichols), 185n12
conservative articles of belief, 187n7
Conservative Ascendancy (Critchlow), 185n8
Conservative Bookshelf (Williamson), 185n11
conservative mind, the, 3
Conservative Mind, The (Kirk), 185n9
Conservative Revolution (Edwards), 184n8
conservative script, 2–3; and capitalism, 11; and truth, 13
conservative think tanks, 149
Conservative Tradition in America (Guttmann), 198n54
conservative vision, 4; basic propositions, 12; and democracy, 13
conservatives, 85; authoritarian vs. libertarian, 86; dichotomous beliefs, 81–86, 92, 102–104; diverse nature, 3; in the Federal government, 61; historical thinkers and, 4, 13; influence of, 1–2; opposition to liberal ideas, 14–27; and resentment, 106–108; and scientific findings, 115–116; secular, 23; shared enemies, and cohesion, 86–90, 92, 93, 94–97, 105–106, 126–127; in the White House, 1–2
Conservatives Betrayed (Viguerie), 193n113
Constitution, United States, 49, 50, 61, 110, 134; and freedom of religion, 112–113; original intent, 71
consumer sovereignty, 125
consumerism, 82, 93; and advertising, 123–124; and arrested development, 120; and creative destruction, 126
Consuming Kids (Linn), 211n22
"Contain the Wealthy and Patrol the Magistrates" (McCormick), 200n90
Contract with America, 115
Contract with America (Gingrich and Armey), 12, 26, 133
Coolidge, Calvin, 88, 118
Coors, as think tank sponsor, 154
Copernicus, 136
Corn, David and Michael Isikoff, *Hubris,* 249n99
Cornog, Evan, *The Power and the Story,* 187n4
corporate bailouts, 27, 48
corporate downsizing, 46, 84, 122
Corporation for Public Broadcasting (CPB), 91

corporations, 121–123; and Christianity, 84–85; as megastructures and mediating institutions, 85, 122–123; news and entertainment, 123; taxes on, 119–120; as think tank sponsors, 154
correlations, 60–71; vs. causation, 60–61, 75; and reverse sequences, 64–71
Corrosion of Character, The (Sennett), 211n32
Corzine, Jon, 180
Costs of Living (Schwartz), 201n106
Coulter, Ann, 73–74, 153, 185n10
counterculture, 94–97; and multiculturalism, 97–98
counterestablishment, 149–156
Cox, Harvey, "The Market as God," 117
Cox, Michael, 126
Cox, Michael and Richard Alm, "You Are What You Spend," 200n89
crash of 1929, 6
Crawford, Alan, *Thunder on the Right,* 209n1
Creationism, 4, 29, 103, 111–112
creative destruction, 39, 49, 81–82, 102–104, 115; and free market enchantment, 125–126; and progress, 145; and resentment, 107–108; social and cultural, 145; and unemployment, 126
Crick, Francis, 136
crime: causation anecdotes, 61–62, 64; causes of, 64; and church attendance, 40; and race, 69
Crisis of Vision in Modern Economic Thought (Heilbroner and Milberg), 202n114
Critchlow, Donald and Nancy MacLean, *The American Conservative Movement,* 185n8
Critchlow, Donald, *The Conservative Ascendancy,* 185n8
Crittenden, Ann, *The Price of Motherhood,* 214n69
Crowd, The (LeBon), 201n106
Cultural Contradictions of Capitalism (Bell), 209n3
cultural diversity, 64
cultural relativism, 100–102
Culture Against Man (Henry), 201n106, 226n98
Culture and Anarchy (Arnold), 216n120
culture of poverty, 68, 69
Cuomo, Mario, *Reason to Believe,* 208n110
Curie, Marie, 136

Dannemeyer, William, 19, 63
Dannemeyer, William, 236n86
Darrow, Clarence, 21–22
Darwin, Charles, 136, 154; *On the Origin of Species,* 139–140
David, 131
daycare, 18
De Bonald, Louis, 13
de Maistre, Joseph, 13, 14
de Toqueville, Alexis, 4, 143, 144, 150, 154
Death of Right and Wrong, The (Bruce), 218n151
Death of the West (Buchanan), 216n99
death penalty, 116
Decatur, Stephen, 50
December 7, 1941, 167
Declaration of Independence, 131, 134, 138, 171
Dector, Midge, 24, 57, 96; "A Letter to the Young," 216n100; *The New Chastity and Other Arguments Against Women's Liberation,* 213n65
Deeds, Creigh, 180
deficit, budget, 27
deindustrialization, 84–85
Deindustrialization of America (Bluestone and Harrison), 210n4
DeLay, Tom, 90; *No Retreat, No Surrender,* 187n7, 239n116
democracy: conditions for, 138; as conservative value, 13, 20–21
democratic capitalism, 33
Democrats. *See also* liberals: budget surplus under, 27; and enchantment, 4–5; identity gap, 5, 160–161; and the intelligensia, 91; and interventionism, 162; as weak on terrorism, 160–161
DeVos, Dick, 40–41
Dewey, John, 73, 101
Diamond, Sara: *Not By Politics Alone,* 203n12; *Roads to Dominion,* 184n8, 220n7
Dickens, Charles, 196n38
discrimination, rational, 36, 70–71
disenchantment, 108–110; and marketplace for ideas, 145–146, 147; and scientific method, 116, 136, 139–140

Disney corporation, 84
divorce, 148
Dobson, James, 185n10
Dole, Bob, 235n23
Dollars and Dreams (Levy), 209n115
domino effect, of democracy, 168
domino theory, and Vietnam, 170
Donahue, Phil, 119
Donohue, William, 19–20, 59, 63, 91, 95, 115, 121, 145
Don't Think of an Elephant (Lakoff), 230n6
Dorrien, Gary, "Inventing an American Conservatism," 186n15
Dorrien, Gary, *The Neoconservative Mind,* 184n8
downsizing, corporate, 46, 84, 122
Dream and the Nightmare (Magnet), 230n10
Druckman, James N., "Political Preference Formation," 184n7
drug abuse: "just say no" campaign, 43; as moral issue, 45
D'Souza, Dinesh, 36–37, 45, 46–47, 69, 70–71, 77, 118; on education, 98; *The Enemy at Home,* 218n150; on health care, 137; *Letters to a Young Conservative,* 192n103, 194n117; on racism, 66, 66–67; on relativism, 100–101; *Ronald Reagan,* 203n15; on taxes, 88; *The Virtue of Prosperity,* 197n45; *What's Go Great About America,* 198n70
Dugan, Robert, 29
Dunn, Charles and J. David Woodward, "The Problem of Defining Conservatism," 186n1
Dunn, Charles, *The Future of Conservatism,* 187n3

Eagle Forum, 150
Eastland, Terry, 43; *Ending Affirmative Action,* 151, 198n69
Eckerd, Jack, 94
economic rationality, 23–24
economics: Christian, 83–85; Keynesian, 88; and other social spheres, 47–49
Economics (Rose), 51
economics, laissez-faire, 40
economics, macro- vs. micro-, 51–52
economics, supply side, 25–27
economics, trickle-down, 25–27, 32
Economics in One Lesson (Hazlitt), 193n113
economy, zero-sum, 45, 46–47; and government taxation, 87–90
Edgeworth Box, 46–47
Edsall, Thomas Byrne and Mary D., *Chain Reaction,* 183, 205n61
education, higher. *See* universities
education reform, 14–15; *Brown v. Board of Education,* 19, 42–43; and consumerism, 120; and multiculturalism, 64; and the new class, 93; and rationality, 35; and spending, 62–63; vouchers, 62
Edwards, George C., III, *Governing by Campaigning,* 184n6
Edwards, Lee, *The Conservative Revolution,* 184n8
Ehrenreich, Barbara, 73; *Fear of Falling,* 214n82; *Nickeled and Dimed,* 120
Einstein, Albert, 136, 154
elections, and voter identity laws, 188n10
elections, by year. *See* under year of election
elites: as contemptuous, 108; and entertainment industry, 119
elites, cultural, 95
elites, new class of, 90–94
elites, political, 91–92
Emerging Republican Majority (Phillips), 183, 220n7
employment: and creative destruction, 126; downsizing and outsourcing, 46, 122; and minimum wage, 16–17; and race, 17, 36–37; of women, 17–18, 89–90; youth and, 17
enchantment, 4–5
enchantment, free market, 117–126; and advertising, 124–125; and creative destruction, 125–126; and market as God, 117
enchantment, promotion of, 131–132; and storytelling, 132–133
enchantment, religious, 109, 110–116; and ingratitude, 120–121; and science, 115–116, 129–130, 135–138
Encounter Books, 152
encumbrances, 43–45, 117–118; discounting, 76–77; and Iraqi people, 77–78, 168–169, 173

Ending Affirmative Action (Eastland), 151, 198n69
"Ending Welfare as We Know It" (Tanner), 203n16
Enemy at Home, The (D'Souza), 218n150
Engels, Friedrich and Karl Marx, *The Communist Manifesto,* 133
Enlightenment, 108, 109, 129
Enron executives, 61, 84, 119–120
entertainment industry, as immoral, 119, 123
entrepreneurship, 134–135
Environment, 37–38
Environmental Action, 91
Environmental Overkill (Ray), 238n108
environmental pollution, 37–38, 50–51; corporate, 64–65, 85; and corporate taxes, 119–120
Equal Rights Amendment (ERA), 18
Erickson, Paul D., *Reagan Speaks,* 230n10
Escape From Freedom (Fromm), 244n45
ethics, absolute, 146–147
ethics, situation, 101–102
Ethics and Public Policy Center, 150
European allies, and Iraq War, 174
euthanasia, 19, 22
evangelical Christians, 13; and church and state, 29–30, 59, 60, 103, 104, 112–113, 143; and feminism, 18; and fight against evil, 21–22, 165; and religious enchantment. *See* enchantment, religious; view of human nature, 23–24
"Evangelical-Capitalist Resonance Machine" (Connolly), 186n2
Evans, M. Stanton, 19; *The Theme is Freedom,* 142
evil, battle against, 21–22, 165; and War on Terror, 164–165, 174
evolutionary theory, 29, 103, 111–112, 139–140
Experiments Against Reality (Kimball), 22, 25, 98, 99, 133, 147, 150
Exxon Mobil, 84

"Fall from Grace" (Orren), 204n41
fallacy of composition, 52
Falwell, Jerry, 2, 18, 29, 63, 85, 89, 114, 120–121, 185n10; on abortion, 59
family, as mediating structure, 85
family, bourgeois, 114–115
family, nontraditional, 115
family values: and counterculture, 95; divorce, 148; and enchantment, 114–116; and feminism, 17–18, 23; and homosexuality, 29, 114, 148; and multiculturalism, 97–98; and taxation, 89–90; vs. technological advancement, 81–83; and welfare reform, 35–36
Fanon, Franz, 98
Faraday, Michael, 136
Father Knows Best (TV show), 138
Fear of Falling (Ehrenreich), 214n82
Federal Bureau of Investigation (FBI), 175
Federalist Society for Law and Public Policy Studies, 150
feminism, 17–18; and counterculture, 95; and evangelicals, 18; as against nature, 24–25; and perversity, 18; and social erosion, 17–18, 23, 114
Feulner, Edwin J., Jr.: *Getting America Right,* 187n7; *Leadership for America,* 185n11
Fierce, Don, 87
Finn, Chester, 120, 124; *We Must Take Charge,* 205n48
Firing Line (TV show), 150
First Amendment, 49, 110; and freedom of religion, 112–113
Fish, Stanley, 98
Fitzgerald, Frances, 20
Fleming, Alexander, 136
Fleming, Thomas, 82
Flynn, Daniel, 99, 143; *Why the Left Hates America,* 217n125
Flynn, James R., *Where Have All the Liberals Gone?,* 192n98
Flynt, Larry, 59
Folbre, Nancy, *The Invisible Heart,* 214n69
food production, 39
Forbes, Steve, 56
Ford, Gerald, 150
Forgotten Americans (Schwartz), 120
Fox News, 185n10
France, 21; and Iraq War, 174
Francis, Samuel, 107–108
Frank, Anne, 60, 131
free market, 31, 40; and Christianity, 83–84; and corporations, 84–85; and creative destruction, 102–104; and enchantment. *See* enchantment,

free market; and encumbered people, 45–48, 117–118; and environmental pollution, 64–65; hypothetical nature of, 117–119; and quality of life, 50; and spheres of justice, 48–51
free speech, 49
Free to Choose (Friedman and Friedman), 200n93, 214n70
freedom, 133–134; bounded, 143–144, 147–148; and Iraq War, 177; as storytelling theme, 142–144; unhampered, 142–143; as universal ideal, 169
Freedom Revolution (Armey), 142
Freud, Sigmund, 123, 154; *Group Psychology and the Analysis of the Ego,* 201n106
Friedan, Betty, 59, 95
Friedman, Milton, 4, 14, 16–17, 20, 24, 31, 37, 45, 48, 51, 62, 84, 92, 119, 122, 123, 125–126, 138
Friedman, Milton and Rose Friedman, *Free to Choose,* 200n93, 214n70
Friedman, Rose, 14, 16–17, 31, 37, 48, 62, 84, 123, 125–126
Friedman, Thomas, 126
Friends of the Earth, 91
Fromm, Erich, *Escape from Freedom,* 244n45
Frum, David, 15, 93–94; *How We Got Here,* 197n49
Fulbright, J. William, *Arrogance of Power,* 249n99
fusionism, 211n34
futility, 22–25, 27
Future of Conservatism (Dunn), 187n3
Future of the Intellectuals and the Rise of the New Class (Gouldner), 214n80

Galbraith, John Kenneth, 124
Galileo, 136
Gardner, Howard, *Changing Minds,* 187n4
Gates, Bill, 134–135
Gay, Peter, *The Enlightenment,* 221n24
gay families, 115
gay marriage, 18
gays: as dangerous to the family, 29, 114, 148; as immoral, 144; and perversity, 19–20
gender. *See* feminism; women
General Motors, 84, 94, 120
genetics, 24–25
George Mason University, 149, 150
Germany, World War II, 169–170
Gerson, Mark, *The Neoconservative Vision,* 184n8
Getting America Right (Feulner), 187n7
Gettysburg Address, 131
Gibson, John, *The War on Christmas,* 223n42
Gilder, George, 2, 16, 18, 38, 69, 84, 87–88, 118, 119
Gingrich, Newt, 2, 7, 26–27, 35, 48–49, 89, 90, 104, 126, 186n12; on student protests, 96; *Winning the Future,* 188n10, 196n40
Gingrich, Newt and Dick Armey, *Contract with America,* 12, 26, 133
Glazer, Nathan, "A Man Without Footnotes," 207n92
global warming, 37–38, 50–51, 152, 154; and corporations, 64–65, 85
globalization, 126
Goldman Sachs, 84
Goldwater, Barry M., 2, 7, 22, 90, 143; *The Conscience of a Conservative,* 13; *Conscience of a Conservative, The,* 88–89; presidential campaign, 13, 20, 41, 65, 105, 135, 177
Goldwin, Robert A., *Left, Right and Center,* 187n7
good intentions, 15
Good Samaritan, 131
Goodman, Paul, 95
Gore, Al, 59, 186n16
Gouldner, Alvin, *The Future of the Intellectuals and the Rise of the New Class,* 214n80
Governing by Campaigning (Edwards), 183n6
government, as enemy, 87–90, 107
Graham, Lindsey, 3, 90, 133
Grant, Bob, 73, 88, 99
Great Depression, 68, 140
Great Society, 129; under conservatives, 1
Green, Mark and Gail MacColl, *There He Goes Again,* 203n14
Greening of America (Reich), 215n93
Greider, William, *One World, Ready or Not,* 210n21

Gresham's Law, 146
Gridlock in Government (Meiners and Miller), 202n114
Gross, Martin, 135–136
Group Psychology and the Analysis of the Ego (Freud), 201n106
Gulf War (Iraq War I), 169
Guttmann, Allen, *The Conservative Tradition in America,* 198n54
Gwartney, James D. and Richard L. Stroup, *What Everyone Should Know About Economics and Prosperity,* 211n33

Hacker, Jacob, 105
Hacker, Jacob and Paul Pierson, *Off Center,* 219n2
Hagelin, Rebecca, 85
Hale, Nathan, 131
Halliburton, 84
Hamas, and Iraq War, 174
Hamilton, Alexander, 4
Hannity, Sean, 104
Hansen, George, 119–120
Hardisty, Jean, *Mobilizing Resentment,* 221n19
Harlan, John, 42, 43
Harris, Marvin, *America Now,* 215n96
Harrison, Bennett and Barry Bluestone, *The Deindustrialization of America,* 210n4
Hart, Jeffrey, 13
Hartmman, Geoffrey, 98
Harvard Law School, 73
Harvard University, 117, 149; Program on Constitutional Government, 150
Hating Whitey and Other Progressive Causes (Horowitz), 198n70
Hayek, Friedrich, 15, 21
Hazlitt, Henry, *Economics in One Lesson,* 193n113
Hazlitt, Henry, "How the Price System Works," 32–33
healthcare: advances in, 137; Canadian, 20; and personal responsibility, 42; reform, 65
Heclo, Hugh, 154–155
Hefley, James, 101, 128–129
Heilbroner, Robert and William Milberg, *The Crisis of Vision in Modern Economic Thought,* 202n114
Heilbrunn, Jacob, *They Knew They Were Right,* 184n8
Helms, Jesse, 19, 89, 90, 121, 138
Henry, Jules, 120; *Culture Against Man,* 201n106, 226n98
Henry, Patrick, 4
Heritage Foundation, 131, 149, 153, 178, 185n10
heroes, 131–132
Herrnstein, Richard, 24
Herrnstein, Richard and Charles Murray, *The Bell Curve,* 44, 151, 192n98
Hesson, Robert, 122
Hezbollah, and Iraq War, 174
High Price of Materialism, The (Kasser), 204n39
Hillsdale College, 131
Himmelfarb, Gertrude, 15, 16, 17–18, 60; on counterculture, 95; on Mill, 146–147, 149; on the new class, 94; *One Nation, Two Cultures,* 202n109; on poverty, 93
Himmelstein, Jerome L., *To the Right,* 184n8
Hirsch, Fred, *The Social Limits to Growth,* 201n106
Hirschman, Albert, 14, 18–19, 22, 25
history, and storytelling, 137–138
History of Political Ideologies, 186n2
History of the Peloponnesian War (Thucydides), 161–162
Hitler, Adolf, 110–111, 169–170; *Mein Kampf,* 133
HIV/AIDS, and personal responsibility, 42
Hoar, William, 89
Hobbes, Thomas, *Leviathan,* 112
Hodgson, Godfrey, *The World Turned Right Side Up,* 184n8, 209n1
Hollywood: as immoral, 103, 119; as new class members, 93, 119
Holmes, Oliver Wendell, 17
Holocaust references, 19, 22, 57, 60
Home Invaders (Wildmon), 221n18
homelessness, 72
homosexual marriage, 18
homosexuality: as dangerous to the family, 29; as immoral, 144; and perversity, 19–20
Hoover, Herbert, 6
Horowitz, David, 22, 25, 42, 66, 153, 170
Hostel (film), 84

How We Got Here (Frum), 197n49
Howard University, 43
Howoritz, David, *Hating Whitey and Other Progressive Causes,* 198n70
Howse, Brannon, 21, 138, 150
Hubris (Corn and Isikoff), 249n99
Huckabee, Mike, 3, 92, 133
Hudson Institute, 150
human nature, 22–25; as economically rational, 23–24, 137
humanism: anecdotes, 56; as evil, 21–22, 56; and situation ethics, 101–102
Humanist Manifesto, 101
Hume, David, 4
Humphrey, Hubert, 73
Huntington, Samuel, 150
Huntington, Samuel, *The Clash of Civilizations and the Remaking of World Order,* 97, 163
Hurricane Katrina, 199n86
Huse, Scott, 111
Hussein, Saddam, 78, 166, 167, 168, 169
Hustler magazine, 59
Hutchinson, Kay Bailey, 3
Hyde, Henry, 90

I Love Lucy (TV show), 138
Ianonne, Carol, 18
idea marketing, 152, 153–154
Ideas Have Consequences (Weaver), 231n18
identity gap, of Democratic party, 160
independence effect, 18
Independent Institute, 153
Index of Leading Cultural Indicators (Bennett), 209n116
India, purchase of petroleum, 51
individualism, 40–45, 47–49, 51–52, 100–102; and conservative vision of America, 53; and encumbered people, 43–45, 76–77; as liberal trait, 96; and personal responsibility, 168–169; and selfishness, 82, 96
individuals, generalizing behavior of, to groups, 51–52
Inquisition, 113
Institute for Political Economy, 150
institutional racism, 66
intelligensia, as new class, 90–94, 107; defining characteristic, 91–92, 92–93
intelligent design, 29
Intercollegiate Studies Institute, 150
Interstate Commerce Commission, 14
interventionism, and party, 162–163
invisible hand, 4, 23–24, 117, 124–125
Invisible Heart, The (Folbre), 214n69
IQ (intelligence quotient), of African Americans, 24, 44
Iran, and Iraq War, 174
Iraq War: costs, 1, 27, 174; and creating reality, 176–177; death toll, 1; and encumbrances, 77–78, 168–169; House and Senate approve, 162; and oil, 51; reasons for, 53, 162, 163; sequelae, 174; stories about, 160–165, 165; as tragedy, 178–179
Iraq War I (Gulf War), 169
Irrational Exuberance (Shiller), 201n106
Isaac, Erich and Rael, 25, 72, 91; *The Coercive Utopians,* 186n42
Isikoff, Michael and David Corn, *Hubris,* 249n99
Islam, 110
Islam, radical, 12
Italy, and Iraq War, 174

Jaffa, Harry, 4
James Watson, 136
Jefferson, Thomas, 113, 138
jeopardy, 27
jeopardy thesis, 18–19
Jerry Springer (TV show), 84
Jesus Christ, 4, 59, 129
Joan of Arc, 131
joblessness: and corporate policies, 46, 84; and race, 17; and youth, 17
John M. Olin Foundation, 150
John M. Olin Institute for Strategic Studies, 150
Johnson, Haynes, *Sleeping Through History,* 230n10
Johnson, Lyndon B., 43, 66, 73, 162, 170
Johnson, Paul, 4
Johnson, Philip, 148; *The Right Questions,* 236n86
Journal of Political Ideologies, 185n12, 209n1
Joyless Economy, The (Scitovsky), 201n106
Judicial Watch, 150
Judis, John B., *William Buckley,* 199n79
"just say no" campaign, 43

justice, spheres of, 47–48; and higher education, 98
juvenile delinquents, 58
juvenile sexuality, 58

Kafka, Franz, 232n32
Kagan, Robert and William Kristol, *Present Dangers,* 163, 170, 171, 172
Kahn, Herman, *On Thermonuclear War,* 195n17
Kaplan, Lawrence, 166, 168
Kasser, Tim, *The High Price of Materialism,* 204n39
Katrina (hurricane), 199n86
Kaye, Angela, 59
Kemp, Jack, 26, 87; *An American Renaissance,* 193n110
Kennan, George, 175–176
Kennedy, D. James, 30–31
Kennedy, John F., 140, 202n114
Kennedy, Ted, 73
Kent, Phil, 72, 89
Kerner, Otto, 66
Kerner Commission Report, 66, 69, 206n63
Kerner Commission Report and the Failed Legacy of Liberal Social Policy (Thernstrom, Siegel and Woodson), 206n63
Kerry, John, 160–161
Keyes, Alan, 42
Keynes, John Maynard, 154
Keynesian economics, 88
killing the messenger, 71–72
Kimball, Roger, 22, 25, 98, 99, 133, 147, 150, 153; *Tenured Radicals,* 233n48
Kinchlow, Ben, 13, 102
King, Martin Luther, Jr., 43, 73
Kingdon, John, 74–75
Kirk, Russell, 198n54
Kirk, Russell, *The Conservative Mind,* 3, 55–56, 185n9
Kirkpatrick, Jean, 91–92
Kondratas, Anna, 42, 85, 115, 120
Koop, C. Everett, "The Slide to Auschwitz," 19
Korten, David C., *When Corporations Rule the World,* 210n21
Kozol, Jonathan, 73; *Savage Inequalities,* 205n48
Kramer vs. Kramer (film), 98
Krauss, Melvyn, 50
Krauthammer, Charles, 172, 186n16
Kristol, Irving, 2, 25, 46, 48, 52, 58, 60, 61, 107, 145, 168, 186n12; on capitalist ideal, 121; on counterculture, 97; on new class, 90–91, 92
Kristol, William, 3, 166
Kristol, William and Robert Kagan, *Present Dangers,* 163, 170, 171, 172
Krugman, Paul, 27, 92
Kruse, Kevin M., *White Flight,* 184n8
Ku Klux Klan, 77
Kudlow, Lawrence, 41, 84; *American Abundance,* 193n116
Kuhn, Thomas, 116
Kuttner, Robert, 73, 92; *Making Work Pay,* 120
Kyoto Treaty, 152

labor unions, 46, 85
Laffer Curve, 26, 32
laissez-faire capitalism, 23–24, 40; and Christianity, 83–84; and corporations, 84–85; and creative destruction, 102–104; and enchantment. *See* enchantment, free market; and encumbered people, 45–48, 117–118; and environmental pollution, 64–65; hypothetical nature of, 117–119; models of, 31; and quality of life, 50; and spheres of justice, 48–51
Lakoff, George, *Don't Think of an Elephant,* 230n6
Lakoff, George, *Whose Freedom?,* 184n7
Lambro, Donald, 19, 87, 106–107
Land of Desire (Leach), 227n113
Lane, Robert, *The Loss of Happiness in Market Democracies,* 202n106
Lane, Thomas, 23, 66, 87
Lareau, Annette, *Unequal Childhoods,* 199n79
Larson, Reed, *Stranglehold,* 211n33
law of unintended consequences, 15, 175
Leach, William, *Land of Desire,* 227n113
Leadership for America (Feulner), 185n11
Leave it to Beaver (TV show), 138
Lebedoff, David, 93
Lebergott, Stanley, *Pursuing Happiness,* 200n88

LeBon, Gustave, *The Crowd,* 201n106
Ledeen, Michael, 173
Left, Right and Center (Goldwin), 187n7
Legal Services Corporation, 91
Lehman Brothers Holdings, 2, 84
"Letter on Toleration" (Locke), 112
Letters to a Young Conservative (D'Souza), 192n103, 194n117
Leviathan (Hobbes), 112
Levi's Children (Scoenberger), 227n113
Levy, Frank, *Dollars and Dreams,* 209n115
Lewinsky, Monica, 142
liberals: as America-haters, 73–74; as communists, 72–73; and enchantment, 4–5, 139–140; as lacking vision, 5, 141; and power, 72; as pragmatists, 140–141; as utopians, 25, 91; views, as false, 14
Libertarians, 52; vs authoritarians, 86
Lienesch, Michael, *Redeeming America,* 183
Limbaugh, Rush, 15, 42, 45, 67, 72, 89, 104, 122, 153, 186n12; on ideal of capitalism, 121; on liberal contempt, 108; on taxes, 87–88
Lincoln, Abraham, 4
Lind, Michael, *Up from Conservatism,* 184n8
Lindblom, Charles, 122
Linn, Susan, *Consuming Kids,* 211n22
Little Engine that Could, 131
Lochner v. New York, 17
Locke, John, 98, 138, 154; "Letter on Toleration," 112
Logic of Collective Action, The (Mancur), 201n106
logical fallacy of composition, 52
Losing America (Byrd), 241n19
Losing Ground (Murray), 209n115
Loss of Happiness in Market Democracies, The (Lane), 202n106
Lott, Trent, 90
Luddites, 107
Lynde and Harry Bradley Foundation, 154

MacColl, Gail and Mark Green, *There He Goes Again,* 203n14
macroeconomics, 51–52
Madison, James, 4
Madoff, Bernard, 61, 207n82
Magnet, Myron, *The Dream and the Nightmare,* 61, 145, 231n11
Mailer, Norman, 83
Making of a Counterculture, The (Roszak), 215n93
Making Work Pay (Kuttner), 120
man, nature of, 22–25, 24–25
Manhattan Institute for Policy Research, 149, 150
Manichean, 20
manifest destiny, 175–176
Mansfield, Harvey, 41–42, 95; Program on Constitutional Government, Harvard University, 150
Marcuse, Herbert, 95; *One Dimensional Man,* 215n93
"Marine's Hymn," 201n102
"Market as God, The" (Cox), 117
marketplace for ideas, 145–147; and conservative think tanks, 150–151
marriage: gay, 18; traditional, 18, 114–115; and welfare, 16
Martha Coakley, 180
Marx, Karl, 59, 129
Marx, Karl and Friedrich Engels, *The Communist Manifesto,* 133
Marxism, 20–21
Massachusetts, colonial, 143
Mattson, Kevin, *Rebels All!,* 185n8
McCain, John, 2, 6, 6–7
McCormick, John P., "Contain the Wealthy and Patrol the Magistrates," 200n90
McDonaldization, 108–109
McDonald's restaurants, 31
McGirr, Lisa, *Suburban Warriors,* 184n8, 214n82
McGovern, George, 73
Mciners, Roger E. and Roger LeRoy Miller, *Gridlock in Government,* 202n114
Meacham, Jon, *American Gospel,* 224n49
media corporations, 119, 123
mediating structures, 85, 122–123
Medicaid, 15, 65
Medicare, 15, 26, 65, 89
Medved, Michael, 60, 63
megastructures, 85
Mein Kampf (Hitler), 133
melting pot, vs. multiculturalism, 97, 99
Menace of Multiculturalism (Schmidt), 210n15
meta-narrative, of conservative storytelling, 133–135

methodology, author's, 185n10
Meyer, Frank, 13, 41, 211n34; "Conservatism," 187n7
Meyrowitz, Joshua, *No Sense of Place,* 200n95
Michels, Robert, *Political Parties,* 201n106
Mickelthwait, John and Adrian Wooldridge, *The Right Nation,* 183
microeconomics, 51–52
Microsoft Corporation, 50, 84
Milberg, William and Robert Heilbroner, *The Crisis of Vision in Modern Economic Thought,* 202n114
military spending, 163–164
Mill, John Stuart, 25; *On Liberty,* 145–147, 148–149, 152–153, 154
Miller, Roger LeRoy and Roger E. Mciners, *Gridlock in Government,* 202n114
minimum wage, 16–17
Miranda rights, 61
Missouri Law Review, 186n12
Mobilizing Resentment (Hardisty), 221n19
models, vs. evidence, 29–34
Mohammed, injunction against depicting, 110
Monsanto corporation, 137
Moore, Roy, 144
moral relativism, 100–102
Morality, 175–176
Mosca, Gaetano, 14
mothers, unwed, 63, 95; and race, 69; and welfare reform, 35–36
Mueller, John, *Overblown,* 241n12
Muggeridge, Malcolm, 22
Muller, Jerry Z., *Conservatism,* 188n9
multiculturalism, 64, 97–100; as countercultural, 97–98; definition, 97; and disenchantment, 109; and weak rhetoric, 141
Muravchik, Joshua, 20, 72
Murchison, William, *Reclaiming Morality in Ameica,* 191n80
Murray, Charles, 2, 16, 24, 35, 39, 66, 67, 90–91, 107; *Losing Ground,* 209n115
Murray, Charles and Richard Herrnstein, *The Bell Curve,* 44, 151, 192n98
Muslims, 110
Myers, David, 116, 147; *The American Paradox,* 201n106
Myth of Separation, The (Barton), 223n40
myths: as distraction, 140; importance of, 131–132

Nader, Ralph, 72, 73
Nash, George H., "The Uneasy Future of Conservatism," 187n3
Nash, Ronald, 16, 21, 23, 33, 45, 51–52, 85, 123–124, 137
National Abortion Rights Action League (NARAL), 114
National Advisory Commission on Civil Disorders, 66
National Center for Policy Analysis, 150, 152
National Council of Churches, 91
National Education Association (NEA), 93
National Federation for Decency, 221n18
National Interest, 150
National Organization for Women (NOW), 95
National Review, 86, 133, 150, 152, 185n10, 187n5; mission statement, 12
National Security Agency (NSA), 175
National Security Council (NSC),75
National Security Strategy of the United States, 2002, 166, 167
nature vs. nurture, 76
Nazi Germany, 110–111
Nazism, and liberalism, 103. *See also* Holocaust references
neighborhood, as mediating structure, 85
Neoconservative Imagination, The (DeMuth and Kristol), 207n92
Neoconservative Mind (Dorrien), 184n8
Neoconservative Vision (Gerson), 184n8
Neo-Conservatives, The (Steinfels), 209n1
Neuhaus, Richard, 85, 150
New Chastity and Other Arguments Against Women's Liberation (Dector), 213n65
New Criterion, 150
New Deal: programs cancelled, 1; unintended consequences, 15
New Right, The (Viguerie), 187n7
New World Order, The (Robertson), 191n85
New York Times, 145, 200n89
Newsweek, 117
Newton, Sir Isaac, 136
Nichols, Ray, "Conservatism and the Right in America," 185n12, 209n1

Nickeled and Dimed (Ehrenreich), 120
Nietzsche, Friedrich, 150
9/11 attacks, 164, 173
1964 Civil Rights Act, 43
1964 election, 13
1929 stock market crash, 6
Nixon, Richard, 61, 97, 170
Nixonland (Perlstein), 185n8
No One Makes You Shop at Wal-Mart (Slee), 199n88
No Retreat, No Surrender (DeLay), 187n7, 239n116
No Sense of Place (Meyrowitz), 200n95
Norquist, Grover, 89; *Rock the House,* 212n36
North Korea, and Iraq War, 174
Not By Politics Alone (Diamond), 203n12
Novak, Michael, 4, 20, 33, 84, 119, 126
nuclear war, surviving, 195n17
Nunberg, Geoffrey, *Talking Right,* 179, 184n6, 184n7
Nye, Joseph S., Jr, 204n41

Oakeshott, Michael, 185n12
Obama, Barack, 1, 2, 5, 6, 6–7, 27, 141, 180–181; presidential campaign, 186n16
Objectivity, Relativism, and Truth (Rorty), 221n24
Off Center (Hacker and Pierson), 219n2
oil, and Iraq War, 51, 163
Olasky, Marvin, 2, 15–16, 87, 91; *Compassionate Conservatism,* 206n76
Olbermann, Keith, 92
Olson, Mancur, *The Logic of Collective Action,* 201n106
On Liberty (Mill), 145–147, 148–149, 152–153, 154
On the Origin of Species (Darwin), 139–140
On Thermonuclear War (Kahn), 195n17
One Dimensional Man (Marcuse), 215n93
One Nation, Two Cultures (Himmelfarb), 202n109
One Nation Under God (Walton), 189n44, 210n11
One World, Ready or Not (Greider), 210n21
Operation Rescue (Terry), 194n3
O'Reilly, Bill, 15, 92, 100
original design, 111
original intent, in the Constitution, 71
Orren, Gary, "Fall from Grace," 204n41
Orwell, George, 191n81
Othello (Shakespeare), 98
outsourcing, of jobs, 46, 84, 122
Overblown (Mueller), 241n12
Ozzie and Harriet (TV show), 138

Packer, George, *The Assassin's Gate,* 240n7
Palin, Sarah, 2, 3, 6, 6–7, 104
Paradox of Choice, The (Schwartz), 202n114
Pasteur, Louis, 136
Pearl Harbor, Japanese attack, 167
pedophilia, and gays, 20
People for the American Way, 91
Perkins, John, *Confessions of an Economic Hit Man,* 227n113
Perlstein, Rick, *Nixonland,* 185n8
personal freedom, 145–150
personal responsibility, 41–42, 121, 143; and social class, 68–69
perversity, 14–15, 27; and affirmative action, 68, 69; and feminism, 18; and homosexuality, 19–20; and Iraq War, 174–175; and social programs, 36, 67–68, 69
philanthropy, private, 15–16, 68
Phillips, Kevin P., *The Emerging Republican Majority,* 183, 220n7
Pierson, Paul, 105
Pierson, Paul and Jacob Hacker, *Off Center,* 219n2
Pierson, Paul and Theda Skocpol, *The Transformation of American Politics,* 185n8, 193n112
Pines, Burton, 96, 106
pirates, Barbary, 50
Pirseg, Robert M., *Zen and the Art of Motorcycle Maintenance,* 215n93
Piven, Frances Fox and Richard A. Cloward, *The Breaking of the American Social Compact,* 201n96
planned obsolescence, 123–124
Planned Parenthood, 63, 91, 114
Plessy v. Ferguson, 42
Policy Review, 150; "So You Want to Start a Think Tank" (Andrews), 153
political act, stories as, 160
Political Brain, The (Westen), 5, 179, 184n7
political elites, 91–92
political parties, as mediating institutions, 85

Political Theory, 186n2
Politics of Injustice (Sasson), 207n82
Politics of Rage, The (Carter), 184n8
pollution, environmental, 37–38, 50–51; corporate, 64–65, 85
Political Parties (Michels), 201n106
poor, undeserving, 15, 16, 120; characteristic behaviors, 70
poor, working, 120
Popper, Karl, 116
population growth, 50–51, 94
Populism and Elitism (Bell), 205n63
Porn Generation (Shapiro), 218n150
pornography, 49, 145, 148, 149
Poser, Richard, 188n10
Postman, Neil, 31; *Amusing Ourselves to Death,* 200n95
poverty: causes of, 15–17, 65–66, 67–68, 84, 93; and class, 68–70, 71–72; culture of, 68, 69; as moral issue, 93, 120; and race, 65–66, 69–71, 71–72, 76–77; and undeserving poor, 15, 16, 120
Poverty of Affluence, The (Wachtel), 201n106
Power and the Story, The (Cornog), 187n4
prayer in schools, 63–64, 84, 143
preemptive war, 166–167
Present Dangers (Kagan and Kristol), 163, 170, 171, 172
Prestowitz, Clyde, *Rogue Nation,* 240n8
preventive war, 166, 167
Price of Motherhood, The (Crittenden), 214n69
Prohibition, 113
Protestant Ethic, 95, 104
Pulp Fiction (film), 84
Pursuing Happiness (Lebergott), 200n88
Putnam, Robert, 115

quality of life, and free markets, 50

race: affirmative action, 24, 41–42, 42; and color-blindness, 42, 43, 44–45, 68; conservative view, 17; and crime, 69; and discrimination, 44–45; and IQ, 24; and poverty, 65–66, 69–70; and unemployment, 17
race riots, 66
racism, 66–68, 76–77; defining, 66–67; institutional racism, 66; rational discrimination, 36, 70–71; and relativism, 101; segregation, 114; and southern strategy, 183n3
rational discrimination, 36, 70–71
rational people, 34–40, 124
rationalism vs. enchantment, 109, 140
Rawls, John, 43–44
Ray, Dixy Lee, *Environmental Overkill,* 238n108
Reagan, Nancy, 43
Reagan, Ronald, 4, 7, 19, 22, 25–26, 26, 34, 55–56, 59, 62, 86, 87, 90, 104, 116, 132–133, 164–165, 185n10, 186n12, 186n15; election, and counterculture, 95; military service, 57; presidential campaign, 135, 183n3; "welfare queen" homily, 176
Reagan Speaks (Erickson), 230n10
Reaganomics (Bartlett), 193n110
Reagan's America (Wills), 203n13, 203n15
Reason to Believe (Cuomo), 208n110
Rebel-in-Chief (Barnes), 184n6
Rebels All! (Mattson), 185n8
Reclaiming Morality in America (Murchison), 191n80
red herrings, 72–73
Redeeming America (Lienesch), 183
Reed, Ralph, 29–30, 42, 89, 106, 141
Reformation, 112–113, 114
regime change, in Iraq, 167–170
Regnery Publishers, 152
Reich, Charles, 95; *The Greening of America,* 215n93
Reich, Robert, 73
Reiman, Jeffrey, *The Rich Get Richer and the Poor Get Prison,* 207n82
religion, freedom of, 112–113
religious enchantment. *See* enchantment, religious
religious right. *See* Christians, evangelical
Reno, Janet, 56
Republican party, southern strategy, 1, 65, 183n3
Republicans, and interventionism, 162
"Rescuing Burke" (Bogus), 185n12
resentment, 106–107
responsibility, personal, 41–42, 121, 143; and abortion, 42, 136; and social class, 68–69
reverse sequences, 64–71
Review of Politics, 186n1
Revolutionary War, 131, 138

rhetoric, 4
rhetorical devices: anecdotes, 55–59; correlations, 60–71; distractions, 71–74; things left unsaid, 75–76
Rhode Island, seventeenth century, 113
Ricci, David, "Political Science and Conservative Ideas," 186n2
Ricci, David, *The Transformation of American Politics,* 239n122
Rich, Frank, 5
Rich, Frank, *The Greatest Story Ever Sold,* 184n6
Rich Get Richer and the Poor Get Prison (Reiman), 207n82
Richard and Helen DeVos Foundation, 154
Richardson, Heather, 153, 154
"Richer is Safer" (Wildavsky), 37–38, 65
Right Nation, The (Mickelthwait and Wooldridge), 183
Right Questions, The (Johnson), 236n86
Right Turn (Rogers and Ferguson), 184n8
Rightward Bound (Shulman and Zelizer), 185n8
riots, race, 66
Roads to Dominion (Sara Diamond), 184n8, 220n7
Roberts, Paul Craig, 26, 36, 72, 150
Robertson, Pat, 31, 89–90; *The New World Order,* 191n85
Robinson Crusoe, 32
Roche, George, 19, 20, 23, 41, 45, 52, 59, 84, 88, 117, 124, 125, 129, 131
Rock the House (Norquist), 212n36
Rockwell, Norman, 133
Roe v. Wade, 19, 212n41
Rogers, Joel and Thomas Ferguson, *Right Turn,* 184n8
Rogue Nation (Prestowitz), 240n8
Ronald Reagan (D'Souza), 203n15
Roosevelt, Franklin Delano, 6–7, 15, 73, 140
Ropke, Wilhelm, 121
Rorty, Richard, 98; *Objectivity, Relativism, and Truth,* 222n32
Rose, Tom, *Economics,* 51
Roszak, Theodore, *The Making of a Counterculture,* 215n93
Rowe, H. Edward, 13, 21, 101, 129
Rumsfeld, Donald, 90
Rutherford Institute, 150
Ryan, William, *Blaming the Victim,* 207n78

Salem witch trials, 113
Sandel, Michael, 43–44, 76
Santayana, George, 198n54
Santorum, Rick, 85, 115
Sara Scaife Foundation, 154
Sasson, Theodore, *The Politics of Injustice,* 207n82
Satan, 120–121
Savage, Dan, *Skipping Towards Gomorrah,* 208n110
Savage Inequalities (Kozol), 205n48
Scalia, Antonin, 90
Schlafly, Phyllis, 7, 18, 58, 101, 114, 135; Eagle Forum, 150
Schlesinger, Arthur, Jr., 73
Schmidt, Alvin, 99; *The Menace of Multiculturalism,* 210n15
Schoenberger, Karl, *Levi's Children,* 227n113
Schoenwald, Jonathan M., *A Time for Choosing,* 184n8
school prayer, 63–64, 84, 143
school vouchers, 62
schools. *See also* education reform
Schor, Juliet, *Do Americans Shop Too Much?,* 201n106
Schumpeter, Charles, 102–103
Schwartz, Barry: *The Costs of Living,* 201n106; *The Paradox of Choice,* 202n114
Schwartz, John E., *Forgotten Americans,* 120
science: neglected in storytelling, 136–138; and progress, 137, 139–140; as vocation, 136–137
scientific method: and disenchantment, 115–116, 129–130, 147; and social problems, 140, 152–153
Scitovsky, Tibor, *The Joyless Economy,* 201n106
Scopes trial, 21–22
script, conservative, 2–3
secular conservatives, 23
segregation, racial, 114
selfishness, and capitalism, 82
Sennett, Richard, *The Corrosion of Character,* 211n32
September 11, 2001, 164, 173

sex, and teenagers, 58
Sex and the City (TV show), 94
sex education, 63, 100
Shakespeare, William, *Othello*, 98
Shalala, Donna, 196n28
Shapiro, Ben, *Porn Generation*, 218n150
Sherman Anti-Trust Law, 14
Shiller, Robert J., *Irrational Exuberance*, 201n106
Shulman, Bruce and Julian E. Zelizer, *Rightward Bound*, 185n8
Siegel, Fred, Robert Woodson, Sr. and Stephan Thernstrom, *The Kerner Commission Report and the Failed Legacy of liberal Social Policy*, 206n63
Simon, Julian, 38, 47; *The Ultimate Resource*, 197n43
Simon, William, 21, 35, 41, 73, 89, 149–150, 153; *A Time for Truth*, 197n47; *The Ultimate Resource*, 201n105
Singapore, 21
Six Books of the Commonwealth (Bodin), 112
Skipping Towards Gomorrah (Savage), 208n110
Skocpol, Theda and Paul Pierson, *The Transformation of American Politics*, 185n8, 193n112
Skocpol, Theda, *Boomerang*, 193n112
slavery, of Africans in America, 37, 99–100, 114
Slee, Tom, *No One Makes You Shop at Wal-Mart*, 199n88
Sleepwalking Through History (Johnson), 230n10
"Slide to Auschwitz, The" (Koop), 19
slippery slopes, 19–20
Smith, Adam, 4, 23–24, 40, 84, 123, 154; *The Wealth of Nations*, 201n106, 231n14
Smith, Mark A., "Economic Insecurity, Party Reputations, and the Republican Ascendancy," 193n112
Smith, Rogers M., *Stories of Peoplehood*, 187n4, 239n1
Smith Richardson Foundation, 153, 154
"So You Want to Start a Think Tank" (Andrews), 153
social class, and poverty, 68–69, 71–72
social erosion, and feminism, 17–18, 23
Social Limits to Growth (Hirsch), 201n106
social problems, and the scientific method, 152–153
social programs. *See also* Medicaid; Medicare; welfare: anecdotes, 56; and perversity, 36, 67–68, 69; and political power, 72; and rationality, 36; and scientific method, 140; and tax cuts, 26, 27, 74; for taxes, 89
Social Security, 26, 89, 154
social workers, 90, 91
socialism, 20–21; as pagan, 83
socialist economies, 20, 21
socialists, liberals as, 72–73
Socrates, 131
Southern Christian Leadership Conference (SCLC), 113
Soviet Union. *See also* Cold War: collapse, 12, 56, 86–87, 163, 186n15; as evil empire, 164–165
Sowell, Thomas, 4, 31, 36
Spencer, Herbert, 14
spheres of justice, 47–48; and higher education, 98
Spheres of Justice (Walzer), 200n92
Spirit of America, The (Bennett), 131
Springer, Jerry, 84, 119
Stanford University, 98, 149
Steinfels, Peter, *The Neo-Conservatives*, 209n1
Stephen, James Fitzjames, 13, 193n105
Stevenson, Adlai, 73
Stiglitz, Joseph L. and Linda Bilmes, *The Three Trillion Dollar War*, 183
stock market crash of 1929, 6
Stories of Peoplehood (Smith), 187n4
Storming the Gates (Baltz and Brownstein), 184n8
storytelling, 132–133, 159; anecdotes, 55–60; contradictions in, 142–144; and history, 137–138; and lack of citations, 57–58, 62; meta-narrative, 133–135; and optimism, 135; as political act, 160; science neglected in, 136–138; and simplicity, 135–136; theme of freedom, 142–144; through think tanks and publications, 150–152; value of, 160, 161
Stranglehold (Larson), 211n33
Stratton, Lawrence, 36
Strauss, Leo, 183n4

Stroup, Richard L. and James D. Gwartney, *What Everyone Should Know About Economics and Prosperity,* 211n33
student protests, 96–98
Suburban Warriors (McGirr), 184n8, 214n82
Suicide of the West (Burnham), 233n47
supply side economics, 25–27
Supreme Court, 63–64; as enemy, 87; and school prayer, 84
Sweden, 21
Swiss Family Robinson, 32
Syria, and Iraq War, 174

Talking Right (Nunberg), 179, 184n6, 184n7
Tanner, Michael, "Ending Welfare as We Know It," 203n16
Target stores, 50
tax cuts, and social programs, 26, 27, 74
tax freedom day, 88–89
taxes, and environmental pollution, 119–120
taxes, and redistribution of wealth, 87–90; benefits of, 89; women as victims of, 89–90
taxes, cutting, 25–27
Tea Party movement, 1
technological advancement: and disenchantment, 108–110; vs. family values, 81–83; social consequences, 93, 102–104, 107–108, 126
teen pregnancy, 63
teenage abstinence, 58
teenage delinquency, 58
television, as detrimental, 115, 119
Telling the Truth (L. Cheney), 198n70
Temperance, in discussion, 154
temperance, in political discussion, 152, 154–155
temperance movement, 113
Tenured Radicals (Kimball), 233n48
terrorist attacks, of September 11, 2001, 164, 173; and hatred of America, 172–174
Terry, Randall, 29, 59; *Operation Rescue,* 194n3
"The Problem of Defining Conservatism" (Dunn and Woodward), 186n1
Theme is Freedom, The (Evans), 142
There He Goes Again (Green and MacColl), 203n14
Thernstrom, Stephan and Abigail, *America in Black and White,* 66, 67, 69, 76–77, 199n70
Thernstrom, Stephan, Fred Siegel and Robert Woodson, Sr., *The Kerner Commission Report and the Failed Legacy of Liberal Social Policy,* 206n63
think tanks, conservative, 149; corporate sponsors, 154
Thomas, Clarence, 90
Thomson, Rosemary, 18
Three Trillion Dollar War (Bilmes and Stiglitz), 183
Thucydides, *History of the Peloponnesian War,* 161–162
Thunder on the Right (Crawford), 209n1
A Time for Choosing (Schoenwald), 184n8
A Time for Truth (Simon), 197n47
Time magazine, 117
To the Right (Himmelstein), 184n8
toleration, 112–113
Tolstoy, Leo, *Anna Karenina,* 98
Toward Liberty (Boaz), 203n16
Tower, John, 125
Transformation of American Politics (Pierson and Skocpol), 185n8, 193n112
Transformation of American Politics (Ricci), 239n122
Treaty of Westphalia, 113
trickle-down economics, 25–27, 32
Truth: and anecdotes, 57; in conservative script, 13, 14, 145, 150; and propaganda, 153–154; as relative, 47–48, 53, 98, 150; unassailable by facts, 154–155, 176–177
Tubman, Harriet, 131
Turning Right in the Sixties (Brennan), 184n8
Twight, Charlotte, 89
Two Income Trap, The (Warren), 214n69
2008 economic crisis, bailout, 27, 48
2008 elections, 1, 6–7, 186n16
2004 presidential election, 1–2, 160–161
2006 elections, 1
Tyrrell, R. Emmett, 38, 135

Ultimate Resource, The (Simon), 197n43, 201n105

"Uneasy Future of Conservatism" (Nash), 187n3
unemployment: and creative destruction, 126; and minimum wage, 16–17; and race, 17, 36–37
Unequal Childhoods (Lareau), 199n79
Unequal Democracy (Bartels), 184n5, 234n49
Unheavenly City, The (Banfield), 22, 68, 71–72
Uniform Crime Reports, 207n82
unions, labor, 46, 85
United Auto Workers (UAW), 73
United States Constitution, 49, 50, 61, 110, 134; and freedom of religion, 112–113; original intent, 71
universities: and absolute truth, 98; canon of, 97–100, 142; as communist, 73, 90–94; conservative centers and programs, 150; first, 113
University of Chicago, 131; John M. Olin Center for Inquiry into the Theory and Practice of Democracy, 150
Unlikely Conservative, An (Chavez), 206n77
Unraveling the Right (Ansell), 184n8, 186n15
Up from Conservatism (Lind), 184n8
Utopia Against the Family (Christensen), 232n30
utopianism, 25, 91

values, primacy of, 128–130; clashing, 147–149
Vicks, as think tank sponsor, 154
Viereck, Peter, 198n54
Vietnam War, 94, 96, 169–171, 176
Vietnam War refugees, 68
Viguerie, Richard, 17, 34, 93, 120, 170; *The New Right*, 187n7
Viguerie, Richard, *Conservatives Betrayed*, 193n113
Virtue of Prosperity, The (D'Souza), 197n45
vision, conservative, 4; basic propositions, 12
vision, liberal lack of, 5
"vision thing," 159
Voeglin, Eric, 183n4
von Mises, Ludwig, 21
voter identity laws, 188n10

Wachtel, Paul, *The Poverty of Affluence*, 201n106
Waldman, Paul, *Being Right Is Not Enough*, 214n82
Walker, Alice, *The Color Purple*, 98
Wall Street collapse, of 2008, 7; bailout, 27
Wall Street Journal, 117, 152
Wallace, George, 107
Wal-Mart, 50, 84
Walton, Rus, 19, 37, 40, 101, 136, 143; *One Nation Under God*, 189n44, 210n11
Walzer, Michael, 47–48, 73, 92, 98
Wanniski, Jude, 26, 32, 50, 61, 119, 138; *The Way the World Works*, 195n17
War, Afghanistan. *See* Afghanistan War
war, preemptive, 166–167, 174
war, preventive, 166, 167
War on Christmas, The (Gibson), 223n42
War on Terror. *See also* Afghanistan War; Iraq War: and Cold War, 164–165, 175–176; Democrats as soft on, 160–161; as fight against evil, 164–165, 165
Ward, Chester, 58
Warren, Elizabeth, *The Two Income Trap*, 214n69
Washington Post, 186n16
Washington Times, 150
Watergate scandal, 96, 97
Watt, James, 17, 87, 111
Waxman, Henry, 73
Way of the WASP (Brookhiser), 219n158
Way the World Works, The (Wanniski), 195n17
We Must Take Charge (Finn), 205n48
wealth, redistribution of, 87–88
Wealth of Nations (Smith), 201n106
weapons of mass destruction (WMD), 166, 167, 175
Weaver, Paul, 33–34
Weaver, Richard, 198n54; *Ideas Have Consequences*, 231n18
Weber, Max, 4–5; on disenchantment, 108–110, 116, 139, 140, 146, 147; on enchantment, 132; on vocation, 136–137
Weekly Standard, 150, 152, 185n10
Weldon, John, 58, 64, 91, 119
welfare, 15–16; anecdotes, 56; and personal

responsibility, 42; and perversity, 36, 67–68, 69; and political power, 72; reform, and rationality, 35–36; as slippery slope, 19; and tax cuts, 26, 27, 74
Westen, Drew, *The Political Brain,* 5, 179, 184n7
What Everyone Should Know About Economics and Prosperity (Gwartney and Stroup), 211n33
Whatever Happened to the American Dream? (Burkett), 196n40
What's Go Great About America (D'Souza), 198n70
When Corporations Rule the World (Korten), 210n21
When Work Disappears (Wilson), 211n32
Where Have All the Liberals Gone? (Flynn), 192n98
Whitaker, Robert, 67
White Flight (Kruse), 184n8
Whitehead, John, 19, 59
Whitewashing Race (Currie, Brown, Carnoy, Duster, Oppenheimer, Schultz and Wellman), 206n74
Who Really Cares? (Brooks), 208n93
Whose Freedom? (Lakoff), 184n7
Why the Left Hates America (Flynn), 217n125
Why We Fight (Bennett), 243n38
Wildavsky, Aaron, "Richer is Safer," 37–38, 65
Wildmon, Donald E., *Home Invaders,* 221n18
Wilentz, Sean, *The Age of Reason,* 185n8
Will, George, 61, 92, 116; *The Woven Figure,* 212n41
William Buckley (Judis), 199n79
William Crawford v. Marion County Election Board, 188n10
Williams, Roger, 113
Williams, Walter, 143, 150
Williamson, Chilton, Jr., *The Conservative Bookshelf,* 185n11
Wills, Garry, 86; *Reagan's America,* 203n13, 203n15
Wilson, Clyde, 107
Wilson, James, 14–15, 34–35, 39, 92, 106; "A New Approach to Welfare Reform," 23
Wilson, William Julius, *When Work Disappears,* 211n32
Winfrey, Oprah, 119
Winning the Future (Gingrich), 188n10, 196n40
Winthrop, John, 143
witch trials, Salem, 113
women. *See also* feminism: abortion rights. *See* abortion; as victims of government, 89–90; working outside the home, 17–18, 89–90
Woodson, Robert, Sr., Fred Siegel and Stephan Thernstrom, *The Kerner Commission Report and the Failed Legacy of Liberal Social Policy,* 206n63
Woodward, J. David and Charles Dunn, "The Problem of Defining Conservatism," 186n1
Wooldridge, Adrian and John Mickelthwait, *The Right Nation,* 183
work ethic, declining, 95, 104
working poor, 120
World Trade Center attacks, 164, 173
World Turned Right Side Up (Hodgson), 184n8, 209n1
World War II: appeasement, 169–170; Holocaust. *See* Holocaust references
Woven Figure, The (Will), 212n41

Yale University, 140
Yeltsin, Boris, 56
"You Are What You Spend" (Cox and Alm), 200n89
youth, unemployed, 17

Zelizer, Julian E. and Bruce Shulman, *Rightward Bound,* 185n8
Zen and the Art of Motorcycle Maintenance (Pirseg), 215n93

About the Author

David M. Ricci, professor and former chairman in the departments of Political Science and American Studies at the Hebrew University in Jerusalem, is also the author of *Community Power and Democratic Theory, The Tragedy of Political Science, The Transformation of American Politics,* and *Good Citizenship in America*. He is a frequent visitor to the United States and has taught at the Pennsylvania State University, the University of Pennsylvania, American University, the University of Tulsa, the Johns Hopkins University, The University of Michigan, and Wake Forest University. He has been a visiting scholar at the Woodrow Wilson International Center for Scholars in Washington, D.C., at the Institute for Advanced Study in Princeton, and at the Brookings Institution.